The Social Contexts of Research

THE SOCIAL
CONTEXTS
OF RESEARCH

SAAD Z. NAGI
The Ohio State University

RONALD G. CORWIN
The Ohio State University

WILEY-INTERSCIENCE, a division of John Wiley and Sons, Inc.

London • New York • Sydney • Toronto

Copyright © 1972, by John Wiley & Sons, Inc.

All rights reserved. Published simultaneously in Canada.

No part of this book may be reproduced by any means, nor transmitted, nor translated into a machine language without the written permission of the publisher.

Library of Congress Cataloging in Publication Data:

Nagi, Saad Zaghloul.
  The social contexts of research.

  Includes bibliographical references.
1. Research   2. Social policy.
I. Corwin, Ronald G., joint author. II. Title.

Q180.A1N24   001.4′3   72-000003
ISBN 0-471-62850-6

Printed in the United States of America.

10 9 8 7 6 5 4 3 2 1

About the Authors

Ronald Corwin (University of Minnesota Ph.D.) is Professor of Sociology, The Ohio State University. He is a past vice-president of the American Educational Research Association and has served as Basic Research Branch Chief, U.S. Office of Education, where he continues to serve on research review panels. He is author of *Militant Professionalism* and *A Sociology of Education* and has published numerous articles on organizational innovation and conflict and problems of professional employees.

Irwin Deutscher (University of Missouri Ph.D.) is Professor of Sociology, Case Western Reserve University. He is a past president of the Society for the Study of Social Problems and has served on various government research review panels. His forthcoming book, *Sentiments and Acts,* expands upon the theme of his chapter in this volume.

Robert L. Hall (University of Minnesota Ph.D.) is Professor of Sociology and former Head of the Department of Sociology, University of Illinois at Chicago Circle, on leave of absence in 1971–1972 as Visiting Scholar at the Center for the Interdisciplinary Study of Science and Technology of Northwestern University. He formerly served for several years as Program Director for Sociology and Social Psychology at the National Science Foundation. His publications include research on social influence processes, small-group performance, and learning in social interaction.

Don E. Kash (University of Iowa Ph.D.) is Director of the Science and Public Policy Program and Professor of Political Science at the University of Oklahoma. He is author of *The Politics of Space Cooperation.* His previous work on the politics of research has been published in *Science* and other journals.

Roger Krohn (University of Minnesota Ph.D.) is Professor of Sociology, McGill University, and author of *Social Shaping of Science.* He has also written papers on the sociology of knowledge and science and on the theory of social organization.

Simon Marcson (University of Chicago Ph.D.) is Professor of Sociology and Special Assistant to the Dean of the Graduate School, Rutgers University. He is author of *The Social Scientist in American Industry; Automation, Alienation and Anomie; The Scientist in Government;* and numerous monographs, papers, and articles in the field of sociology of science.

James P. McNaul (Stanford University Ph.D.) is an Associate Professor of Organizational Behavior, College of Administrative Science, The Ohio State University. His principal research interests are the behavior of professionals in complex organizations and organizational adaptation to environmental change.

Saad Z. Nagi (Ohio State University Ph.D.) is Mershon Professor of Sociology and Public Policy, The Ohio State University. He has served on the research review panels of various government agencies and is author of *Disability and Rehabilitation: Legal, Clinical, and Self Concepts and Measurement;* and contributor to a number of professional journals in the social sciences and the health fields.

William Petersen (Columbia University Ph.D.) is Robert Lazarus Professor of Social Demography, The Ohio State University. He is author of 10 books and monographs and 80 articles concerning population and social policy. His most recent books are *Japanese Americans: Oppression and Success,* and *Readings in Population.*

Norman W. Storer (Cornell University Ph.D.) has served on the faculty of Harvard University and was formerly a staff associate with the Social Science Research Council. He is currently Professor and Chairman of the Department of Sociology, Bernard Baruch College, City University of New York. His publications include the *Social System of Science* and papers on the coming changes in science and in basic and applied research.

Richard Tybout (University of Michigan Ph.D.) is Professor of Economics, The Ohio State University. He edited *Economics of Research and Development* and has published widely on the contractor system, government and invention, technological change, and the economics of research.

Howard Vollmer (University of California Ph.D.) is Professor of Sociology, American University. He was formerly a Program Manager for Stanford Research Institute. He is co-editor (with Donald Mills) of *Professionalization* and is author of numerous papers on the productivity of research scientists and research management.

Preface

The idea for this volume grew out of collaboration on an essay on educational research which appears in the last chapter. The plan of the work was guided by two primary interests. The first is a substantive interest in the social organization of research and its place in society. Research, as a social institution, has been discussed only tangentially in writings on science and on technology. Some recent publications have focused on particular aspects of the subject, but after examining the state of available literature on research, we became convinced of the need for a comprehensive analysis of the way in which social contexts influence the research process. Such an effort seems particularly timely in view of the many recent controversies in universities, government, and industry regarding the contributions, purposes, and means of financing and organizing research.

The paucity of material to acquaint future researchers with their anticipated roles, the constraints on research, and other aspects of the social environment within which research is conducted, provided a second stimulus for this volume. There is a corresponding vacuum within the research training programs of most disciplines. In the main, curricula in the various disciplines are built around their theoretical content, methods, and techniques. We hope the material assembled in this volume will help provide a broader understanding of research roles and the forces that shape both the work environments and curricular developments in this area. This volume, then, should be of interest to professors and practicing researchers in a variety of social science disciplines, educational research, and public administration.

The volume is organized into twelve chapters. In addition to the introductory and the concluding chapters, the ten other chapters discuss research within five contexts. In Chapter 1, entitled "The Research Enterprise," the editors provide a definitional framework and present some of the major themes and issues in the literature. Within a *context of values and ideologies,* Roger Krohn analyzes "The Patterns of Institutionalization of Research in Chapter 2, and Howard Vollmer discusses "Basic and Applied Research" in Chapter 3. Chapters 4 and 5 consider research within a *context of control.* The first of these chapters, by Don Kash, deals with "Politics and Research"; and the second, by Richard Tybout, examines "Economics of Research." A discussion of research within an *organizational context* appears in Chapter 6 on "Research Settings" by Simon Marcson; and Chapter 7 on "Agencies of Research Support" by Robert Hall. Two major aspects of the *operational context* of research are discussed in Chapter 8 on "Relations among Scientific Disciplines" by Norman Storer, and Chapter 9 on "Relations between Researchers and Practitioners" by James McNaul. The *context of ethics* and other aspects of the professional relationships of researchers to subjects and data constitute the sixth part in the organization of the book. Included in this part are Chapter 10 on "Forbidden Knowledge" by William Petersen, and Chapter 11 on "Public and Private Opinion" by Irwin Deutscher. The volume concludes with a case study to illustrate the utility of the frameworks and concepts developed throughout the various chapters in the analysis of a research field. Chapter 12, by the editors, presents "The Case of Educational Research."

We have attempted to avoid the usual disconnectedness characteristic of collections of original contributions. The outlines prepared for the organization of the book were aimed at developing an integrated and coherent framework. We believe the ways the contributors have brought these plans to life have fulfilled this objective by preserving coherence and continuity throughout the volume. For each chapter to be a meaningful unit in itself required that some points be discussed by more than one author. Nevertheless, the fact that these points are discussed within different contexts and from differing perspectives avoids undue repetition.

Even a limited review of literature on research would reveal the lack of data and empirical evidence concerning many of the theses advanced. Consequently, to varying degrees, the chapters in this volume constitute ground-breaking conceptual efforts where authors had to depend more on illustrative than verificational material. The authors not only bring several disciplinary perspectives to the volume, but they also represent a broad range of experience with research in different settings. We hope that the frameworks developed and the hypotheses presented will generate more studies and evidence on the topics discussed.

We are grateful to the contributors who have joined us in this venture and to the many students of research whose ideas stimulated our interests and guided our work. We want also to express our appreciation to Betty Wisberger, Lois Brooks, and Lynn Doherty for typing and proofreading numerous drafts of chapters with excellence and continuing good spirit.

SAAD Z. NAGI
RONALD G. CORWIN

Columbus, Ohio
December 1971

Contents

The Social Contexts of Research

CHAPTER ONE

The Research Enterprise: An Overview

Saad Z. Nagi and Ronald G. Corwin, The Ohio State University

What does "research" mean? Even a limited survey of the usage of the term is enough to show that it is applied to activities as varied as the study of form and content of literature, the authentication of historical documents, the derivation of mathematical formulas, the development of technical models and prototypes, the collection and analysis of data in experiments and surveys, and the formulation of laws and theories. Even if all such pursuits were enumerated, however, the definition would not be complete. Research has become so broad and complex that it cannot be understood or appraised without reference to the people involved and to the contexts of their work. This volume is conceived accordingly, and its subject is the social organization of research within the structure and processes of society.

In any anthology the various contributions are addressed directly or indirectly to a theme or themes that unify the whole. Here, they are the major themes in the social science literature on research. In this chapter we present some of the themes that cut across those of the succeeding chapters. First, however, the definitions of research activities need to be examined and clarified.

1

DEFINITIONS AND CLARIFICATION OF BOUNDARIES

One common theme in research activities is that all relate to the accumulation of knowledge, whether scientific or nonscientific, theoretical or practical. The overlap among processes involved in developing, disseminating, and using knowledge obscures the differences among them. The definitional boundaries of research will be sought by distinguishing them from—and identifying the areas of overlap with—"knowledge," "science," "learning," "communication," "practice," and "development." We know how difficult it is to construct analytical definitions. Nevertheless, as Cohen points out, to define is no more than to decide to use a word in a certain sense. Diverse definitions of a term follow from the likelihood that various analysts are concerned about different aspects of its referent, so that "only when one denies a material proposition that someone else affirms do we have real contradiction."[1]

Knowledge, Science, and Research

Knowledge "has been broadly conceived as to refer to every type of idea and every mode of thought ranging from folk belief to positive science"; it "has often come to be assimilated to the term 'culture.' "[2] As used here, it takes in all constructions of reality that refer to objects, meanings, ideas, and occurrences. Although knowledge is intricately associated with cognition, it would be nihilistic to define knowledge in terms of personal perceptions. Such perceptions sometimes include deranged evidence in various prejudicial "worlds of individual opinions," and sometimes deranged thought processes in the "worlds of sheer madness and vagary."[3] *Claims to knowledge are here restricted to communicable and public constructions of reality within systems of widely shared and accepted thought processes and evidence such as theology, philosophy, and science.*

Science differs from theology and philosophy in the nature of questions posed, basic premises, rules of evidence, and ways of knowing. Russell contends that "all *definite* knowledge belongs to science; all *dogma* as to

---

1 Morris R. Cohen, *Reason and Law*, Collier Books, New York, 1961, p. 10.
2 Robert K. Merton, *Social Theory and Social Structure*, Free Press, New York, 1957, p. 467.
3 William James, quoted in Burkart Holzner, *Reality Construction in Society*, Schenkman, Cambridge, Mass., 1968, pp. 4–5.

what surpasses definite knowledge belongs to theology"[4] [emphasis his]. The "no man's land" between these two systems of knowledge he ascribes to philosophy—"almost all the questions of most interest to speculative minds are such as science cannot answer, and the confident answers of theologians no longer seem so convincing." Science differs from theology also in that the latter ultimately appeals to authority of tradition or revelation. Science differs from philosophy in the nature of proof. While logical consistency and deductive reasoning are the primary elements of a philosophical system, sensory observation to test the correspondence between theories and the empirical world is essential to scientific knowledge.

Science comprises constellations of facts, theories, and methods.[5] It "involves the discovery through processes of controlled inference that something is a sign of something else; it is statable in a propositional form; and it is capable of being verified through sensory observation by anyone who is prepared to make the effort to do so."[6] Science includes both products and processes of inquiry. Thus scientific research can be defined in terms of processes and activities by which scientific knowledge is tested, modified, and expanded. Research of this nature, in the context of society, is precisely the subject of this volume.

Learning, Communication, and Research

A definition of research can be restricted according to the modes of activity involved as well as the kind of knowledge produced. Ideally, research begins with theory and feeds back into theory. However, accomplishments in science, as in other complex activities, are realized in phases. Many efforts do not span the full cycle of research but are rather concentrated into certain phases—as in reviewing and organizing literature, collecting descriptive material, synthesizing and interrelating facts and generalizations, resolving anomalies, and constructing new paradigms. Learning and communication are often confused with research because any of the phases of systematic inquiry include both the acquisition and reporting of gradually increasing knowledge. Thus much of the intellectual procedure that has come to be known as the scientific

---

4 Bertrand Russel, *A History of Western Philosophy*, Allen and Unwin, London, 1946, p. 10.
5 Thomas Kuhn, *The Structure of Scientific Revolutions*, Univ. of Chicago Press, Chicago, 1962, p. 1.
6 Ernest Nagel, "Problems of Concept and Theory Formation in the Social Sciences," in *Philosophy of the Social Sciences*, Maurice Natanson, Ed., Random House, New York, 1963, p. 202.

method is common to all scholarly pursuits. This overlap has prompted some to conclude that "little agreement exists as to what kinds of human behavior constitute research."[7]

It would be difficult to distinguish research from learning and communication within a particular individual's activities, especially for someone who contributes new knowledge. However, as a class of activities, research differs from learning and communication when the latter two are ends in themselves. On the one hand, learning produces minds educated into existing knowledge, whether or not these minds contribute to its expansion, and communication produces reports that may or may not contain new knowledge. On the other hand, original contributions to knowledge are generally the aims and often the products of research. These contributions may fall within one or more of the phases that make up the cycle of inquiry which, as mentioned above, begins with theory and feeds back into theory.

Practice, Development, and Research

Research activity also needs to be distinguished from the kinds of enterprise that result when knowledge from research is put to use. In "practice," knowledge is used as means to such ends as technological and organizational developments or policy decisions. In an excellent discussion of the recurrent issue of relationships between theory and practice, Jonas distinguishes knowledge that enters into the setting of ends from that used in selecting means.[8] For example, knowledge that underlies establishing priorities among exploration of the moon, the building of supersonic transports, or the construction of more hospitals differs fundamentally from that applied to implement whichever goal has been selected. One requires judgements based on values, and the other, an understanding of processes. Within the latter category, Jonas identifies three types of knowledge. First, "knowledge which pronounces on possibility in principle" and which rests on universal laws. Second, knowledge "which maps, still in the abstract, possible ways of realization." This type is composed of "more complex and more specific causal patterns," embodying universal principles and "providing models for rules of action." The third type is knowledge involved in "the discernment of the course of action most practicable in the given circumstances." Such knowledge

[7] John L. Kennedy and G. H. Putt, "Administration of Research in a Research Corporation," Office of Technical Services, U.S. Department of Commerce, Washington, D.C., April 1956, p. 1.
[8] Hans Jonas, "The Practical Uses of Theory," in *Philosophy of the Social Sciences*, Maurice Natanson, Ed., Random House, New York, 1963, pp. 119–142.

"of what to do now is entirely particular, placing the task within the context of the whole concrete situation." To put the matter concretely, if travel to the moon is the aim, the means require first an understanding of action and reaction, then a chemistry of fuels and knowledge of their behavior, and finally a choice among them which depends on payload, ignition reliability, firing duration, safety, and so forth. In essence,

> We have here a scale descending from the simple to the complex, and at the same time from theory to practice, which is complexity itself. . . . The first two steps are both within theory, or rather, they each *can* have their developed theory. The theory in the first case we may call science proper, as in theoretical physics; the theory in the second case, derivative from it in logic, if not always in fact, we may call technological or applied science—which it must be remembered, is still "theory" in respect to action itself, as it offers the specific rules of action as parts of a reasoned whole and without making a decision. The particular execution itself has no theory of its own and can have none.[9]

Theoretical knowledge, whether "basic" or "applied" falls within the domain of science and is judged as true or false. However, practices can be judged only as right or wrong, successful or unsuccessful, and therefore must be approached with the various advantages and disadvantages in mind.[10] We limit the term research to activities involved in extending either basic or applied knowledge, using "development" for the application of knowledge in technology or other practices. These distinctions are neither simple nor clear-cut, for problems encountered in the application of knowledge are often an important stimulus to new theories. Also, there are similarities in experimental approaches to what Ziman refers to as "scientific Technology" and "technological Science" that further complicate the problems of differentiation.[11] This complexity accounts, at least in part, for the currency of such self-contradictory labels as "action research."

Basic and Applied Research

Distinctions between basic and applied research have often been predicated on the motivations of investigators or of their sponsors. Definitions used by the National Science Foundation combine the sponsors' motiva-

---

[9] *Ibid.*, pp. 129–130.
[10] Michael Polanyi, *Personal Knowledge: Towards a Post-critical Philosophy*, Harper, New York, 1964, p. 178.
[11] John Ziman, *Public Knowledge: The Social Dimension of Science*, Cambridge Univ. Press, Cambridge, 1968, p. 25.

tions with other criteria such as "originality," "advancement of scientific knowledge," and "the role of sponsors in identifying the research problems."[12] The source of support, being the easiest to identify, has become the most common basis for distinguishing basic from applied research. Thus while research supported by certain divisions in the National Science Foundation might be categorically considered "basic," research supported by the Department of Defense, Public Health, or other mission-oriented agencies also might be categorically considered "applied." Although motives and sources of funding are associated with one or the other type of research, a clear and consistent differentiation is not afforded by either criterion or by the two combined. Many people engage in research with two objectives—to advance theory and to contribute to the understanding of applied problems. For example, a study of how certain gases behave at high temperature and velocity might be undertaken with a view toward improving the design of combustion chambers in rocket engines.

The *products* of inquiry do not necessarily derive from the motives for selecting a problem, or the appropriations from which a study is financed. More fundamental distinctions between basic and applied research can be made when criteria are based on the types of knowledge produced rather than on the researcher's values and attitudes or the sponsor's mission.

Following Jonas's distinction between basic and applied theoretical knowledge, quoted earlier, it can be said that basic research consists of activities leading to the discovery of a discipline's universal principles and constitutive laws, while the products of applied research are the "more complex and more specific causal patterns embodying the first principles and providing models for rules of action." How can the two types of theoretical knowledge be identified? Two criteria can be applied: (*a*) the ways used in codifying knowledge, that is, the models or forms of theory construction; and (*b*) the nature of the phenomenon being explained and whether it is strictly of theoretical interest or constitutes a social or a technical problem.

Two models for theory construction have been identified in the literature. In describing the various theories in physics, Einstein observes that

Most of them are constructive. They attempt to build up a picture of the more complex phenomena out of materials of a relatively simple formal scheme from which they start out . . . along with this most important class of theories there

---

[12] See Chapter 3 by Howard Vollmer in this volume.

exists a second, which I shall call "principle-theories." . . . The advantages of the constructive theory are completeness, adaptability and clearness; those of the principle theory are logical perfection and security of the foundation.[13]

Kaplan uses similar distinctions to specify two parallel forms—the "hierarchical" and the "concatenated." A hierarchical theory is one

. . . whose component laws are presented as deduction from a small set of basic principles. A law is explained by the demonstration that it is a logical consequence of these principles, and a fact is explained when it is shown to follow from these together with certain initial conditions. The hierarchy is a deductive pyramid in which we rise to fewer and more general laws as we move from conclusions to premises which entail them.[14]

In contrast, the concatenated or "pattern" type is one

. . . whose component laws enter into a network of relations so as to constitute an identifiable configuration or pattern. Most typically, they converge on some central point, each specifying one of the factors which plays a part in the phenomenon which the theory is to explain.[15]

In the hierarchical model (aside from the overlap necessary for deductive processes), both dependent and independent variables vary among propositions. The types of propositions would be such as: If A then B, if B then C, or if C then D. This allows the derivation of new propositions as conclusions in the form: If A then C or D, and so on. In a theory of the concatenated type, the dependent variable is generally held constant, for the function of the theory is to explain variance in the dependent variable through a configuration of independent variables. When Y is a phenomenon to be explained, the propositions in this type of theory represent probability or tendency statements that relate $A, B, C, D \ldots N$ to Y. To illustrate the differences between these two approaches to theory building, let us consider the phenomenon of unemployment and how knowledge about it relates to each. Variability in unemployment can be used to test hypotheses derived from several hierarchical theories in economics, sociology, political science, or other disciplines. Each hypothesis accounts for only part of the variance in unemployment. The primary function of such inquiries is to extend the range and scope of hierarchical theories, but explanations of unemploy-

---

[13] Albert Einstein, quoted in Abraham Kaplan, *The Conduct of Inquiry*, Chandler, San Francisco, 1964, p. 299.
[14] Abraham Kaplan, *The Conduct of Inquiry*, Chandler, San Francisco, 1964, p. 298.
[15] *Ibid.*, p. 298.

ment itself within any given theory of this type remain segmental. In contrast the objective of a concatenated theory of unemployment is to attain as much closure as possible by accounting for as great an amount of the variance in that phenomenon as possible.

The basic structures of theories are often obscured by the narrative, compared to mathematical or other formal styles of presentation. This is particularly the case in the social and behavioral sciences. Furthermore, attempts to build hierarchical theories in these disciplines have met with only limited success, in part because many cause-effect relations are reversible and are characterized by low probabilities.[16] However, approximations of such theories can be exemplified in theories of learning, exchange, symbolic interaction, and formal organization. Explanatory systems focused on such phenomena as poverty, delinquency, or unemployment provide examples of the concatenated type. The focal substance of a concatenated theory need not be a social or a technical problem but can be a phenomenon primarily of theoretical interest.

The hierarchical model is better suited for codifying the principles of developed fields; the basic premises and axioms in such theories are highly abstract; and work at this level is more likely to be analytical than empirical or synthetic. Contributions to the expansion of this form of knowledge are the products of *basic* research. However, as pointed out earlier, a hierarchical theory can give only a partial explanation of any concrete phenomenon such as a social or a technical problem.

When concatenated theories are focused on social or technical problems, the yield is applicable knowledge. Organized knowledge can be applied in developing products or solving problems only "if the task is so subdivided that it begins to be coterminous with some established area of scientific or engineering knowledge."[17] Success and efficiency depend largely on whether or not knowledge about particular elements of the product or the problem is comprehensive and concrete. The concatenated models are more suited for codifying knowledge needed for these purposes. Each element in the product or problem becomes the focal point in a pattern that provides as comprehensive an explanation as possible. And, concatenated models can also incorporate knowledge at such a concrete level as to provide directions for application. Activities leading to the expansion of this type of theoretical knowledge constitute *applied* research.

Systems analysis has become the usual term for the process of breaking down a complex problem into detailed components, applying the knowl-

16 *Ibid.,* p. 298.
17 John Kenneth Galbraith, *The New Industrial State,* Houghton-Mifflin, Boston, 1969, p. 12.

edge related to each of these components, and recombining the components into a new whole. By such a process knowledge from the various disciplines relevant to the product or problem can be identified and applied. It is no accident that emphasis upon knowledge applicable to the solution of social and technological problems has given impetus to systems analysis and led to the criticism of university research and teaching as organized within "departments representing the narrow academic discipline."[18] However, while the type of coordination characteristic of the systems approach has demonstrated remarkable success in hardware technology, its effectiveness remains to be shown in helping to apply existing knowledge to the solution of social problems.

SOME MAJOR THEMES FROM SOCIAL SCIENCE

Ideas related to a phenomenon as complex as research can be organized in many ways that vary in coherence, in conceptual scope, and in the range of information encompassed. We believe that the organization we have selected for this volume as a whole represents the most useful way of presenting available material on research. Nevertheless, there are important themes that underlie the discussions in several chapters or cut across their subject matter, and therefore are not highlighted in any of the chapters. Four such themes are reviewed here: the functions of research, growth and structural change, the openness of the research system, and the role of competition and incentives in the system.

The Functions of Research

The functions of research are conveyed primarily by its product—the extension of scientific and other forms of knowledge. The functions of knowledge, however, are also the subject of a long and complex debate. In the analysis cited earlier, Jonas contrasts the classic positions of Aristotle, as expressed by Thomas Aquinas, and of Francis Bacon.[19] For Aristotle and Aquinas, knowledge is to be honored if it contributes to the knower's fulfillment. In contrast, Bacon was concerned whether or not knowledge helped to solve human problems. The issues and positions have not changed much since these statements were made. Indeed, the

---

[18] John S. Steinhart and Stacie Cherniack, *The Universities and Environmental Quality: Commitment to Problem Focused Education,* Office of the President, Washington, D.C., September 1969, p. 7.
[19] Jonas, *op. cit.*

highly accelerated growth in scientific knowledge, as well as the phenomenally successful application of its findings in physical and biological disciplines, has focused increasing attention on these old questions.[20] Views and interests such as those expressed above point up a number of overlapping purposes for knowledge and implicitly for research. Jonas identifies the "fulfillment of man" as the grounds common to both of the classic positions. Knowledge is also connected with "power" and "prestige." And finally, knowledge has "practical uses" and can be applied for the betterment of the conditions of mankind.

How man can be fulfilled is a philosophical question, not to be answered with scientific concepts and techniques. Of the three types of knowledge identified by Scheler—"knowledge born of a desire to achieve control over nature, knowledge born of a desire to cultivate and refine the personality, and knowledge born of a desire to achieve salvation"— he contends that there has been an increasingly one-sided emphasis upon the first in modern Western societies,[21] and thus, by implication, a failure to further fulfillment. Jonas, identifies two differing conceptions of fulfillment as espoused by Aristotle and Bacon. They can be distinguished by the types of scientific knowledge that lead to each.[22] The enoblement of the knower is achieved through intellectual communion with the "most perfect objects" whose being "is indeed the condition of their being 'theory' in the classical sense of the word." This kind of knowledge, the basic abstract principles of the disciplines, leads to fulfillment through the wisdom and understanding it confers and thus possibly to an increase in the knower's moral freedom from the necessity of common things, even without improved control over them. In contrast, for Bacon the "fruits" of knowledge are not only for the knower but for the whole of mankind. For knowledge to bear fruit, thus, it must deal with common things in their own terms. Man is brought to his own not by rising above common things, through knowing about them and related necessities, but by "delivering the things into his power." Fulfillment, as Bacon conceived it, is achieved through the development of applicable knowledge and its actual application to practical ends.

Knowledge and its extension bring *power* and *prestige* to individuals,

[20] For example, see *Knowledge and Power: Essays on Science and Government,* Sanford A. Lakoff, Ed., Free Press, New York, 1966; J. S. Steinhart and Stacie Cherniack, *op. cit.;* Committee on Government Operations, *The Uses of Social Research in Federal Domestic Programs,* Washington, D.C., April 1967; and The National Academy of Sciences, *Basic Research and National Goals,* Washington, D.C., 1965.

[21] Max Scheler, quoted in Werner Stark, *The Sociology of Knowledge,* Routledge and Kegan Paul, London, 1967, pp. 117–118.

[22] Jonas, *op. cit.*

as well as to groups and nations. As government and industry have become increasingly involved with science, the influence of successful scientists has extended into politics and the economy. Despite the norm of disinterestedness so eloquently argued by Bacon, knowledge makes some individuals and nations superior to others in power, wealth, and prestige. National prestige is often involved in questions of science and educational policies. Among advanced nations science has been crucial in competition for international influence. In the United States, where scientists are reluctant to accept governmental constraints, the sciences have developed, nevertheless, in accordance with national policies,[23] and in the Eastern Bloc political control is even greater. The high priority that governmental policies in the various nations give to applied research and technology has not been necessarily detrimental to the advance of science. Such forms of recognition as Nobel prizes provide nations with a worldwide measure of their relative standing in prestige. The great increase in the number of American laureates (Table 1),[24] although in part attributable to the immigration of European scholars during the 1930s and the 1940s, was attributable in large measure to competition for the prestige and power that scientific knowledge brings.

Table 1   Nobel Prizes in Science

Country	1901–1930	1931–1960
Austria	3	4
Denmark	4	—
England	15	18
France	11	—
Germany	27	14
Holland	6	—
Italy	2	2
Sweden	6	2
Switzerland	3	5
United States	6	33
U.S.S.R.	2	2

Science and technology, however independently they may have developed in the past, are both closely linked to the *practical application* of new knowledge. According to Galbraith, the relation today between

23 Gene M. Lyons, *The Uneasy Partnership: Social Science and the Federal Government in the Twentieth Century,* Russell Sage Foundation, New York, 1969.
24 H. W. Bode, "Reflections on the Relations between Science and Technology," in *Basic Research and National Goals,* National Academy of Sciences, Washington, D.C., 1965, pp. 52–54.

the industrial system and what he calls "the educational and scientific estate" parallels the earlier relationship with banking and finance, for knowledge and qualified talent are no less important than capital to corporations.[25] Decisions concerning science and technology are thus not left entirely to researchers or professional associations. Moreover, most nations have policies with more or less explicit priorities in public support, which shape both individual researchers' careers and whole disciplines.[26] Although influenced in varying degrees by scientists, these policies are typically made in councils preoccupied with social and technological problems. In order to justify support for basic research, attempts have been made to document the relations between basic and applied research, and between science and technology.[27] Official emphasis on the application of knowledge is not shared by scientists themselves, most of whom still prefer basic research if indeed they do not, in Snow's words, pride themselves on the fact that their findings could not have any practical use.[28] "This preference seems almost incomprehensible to management experts, because they fail to see that the scientific loyalty is not just towards a prestigious professional group but to an ideology."[29] Young scientists are trained to make contributions that their peers will find significant, and this emphasis in the universities explains why they are typically in controversy with the national policy as defined by other norms.

Growth and Structural Change

If science was once "a relatively simple social system,"[30] the same could not be said for the system of research today. During the three decades from 1940 to 1970, research grew in both volume and complexity far faster than the most optimistic expectations. Although the greatest expansion was in the pursuit of applicable knowledge, basic research also grew rapidly, as a result of both increased direct support and indirect support from subsidies for applied research. Growth was accom-

25 Galbraith, op. cit., p. 282.

26 See examples of national policies in several countries in Lawrence W. Bass and Bruce S. Old, Formulation of Research Policies, American Association for the Advancement of Science, Publication No. 87, Washington, D.C., 1967.

27 See for example, The Illinois Institute of Technology Research Institute, Technology in Retrospect and Critical Events in Science, A report prepared for the National Science Foundation, 1968.

28 C. P. Snow, The Two Cultures: A Second Look, Cambridge Univ. Press, Cambridge, 1965, p. 32.

29 Ziman, op. cit., p. 25.

30 Norman Storer, The Social System of Science, Holt, New York, 1966, p. 4.

panied by dramatic changes in the structure and organization of research activities.

Hagstrom likens the traditional activities in basic science to medieval economic organizations—free collaboration analogous to free partnerships, and professor-student relations similar to those between master and apprentice.[31] "In most academic fields outside the natural sciences, the dominant pattern of academic work in the past has been that of the researcher-writing-a-book-from-library-sources."[32] In an early stage of scientific invention, "a barn or an attic and a small bank account, coupled with a rare combination of imagination, toughmindedness, and perseverance, were sufficient."[33] The major transformations in this traditional picture were associated with an accumulation of knowledge at a rapid and increasing rate; a rise in costs of research, with a consequent dependence on special support; new research techniques requiring particular skills; and following from the emphasis on applied knowledge, a rise in interdisciplinary research.[34] The influence of these trends on the organization of research can be illustrated with three central features: the infusion of new roles, the spread of organized research, and changes in the roles of scientists.

New Roles in Research

Developments in research technology have combined with increased support to alter the classic professor-student research teams. The expensive and complex equipment used in the natural sciences requires highly skilled operators, who may or may not be involved in the substantive issues of the research. The field of computer analysis offers other examples of these new technical roles. The facilities are usually centralized and analysts assist with computations of data for researchers from various disciplines in the case of universities, or various organizations in the case of government or industry. These analysts may engage in substantive studies within their own specialties (data and information systems, in this case), but in the research of others their role is purely to provide technical services.

---

31 Warren O. Hagstrom, *The Scientific Community*, Basic Books, New York, 1965, p. 140.
32 Lewis A. Coser, *Men of Ideas: A Sociologist's View*, Free Press, New York, 1965, p. 287.
33 James B. Conant, quoted in Coser, *op. cit.*, p. 297. Although science might have been characterized in its early history by limited facilities and means, large-scale experiments and scientific expeditions were organized in several countries with the support of private and public funds.
34 Hagstrom, *op. cit.*, p. 140; and Coser, *op. cit.*, p. 297.

From the standardization of many tasks, there have evolved other new roles in research, as in the surveys now common in the social and behavioral sciences. After the "principal investigator" has delineated the problem and devised and tested appropriate insruments, the task of collecting data is usually assigned to specifically trained interviewers. Other subordinates code the data and otherwise prepare them for analysis. The technical skills acquired by persons in such roles can be easily transferred from one study to another, and often from one social discipline to another, so that research organizations try to use these persons efficiently by distributing their time among several studies.

Such new roles have developed along with the large-scale research made possible by increased funding. With specialization and role differentiation, the scientist can spend more of his time and effort in planning studies and analyzing the results. Senior investigators can also engage in several studies simultaneously, with a consequent acceleration of research in general. As the costs of research are increasingly paid from public support, with consequent emphasis upon accountability, a number of new roles have developed such as research administrators, grant officers, and managers. As noted later, the infusion of new roles in research has not been without cost to the scientists.

Organized Research

Although individual studies funded separately for limited periods still prevail in university research, most research is presently organized in special institutes, centers, or laboratories, where continuity can lead to cumulative results. The "routinization" of invention and discovery "occurs not because invention and discovery flow automatically, so to speak, from large research organizations but because contributions can be made mainly by those who have access to the facilities provided by large-scale organizations."[35]

The indirect consequences of organized research and specialization have not been studied in detail, but some eminent scientists believe that creativity can be thwarted by a commitment to organizational objectives.[36] Yet it is only from the outside that scientists "seem to be far more bureaucratized, far more like officers in so many little armies, than many professional workers, such as doctors, lawyers or architects, who often still perform their duties as individuals in private practice."[37] This

35 Coser, op. cit., p. 297.
36 See James B. Conant, quoted in Coser, op. cit., p. 304; and Alvin M. Weinberg, quoted in Hagstrom, op. cit., p. 143.
37 Ziman, op. cit., p. 127.

impression may be deceptive, for the scientist is usually given great freedom in choosing the topic and manner of his research. Policy makers in industrial and other applied laboratories, recently sensitized to the special requirements of scientists, have restricted their activities less than formerly.[38] Scientific knowledge grows, it is believed, with the stimulation of individuals' ideas and discoveries which routinization may hinder or destroy. In industry, it is true, the autonomy of scientists and their orientation toward their professional colleagues are often in conflict with the larger aims of the organization. Accommodations are achieved by (1) industrial managers' acceptance and support of basic research and by the scientists' acceptance of applied functions, (2) an adaptation of professional norms to the organizational controls in a joint role of "scientist-administrator," or (3) the development of "professional ladders" whereby scientists can secure advances in status without becoming involved in administrative duties.[39] Concern about autonomy and professional prerogatives has also intensified power struggles in interdisciplinary research on university campuses.

Relations of power become involved in making decisions about the selection of problems and techniques and the necessary tests for validity of results. Each kind of specialist approaches the problem area from his own perspective and is often incapable of understanding the approaches of others; he may interpret the arguments of others as devices to win power and they may be precisely that.[40]

It has been suggested that these power struggles can be resolved by establishing clear lines of authority, or by institutionalizing an interdisciplinary area as a new specialty.[41]

The Scientist's Role

While the introduction of new roles to research has saved the typical scientist much time and effort, he has usually had to take on new administrative tasks. Scientists have become fund raisers, recruiters, coordinators, negotiators, and trouble shooters. They must relate to agencies that support research; to administrators in industry, government, or universities; and to the nonscientists who often control access to data. The role of scientist-consultant has developed around commercial research organizations whose number grew with the governmental funding of

38 Coser, *op. cit.,* p. 303.
39 William Kornhauser, *Scientists in Industry,* Univ. of California Press, Berkeley, 1962.
40 Hagstrom, *op. cit.,* p. 148.
41 *Ibid.,* p. 148.

applied research and development in defense, space, health care and, more recently, environmental and social problems. However marginal many of these roles and institutions may seem to the closed social system of science, as traditionally defined, they are now integral parts of research. Yet these are roles for which the professional norms of science give little guidance and to which recruits into science are rarely introduced during graduate education.[42]

Another form of differentiation has evolved in most sciences with the expansion of empirical research. The work of some scientists consists largely of developing concepts and theories, with little or no involvement in empirical research. Others concentrate on the search for new evidence. Thus the gap has sometimes increased between empiricists and theorists. In some instances this role differentiation derives from differences in the capabilities of scientists and relates to their status in scientific communities.[43] It should be noted, however, that the differentiation is of roles and contributions, and not of persons, many of whom engage in both spheres alternately or simultaneously, especially among natural and biological scientists.

Openness and Closure

By "closure" we mean clearly defined boundaries that differentiate and insulate the social system of research from other systems, a high level of normative consensus, resistance to change, and limited mobility in status. "Openness" depicts the other end of a continuum. Implicit in much of the discussion so far is the idea that the diverse functions of research and the patterns of growth and differentiation of its activities have blurred the boundaries of the science community, promoted normative conflicts, and helped generate social and intellectual change. These three dimensions of openness-closure in research are discussed successively, followed by a section on "mobility, incentives, and competition."

[42] Coser echoes concerns expressed by Conant and others that the demands of the new roles of scientists and the specialization resulting from the knowledge explosion and organized research may have detrimental effects upon the development of the breed of the intellectual-scientist-generalizer. Yet, he concludes with the reassuring note that "there are good reasons to believe that a breed that has producd Robert J. Oppenheimer, Linus Pauling, and James Conant is nowhere near extinction." See Coser, *op. cit.,* pp. 287–312.

[43] John J. Beer and W. Davis Lewis, "Aspects of the Professionalization of Science," *Daedalus,* **92,** 4 (Fall 1963), 764–784.

consensual model may apply better to the more advanced natural and biological sciences than to those that are less developed.[54] Disciplines tend to depreciate empirical research in their earlier stages,[55] when the threat posed by openness in research, in contrast to conceptual and theoretical activities, is likely to be greatest.

In short, analysts who concentrate on the internal consistencies within the normative structure of science may obscure the diversity of norms in research. As in all social systems, there is tension between the search of members for internal autonomy and the external pressures on the system. An important challenge to the norms of science comes, especially in quest for applied knowledge, from the openness of research to economic and political influences of the laymen who both sponsor it and consume its findings.[56] Typically, these patrons are neither committed to scientific norms nor qualified to bestow scientific recognition. The alternative rewards they offer comprise a blend of scientific and nonscientific criteria such as visibility, influence, and economic gains. Some of the tensions between basic and applied researchers arise from this type of openness in applied research.

Tension varies with the research setting. Those who desire the researcher's traditional autonomy find university settings most compatible, although to a lessening degree in the centers and institutes that are proliferating there. Those whose research is dependent upon organizing large-scale programs find the facilities of government or industry better suited.[57] The loyalty of scientists to the large organizations that house or sponsor their work often conflicts with their orientation to disciplines and peers, especially when the organizations' requirements contradict established scientific norms such as whether or not research findings may be kept secret. Another type of conflict is generated by the fact that the social conventions of science are often incompatible with the administrative coordination of any large-scale operation. Conflicts between researchers and their supervisors in university, government, and industrial laboratories are of two types: technical, over the means and ends of scientific work; and administrative, over procedures, policies, and the allocation of resources. Researchers in lower positions more frequently engage in the former type of conflict—those in higher positions in the latter.[58]

54 See Ziman, *op. cit.;* and Chapter 8 by Norman Storer in this volume.
55 Hagstrom, *op. cit.*
56 Storer, *op. cit.*
57 Roger Krohn, "The Institutional Location of the Scientist and His Scientific Values," IRE, *Transactions of Engineering Management,* **EM8** (September 1961).
58 William Evan, "Superior-Subordinate Conflict in Research Organizations," *Administrative Science Quarterly,* **10** (June 1965).

Structural Boundaries

Abstract principles and theories define the scientific *disciplines,* the members of which constitute relatively closed communities whose well-defined boundaries help to distinguish the members of one discipline from those of others and of scientists as a category from the rest of society. This closure enables peers to exercise great influence in the selection of problems to be studied and the techniques to be used. In turn, scientists become predisposed to communicate their findings mainly to their colleagues.[44] By contrast, research activities are organized into research *fields* which comprise subdisciplines (such as high-energy physics), or an area of studies concerning a technological or social problem (space programs, health care, education, and so on). Research on technical or human problems is usually multidisciplinary but is often dominated by one discipline.

Different disciplines are closed to varying degrees, depending on the characteristic balance between a discipline's internal structure and the external pressures on it. In mature disciplines researchers use their established paradigms to identify central problems and criteria for assessing the significance of findings. Thus a high level of theoretical development is typically associated with self-sufficiency and insulation from outside influences. Scientists in disciplines still lacking formal paradigms, however, often derive their research topics from social problems, and their criteria of significance from quasi-scientific measures. Maturity and external pressure together provide the basis for a meaningful typology of disciplines with respect to members' autonomy and insulation (Table 2). Of the four examples astronomy can be expected to enjoy the greatest insulation and autonomy, and sociology the least.

Table 2 A Typology of Disciplines Based on Level of Development and External Pressure

Level of Theoretical Development	External Pressure	
	High	Low
High	Physics	Astronomy
Low	Sociology	Linguistics

Research fields that constitute specialties within disciplines are no less insulated than the disciplines themselves. In contrast, the boundaries of multidisciplinary research fields, especially when the subject is a techno-

44 Storer, *op. cit.;* and W. O. Hagstrom, *op cit.*

logical or a social problem, are more permeable and less protective of members from outside influences. The proliferation of technical and other nonscientific roles in research contributes to greater openness of research fields in comparison to scientific disciplines.

According to some analysts, the insulation afforded basic scientific research through the traditional departmental structure in universities has helped to advance the development of the sciences. The autonomy of departments shelters their members from social pressures to direct their energies to urgent probelms for which no solutions currently exist, thus permitting them to concentrate instead on "problems that only their own lack of ingenuity should keep them from solving."[45] Other commentators have argued, on the contrary, that high-level contributions to science derive in part from the "hybridization" of scientists who move across disciplines.[46] Such new sciences and theories as bacteriology and psychoanalysis originated from the practical concerns of academically marginal persons who evolved hybrid roles bridging the gap between theory and practice.[47] German medical research lost in efficiency when its isolation from practicalities shut it off from such new developments.[48] In social science research on illness, the most innovative studies were also conducted in academically marginal settings.[49]

The first of these views may be more applicable to advanced sciences, in which researchers are guided by highly developed theories. However, less developed disciplines depend on practical problems to stimulate research questions. Seemingly, the structural and intellectual gaps that result from removing these latter disciplines too far from practical issues threaten scientific advancement no less than too much openness. In the optimum situation the *insulation* of scientists from undue demands does not entail their *isolation* from the real world.

Normative Conflicts

The norms of the scientific community revolve around: *universalism*, or the postulate that scientific laws are the same everywhere; *organized*

skepticism, or the principle that scientists are responsible for the results on which they base their work; *communality*, or the ness to share knowledge freely and in particular to contribute t knowledge; and *disinterestedness*, or the banning of ulterior m scientific work.[50] It is presumed that there is consensus among about these norms and that the norms are consistent and mutua forcing. Aspiring scientists commit themselves to these values th long period of graduate training and professional socialization wh tinues within a milieu relatively insulated from extraneous no the social sciences, however, a nonscientific influence is often through training in the humanities, whether in graduate or underg courses.

But, the increase of personnel in nonscientific roles has intr other normative patterns, for such persons are seldom strongly con to the goals of science. They generally see their obligation to em rather than to the scientific community. "If commitment to the and values of science is necessary in research groups, professional so must be in control to give the groups their orientation."[51] Moreo consistencies among some norms themselves generate disagreen For example, scientists must make new knowledge available to as soon as possible, but must also avoid rushing into print; sc must strive to know their field and the work of contemporarie predecessors, while remembering that too much reading stifles cre

In view of such inconsistencies, some writers have rejected the con model, substituting for it normative conflict as a useful framewo analyzing research. Rather than the harmonious integration tha functionalist sees, there are several contradictions among norn that researchers must choose among equally accepted routes to e valued goals.[53] For example, to emphasize conceptual and theo contributions is one way to compensate for the lack of rigor in odology. Such incompatabilities are so central that most discip have broken into research subcultures, each with different pri accorded competing goals, and each with its own journal or jou When the tension over normative issues reinforces substantive ences, new specialties may break away from established disciplines.

[45] Kuhn, *op. cit.*, p. 37.

[46] Coser, *op. cit.*

[47] Joseph Ben-David, "Roles and Innovations in Medicine," *American Journal of Sociology*, **65** (1960), 557–568.

[48] Joseph Ben-David, "Scientific Productivity and Academic Organization in Nineteenth Century Medicine," *American Sociological Review*, **25** (1968), 828–843.

[49] Gerald Gordon and Sue Marquis, "Freedom, Visibility of Consequences, and Scientific Innovation," *American Journal of Sociology*, **72** (September 1966), 195–202.

[50] See Merton, *op cit.*, pp. 543–545; Storer, *op. cit.*, pp. 86–90.

[51] Hagstrom, *op. cit.*, p. 150.

[52] Merton, *op. cit.*

[53] Gunnar Boalt, *The Sociology of Research*, Southern Illinois Univ. Press, Carbor Ill. 1969. It should be noted that whereas Merton's reference is to science, Boalt'i cussion is about research.

Resistance to Change

Conflicts in norms often arise over change, whether social or intellectual, that some advocate and others oppose. That scientists resist change in the social structure of research is implicit in the above discussion. True, in the early stages of its development, when science was a marginal institution, it was markedly open to innovation.[59] Not surprisingly, conventions become harder to challenge once they are established, especially since the norms and values espoused by the scientific community are upheld not merely for social convenience, but because their violation is believed to subvert efforts to advance knowledge, a fundamental life goal of all scientists.

Substantive change is sometimes just as threatening to the scientific community as normative change. No one has described the resistance to new theories and findings more forcefully than Kuhn.[60] In his terms a "scientific revolution," a change in paradigms, is analogous to the overthrow of a government. It may be, indeed, that resistance prevents the surrender of scientific perspectives until an approved substitute is available, but usually opposition to change is closely related to competition among adherents to different "schools" for influence in scientific circles.

The metaphor likening a new set of paradigms to a political revolution might be questionable, for "the new theory seldom displaces a true government-in-being over the whole realm," and "scientific consensus before the breakthrough is vague and cautious."[61] Ziman identifies four stages characteristic of scientific developments: (1) conjecture, with heavy reliance on philosophical or even theological principles, interpolated with the conventional wisdom of other disciplines; (2) discovery, stimulated by technical developments, a pioneer's creativity, objective observations, and a challenge to the philosophical ideas by numerous contradictory and highly speculative theories; (3) a breakthrough to a general explanatory pattern, which both elucidates some phenomena and guides new investigations of other problems in the field; (4) finally, a classic epoch, when pieces of the puzzle are assembled, "usually by industrious pupils of the participants of the original revolution."[62] Heightened resistance might be expected during two stages in this process: the stage of discovery, "for the new ideas meet inevitable resistance, not only from the Old

---

59 See Chapter 2 by Roger Krohn in this volume.
60 See Bernard Barber, "Resistance by Scientists to Scientific Discovery," *Science* (September 1965), 596–602; and Thomas Kuhn, *op. cit.,* pp. 110–134.
61 Ziman, *op. cit.,* p. 54.
62 *Ibid,* pp. 51–52.

Guard, governed by a conventional conservatism dating from the semi-philosophical or theological era, but also from the disappointed rival theorists who are reluctant to give up the hope of themselves providing the successful interpretations"; and the third stage, when a breakthrough is incipient and threatens a pattern of thought after it has hardened and become the "conventional wisdom of the field."[63]

Scientific communities develop mechanisms—as exercised, for instance, by editors of journals and gatekeepers of other means of communication —for keeping controversy within bounds. Efforts are often made to neutralize severe disputes and to insulate the scientific community from their effects, even though this may restrict the dissemination of valuable information.[64] Too much zeal in restoring tranquility can be dysfunctional, however, since "creation and preservation of a free consensus is the overriding aim of science," and it cannot be served by what amounts to censorship.[65]

Mobility, Incentives, and Competition

Notwithstanding ideals of "humility," "disinterestedness," and "equality" among scientists, there is an elaborate stratification in science and research. Similarly to humans in other walks of life, scientists seek recognition, although different forms of recognition, judged by criteria related to "significant others" whose judgment is valued. These factors contribute significantly to the dynamics and productivity of science and research.

Scientific careers constitute a typical progression through a series of statuses, linked to contributions to science through research publications acknowledged by one's peers, to memberships on committees and other functions in professional associations, and to a series of jobs of rising remuneration. Organizations employing scientists provide opportunities for promotion as signified by gradations of professional rank or by the various titles used in research appointments. Local recognition can be distinguished from that in the wider scientific community or society as a whole, for the criteria are related but not identical. While in settings such as the better universities criteria for mobility are often based on a wider recognition, particularly from peers in one's specialty, in many settings mobility is largely determined by criteria of primarily local significance. Conflicts between criteria of recognition in local situations

[63] *Ibid,* p. 52.
[64] Hagstrom, *op. cit.,* pp. 279–281.
[65] Ziman, *op. cit.,* p. 135.

and those espoused by the larger community contribute greatly to the geographical mobility of scientists, especially those strongly committed to scientific goals.

As in other occupations, the pattern of social mobility in science and research is a product of many personal and structural factors; among them are elements of ascription in the system, the status dimensions or avenues for mobility, the structure of authority and the role of "invisible colleges," and incentives that motivate scientists and the role of competition in productivity and other achievements. These are discussed in turn.

Elements of Ascription

In a system built around scientific discoveries, one would expect that those who make significant contributions ultimately are recognized; and in general, the pattern of mobility in research and science is based on achievement. However, other criteria border on ascription; in particular, the prestige of the institution from which a person obtains his doctorate, which casts a positive "halo" on its graduates.[66] Such prestigious institutions usually have resourceful graduate schools, select the best students, and train them by the most productive scientists. However, as one study shows, while the prestige of the institution where a scientist received his doctorate is correlated with that of his current affiliation, the relationship of the former institutions to *productivity* is weak.[67] "Powerful patrons" are also important in moving protégés and new initiates in science, so that those who lack patrons must try to bring their names and work to the attention of the legitimizing elite by different means such as participation in conferences and other forms of communication.[68]

Since there are generally fewer scientific prizes than scientists to qualify for them, some persons are bound to be unrecognized who have contributed as much as the recipients. Such an inequity is viewed by some analysts as functional in that the result is to create and maintain a highly visible class of eminent scholars whose findings the community will closely scrutinize, thus identifying more effective channels of communicating scientific discoveries than the publications of obscure researchers, however deserving.[69] These views ignore the cumulative effects

66 Diana Crane, "Scientists at Major and Minor Universities: A Study of Productivity and Recognition," *American Sociological Review*, 30 (October 1965).
67 Lowell L. Hargens and Warren O. Hagstrom, "Sponsored and Contest Mobility of American Academic Scientists," *Sociology of Education*, 40, No. 1 (Winter 1967).
68 Ziman, *op. cit.*, pp. 129–134.
69 Robert K. Merton, "The Matthew Effect in Science," *Science*, 159 (Jan. 5, 1968).

of inequities on the motivations of members of a system in which recognition is presumably based on achievement.

Status Dimensions and Authority Structure

In addition to income and to formal authority associated with the specific positions scientists occupy in their respective settings, two status dimensions are particularly important—intellectual influence and social influence. While the first rests on scientific contributions and the recognition of peers, the latter derives from positions of authority and connections with political and economic bases of power outside science. This dual system of stratification and mobility is not unique to research and the scientific community. Indeed, knowledge and social influence serve as alternative bases of authority in most organizations.[70]

It is commonplace that intellectuals, although attracted to power throughout history, typically relate to government with uneasiness on both sides.[71] Most scientists still seek to advance primarily in their fields, with a measure of security and insulation from undue pressures, but many others have tried to influence the practical affairs of society. The scientists who advise presidents and legislative bodies are only the most visible of those at the various levels of government and industry.

Some criteria for mobility in scientific careers reflect the ideals and evaluations of so-called "invisible colleges."[72] Comprised of small groups of prolific scientists at the core of a large number of occasional collaborators, these reference groups constitute circles of power which influence the allocation of research funds and the fate of new ideas and research strategies. Invisible colleges are continually engaged in informal assessments of their members.[73] This is not meant to imply that a scientific discipline is necessarily controlled or dominated by a single "power elite." The degree to which intellectual influentials in the various disciplines and research fields are also the social influentials is not entirely clear. There seem to be hierarchies of influentials in both spheres; and the intellectual leadership often includes competing schools of thought, theoretical orientations, epistemological positions, or interests in particular substantive areas. Given the openness of many research fields and the interdisciplinary nature of some, the dominance of a

---

[70] For example, see Alvin Gouldner, "Organizational Analyses," in *Sociology Today*, R. K. Merton et al., Eds., Basic Books, New York, 1959, pp. 400–428.

[71] See Coser, *op. cit.*, pp. 135–138; and Gene M. Lyons, *op. cit.*, pp. 1–16.

[72] D. J. deSolla Price, and D. Beaver, "Collaboration in an Invisible College," *American Sociologist*, 21 (November 1966), 1011–1018.

[73] Ziman, *op. cit.*, p. 133.

monistic power structure is not likely except when a field emerges as a unified specialty (which even then, however, tends to carry over diverse perspectives from the contributory disciplines).

The existence of elements of ascription and of invisible colleges reveals that more is involved in the recognition accorded scientists than purely objective appraisals of their work. There is always an underlying dimension of power that is manifested in disproportionate control over the bestowal of recognition. The key to understanding the system is not to be found exclusively in the criteria used to *identify the particular works* deserving recognition but also in the influence-structure and decision-making process responsible for *establishing and applying the criteria.* This influence-structure explains why the contributions of researchers who are low in the status hierarchy may go unrewarded, why the institution in which a scientist did his graduate work has so much bearing on his present position, and why early recognition is related to productivity. The authority structure in science and the "circulation of elites" also help explain the rise and fall of certain fads and fashions in research.

Incentives and Competition

Of the writers who attempted to identify the major factors in the progress of science, some credited the perspective of "great men," and others argued convincingly that the *Zeitgeist*, the social milieu of the scientific culture, largely accounts for discoveries.[74] Certainly, scientists bring to their fields their individual capabilities and motivations to solve problems and overcome greater and greater challenges. However, the influence of the intellectual climate and the level of knowledge already accumulated cannot be overlooked. In addition, the social environment affects scientific advancement through the nature and structure of incentives and other social forces that motivate scientists.

Motivation and mobility within science may be explained in part within an "exchange" framework; knowledge is exchanged for recognition by other scientists. Exchange, however, does not explain why highly respected scholars seek higher positions of social influence. Additional explanations may be sought in the tendency toward "status congruency" —the relative standing an individual attains on the important status dimensions. An advance along one status hierarchy may merely highlight disparities in the overall status pattern. Since lower standing in one or more dimensions detracts from higher achievements on others,

[74] Edwin G. Boring, *History, Psychology, and Science: Selected Papers,* Robert I. Watson and Donald T. Campbell, Eds., Wiley, New York, 1963, pp. 5–25, 29–49.

scientists at certain points in their careers can be expected to pursue or respond to opportunities that enhance their positions along the dimensions in which they are low. From this perspective mobility is viewed as a function of a complex set of statuses and the motivation to enhance the total set.

The influence of colleagues on researchers' productivity is important. Incentives to advance basic knowledge were found to be associated with the values held by the peer groups of a sample of scientists, their integration in these groups, and their isolation from other influences.[75] However, social acceptance is not the only factor through which researchers are motivated by their colleagues. Competition is a basic force in the productivity of researchers and the shaping of research developments. Competition, aggravated by crowding in a discipline or a research field, motivates scientists to explore new and uncharted courses. Growth in applied research has been attributed more to changes in the supply of basic scientists than to growing industrial demands.[76] And, the emergence of the subdisciplines of experimental psychology and molecular biology has been credited to young scientists who moved from the more crowded fields of physiology and physics where fewer opportunities for recognition existed.[77]

Competition among academic institutions and research organizations has also affected scientific productivity. To attract distinguished researchers, universities and laboratories have improved their facilities and supported new fields, sometimes with heavy subsidies. For instance, competition generated by decentralization of institutions was largely responsible for shifting the leadership in medical research from France to Germany and later to the United States, and not merely the national values and wealth.[78]

The foregoing discussion of social forces and conditions was not intended to establish alternative explanations of productivity in science and research. All of the factors mentioned are believed to contribute in varying degrees under certain conditions. Better conceived as links in a concatenated pattern, all must be examined to explain the motivation of

[75] Barney G. Glaser, "Differential Association and the Institutional Motivation of Scientists," *Administrative Science Quarterly,* 10 (June 1965).

[76] D. S. Cardwell, "The Professional Society," *Science and Society,* Norman Kaplan, Ed., Rand McNally, Chicago, 1965.

[77] Joseph Ben-David and Randall Collins, "Social Factors in the Origins of a New Science: The Case of Psychology," *American Sociological Review,* 31 (August 1966), 451–465.

[78] Ben-David, *op. cit.,* 1968, pp. 828–843; and Joseph Ben-David and Abraham Zloczower, "Universities and Academic Systems in Modern Societies," *European Journal of Sociology,* 3 (1962), 45–84.

scientists and development in science. Many more data are needed to assess the relative bearing of these factors and to identify the conditions under which they influence the processes of science.

ACKNOWLEDGMENTS

Acknowledgment is due to Edward Z. Dager, William Petersen, and Donovan L. Clark for their many helpful, substantive, and editorial suggestions.

CHAPTER TWO

Patterns of the Institutionalization of Research

Roger G. Krohn, McGill University

Since World War II large-scale government and industrial support and purchase of research have set in train pervasive changes in the revered tradition of science. Many wonder what is happening to science and worry that the principal, the creative core, of science is threatened. More specific questions—in the 1950s about how to organize new, larger group and team projects and in the 1960s about priorities in the no longer accelerating support of research, the problem of the "criteria of scientific choice,"—are constantly asked.[1] All these questions, general and specific, indicate the basic, puzzling, change in American science.

One difficulty in this discussion of the problems of modern science is that they are viewed as the result of rapid growth, rather than in terms of qualitative or structural change. They are seen in terms of a traditional model of science that participants consider really self-evident. Most tersely put, the model assumes a community of independent scientists, working out of private, idiosyncratic motives (curiosity), with the

[1] Alvin Weinberg, "The Criteria for Scientific Choice, I," *Minerva*, 1 (1963), 159–71.

justification of knowledge for its own sake. Questions about change, in terms of the traditional model, lead to a dichotomy of past and present, of "little science" versus "big science."[2] However, this is not the first major change in science but the third, counting the original "revolutionary" introduction of critical, empirical scholarship in the sixteenth and seventeenth centuries. And neither everything nor nothing is changing in science, as the dichotomy assumes. To aid in sorting out these issues, we outline three stages of Euro-American science based on an analysis of its internal and external relations. Readers familiar with the exchange theory of economic anthropology and the sociology of knowledge will see the source of the questions and concepts.[3]

What is science? It has been much described as a viewpoint, as a method of inquiry, and more recently as a social system. Risking oversimplification, we can say that two assumptions constitute the beginning of the scientific viewpoint. These are that knowledge is universal, there is one "truth," and that this truth can be "discovered" at a moment in time, and thus sharply revised. The first of course had a long history in Europe, but the second was the key element in the knowledge revolution of the sixteenth and seventeenth centuries. Previously Europe, similar to the rest of humanity, had assumed that knowledge was a received, stable, collective wisdom. We are beginning to see that these stable and volatile views of knowledge are not ultimately incompatible, as in the arguments of Kuhn and Horton.

Socially, science is simply a number of people with this viewpoint, making investigations and exchanging "discoveries" for their mutual edification and in the expectation that they are changing the knowledge of all humanity. Scientific method is the visible and communicable procedure and technique derived during investigations that make discoveries. It becomes a set of guidelines for further investigations and for establishing their context of credibility. Or, as Kuhn says, the rules are derived from the paradigm.[4] Note that scientists (or spokesmen or phil-

---

2 Derek J. De Solla Price, *Little Science, Big Science*, Columbia Univ. Press, New York, 1963.

3 Useful introductory volumes in economic anthropology are, *Primitive, Archaic and Modern Economies: Essays of Karl Polanyi*, George Dalton, Ed., Doubleday, Garden City, N.Y., 1968; Manning Nash, *Primitive and Peasant Economic Systems*, Chandler, San Francisco, 1966; Cyril S. Belshaw, *Traditional Exchange and Modern Markets*, Practioners, in Larry T. Reynolds and Janice M. Reynolds, Eds., McKay, New York, 1970. of Knowledge in the United States of America: A Trend Report and Bibliography," *Current Sociology*, 15 (1967), 1, for a good current bibliography; and Karl Mannheim, *Ideology and Utopia*, Harcourt, New York, 1964, the outstanding classic in the field.

4 Thomas S. Kuhn, *The Structure of Scientific Revolutions*, Univ. of Chicago, Chicago, 1962, p. 43.

osophers of science) have more typically declared science to be defined by its method. The argument here is that this belief arises from the internal controls of science and its self-distinction from "intuitive" systems of knowledge, rather than from actual and implicit scientific practice.

Our discussion focuses on science as a system for the exchange of discovered information. This exchange model of science raises other questions. Manifestly, scientific information and ideas are not all of equivalent value. How are values put on them? Those related to existing theory are more valuable than isolated bits, and those eliciting a new range of interpretation and discovery are more valuable again. This is different from "basic" versus "applied" and "fundamental" versus "derived" sciences. The last-mentioned concepts will be explained here in terms of the academic system of science, and the prestige hierarchy of disciplines rather than their actual role in the process of discovery.

Science also developed norms for the exchange and presentation of information and for the assignment of credit for valuable discoveries. According to Mauss, systems of "prestation" (institutionalized gift exchange) have three common moral obligations: to give, to receive, and return a gift.[5] Apart from the modified obligation to acknowledge rather than to return a published "contribution" in science, because information unlike goods and services is not consumable, these are also the rules of science. In fact, the obligation to receive news is so fundamental, perhaps because reinforced by opposition to "traditional" knowledge, that the need for stable theory was only unconsciously recognized and paradigms had to be implicitly defended against premature change.[6] Similarly, the production of information has everything to do with its validity and use, hence the rigorous standards of honesty and rules of disclosure of the methods used in producing data. As an aside, note that the history of concepts, assumed to have nothing to do with their possible validity, is not part of this mandatory history.[7]

The point here is not to attempt to derive the complexity of science from this simple model but merely to establish an initial perspective. Primarily, we focus on the relations of scientists to each other and to their sources of support. We do not want to assume that we know precisely what science is, but to attempt to establish that from the behavior of scientists. We look at the self-definitions and social

[5] Marcel Mauss, *The Gift,* Cohen and West, London, 1954.
[6] Kuhn, *The Structure,* p. 76.
[7] For this and other reasons traditional science carries an antisocial theory of knowledge. Accordingly, the sociology of knowledge was invented, by Marx, against an "objectivist" opponent, that is, with a scientifically phrased social ideology.

arrangements of science as the products of this activity and pattern of relationships. We have described the internal system of science as one of information exchange and suggested that the scientific ethic, the standards for the public presentation of findings, the method of observation, the assignment of value to information, and the assignment of prestige to the presenter can all be derived from this elementary model of science as a viewpoint toward the creation of knowledge and a social system for its exchange and communication.

THE EXTERNAL SYSTEM OF SCIENCE

It is characteristic of scientific investigators, even in the early phases, that they have so often been involved in exchange in another direction, with parties giving financial or other support. Paradoxically, the more intensely the investigator is involved in his work and with communication with colleagues, the more he requires the material, political, and ideological support of outsiders. This has created an external system, with its own reciprocities, ethic, and prestige and power system, which has a great deal to do with what goes on inside science. Much of the change, contradiction, suppression of data and ideas, and fixed principles in the history of science has been generated in the contact, contrast, and negotiation between the internal and external relations of science. External parties have confronted scientists as givens to which they must adapt, or with whom they must negotiate, or to whom they must explain themselves. Scientists have maintained a certain independence, not as large as they think, which has been prerequisite to its specific character but has not been necessarily entirely beneficial from the viewpoint of its progress and social utility. And it has continuing vital and determining relations with outsiders which we need not assume to be uniquely, or even dominantly, a limitation. These external relations of science have been largely taken for granted, socially invisible, or when identified have been blamed for interfering with scientific autonomy. In short, science has assumed itself to be much more autonomous than it is, or in fact could possibly be.

While internally science has developed on the single principle of the exchange of new information, it has been supported for various reasons and through various types of exchange. Historically, these can be seen to have occurred in three dominant phases. From its beginnings in the sixteenth century to the mid-nineteenth century, scientific investigations were self-supported by amateurs or by interested patrons in a complex set of idiosyncratic arrangements. From the mid-nineteenth century, first in France and Germany and later in the United States and England, research science was conducted within and supported by universities and other higher schools. Since World War II, especially in the United States, science has been ever more decisively shaped by the predominant governmental support of research. It is the emergence of this third phase, under the title "big science," that is the cause of the current debate about priorities in science, criteria (nonscientific) of scientific choice, about the relation of basic to applied research, and so forth.

The contrasts between these phases in the relations between scientists and their supporters, the definitions and ethic that develop out of this reciprocity and power relation, the emergent or secondary structures to which these relations give rise, and the concept of science that develops out of these processes are explored in this chapter. There is a logic in the connection between the internal and external relations of science. That is, not every pattern of relation between the principle of information exchange and that of the exchange of information for something else is possible. The dynamics of these interlocking systems, and the transition between the unlocking of one systematic principle and the locking into place of the next, produce both the particular patterns of science and its problems.

In addition to the internal and the external systems, the model describes the collective relation of science to society. The latter includes the relation of science to other institutions, the public concept of science and the behavior it expects, and the scientists' publicly presented image and the terms in which they expect to be treated. Finally, science is also historical. For example, it developed in opposition to some opponents, compromised with others, and defined itself against past "errors." This has meant, for one thing, that science as a social movement has had a "naturalistic" as opposed to a "supernatural" ideology, and an impersonal rather than a personal metaphor. The elements of the paradigm are summarized below:

I. The internal system
   A. Scientist to scientist reciprocity
   B. Ethic of the relation
   C. Emergent structures
   D. Self-concept generated
II. The external system
   A. Reciprocity of scientist and his support: three historical types

        B. Definition and ethic of the relation
        C. Emergent structures
        D. Concept of science
  III. The relation of science and society
        A. Exchange with other institutions
        B. Public concept of science
        C. Emergent structures
        D. The presented image of science
  IV. Historical process
        A. Internal development
        B. Dialectics of opposition
        C. Continuity, accretion, and residual elements
        D. The "elective affinity" of science to other institutions

The paradigm contains certain assumptions in addition to that of partial discontinuity between its internal and external systems. Because science is not all of one piece, change can be initiated at levels I, II, or III, and, for example, the internal system of science can be—and has been—accommodated to more than one external system. It also assumes that levels I, II, or III can be dominant, carry greater implications for other levels at any one phase (namely, I in early science, II in academic science, and III is now emerging). These distinctions are meant to help in resolving the contrasting opinions of what is basically happening by postponing the question of whether it is good or bad, or old or new, until we can describe basic structure. We can then see stability in the constant—even though ever more complexly developed—principles of the search for and exchange of scientific information. And we can see basic change in the shift (now the third) to new structures in the external relations of science, and in its material and ideological support.

Amateur Science in Europe

The decisive break from classic and scholastic learning, to what has become "the scientific mentality," occurred between the mid-sixteenth century—in 1543 Copernicus' *De Revolutionibus* and Vesalius' *De Fabrica Humani Corporis* were published—and the early seventeenth century, which saw the work of Gilbert, Kepler, Galileo, Bacon, Descartes, and Harvey, among the more important figures. The actual nature and scope of these departures is itself a complex question, one just beginning to be opened, but it is clear that it was seen as a "new learning" by participants. Socially, these departures of interpretation and technique also bear the marks of revolution. The originators were not in established centers of learning, but rather amateurs whose studies, although perhaps full-time, were largely unpaid. Some were university teachers (Galileo, Descartes), others were clerics (Copernicus, Mersenne, Kepler), physicians (Gilbert), and still others were patronized by nobles or kings as ornaments of the family or court (Tycho Brahe, Galileo). Others, especially later in the century, were men of independent wealth (Robert Boyle, van Huygens). They have in common sufficient wealth or leisure for their substantial avocation and a lack of career or higher commitment to established institutions, especially universities.

From the beginning these men had developed a new faith in critical and current thought and in their own experience as opposed to traditional authorities. This assumption that knowledge could be reappraised and new discoveries found we could call an "open" system of knowledge, as opposed to systems with built-in devices against change.[8] One dimension of this openness of the new philosophy was that practitioners constantly sought each other's company and communication. Letters, tracts, travel and conversation became frequent and essential to any one man's work. Although these men were individualists, necessarily forcefully so, to the point of risking heresy, their work and thought were still as social as that of the institutional and authoritarian traditions. In one sense more so, because one person's observations or particular notions often entered another's thinking before conclusions were reached and formulated on paper. In our time, this reaches a direct and complex interrelation in constant cycles of isolated work and intense communication, as dramatically described, for example, by Watson in *The Double Helix*.[9] This use of selected elements from others' work in the volatile stages of thinking, as opposed to the deductive consolidation of conclusions, is a continuity in science important to mark. According to the interpretation given here, these elements of data and concept are the items of exchange in the social system of science.

The centrality of communication in science is indicated in that the first special organs of science, the scientific societies, had their origins in spontaneous private meetings, for example, in the monastery cell of Mersenne, or at Gresham College in London. The latter meetings, to-

8 Robin Horton developed the parallels in the logical structure of native African religions and modern science, together with the devices for logical closure in the native religions and for openness in science. See his "African Traditional Thought and Western Science," *Africa*, Parts I and II (January and April, 1967), 50–71, 155–87.
9 James D. Watson, *The Double Helix: A Personal Account of the Discovery of the Structure of DNA*, Atheneum, New York, 1968.

gether with similar ones of an Oxford group, evolved into the Royal Society. As Ornstein says, it was an association "not of scholars and learned men pre-eminently, but of amateurs interested in experimental science." Bishop Sprat, historian of the Royal Society, took pleasure in this absence. "It suffices if many be plain, diligent and laborious observors who though they bring not much knowledge, yet bring their hand and eyes uncorrupted. . ."[10]

As the above quotation begins to indicate, the norms of careful, accurate observation and the limitation of theorization to observation and experiment was already part of early science. For example, Tycho Brahe's astronomical observations were carried out in meticulous detail. The members of the Accademia del Cimento (experiment) were certainly protopositivists. "Their measurements were most careful; many measuring instruments owe their origin to them. [They did not] draw the false conclusions which would seem inevitable. But their aim was to be exclusively and solely experimental physicists, and therefore they contributed only to the determination of definite facts, but not to the development of fertile physical theories."[11]

The scope of their interests was very wide, so wide that the projects "defy classification," touching on and crisscrossing most current disciplines. Nor did individuals or societies move toward specialization, not even the long-lived Royal Society. In this variety the practical was mixed with the theoretical, some members bringing problems directly from business life. For example, Sir William Petty, a clothier, investigated "The Philosophy, i.e., The History of Shipping and Clothing and Dyeing."[12]

The central social dynamic of early science, as is revealed in the importance of communication and the stress on the reliability and honesty of research results, is the exchange of information for information. This was the essential reciprocity of the private meetings and correspondence, and of the early scientific societies as the first institutionalization of this exchange. In the Royal Society the core of each meeting was a demonstration or experiment prepared in advance by individual members. In the Academie des Sciences, the experiments were done collectively and originally at meetings by the members. (This is an interesting contrast because it seems related to the royal support of the Academie as a body.)

---

[10] Thomas Sprat, *The History of the Royal Society of London for the Improvement of Natural Knowledge* (1667), reprinted by Washington Univ. Press, St. Louis, 1958, p. 72.
[11] Martha Ornstein, *The Role of Scientific Societies in the Seventeenth Century,* Univ. of Chicago Press, Chicago, 1928; Ornstein, pp. 89–90, quotes F. Rosenberger, *Die Geschichte der Physik in Grundzugen,* Braunschweig, 1882–1890.
[12] Ornstein, pp. 103–104.

Rare or expensive instruments were also shared. Soon after their founding, the societies published journals.[13] The private correspondence carried on by Oldenburg, secretary of the Royal Society, became inadequate in 4 years, and the *Philosophical Transactions* were published. Later the Society also published books.[14]

The "publication" of scientific information puts it into another exchange system, a redistributive system in which one receives "credit" for his "contribution."[15] This credit has not only a prestige significance but, more basically, "recognizes" the giver as a member of science. One who does not contribute is not a scientist. If well informed, he may be a follower of science. This was not explicit in early science, in which anyone who followed scientific affairs might be named among the virtuosi.[16] Then sympathizers and friends were of course important to the fledgling private activity trying to become a public institution. In both early and later science, there was much more than personal prestige and reward involved in "recognition." An individual's credibility and influence are based on past contributions, and this in turn influences the flow of ideas and the process of scientific decision making. Perhaps the differing structures, but yet unclear ethics, of the private, reciprocal, "informal" system and the public, redistributive, "formal" system may account for many of the quarrels and misunderstandings in early science.[17]

The publication of the *Transactions* had the additional advantage of regulating the exchange, of aiding in the establishment of priority, and protecting members from plagiarism.[18] This early concern with priority, together with the quarrels over credit, such as that between Newton and Leibnitz over the invention of the calculus, has encouraged Hagstrom to view the relations of early science as the exchange of information for prestige or recognition, which he finds characteristic of contemporary

13 The publication of journals introduces a second exchange system in the internal relations of science. In private, "informal," communication we find individual to individual reciprocity under the assumption that the information is only for the personal use of the recipient. If he passes it on he is obligated also to pass on the credit for its discovery. [It is in Robert Paines' vocabulary a "signed message." See his suggestive analysis of gossip, scandal, and rumor as part of a community information exchange system, "Informal Communication and Information Management," Memorial Univ. of Newfoundland, St. Johns, Newfoundland, 1970 (mimeo)].
14 Dorothy Stimson, *Scientists and Amateurs:* A History of the Royal Society, Sigma Books, London, 1949, p. 66.
15 On the concept of redistribution, see Karl Polanyi et al., *Trade and Market in the Early Empires,* Free Press, New York, 1957, p. 250.
16 Stimson, p. 27.
17 Stimson, p. 66.
18 The frequent disputes about credit for contributions and the lack of a well-understood ethic concerning credit and acknowledgement are referred to by Stimson, p. 66.

science. However, it seems that, apart from the comparative rarity of such disputes considering the volume of peaceful communication and acknowledgment that does occur, the ethic and demeanor of early scientists is not understandable in these terms. Meetings were not conducted in the spirit of braggadocio, pride, and competition of a Potlatch,[19] but rather in a sober demeanor and in the interest of straightforward and efficient communication of the information itself. This impetus is also reflected in the style of early scientific writing.

The scientific virtuosi complained about the elaborate and pedantic style of university professors and learned men, a style understood only by the learned. The virtuosi addressed themselves to the general public. "The facts of their investigations and the reports of their experiments should be as direct, straightforward and explicit as the investigations and experiments themselves."[20] Sprat characterized it as a "naked" directness and simplicity of expression, which is not a bad characterization of scientific writing to this day. Prestige seeking would be just the wrong motive to explain the pressure toward strict honesty in the presentation of findings, the simple style of the writing, and the developing controls for citation and acknowledgment in science.

The amateur status, the large degree of independence, and the free, unstructured, even directionless, character of their investigations are all related to self-support by the devotees of experimental learning. Notwithstanding the partial governmental support of the scientific societies in France, Italy, and Germany,[21] and the occasional patronizing of individuals by wealthy or noble persons, it seems that the main support of research all through the seventeenth century came from investigators themselves. This was certainly true of all the activities of the Royal Society, and England was the center of scientific advance in the seventeenth century. The Society was continually preoccupied with its financial difficulties, "Which more than once threatened its very existence."[22] When the center of scientific developments did move from England and France to Germany, it was precisely because of substantial support of science by the German states through their universities.

---

[19] The competitive gift-giving ceremonies of the Kwakiutl Indians of British Columbia have often been described. A basic source is Helen Codere, *Fighting with Property,* Monograph 18, American Ethnological Society, J. J. Augustin, New York. 1950.
[20] Stimson, pp. 108–109.
[21] The Academica del Cimento was supported in its direct expenses by the Medicis from its foundation. Only the Academia des Sciences had substantial governmental patronage, including a pension for 20 to 30 full-time investigators and a general fund of 21,000 livres.
[22] Ornstein, pp. 106–107.

The exact terms of the early patronage of science and of individual investigators are difficult to determine; they were no doubt various, and predominantly temporary as mood and convenience affected both patron and clients. That the relations of patron and client in science were never institutionalized, never defined by norms of proper relationship, sanctions, and agencies of control, seems to indicate lack of any pervasive effect of the patronage system on the social patterns of amateur science. The Royal Society, however, does illustrate the dynamics of amateur and philanthropically supported science. Because the Society was entirely self-supported, by membership fees, gifts, and bequests, and not by government, it could never establish a scientific criterion for membership. Since a considerable prestige adhered to the Society, prestige reasons to belong were quite powerful. At times, as toward the end of the seventeenth century, the Society became almost purely a gentlemen's social club.[23] From 1687 to 1696 the Society published no books, and for 3 years, 1688–1690, even the *Philosophical Collections,* as *Philosophical Transactions* was then called, was not published. Never in its long history, until late in the nineteenth century, did the ratio of gentleman dilettantes to serious investigators fall below two to one.[24] And this was in spite of efforts in 1674 and again in 1730 to tighten membership requirements.[25]

Ben-David argues that it was exactly the independence and self-support of the bourgeois scientists of Europe that allowed its continuous development. In Italy the academies decayed as a result of the incorporation of noble amateurs and fanciers of science.[26] This process very nearly ended the Royal Society as well; perhaps the self-support by scientists such as Wren, Boyle, Wilkins, Wallis, and Newton, who also made timely gifts to the Society, was basic to its survival.

There was also a positive side to the prestigious amateur members, who defended the Society before a suspicious and critical public. Bishop Sprat's *History of the Royal Society,* written only 5 years (1667) after its establishment, was in fact a defense of the Society against accusations that the Society was antiuniversity, antichurch, and in violation of common sense. However, the Society's lack of internal criticism and control, because of varied membership, also provided excellent targets for critics who found a great deal worthy of ridicule—for example, the observations of animal life on the moon, of human constructions

23 Stimson, p. 155.
24 Stimson, p. 144.
25 Stimson, p. 149–150.
26 Joseph Ben-David, "The Scientific Role: The Conditions of its Establishment in Europe," *Minerva,* **4**, 15–54, especially 30–36.

there, and speculation about travel to the moon. An Oxford orator gibed that the virtuosi "can admire nothing except fleas, lice and themselves."[27] No doubt the critics wanted to do more than to expose triviality, but rather to defend established learning and institutions and the very categories of offended common sense.

The dilemma of the members was no doubt great; efforts to tighten membership requirements and to screen articles for significance went against the necessity of admitting members who would support the Society financially and socially. And, once members, how were they to be prevented from speaking at meetings or occasionally publishing articles in the *Transactions?* The same dilemma appeared in another way. The society had constant problems in collecting dues from members and made never successful efforts to become more strict.[28] If members who gave the Society the prestige of their names neglected to pay their fees, how could the Society enforce collection from others?

It seems that a certain diffuseness, lack of self-criticism and control, and conversion of scientific values to prestige purposes were the inherent maladies of amateur science.

This brief analysis of the dynamics of support and prestige in the Royal Society also illuminates something of the general place of early science in society. The work of the Royal Society was criticized as either trivial or dangerous and was, no doubt, both. The first investigators began their work largely independently of the churches and their universities, which had enjoyed a monopoly of official "knowledge." The new philosophers were more than self-preoccupied hobbyists but, in fact, were contesting the intellectual monopoly of the church. However, the new learning was not an explicit and direct challenge to the churches in the sense that a revolutionary party is to a government. This allowed a blurring of issues, compromises and truces, and a gradual change that is in fact not yet over today. However, even the more limited claim for space the new learning in effect made for itself created a "battle of the books," between the new and the old learning in which Bishop Sprat's *History of the Royal Society* also had a part.

The formative and continuing influence of this contest on the future of science is not to be underestimated. The trial of Galileo in 1632 obviously set the beginning separation of experimental knowledge and the Roman Church. Church commitment to opposition did not stop scientific inquiry, even in Italy, but it clearly defined the issue. More importantly, no European university accepted scientific studies until the

---

27 Stimson, p. 77.
28 Stimson, p. 104.

new state-supported universities of the Protestant German states of the mid-nineteenth century. That science had to find its place in socially interstitial areas, outside the universities, affects science, the universities, and the relation of the fields of learning to this day, most obviously in the split of humanities and the sciences.

The insurgent new learning rapidly shifted from Latin, the language of established learning, to the vernacular. This change of language involved a shift in mental style, a shift in class base—to the humbler but rising classes—and in recruitment paths into science. These new paths gave direct access to the new learning through self-education and apprenticeship rather than through the universities, thus omitting a phase of potential thought control (and perhaps also of intellectual discipline). Leibnitz, a missionary for science in Germany and founder of the Berlin Academy, realized this fully.[29] He opposed Latin in school and university because education should reach everyone, and because Latin "was allied to the old thought, while the vernacular was the mouthpiece of the new times."[30] Leibnitz lacked all respect for the old learning, trivialities were veiled by complex language, and nothing was proposed without ancient authority. He could learn more "in a book on carpentry . . . than in learned works."[31] Leibnitz's scepticism carried even to books as a vehicle of communication. "He felt that only by co-operation with men who sympathized with and shared his attitude could his ideas ultimately prevail."[32] This is the profile of a true revolutionary.

Similar to all revolutionary movements, science was shaped by the conflict. Both in the definition of its fundamental terms of explanation and in the terms of its bases of belief, the new knowledge formed itself as a countersystem to the old knowledge. Its "naturalistic" terms of explanation contrasted with "supernaturalism." Its current, disciplined observation contrasted with the traditional, but various, interpretations of the ancient texts. The knowledge of the past was intricately deductive; that of the present was directly inferred from observed facts. As Rosenberger says of the Accademia del Cimento, ". . . their aim was to be exclusively and solely experimental physicists, and therefore they contributed only to the determination of definite facts, but not to the development of fertile physical theories."[33] Where religious and philosophical authority supported the suppression or reconciliation of ex-

29 Ornstein, p. 177.
30 Ornstein, p. 181.
31 Ornstein, p. 182.
32 Ornstein, pp. 182–183.
33 Quoted by Ornstein, p. 90.

perience when it conflicted with knowledge, the naturalists demanded the acceptance of new knowledge. For the traditionalist, emotional conviction under the name of revelation or intuition carried authority, but for the new science, emotion could only be a blind to observation and a distraction from truth. And somewhat paradoxically, traditional and collective wisdom implied that the truth was presently available, but the new thought said that although truth could be increasingly approximated it would only be complete in the future. The implications of all this are very great, for none of it is itself systematically and empirically derived. Rather, these doctrines are also a priori assumptions, the unconsciously derived and socially useful counterideology of a social movement. Currently, the traditional character of science is being critically reexamined and, of course, precisely this is prerequisite to a sociology of science that will be an empirical theory of knowledge and not only a gloss on the common sense of institutional science.

In bold outline we find the first attempts at a new, critical scholarship conducted by scattered individuals who assumed that careful current investigation could discover truths against the received wisdom of the ancients and of venerable institutions. The material resources and apparatus of these investigations were supplied, or solicited from sympathizers, by the same people who carried them out. They generated their own institutions around meetings and cooperative investigations, the exchange of discoveries and equipment, and the public communication of results. Subsidies by individual or governmental patrons, although perhaps often strategically important at times, did not seem to have had major structural consequences for science. The patronage system was never regularized into a sustaining and controlling external system for science. If it had been, science might have become totally under control of dilettantish fanciers and only the plaything of prestigious circles. Rather, science had the independence, if also the marginal existence, of self-support. It was this that allowed sufficient autonomy to break the categories and offend the logic of common sense, to make discoveries and recognize and accumulate them into an increasingly persuasive body of knowledge, one impossible to set aside. Even then this happened primarily in the countries of North Europe, broken off from the Roman Church, with Protestant minorities and insurgent commercial classes.

Even though support for science might come from a ruling family (Medicis) or a king's official (Colbert under Louis XIV), this is still better considered support by sympathetic individuals, themselves interested in science, than a matter of government policy. Science in this sense was not related to society. When not seen as heretics or critics of traditional learning, scientists were seen as cranks, mere hobbyists, or "wanderers."[34] When they specifically challenged theological doctrines, they fell into conflict with the church, or religion broadly, over the right to interpret nature for the public. The high charter of science was formed by a claim of intellectual autonomy, by conflict with orthodoxy, by a compromise which excluded the study of man, and by implicit derivation from the practice of science itself. It is this nonempirical, but apparently "functional" charter, seeing that science did obtain a measure of freedom and has progressed, that now begins to be subject to critique and challenge.[35]

Academic-Professional Science

Amateur science developed little specialization or control over the scientific qualifications of members. Academic science was organized into "disciplines" for which there were formal criteria of membership and control over publication. The key steps toward professional science —the establishment of science in universities and of professional scientific societies—were taken in Germany between 1810 and 1830. The causal relation is unclear, but the close connection of university science and professional scientific societies is clear in their mutual disciplinary organization.

Specialized scientific societies were established in England; twelve societies began between 1788 and 1839, without the concurrent establishment of science in the major universities. The founding of the Gesellschaft Deutscher Naturforscher und Ärzte in 1822 was a definite step toward professional science. It was agreed at the first meeting in Leipzig that "the actual members of this assembly can only be those who have published" scientific papers, that is, independent work beyond the doctoral dissertation.[36] It is also significant that the lack of a dominant scientific center in Germany, and the hope to give the association a national character, decided them to meet each year at a different local center of science.[37] This format, unlike that of amateur societies, was then broadly imitated in England, France, Italy, and the United States. In

---

[34] Ornstein, p. 122.

[35] Roger G. Krohn, "The Secularization of Science," *The Sociology of Sociology: Analysis and Criticism of the Thought, Research, and Ethical Folkways of Sociology and Its Practitioners,* in Larry T. Reynolds and Janice M. Reynolds, Eds., McKay, New York, 1970.

[36] Everett Mendelsohn, "The Emergence of Science as a Profession in Nineteenth Century Europe," in *The Management of Scientists,* Karl Hill, Eds., Beacon Press, Boston, 1963, p. 24.

[37] Mendelsohn, p. 25.

England, The British Association of the Advancement of Science was established in 1831.

The key point here is that the societies on the German model had formal scientific criteria of membership and were open to anyone who qualified. The amateur societies, however, had more limited membership and tended toward prestige criteria, such as the Royal Society, or personalist criteria, such as the Lunar Society of Birmingham, which died with the original network of friends.[38] When the detailed history of early professional societies has been written, they will no doubt be found to have developed standards of criticism and rules of evidence and argument that have been critical in making science coherent and cumulative, while keeping the capacity for basic change. Amateur science was intellectually open, to a fault in fact. Other intellectual systems have been rigorous and cumulative but closed to change. The question of just what are the social mechanisms combining logical standards of self-consistency and openness to shifts of basic assumption as well as explicit theory should be addressed to these nineteenth century scientific societies.

Science as an investigative enterprise, as opposed to a subject to be taught, did not enter European universities until the 1820s, and then it did not first enter the old, respected, self-governing universities of England or France but the new, state-supported Ecole Polytechnique in France, and newer, state universities of Germany. The older, major universities of Heidelberg, Leipzig, and Freiburg resisted until after the lesser universities of Giessen, Halle, Gottingen, and the new University of Berlin had founded science professorships.[39] The resistance of British universities, of Oxford and Cambridge, was particularly strong, perhaps because they were in clerical and aristocratic control and were used to defend establishment prerogatives and to control access to prime civil service appointments in the face of the rising bourgeoisie, who were identified with science.[40] This class interest thesis is less applicable to French universities after the revolution, and to Germany, where the bourgeoisie were much less a threat to the nobility. More basically, the new and the old learning contained fundamentally opposed principles. The new learning assumed that knowledge was being discovered today by independent scholars, and the old learning assumed that true, basic

[38] Robert E. Schofield, *The Lunar Society of Birmingham: A Social History of Provincial Science and Industry in Eighteenth Century England,* Clarendon, Oxford, 1963, p. 418.
[39] Friedrich Paulsen, *The German Universities and University Study,* translated by Frank Thilly and William W. Elwang, Longman's, Green, New York, 1906, p. 443.
[40] This is suggested by Cardwell at several places. Donald S. L. Cardwell, *The Organization of Science in England: A Retrospect,* Heineman, Toronto, 1957. See especially pp. 29–36, 80, 132, 184–186.

knowledge had always been known and was safeguarded by men of learning in universities. The one threatened to degrade or displace the other.

The first time that a major group of scientific scholars taught at university level was at the Ecole Polytechnique (1794). Later, (1810) at the new University of Berlin, professorial chairs for science were established as part of humane learning. The most decisive development in university science did not occur until Leibig, having been impressed by the laboratory teaching-research at the Ecole Polytechnique, set up a research laboratory in chemistry at the University of Giessen.[41] Here not only was a great research scientist teaching, but his students were involved in his research and did their own research under close direction. This key innovation, of students doing serious research as apprentices, and in organized but open-ended situations, was fundamental to the contribution university science was to make. For one, this close work with a respected master forged master-disciple ties which were a powerful socializing force in science as profession and ideology. The enthusiasm of German-trained scientists was a great force for university reform in England, the United States, Russia, and other countries.[42]

The introduction of research-teaching laboratories and seminars in German universities took place within a growing university system of about 20 German speaking universities competing for talent and developing new disciplines. Ben-David argues that this period of competitive growth and development, from the 1840s to the 1860s, was the basis of the productivity and prestige of German science during the last half of the nineteenth century. Two main reasons have been suggested for the resources and talent that went into science in Germany in this period. First, a great deal of pride was invested, both by government and by the educated public in German intellectual and scholarly life, partly because of the defeats the German states suffered in the Napoleonic Wars. Paulsen cites the words of Wilhelm von Humbolt's report on the University of Berlin to the King, "The state, like the private citizen, always acts wisely and politically, when, in times of misfortune, it uses its efforts to establish something looking to future good and connects its name with such a work."[43] Second, economic and political careers were not as rewarding as in France and England, and this directed high talent into German science. These great professors were much of the reason for the enthusiasm and richness of German university life: "Our

41 Mendelsohn, p. 11.
42 On England, see Cardwell, p. 46ff and on the United States see Lawrence R. Veysey, *The Emergence of the American University,* Univ. of Chicago Press, Chicago, 1965.
43 Paulsen, p. 55.

thinkers and investigators not only write books for us, but are our personal instructors, men whom we meet face to face."[44]

Whatever the reasons, Germany had hundreds of professors of science with full salaries free to give much of their time to research, and original research was now required to be a university teacher. Research no longer rested on individual initiative but was fully instituted in a system with high motivation and stable support, a near-perfect situation for recruitment and socialization, which allowed cooperative and flexibly organized research. However, the system also had latent problems even in the beginning, which became apparent only to perceptive observers such as Paulsen and Weber in the early twentieth century and became subject to a systematic critique only in recent years.[45]

We touch on these limitations after mentioning two further features. First, although the German system was highly professional in the sense of standards of entrance, internal autonomy, self-criticism, and so forth, research was still not a full-time and stable career. Even the full professor (ordinaribus) was paid as a teacher and, in fact, fees from students attending his lectures were a substantial portion of his total income. (Paulsen defended the honorarium staunchly against criticisms that the system had led to abuses.)[46] Also the privatdocent, upon whom many placed great emphasis as the "power and life of the university,"[47] was actually a fee-taking, licensed teacher not paid by the university. The privatdocents hoped to become professors, but because the ranks of the privatdocents increased far faster than that of salaried professors, this was by no means regular. [48] Finally, there were the *rentenintellectuell-entum*, scholars with private financial resources. The prestige of the scholarly career was such that many subsidized their professor's salaries or student honoraria for living expenses. The wealth of many families was such that scholarly members "could survive the long period of unpaid preparation and waiting for an appointment to an intellectual post which did provide an income."[49]

Why this was so leads us to our second point, that prestige can be seen as the common coin of German university life. This was true in the relations between the universities and the states, which took great pride

44 Paulsen, p. 5.

45 Joseph Ben-David, *Fundamental Research and the Universities: Some Comments on International Differences*, OECD, 1968, pp. 29–45.

46 Paulsen, p. 87ff.

47 Alexander Busch, "The Viscitudes of the Privatendozent: Breakdown and Adaptation in the Recruitment of the German University Teacher," *Minerva*, 1, 319–41. This phrase is cited on p. 320.

48 Busch, p. 327 and 332ff.

49 Busch, p. 332.

in the fame and respectability of their universities, to the point that the founding of the University of Berlin could be viewed as a reaction to the defeat of Prussia by Napoleon. Also, within universities support of science in particular and the philosophical faculty generally was well supported as the most prestigious faculty within the university.[50] Here, prestige is converted into money by universities and scholars, and money is converted into prestige by the state and by universities.[51] The same exchange is made by the individual scholar who is willing to live on a low income or to subsidize his career for the sake of a place in a prestigious institution. This helps to explain the unique place of universities and university scholarship in German life and their substantial support before any equivalent economic advantage in scientific excellence was apparent. It also helps to explain the rigidities and other disadvantages of the German university system so well outlined by Ben-David.[52]

The Interaction of Science and the Universities

None of the older, major universities of Europe adopted the new sciences voluntarily. In France the old universities were abolished in 1793 and mathematics and some sciences were established in the new Grand Ecoles. In Germany scientific studies were introduced by the new state University of Berlin. In England, where the private universities had a very real autonomy as self-governing corporations, science was not a basic part of university education until more than a century later. Major movements of agitation and reform were necessary to force the study of basic science into even the University of London, not in control of the Anglican church. And the reform of the entrenched system of examinations, so antithetical to higher scientific training, and so basic to British higher education, required further struggles.[53] The universities had to be captured, taken over by the scientific movement. In France, this was part of a political revolution, and in Germany it was part of a nationalist and "spiritual" insurgence. Academic autonomy, now thought to be fundamental to science by its most tradition-minded spokesman,[54] had it remained inviolate would have precluded university science.

[50] Paulsen, p. 48.

[51] On the concept of the conversion of values (items) from lower to higher spheres of exchange (prestige levels), see Paul Bohannon, "Some Principles of Exchange and Investment Among the Tiv," *American Anthropologist*, **57**, 60–70.

[52] Ben-David, *Fundamental Research;* and also, "The Universities and the Growth of Science in Germany and the United States," *Minerva* (Autumn 1968), 1–36.

[53] Cardwell, p. 132.

[54] See Michael Polanyi, "The Growth of Thought in Science," *Economica,* (November

The cultivation of original research succeeded in bringing the universities back into the center of cultural life for the first time since they were the "intellectual powerhouses" of the Middle Ages. This occurred whether research only took a place among other university purposes, as in Great Britain and until recently in the United States, or whether it became the predominant and distinguishing purpose of university life, as in Germany. The universities also became less autonomous, self-contained, and idiosyncratic in their own cultural style; compare Oxford and Cambridge as recent and partial converts, with the greater homogeneity and interchangeability of German and United States universities. Internally, universities were transformed by their most prestigious branch. In Germany science became the model of all faculties, and in the United States original scholarship was attempted by all the professional schools. The problem now runs the other direction; the control of undergraduate education by professionally oriented graduate departments is currently part of the problems of universities in the United States.[55]

Certain important effects have become conspicuous as the university has become the new locale for science and as the new academic-science compound has become dominant. Science, with its historical particularities, has become established as the dominant model of knowledge of the European world. It inherited the concept of the pursuit of truth for its own sake as a high calling and a systematic scholarly tradition. On this latter point, Busch points to a less obvious effect. A new intellectual movement of systematic, detailed scholarship coming from classic philology, archeology, and philosophical idealism was carried into science, helping to develop the stringent standards that German research became famous for. The social energy for these intellectual currents in turn was the self-emancipation of the bourgeoisie.[56] The reform and upgrading of academic standards began at the University of Berlin, which required the *habilitation* of the prospective university teacher. Habilitation required the presentation of original scholarly work, participation in a colloquium of full professors, and a trial lecture in addition to the doctor's degree in order to obtain the *venia legendi*, permitting one to teach in the university. This must be seen as part of the earlier, broader impetus rather than from scientific practitioners alone.

1941); "Freedom in Science," *Bulletin of the Atomic Scientists,* **6,** (1950) 195–198, 224; "The Republic of Science: Its Political and Economic Theory," *Minerva,* 1 (1962), 154ff, a sample of Polanyi's many writings on the subject; and, Price, *Little Science, Big Science.*

[55] Christopher Jencks and David Riesman, *The Academic Revolution,* Doubleday, Garden City, New York, 1968, pp. 244–247.

[56] Busch, p. 322ff.

University science also encouraged the emergence of a certain cultish enthusiasm, a sacralization and mystique of research that has been basic to its history and progress. Research was not a mere profession as the others were, but a special calling "of whole-souled self-abandonment."[57] This presented the danger that the conviction that one was discovering the universal and permanent "truth" would verge into sectarian conviction and contention, but converts to new theories have been won, devotees to older theories forced to give way, and science has been able to change its theories. However, the principles of scientific method have been erected as permanent truths by some philosophers and spokesmen of science. And the values and ethic of the scientific community have been conceived as a permanent and higher morality and even a more general model for society. The positive and negative consequences of this faith are complex, and we will not attempt an appraisal here. However, the analysis of science as first a social movement, and then as a sacred institution with its own ritual and belief, is necessary before we can understand science and the changes it is undergoing today.

American Academic Science: A Further Transformation

American academic science began in the 1870s and 1880s during the great era of German science, and in large part in conscious imitation of the German example. However, for a complex of reasons, well outlined by Ben-David and Veysey, American university science led to a transformation of the universities beyond that occurring in Germany. This in turn has helped science to take a central place in American society.

The major innovations of the Germans were taken over by the Americans. Teaching and research were combined in a role of the professor, who could live on his teaching salary and devote part of his time to research; research and scholarly facilities were located in the university and given a minimum capital support; advanced students were involved in the professors' research and learned science by the apprentice system; and an original contribution in research became the qualification for university-level teaching. However, other key features of the academic tradition either could not be or were not imitated.[58] Thus departments of several professionally qualified and formally equal professors replaced the single professorial chair in a discipline, with research institutes under the professor's total control. The university department thus became the autonomous and effective unit of the scientific disciplines and of the

[57] G. Stanley Hall, quoted by Veysey, p. 149.
[58] Ben-David, "The Universities and the Growth," pp. 7–8.

universities. This meeting point of internal and external systems allowed flexibility in the scientist's choice of loyalty and orientation and is the background of "local" versus "cosmopolitan" loyalties in the American system. The departmental organization also allows the flexible rearrangement of specialties as compared to Germany.[59] Also, since young Ph.D.'s were hired as junior but salaried professors, the research career was regularized and much less problematical, the time of risk ad self-support being largely confined to the graduate student years.

A second major change was the separation of unspecialized undergraduate education from specialized, professional graduate education. In Germany the single-degree, 3-year program was too little specialized for training professional researchers, but it was much too specialized for training general students.[60] In the United States the separation of levels of university work was then also applied to the professional schools which also established graduate programs. This, plus the lack of such unique prestige of faculties of arts and science as the faculty of philosophy had in Germany, meant the softening of the distinction between basic and merely practical research as occurred there. This, as Ben-David has pointed out, has favored broader application of the scientific approach in American society.[61] In effect then, in the United States the universities were, partly unconsciously, tailored more closely to the purposes of research, with more traditional features not favorable to science dropping away.

Besides the selective imitation and adaptation of German science, other features of the American environment were also favorable in some ways. Ben-David stresses the "ecology" of higher education in the United States, universities being still more decentralized and in an even more open and larger competitive system than in Germany.[62] In this situation, containing both private and state universities, university presidents were led into an entrepreneurial pattern of mobilizing resources and looking for markets for university services. Instead of this being the corruption of university and scholarly ideas, as it appeared to European and more orthodox American academicians such as Veblen, Wilson, and Caplow and McGee, Ben-David argues that this allowed United States science to escape the somewhat confining conceptual and institutional boxes of European academic science.[63]

Compared to Europe, especially after World War II, American science

59 Ben-David, "The Universities and the Growth," p. 4.
60 Ben-David, *Fundamental Research*, p. 32.
61 Ben-David, *Fundamental Research*, pp. 43–46.
62 Ben-David, The Universities and the Growth," pp. 16–19.
63 Ben-David, *Fundamental Research*, pp. 58ff.

showed at least three distinct contrasts. Organized research groups of professional scientists were developed without rigid internal hierarchical patterns. There was less assumption that collective research was inhospitable to creativity, or that it should be under the secure control of a master scientist. Second, a strengthening of disciplinary loyalties and increased job mobility led scientists to identify more with their profession and less with their university. And third, the increased mobility extended to an exchange of scientists between universities and government and industry. This and other kinds of communication between them assisted in the increasingly rapid applied and technical exploitation of basic advances in science. These were key departures from the academic system and opened the way to the basic structural changes and stresses of the 1960s.

Academic-Professional Science and Society

Compared with amateur science, academic science was firmly within the constellation of national institutions. With the establishment of scientific professorships and research institutes in universities and recognized national professional and disciplinary associations, science had a legitimate place in society. Institutions or individuals that found occasion to consult scientific opinion, or to conduct other business, found devices by which to do so. And science had, thanks largely to the support from undergraduate education, a modest but secure flow of resources, a continuous center of operations, and substantial capital investment in public facilities, libraries, laboratories, and so forth. And it had an ideal source of recruits through scientists' own college and university classes. Internally, science had developed much further in the directions laid down in the amateur period. Theories became more comprehensive and self-coherent, and scientific opinion was decisive in its own area of competence, as was established by the victory of Darwin's theory of evolution over religious-philosophical opposition. Modifying this conceptual and formal autonomy of science was a flux of forces determining the size and direction of research support, including the effects of endowments, the force of particular personalities, the fate of particular universities and institutes, and so forth. However, scientific opinion was free of public opinion across the broad front of the natural sciences and even showed signs of a commanding ideological position. Science became the authority for many things, legitimately and illegitimately.

Science was still socially marginal, however, an appendage to higher education which was itself without independent leverage in society. The conceptual and ethical side of this marginality and isolation begins in a

sharp self-distinction of science from society. Scientific knowledge is opposed to common sense, scientific method to loose inference, the pure motive of curiosity and search for truth to the complex of mundane emotions that govern other activities, and the honor, honesty, and co-operativeness among scientists to the easier morality of the rest of human interchange. Scientists had set themselves and their science as a world apart in a vocabulary normally secular but which was clearly sacred in in emotional tone. This point hardly needs demonstration by quotation; all readers are aware of the completely self-serious "sacred" tone that pervades scientists' discussion of their moments of insight and discovery, the ethic of their relations with colleagues, and the governing values of the scientific search.[64] This cultish mystique of science has been taken for granted, never questioned or felt to require explanation. The point is not to attempt here an analysis of the historical and institutional sources of the scientific sect but to suggest further implications of the history of science as a social movement and directions for further study. The academic phase of science could be viewed as another denomination struggling for adherents, having devices of exclusion for unbelievers, and granting rights to those qualified to interpret the truth. This move-ment become institution has struggled for and gained the intellectual monopoly for the interpretation of nature; the autonomy and power to interpret man and his institutions is still in contest. That many of the early converts to "natural philosophy" were clergy and that they suc-ceeded in reconciling the new epistomology and new theories of nature with their theology only reinforces the imputation of a strong continuity of motives between religion and science.

This view of the parallels between the development of religious-philosophical movements and science, in spite of its deliberate self-distinction, connects at many points with the communication-exchange model we primarily employed. For example, the claims of scientists for legitimacy and prestige were necessary for the conversion of prestige to money and other social support on which science was based in the aca-demic era (Bohannon, etc.). It was in Germany where, among European countries, knowledge (*Wissenschaft*) was given the broadest definition and

---

64 Perhaps the most extreme example is the writings of the people associated with the Society for Freedom in Science. See its, *The Society for Freedom in Science, Its Origins, Objects and Constitution,* Potter Press, Oxford, 1953; and "Occasional Pamphlets," No. 1–13, 1945–1952. See also J. R. Baker, *The Scientific Life,* Macmillan, New York, 1943; and C. D. Darlington, *The Conflict of Science and Society,* Watts, London, 1948. The Society was founded in response to J. D. Bernal's proposals for a nationally organized and supported applied and basic science program. See J. D. Bernal, *The Social Functions of Science,* Macmillan, New York, 1939.

the most profound respect, that science was first given systematic support as "an end in itself." In England and France, where national, institutional, and personal prestige were gained on economic, political, and military grounds, science was confined to individual philanthropy and limited to irregular governmental support. The case of England is especially clear; there science was shaped by the powerful utilitarian arguments that had to be launched in its behalf in London, Oxford, and Cambridge universities.[65]

In spite of its intellectual and social success, academic science had its limitations and its problems, in part the result of the above self-reverential attitude. The limitations are only now in retrospect begining to come to systematic attention.[66] However, they were not invisible to a sensitive student of universities such as Paulsen, writing in 1902, the late golden age of German science according to the chronology of Ben-David. Paulsen clearly outlined the professor's conflict of commitment to teaching and research, which begins in the research professor putting his greater, or nearly exclusive, effort into research, which for personal and professional reasons he finds more rewarding.

It may even happen that he regards teaching as a burden, as a task that interfered with his true vocation and which he feels himself justified in performing as best he may. . . . he will then read off his notes or talk like a book, like a book not caring whether the hearer can or is willing to follow him. And when he meets with poor success . . . he consoles himself by throwing the blame upon them; they are too dull to feel a yearning for true science. And at last he comes to look upon his lack of success in teaching as a sign of superiority; whatever is truly valuable is always a matter for the few . . ."[67]

Paulsen goes on to mention the dangers to students in specializing too early, through being involved with the professor's research, and failing to obtain a proper perspective of the whole discipline. In lecture courses teachers discuss not what students need but what they themselves are investigating.[68] "The university system" also has dangers for science, including "a kind of pseudo-productivity," of quantity not quality, deriving from competition for positions. This competition also influences the criticism and citation of scientific work by creating artificial and venomous controversies, or by currying favor with one party in an argument,

[65] Cardwell, p. 56, 140ff.
[66] See Ben-David, already cited, and his "Roles and Innovation in Medicine," *American Journal of Sociology*, **65** (1960), 828–843. See also Busch and Krohn, both cited.
[67] Paulsen, p. 171.
[68] Paulsen, p. 173.

and so forth.[69] Evidently, professionalism was combined in Paulsen's mind with "the university system," but the point here is the rather remarkably similar portrait of troubles he paints and the criticisms current American critics make of their system. One thing Paulsen does not see in German universities at the turn of the century is any tension between teachers and students. He attributes this to "the entire freedom" of the students to choose their teachers, and to the fact that the professor is not the examiner, which makes them "fellow soldiers."[70] The professors, on their side, show a spirit of confidence and are willing to be helpful whenever asked. This is in sharp contrast to the current American system of higher education. The final problem Paulsen sees in the science of his day in, "an undercurrent of hostility to the scientific activity of our universities." He sees this as the result of disappointment in science for its failure to redeem its promise to "supply a complete and certain theory of the universe and a practical world-wisdom . . ."[71] As philosophy replaced religion, science has claimed and been given the place of philosophy in answering these questions and providing these guidelines. However, it becomes more evident that science does not provide a world view, "nor satisfy the hunger for knowledge, . . . nor . . . personal culture." Paulsen asks whether the unbelief in science of the followers of Nietzsche is a sign of its ultimate bankruptcy and abdication, or a "demand for ideas, the long suppressed demand for philosophy that is coming to life again, but is not yet quite sure of its path and goal."[72]

The Government-Professional Research System

Since World War II the United States has, without knowing it, moved decisively into a new system of science. Scientific contributions to the war effort, such as radar and the atomic bomb, convinced a skeptical government that high technology and its basic background sciences would be critical to the military and political posture of the United States after the war.[73] (Greenberg gives a sharply lined account, emphasizing the mutual distance of science and government before the war, and the war's key role in creating close relations in 3 or 4 years.) We argue that this large infusion of primarily government but also industrial support has meant much more than an increase in the scale of United States science. It has meant a qualitative change in the structure

---

[69] Paulsen, pp. 173–174.
[70] Paulsen, pp. 184–185.
[71] Paulsen, p. 66.
[72] Paulsen, p. 67.
[73] Daniel S. Greenberg, *The Politics of Pure Science*, World, New York, 1967.

of science and in its place in society. In the language used here, science has a new "external system" based primarily on the direct support of individual scientists' work by agencies of the federal government, and a new central place in society based on military, industrial, and medical technologies. Opinions on the basic health of science in this new era range from the extremely optimistic (Ben-David), to the slightly less so (Hagstrom), to the pessimistic (Price), to the gloomy (Polanyi).[74] We have argued that one difficulty in answering this question has been the lack of a clear distinction between the internal and external relations of science, and that it is its external relations that are bringing science into a third distinct phase. The first two allowed scientists a partial but effective autonomy to phrase their own questions, to address them by self-developed techniques, to exchange information on internal criteria, to conduct self-persuasive argument, and to change cumulatively the consensus of opinion. The question now becomes: Compared with the self and philanthropic support of the amateur era, and the modest but broad subsidy and largely symbiotic relation of teaching to research in the academic era, what are the precise implications of centrally allocated, largely "mission-directed," and individually contracted research for the internal system of science? Given the prolix, but amorphous and dispersed knowledge of contemporary American science, we can only attempt a partial answer and emphasize a few points.

The pervasive changes to be described have occurred in spite of the conscious and particular intention of university scientists to accept government support only on the basis of their traditional values and work patterns. Most basically, the autonomy of science and the independence of individual scientists was preserved by the peer referee system whereby the government, in granting specific support or making contracts, was taking scientific and specialist advice rather than exercising its own discretion. This looks like, and is, a brilliant device to mesh hierarchical agencies with specific purposes with the individualist-equalitarian pattern and open goals of science. The referees chosen were naturally the "most eminent," highly qualified scientists. However, these previously largely symbolic prestige rankings within science were now given a powerful material interest and political significance. This is a key element in the creation of a now finely graded prestige structure involving universities, departments, disciplines, specialties, and individual scientists. Over this finely graded prestige structure is a national "leadership," centered in the President's Scientific Advisory Committee, which

---

74 For Ben-David, Price, and Polanyi, see works already cited. See Warren O. Hagstrom, *The Scientific Community,* Basic Books, New York, 1965.

gives advice to the federal government and also serves as spokesman for American science.[75] At the very least, this confounding of scientific judgement with career interests opens the way for controversy, as in the case of the federal denial of the Midwestern Universities Research Associations's (MURA) proposal for a low-energy fixed-field alternating gradient synchrotron. Technically, it is of course complex, but at the core of the controversy was a difference of opinion between a group of Midwestern scientists and those on the East and West Coasts on the research potential of accelerators based on different physical principles. When MURA's proposal was turned down, it was not taken as a purely scientific judgement; careers were at stake, and MURA scientists conducted a political campaign through members of Congress to have it reversed.[76] Political means were taken to reverse a scientific judgement by colleagues, and this in the scientific specialty, particle physics, supposed to have as close a relation between data and theory and as much theoretical consensus as any.

To get at the principal forces operating here, it is necessary to see that the new prestige and power hierarchy of science is not the result of an increase of scale alone, as is suggested by "big science." Rather it is that, unlike in the academic era, these resources have been selectively poured in at the top—top universities, specialties, and individuals—of the traditional symbolic, reputational prestige pattern of science to make it a prestige structure in which the stakes are very great. Academic support, however, had an inherently equalitarian dimension. Every scientist employed by a university had the privilege-obligation of combining research with his teaching, access to student apprentices, and so forth. He obtained a basic minimum support for his research in his teaching salary. These teaching duties might vary from onerous to light, but this is nothing like the difference between obtaining or not obtaining a research grant, having or not having research assistants and access to equipment and installations, and so forth. Now, however, it is necessary to seriously play the prestige game, to obtain grants, to work on currently important problems, and publish rapidly in order to be in the federally supported areas of science at all. Jobs, research opportunities, access to equipment, students, and so forth, depend directly upon the opinion of fellow specialists. Success breeds success in a feedback process until science becomes a clear hierarchy which allocates resources and privileges.[77] Hagstrom sees the prestige system as central to the *nature*

[75] Greenberg, pp. 15–16.
[76] Greenberg, pp. 246–69.
[77] F. Reif, "The Competitive World of the Pure Scientist," *Science,* 134 (1961), 1959–1964; and F. Rief and A. Strauss, "Impact of Rapid Discovery upon Scientific Careers," *Social Problems,* 12 (1965), 297–307; and Hagstrom, pp. 69ff.

of science; it *is* an exchange of information for recognition. In the present interpretation this is most pronounced in current science, especially in the disciplines studied by Hagstrom, primarily mathematics and physics, which includes a large part of his sample and is basic to his argument.[78] It is tempting, then, to read this central prestige mechanism back into the history of science, supported by incidents of worry and conflict over plagiarism, simultaneous discovery, and anticipation. However, that claims for credit are made after a discovery does not necessarily mean that prestige is the single or dominant motive for the work in the first place.

The new government-professional research system has had many other consequences, much discussed in popular commentary on science and the universities. Successful scientists in the well-supported disciplines are oriented more to specialist colleagues and to granting agencies than to their universities. The scientific career is increasingly a series of applications, grants, publications, and discoveries, which may take the scientist to several universities rather than through a progression of ranks within one university. This has meant a very great departmental autonomy within universities, and a decentralization of control to the point where coherent university-wide policy is jeopardized. Responding to these problems, the National Science Foundation began a program of institutional grants designed to strengthen universitywide control and programs.[79]

In a second development graduate schools have come to dominate universities and to shape undergraduate education into preprofessional programs.[80] Older discontinuities, created in the adaptation of universities to science, such as having a research degree (Ph.D.) as a teaching qualification, become increasingly troublesome when scientists become more exclusively oriented to research careers. This is not only a matter of commitment to teaching by research professors but also of its nature and direction. At a time when students are more committed and demand more response to their sense of priorities, the universities are most committed to the scientific prestige race and more dependent on the federal support to which it gives access.

Third, along with the decentralization within universities, there is a decentralization within science. As Hagstrom ponts out, current differentiation of disciplines and specialties has meant a qualitative change in the organization of science. "There are no universal scholars, and interdependence between disciplines and even among specialists within

[78] Hagstrom, p. 6.
[79] Harold Orlans, Ed., *Science Policy and the University*, Brookings Institution, Washington, D.C., 1968, especially the articles by Price, Page, and Panofsky.
[80] Jencks and Riesman, pp. 245–250.

disciplines is small."[81] This causes problems in the organization of university instruction, in allocating research support, and for the place of science in the larger culture. Hagstrom quotes Oppenheimer:

> We so refine what we think, we so change the meaning of words, we build up so distinctive a tradition, that scientific knowledge today is not an enrichment of general culture. It is on the contrary the possession of countless highly specialized communities who love it. . . . Today (as opposed to Plato's Greece) it is not only that our kings do not know mathematics, but our philsophers do not know mathematics—and to go a step further—our mathematicians do not know mathematics.[82]

Oppenheimer and Hagstrom take this to be a natural consequence of the sheer size of the scientific enterprise and of the limits of the individual human mind, and to be sure that is an impressive discrepancy. However, it may also be related to the fact that support is given to individual scientists on the basis of a series of separate decisions on which research seems "inherently" worthy or applicable. Thus there is little occasion to consolidate science, to develop coherent larger pictures, or to organize theoretically comprehensive research programs. Few organizations mediate between individual scientists and the national agencies that disperse the current largess. We have now a peculiar juxtaposition between the historically decentralized science of the amateur and academic eras and the national support that World War II produced. Perhaps this juxtaposition of the top and the bottom, the large-scale and the small, has produced the "countless highly specialized communities" which *seem to be* defined by the range of the individual's competence and by the number of people who can usefully be in personal and written communication.[83]

The first and most obvious effect of federally supported science was the opening of new career possibilities. More generous research support and partial or temporary release from academic duties meant that concentration on research no longer meant less income or certainly no increase. Many benefits—financial, consulting opportunities, political participation, travel, and others—became tied in with scientific prestige. Science generated an elite of research- and government-oriented scientists in the most prestigious universities and departments which in turn obtained most of the research funds.[84]

---

[81] Hagstrom, p. 224.
[82] Hagstrom, p. 226.
[83] Price argues that this is on the order of 100 people, or a "small number of hundreds." See Price, pp. 71, 84–85.
[84] For example, out of some 2000 possible contenders, 10 universities received 40 per-

Centralized support for science has also affected the size, style, and even substance of the scientific areas and disciplines. Most obviously, defense, medical, and agricultural technologies have had strong ideological and political support, and so have the applied sciences behind them. However, differences in the organization of support have been as important in shaping the sciences as those of scale. Support for the agricultural sciences has not been as exclusively federal as the other two, nor has it been allocated by the peer review and individual project system, but rather to states by the federal government and to schools of agriculture by the states. On the one hand, this has resulted in a nonelite structure and much routine research that is the object of condescension from elite pure scientists.[85] On the other hand, it has resulted in a broad geographical spread of competence in the agricultural sciences, in pervasive "grass roots" improvement in agricultural technology and practice that contrasts markedly with the disjunction in medicine between high technology, for example, heart surgery at elite centers, and primitive public health technique and practice.

In contrast, support for the defense-related physical sciences and for the biomedical sciences has been allocated primarily by the federal government, and by the peer review system and individual project system. This has given rise to an ever greater dominance of the great private universities in the Northeast Coast and Chicago areas, and the public universities in California. The National Science Foundation's attempt to counteract this concentration, to develop other "centers of excellence" does not recognize the powerful focus toward elite dominance; it deals with a symptomatic problem but not with the basic process.[86] Agriculture on the one hand, and physics and biomedicine on the other, illustrate contrasting support systems with very real consequences for science.

Because physics was basic to the atomic bomb and because physicists had had to convince a barely responsive government of this potential, physics has benefited mightily, acquiring powerful national political influence and receiving, for example, governmental largess for elemen-

cent and 100 institutions received 90 percent of federal funds for science in 1964. See Greenberg, p. 19.

85 See R. Krohn, *The Social Shaping of Science: Institutions, Ideology, and Careers in Science*, Greenwood Press, Westport, Conn., 1970, on the differences of federal, state, and philanthropic support to the Divisions of the University of Minnesota. See Christian K. Arnold, "The Government and University Science: Purchase or Investment," Orleans, pp. 99–100, on the relation between elite centers, broadly based scientific competence, and patterns of support in agricultural and other sciences.

86 See Howard E. Page, "The Science Development Program," in Orleans, for a description and commentary.

tary particle physics, paradoxically its most expensive and least fore-seeably applicable branch.[87] Chemistry, however, which had much the largest number of scientists because of its broad industrial relevance, did not fall under a single government agency or mission. It received far less government support and no overall planning or development as physics at least implicitly received through the Department of Defense and the Atomic Energy Commission.[88] Again, this discussion is meant only to suggest the internal impact on disciplines of the circumstances of federal organization and policy, that it is pervasive, and that the consequences have thus far hardly been described. They have been the subject of commentary by participants and journalists but not of systematic and theoretically informed inquiry. This is in turn a consequence of the particular patterns of development and support of the social sciences.

The external system of science has changed; science has new, larger, far more centralized and deliberate (interested) support from govern-ment than the universities provided. Internally, science is larger, has developed powerfully in certain directions, but has it also qualita-tively changed? If so, where would we look and how would we ascertain this change? Some major elements of change are implicit in the above discussion. It seems that publication, as evidence and goal of research, is rivaling the conduct of the research itself as a motive, which seemed so necessary during the amateur and academic eras. Now rapid, repetitious, and trivial publication is acknowledged by everyone. The first scientific societies in founding journals sought more ready and direct exchange of information, but as amateur societies they found critical editorship difficult. Scientific communication was made more efficient by the first German and British professional science associations. Professionally edited journals were designed to screen out redundant, careless, or irrelevant information—to screen "noise" out of the scientific com-munication system. Now that noise is apparently again increasing in volume, perhaps we should look for internal changes that are also al-tering the pattern of motives for scientific work.

My own interpretation is that this shift is not yet total or even de-cisive. A study I did at the University of Minnesota found that one-third of its physical and biological scientists showed career and attitudinal patterns that clearly marked them as "intellectuals," by which I mean that they treated the research process as a goal rather than as a means to career, organizational or other ends.[89] Nor is it easy to interpret the

87 Greenberg, pp. 68ff.
88 Greenberg, pp. 153ff.
89 R. Krohn, *The Social Shaping of Science,* Chap. 6.

always emerging and shifting "invisible colleges" as in the first instance prestige-seeking mechanisms. They seem to be more responsive to shifts in the frontiers of scientific advance than to prestige ranks within the community of science. Unlike the specialties, which do have acknowledged prestige associations,[90] they are information exchange systems first, and flow with its availability and relevance.[91] That they are precisely "invisible" means they do not make prestige claims over against each other. Perhaps it is the organizational and hierarchical rigidity of the recognized specialties that has impelled the search for a more flexible format for direct communication. They may be a new version of the early societies in modern guise.

One test of the present argument would be a comparative study of the specialties and the "invisible colleges" to see if information does not follow prestige in the former and prestige follow information in the latter. Another test would be to compare the formal communications of science, publication and presented papers, with the informal system, not only exchange networks ("colleges") but also the constantly generated dyadic exchanges of information, between departmental colleagues, excolleagues, and at conferences and meetings. This is the way much, at least, of the business of science gets done. "Publication" seems to involve a "redistributive" exchange system which demands a political and status hierarchy, while personal exchanges involve a gift exchange system in which prestige is only one component among a flexible complex of motives and reciprocities.[92]

If prestige does become the personal goal of scientists who would normally be the intellectual elite, and if it does become the socially dominant consideration in the exchange of scientific information, then, for the first time since the birth of this self-critical and socially autonomous search for knowledge, it would again be a socially dependent system, that is, not science. This would be accomplished by external support being both mandatory for the individual and completely geared in with science's prestige system. The government-supported, professional research system of the United States has a new kind, certainly, if not new level of external determinism. This is evident in its

90 Hagstrom, pp. 167ff.

91 Nan Lin et al., "A Study of the Communication Structure of Science," and William D. Garvey et al., "Some Comparisons of Communication Activities in the Physical and Social Science," Report No. 10 and 11, Center for Research in Scientific Communication, Department of Psychology, Johns Hopkins Univ., January 1970 (mimeo).

92 Nan Lin et al., found that two-thirds to three-quarters of scientists in their sample of 277 scientists knew and had continuing exchange with the authors of what they considered the major papers in their area of work. See pp. 33–37.

finely calibrated prestige system, in the political determination of the direction and speed of scientific activity, in the shift in the criteria of support from the declared purpose of the researcher to the judged theoretical significance of his work, and in the fading of the academic distinction between basic and applied research. These developments are not all bad. The noted Israeli sociologist of science, Ben-David, persuasively argues that this new, more open, entrepreneurial, and government-supported system is in fact more important to American science's great productivity than its sheer scale, which many academic traditionalists, especially Europeans, prefer to think.[93] However, even Ben-David sees "negative aspects." One of these is the delicacy of the balance between the "internal structures and traditions of scientific and scholarly creativity and the demands of the economic and political powers."[94] I would like to mark carefully the difference between this point and the worries of academic traditionalists who see "big science" as nearly a contradiction in terms, and all departures from individual autonomy, equalitarian ethic, devotion to "pure" research, and the total autonomy of the basic disciplines as destructive of the creative impulse. Academic science had, and has, its limitations, and very severe ones. It was often as closed organizationally—to the formation of new specialties—as it was open theoretically and intellectually.[95] And it had its metaphysics, which gave rise to objections to Pasteur's, "vitalist" bacteriology and to Freud's social physiology[96] and its epistemology. The point is not to declare for past or present, but to see that science is again being transformed by a new system of support and a new place in society.

CONCLUSIONS

Although this chapter has presented a model of the internal and external changes that constitute science and its support system, its primary purpose has been to create a sense of problem, to open questions at a new level rather than to answer them. The major thesis is that we do not understand science and that the traditional belief that there is one

---

93 Ben-David, *Fundamental Research,* pp. 30–32.
94 Ben-David, "Universities and the Growth," pp. 32ff.
95 By good fortune academic problems did not kill science, but rather universities made their own contribution, including teaching-research, a rationale for independence and habits of systematic work. The question now is, What is to be the new exchange between science and society? How can it be made a mutually rejuvenating exchange rather than an enervating embrace?
96 Ben-David, "Roles and Innovations."

known and most favorable situation for science is ill-founded. The sense of unilineal development characteristic of science's self-concept is at best oversimple. Rather, the center of science has moved like a skipping stone across Europe, then to North America, and it may well move again. This is because scientific institutions have not been and are not perfect. As contradictions in those of one locale slowed development, the spirit of investigation and exchange that is science has found another locale. Basically, Europe provided a cultural homogenity, including a monistic, or universal, theory of truth, plus a structural diversity that allowed this progress by elective affinity.

We have seen three major phases in sciences thus far. In the amateur era, that first *dispersed* questioning of the old learning in the favor of a new one later gathered first in Italy, then England, the Low Countries, and prerevolutionary France. Science was next incorporated in the universities, first decisively in Germany and then in the United States in a way that transformed both the universities and science. Neither country had been especially active in the amateur era of science. Finally, through a warborn reciprocity that overcame or set aside all the basic doctrines, a mixed system of government support and academic location for science released a third burst of scientific and organizational creativity. This system also seems to have its contradictions, which are straining the creativity and adaptiveness of government, universities, and science. As is characteristic, science seems to be on an escalating cycle of change: three centuries for amateur science, one for academic, and now in 30 years the American government-university crossbreed seems ready to crystallize into a new set of arrangements.

Two separate principles of change seem implicit in this history. In its external relations science has proceeded by the selective affinity described above, by a series of lucky accidents, whereby the scientific system changed from one to another pattern of support, each adding an element of its own. The open amateur system allowed the creation of a socially independent, self-critical, yet systematic pattern of learning and communication. The academic system provided far greater and more regular support, intellectual discipline, a symbiosis of students and teachers, a permanent place of operations, a professional career structure, and a justifying ideology. Government has provided massive support, social relevance, and a central place in society.

Internally, science exhibited no shift of structure, but a constant accumulation on a single social principle, the exchange of information for information. It developed a system of "prestations," with the three obligations—to give, to receive, and to return a gift—and with the formal autonomy reserved to the individual of what he was to give and to what use he would put gifts received. Implicitly, this ethic was important in its application to dyadic ties and small networks of colleagues ("informal communication") who exchanged with and supported each other in a very interested way. This achieved a great flexibility and avoided the necessity for science to think and to change its mind all at once (while maintaining a self-consistent, noneclectic view of the world), an impossible achievement. However, a pressure toward self-consistency—to fit with current theory or to challenge it—is implicit in the responsibility of publication, especially after the founding of professional journals.[97] Since that time, scientists have been less free to be "wrong" in print.[98] Dyadic exchange, together with the doctrine of individual autonomy, has allowed self-convinced, opinionated individuals or groups to do new work and to communicate until they are ready to submit their contribution to criticism.[99] It therefore continues to be important to science along with the growth in publication.

Just as the rules of exchange and the doctrine of individual autonomy have important indirect effects, so also does the assumption of a single, coherent but changing truth. The call of intellectual order is prerequisite to a cumulative knowledge system, but the doctrine of change allowed argument and tension over concepts and assumption without sanctioning struggle to win at any price. Thus even though scientists have not been completely aware of the complex effects of their simple social faith, it has in fact been continuous in its many-sided amplifications.

Science is now facing a complex and pervasive set of changes in its shift

[97] This responsibility results from the unilateral character of publication, whereby the message carries little of its context and the response is much more delayed than in conversation. In dyadic exchange the giver can be questioned and only limited numbers are inconvenienced by misleading or incomplete notions. To publish, because science is a system of prestation, is to demand to be read. And, because publication is redistributive exchange, the receiver is not in contact with the contributor; he cannot question directly or sanction him. Because publication is both one-way and carries little of the context of the information, it requires a formula of credibility.

[98] The Velikovsky affair was a case of the seeming opinionated rejection and even suppression of an unorthodox theory, a cataclysmic theory of the earth's history. See I. Velikovsky, *Earth in Upheaval*, Doubleday, Garden City, New York, 1955; and *Worlds in Collision*, Dell, New York, 1965. Polanyi said, in defense of the reaction of his fellow scientists, "The theory has to be plausible." He admitted that this could result in the rejection of good work, but the alternative was theoretical anarchy. See Michael Polanyi, "The Growth of Science in Society," *Minerva*, 5, 533–545.

[99] James D. Watson's *The Double Helix* gives an excellent insight into the operation of dyadic exchange during the course of a discovery (of the structure of the DNA molecule) and its relation to publication. One facet of this was that confidential communication with sympathetic people was essential before the responsibility of public defense was taken on.

from a laissez-faire system with widely dispersed and nonpolitical support and politics. As Greenburg points out, "the new politics" of science was delayed by a number of circumstances until the early 1960s even though the large government support that necessitated them began during and after World War II.[100] This new politics includes the deliberate allocation of support among the fields of science, a reconciliation of current merit in the allocation of support for research with regional development of scientific abilities, and the avoidance of conflict of interest in the multiple roles of scientists as proposers and referees for research support and advisers of government. These and other normal political issues had been held aside, on the side of science, by rapidly growing research funds during the 1950s, which meant that the requests of all the sciences could essentially be met. And, on the side of government, the immunity of science was gained by its moral credibility—by the supposed asceticism of academics and high internal ethics of science. Also, scientific spokesmen had built up very positive personal ties and great prestige with government during World War II. Then the sacred image of science was fully redeemed by the miraculous appearance of the promised atomic bomb. However, by the mid-1960s the Mohole scandal and the MURA controversy proved that conflict of interest and the confounding of technical judgement with politics was possible in science as in the rest of political life. The reluctance of the National Institutes of Health to impose accounting responsibility on its grantees led members of Congress, not already so inclined, to take scientists at something less than their self-presentation.[101] With the leveling off of federal support for science in the mid-1960s, the relations among the sciences could no longer be smoothed with more for everybody. This has meant a political impetus also from scientists, who now must learn to combine scientific judgement with social and political purposes. The decisions made implicitly in the "old politics" increasingly now will have to be part of open and accountable politics; and informal controls, or controls foregone altogether, will have to be formally provided.

Philanthropic support of the amateur and academic eras, and the state support of science "as an end in itself" (as basic research) which, as Ben-David points out, is also philanthropic,[102] has its own dangers for science. Philanthropy is the converson of money to spiritual-prestige values, and prestige definitions can lead to very great rigidity and definition of purpose. The dangers in a unique dependence on government

100 Greenberg, see especially his concluding chapter.
101 Greenberg has extensive discussion of all three episodes.
102 Ben-David, *Fundamental Research and the Universities; Some Comments on International Differences,* OECD, 1968.

support seem more obvious: How can science retain a critical measure of autonomy, self-discipline, and sense of direction? It is probably safe to say that no government has yet supported science on a modern scale and allowed it broad and intellectually autonomous development. The United States certainly does not seem to be immune to a narrow and direct use of science on government's terms.

However, the relations between science and government may prove less difficult, because better defined, than between science and the universities. Direct contracts and grants by government agencies to scientists have meant a loss of control by universities over their own growth and direction. And the requirement of a research degree (Ph.D.) for teaching positions is causing increasing tension as an oversupply of Ph.D.'s goes down the academic ladder to two-year and open admission colleges.[103] The older problem of administrations and departments engaged in the scientific prestige race, with undergraduates a weak constituency with accumulating grievances, is still with us. There is little doubt that undergraduate education has long subsidized graduate-level teaching and free time for faculty research. One result of the control of undergraduate education by graduate-level education is the constant pressure of personal and career interests of research professors toward graduate training and research programs.[104]

There is a problem still more basic. Science was first able to be an open, progressive system of knowledge precisely because it was socially marginal, and since then, by way of compromise, it has been confined to the natural sciences. (This assumes that the social sciences do not yet have effective intellectual autonomy, that is, the power of self-definition —the ability to develop a theory independent of conventional definitions and ideologies). Now science is not socially marginal, but central to national military power, industrial wealth, and human health. And the social sciences seem to be entering a phase of social criticism which, if combined with self-critical scientific scholarship, may be the prelude to the discovery of the principles of society as opposed to the restatement of its assumptions. The old compromise may now break down. We may no longer be able to have an open, progressive system of knowledge and a closed, paradigmatic society. This is a basic turning point toward which many decisions are beginning to accumulate.

---

[103] Fred M. Hechinger, "Ph.D.: It has Become a Problem Degree," News of the Week Review Section, *The New York Times,* July 19, 1970.
[104] Jencks and Riesman, p. 245.

CHAPTER THREE

Basic and Applied Research

Howard M. Vollmer, American University

In discussing "basic research" we use essentially the definition of the National Science Foundation and refer to "original investigations for the advancement of scientific knowledge that do not have specific objectives to answer problems of sponsoring agencies or companies, although these investigations may be in fields of present or potential interest to the sponsoring organizations."[1] In contrast, "applied research" is defined as "research activities on problems posed by sponsoring agencies or companies for the purpose of contributing to the solution of these problems." Thus we define both basic and applied research in terms of the intent or

[1] The essence of this definition is presented in National Science Foundation, *Basic Research, Applied Research, and Development in Industry, 1965*, NSF 67–12, Washington, D.C., 1967, p. 101. As C. V. Kidd has pointed out in "Basic Research—Description versus Definition," *Science* (February 1959), 368–371, there is no precise way to define basic and applied research that would be agreed upon by sponsors, managers, and researchers alike and that would provide a definitive basis for determining the exact amounts of funds spent on the two different kinds of research. At the same time, Kidd agrees that basic and applied research can be described in general impressionistic terms that are adequate for investigators of administrative considerations such as those discussed in this chapter.

purpose of *sponsors* who provide the money to support specific research projects. They supply money to support research either because (in the case of basic research) they believe that projects generated by scientists will themselves ultimately be of benefit to society or mankind in general, or because (in the case of applied research) they believe that the talents, techniques, and findings of scientific research will help in the solution of an immediate problem.

These definitions say nothing about the intent of the scientist who conducts the research. He may—and in many cases does—engage in applied research because the specific problem posed to him by a sponsor happens to coincide closely enough with his own areas of scientific interest so that he feels he is able to pursue his interests and the practical interests of his sponsor at the same time. In such cases the scientist may think of this kind of activity as a mixture of basic and applied research. In many of these cases the scientist is likely to resist the appellation of either "basic" or "applied." He may actually be "bootlegging" basic research interests within a sponsor-defined category of applied research.[2]

Nor does a definition in terms of the sponsor's intent—or even in terms of the intent of the researcher—necessarily indicate the overall "scientific merit" of the research activity. Indeed, there are notable examples of contributions to scientific knowledge that have come out of essentially applied research activities for commercial or government sponsors, such as from the work of Louis Pasteur or from the Manhattan Project.[3] Conversely, many theses and dissertations that are subsequently unreferenced in the scientific literature and that gather dust on the shelves of university libraries testify to the lack of scientific utility in much of what is commonly accepted as basic research.

In spite of objections to a distinction between basic and applied research that derive from the above considerations, there is still a value from a societal point of view in making this distinction in terms of the intent of the sponsor. On the one hand, we know that well over half the research activities of scientists in the United States is supported by agencies of the federal government. These agencies and Congress justifiably call for an accounting of public funds spent for scientific purposes, as well as for other purposes.

---

2 See D. S. Greenberg, " 'Bootlegging': It Holds a Firm Place in Conduct of Research," *Science,* 153 (August 1966), 848–849; see also H. M. Vollmer, *Adaptations of Scientists and Organizations,* Chapter X, "Hedging and Bootlegging," Pacific Books, Alto, Calif., in press.

3 An analysis of the contributions of those in applied roles to innovation in the medical sciences is contained in J. Ben-David, "Roles and Innovations in Medicine," *American Journal of Sociology,* 65 (May 1960), 557–568.

One of the simplest ways to account for these funds is to determine the proportions that are spent by various agencies with the intent of advancing science in areas of particular interest to the sponsoring agencies in comparison to the funds these same agencies spend to obtain scientific answers relevant to the solution of their more immediate problems. It is an important matter of public policy to determine what the ratio of basic to applied research should be for each sponsoring agency.[4] It is also an important matter for corporate policy to determine what this ratio should be for funds provided by business corporations, by foundations, and by other institutions in the private sector. There is a general clamor today in many public and private organizations to give closer attention to the "cost effectiveness" or more immediate payoff from research activities—in other words to increase the ratio of applied research to basic research (without necessarily decreasing the overall amount of basic research). Increasingly disturbing problems of overpopulation, environmental pollution, urban decay, poverty, intergroup conflict, and a host of related concerns press for solution. Scientific talent is increasingly looked to for assistance on these matters by public and private organizations in our society.

Somewhat paradoxically, a similar concern comes from modern youth, many of whom consider themselves to be alienated from the existing "establishment." Their cry is for more relevance in their education. They tend to be impatient with abstract theoretical discussions in their classes; they want to see both theory and research more closely related to the social and economic concerns of the day. They are unimpressed by "research for the sake of research." Although many do not recognize the issue precisely in these terms, many young people are actually calling for more emphasis upon applied research in the allocation of our national resources.

Even among scientists themselves, who value so highly their traditional independence to pursue scientific curiosity wherever it may lead without considering practical applications, there is today increasing concern with the uses of their research findings. Insofar as they share the moral concerns of many others in the larger society, scientists want to see the results of their research used for the benefit of mankind, not for its destruction. In recent years they have expressed this concern in professional journals

---

4 For a general discussion of public policy regarding the support of basic versus applied research, see National Academy of Sciences, *Basic Research and National Goals*, U.S. Congress, U.S. House of Representatives, Washington, D.C., 1965. For a discussion of increasing pressures toward the application of research findings in a federal government agency, see J. Walsh, "NIH: Demand Increases for Applications of Research," *Science*, **153** (July 1966), 149–152.

and in more general interdisciplinary publications such as the *Bulletin of the Atomic Scientists;* and many have taken more active roles in symposia and public forums on this subject. Most scientists are in no mood to abandon their traditional orientation toward their work and the freedom from day-to-day concerns and administrative controls that accompany this orientation. Yet they recognize the need for more attention to relevance in their work.

However, there are severe barriers to the accomplishment of this common goal—the desire to bring the talents of scientists to bear more effectively on the solution of the social and economic problems of the modern age. These barriers are essentially of two kinds. One is the cultural and attitudinal constraints that inhibit many of the most competent scientists from becoming involved in applied research. The other is organizational in nature; applied research requires different patterns of decision structure, of control over research activities, and of relations with colleagues than does basic research. These patterns must be understood and accepted both by scientists and by research managers if applied science is to grow and become more effective in the future. In this chapter we devote closer attention to these cultural-attitudinal and organizational factors before we consider the future prospects for both basic and applied research.

THE PREFERENCE FOR BASIC RESEARCH

There is no question but that the vast majority of scientists in the United States prefer basic to applied research. This finding was supported strongly by data from a nationwide survey of the attitudes and activities of over 3,600 scientists we conducted in 1965.[5] The scientists were randomly selected from professional society membership lists for the disciplines of biology, chemistry, mathematics, and physics. Overall, 61 percent of the scientists said that they preferred to engage in "research emphasizing contributions to scientific knowledge" (which we categorized as "basic research"), while only 7 percent said that they preferred to engage in "research emphasizing solution of problems for industry or government" (which we categorized as "applied research"). The remaining 32 percent of the scientists said that they preferred "research giving equal

5 This survey was part of a 5-year study sponsored by the Behavioral Sciences Division of the Air Force Office of Scientific Research. The methodology of the survey is described in detail, along with preliminary data summaries in H. M. Vollmer, *Work Activities and Attitudes of Scientists and Research Managers: Data from a National Survey,* R & D Studies Series, Stanford Research Institute, Menlo Park, Calif., 1965.

emphasis to solving problems and to contributing to scientific knowledge" (i.e., "mixed research").

At the same time we found that 62 percent of the scientists said that they actually were engaged primarily in basic research, while 16 percent said that they were engaged primarily in applied research, 17 percent were engaged in a mixture of basic and applied research, and the remaining 6 percent indicated "other" pursuits. The preference of all scientists for basic research activities become even more evident when we see that even among those who are primarily engaged in applied research the majority still would prefer to be engaged in basic research, as is shown in Table 1 (showing data only for scientists with doctor's degrees, to control for possible effects of degree level):

Table 1

	Scientists Primarily Engaged In		
Prefer to Engage in	Basic Research (2051)	Mixed Research (467)	Applied Research (379)
Basic research	88%	73%	55%
Mixed research	12%	25%	21%
Applied research	1%	2%	24%

We broke the responses down further to see if the picture would be different among doctoral-level scientists employed in industrial firms in contrast to those on the staffs of universities. The pattern of preferences is quite similar in both employment situations. Although there are larger proportions of scientists in industry who indicate a preference for applied research or mixed research than there are in universities, the majority in both situations still prefer to engage in basic research, as may be seen in the Table 2.

What is the primary source of this overwhelming preference for basic research among most scientists? There is ample evidence from many studies that the main source of this preference is in the graduate and undergraduate education that scientists receive in a university environment.[6] The total culture surrounding a scientific education and the values and ideology transmitted through the educational process differ from the values transmitted to students in other disciplines. Thus Becker and Carper in a notable study showed that

6 Edward Teller, Arthur Kantrowitz, and Hendrik W. Bode have all pointed out that a basic research orientation in most universities can detract from education for applied research; see their essays in National Academy of Sciences, *Basic Research and National Goals.*

Table 2

Prefer to Engage in	Engaged in		
	Basic Research	Mixed Research	Applied Research
Scientists in universities	1518	116	73
Basic research	87%	78%	73%
Mixed research	13%	22%	12%
Applied research	1%	1%	15%
Scientists in industry	144	240	248
Basic research	86%	73%	53%
Mixed research	13%	25%	21%
Applied research	1%	2%	26%

. . . physiology students feel themselves part of a larger group, devoted to building the edifice of science, and pride themselves on their participation in this endeavor and on the ultimate value of their work to society in the cure and prevention of disease. Nevertheless they sharply differentiate their work from that of physicians and of other scientists involved in this enterprise. They feel that they make the important scientific discoveries on which medical practice is based, medicine itself being more empirical and superficial; one student put it metaphorically: "We write the music that the doctors play."[7]

Becker and Carper pointed out that this ideology among those being trained as basic scientists in physiology differs markedly from the attitude that engineering students develop toward their work:

The ideology tells them that anyone called "engineer" has learned to reason so rationally and effectively that, even though this has been learned only with reference to technical problems, it operates in any line of endeavor, so that *the engineer is equipped to solve any kind of problem in any area quickly and efficiently* (emphasis added).[8]

There are even differences among scientific disciplines in the emphasis given to making contributions to fundamental scientific knowledge versus the emphasis upon practical problem solving. For example, our survey data showed that biologists and physicists, and to a lesser extent, mathematicians, are much more likely to say that they prefer basic research to applied research than are chemists (Table 3).

The main explanation for these differences among the values expressed

[7] H. S. Becker and J. Carper, "The Elements of Identification with an Occupation," *American Sociological Review,* 21 (June 1956), 342.
[8] *Ibid.,* p. 343.

Table 3

Prefer to Engage in	Biologists (1250)	Physicists (973)	Mathematicians (724)	Chemists (746)
Basic research	78%	62%	54%	36%
Mixed research	20%	31%	36%	48%
Applied research	1%	6%	10%	16%

in different scientific disciplines appears to lie in the fact that more students of chemistry are headed for industrial employment where they will essentially be engaged in applied research.[9] They know this, their professors know this, and their value system is adjusted accordingly. (In our survey sample we found that 69 percent of the biologists, 44 percent of the physicists, 60 percent of the mathematicians, and only 30 percent of the chemists were currently employed in academic institutions.)

The effects of the academic culture in determining the preference of students for basic research becomes even more evident when one examines the difference in attitude between those who hold doctor's degrees (mostly Ph.D.'s) and those with master's or bachelor's degrees as their highest level of formal academic attainment. Although our survey did not provide enough cases of nondoctors among the biologists to make a meaningful comparison, the data in Table 4 show that for the other three disciplines those with doctor's degrees were uniformly more likely to prefer basic research in comparison to those who had not attained the doctoral level.

Table 4

Perfer to Engage in	Physicists		Mathematicians		Chemists	
	Doctors	Non-Doctors	Doctors	Non-Doctors	Doctors	Non-Doctors
Basic research	68%	42%	66%	26%	47%	22%
Mixed research	28%	44%	29%	53%	44%	53%
Applied research	3%	15%	5%	21%	9%	24%

It is likely that two processes operate to yield the result that in any scientific discipline those who attain doctor's degrees are more likely to value basic research than those who do not attain doctorates. One could be a process of selective recruitment; that is, those students who value what their professors tend to value—namely, basic research—may be more likely to be admitted to doctoral programs. In such cases the

[9] For a definitive analysis of chemistry as a professional category, see A. L. Strauss and L. Rainwater, *The Professional Scientist* Aldine, Chicago, 1962.

rationale is frequently heard that nonconforming students in the sciences are "really not scholarly in their interests and attitudes"; "they are good enough for industry (i.e., applied research) but not suitable candidates for a doctoral program." The other main process is probably that of continuing socialization into the academic norms and values of basic research *after* the student becomes a doctoral candidate. Hagstrom has shown in his analysis of scientific communities in universities that graduate students frequently take professors as significant role models, and that, moreover, the typical relationship between professor and student in advanced research training is not one of free collaboration but rather one more like that of master and apprentice. He reports that a majority of the faculty in the physics and chemistry departments he studied said that the professor really selects most dissertation topics for his students. Hagstrom cites a prior study by Berelson that has indicated that only 2.5 percent of his sample of scientists said that students select most dissertation topics.[10] Thus the very subject that a science student selects for his major effort at the doctoral level is likely to be a reflection of the basic research interests of his principal academic mentor, as is the way he is graded and evaluated in his oral and written examinations.

The fundamental commitment of many universities to basic research in their ideology and culture and their inability to incorporate applied research interests within their institutional framework has been illustrated in the course of developments regarding the relationship between Stanford Research Institute (a primarily applied research organization) and Stanford University in California. Underlying a controversy about the place of military research in a university-affiliated institution was a more fundamental question concerning the appropriateness of any kind of affiliation between an applied research activity and a university. Illustrating the existence of this underlying issue, the faculty-dominated majority of a student-faculty committee at Stanford University summarized its opinions on University relations with Stanford Research Institute in April of 1969 by writing:

For its part, the University has its own primary mission to further basic research and teaching. This is a large enough task, and requires a sense of purpose and mode of operation which is essentially different from the methods of a more action-oriented, problem-oriented, market-oriented institution engaged in applied contract research.

Given these facts the present relationship between Stanford University and

[10] W. O. Hagstrom, *The Scientific Community*, Basic Books, New York, 1965, p. 125.

Stanford Research Institute is an anomalous and ambiguous one. We are unanimous in recommending that it should not be continued in its present form.[11]

Following this report by the student-faculty committee, the Board of Trustees of Stanford University decided in May 1969 that formal ties between the University and the Institute would be terminated, reasoning that

. . . to affiliate the Institute more closely with the University, as many advocate, would embark Stanford upon a program of applied contract research in manner and scale completely foreign to our concept of an educational institution of high quality. Not only this, but in the process, the Institute as a viable organization would, in our view disintegrate and its highly skilled personnel be dissipated.[12]

The alleged lack of fit between applied research and university activities as they are presently constituted has been brought out even more by the situation that developed at the same time with regard to the Stanford Electronics Laboratories. These are on-campus laboratories not affiliated with Stanford Research Institute. However, a group of researchers in the laboratories decided to leave the University, asserting that the majority of the faculty at the University were unsympathetic with the kinds of applied research activities the laboratories engage in. Thus in an open letter, Professor William Rambo, Director of the Stanford Electronics Laboratories, stated:

It is my view that the University Community has demonstrated an incapacity to understand the nature and import of certain areas of research, particularly applied research. It is unable, or disinclined, to provide a suitable environment for such research, or to accept those who engage professionally in it.[13]

Professor Rambo stated further in the same letter that

Many of the professionals in our laboratories have regularly taught courses, advised students, guided thesis research, etc. This academic participation has been entirely appropriate since the abilities of these individuals have surely supple-

---

[11] Stanford University, "Report of Stanford-SRI Study Committee," *Campus Report Supplement,* No. 5 (April 14, 1969), 17.
[12] Stanford University, "Statement by Board of Trustees of Stanford University," May 13, 1969, pp. 1–2.
[13] A letter from William R. Rambo, Director, Stanford Electronics Laboratories to Charles A. Anderson, President, Stanford Research Institute, May 6, 1969, pp. 1–3.

mented, and in some areas extended, the capacities of our faculty to provide the broadest opportunities for an engineering education. But despite the efforts of many here at the University, these professionals have also operated in a structured second-class-citizens role.[14]

Thus even in the field of engineering education, where there has traditionally been more emphasis upon a practical, problem-solving orientation than in the physical sciences, there are indications that applied research activities are having to yield to pressures to conform to the value system of basic research that predominates in a large number of academic settings.

In the basic research-oriented culture of universities, there tends to be a commitment among researchers to (1) members of one's scientific profession rather than members of an employing organization as the significant reference group; (2) a career in scientific work rather than moving into management positions with "permanent" administrative responsibilities;[15] (3) a strong emphasis on freedom of the researcher to select the topics he will investigate;[16] and (4) a strong emphasis on the opportunity to publish research findings in scientific journals.[17] These values are

---

[14] *Ibid.*

[15] There have been several studies describing different kinds of career orientations among scientists. D. Marvick, in *Career Perspectives in a Bureaucratic Setting,* Michigan Government Studies No. 27, Univ. of Michigan, Ann Arbor, 1954, identified "specialists," "institutionalists," and "hybrids." See also A. W. Gouldner, "Cosmopolitans and Locals: Toward an Analysis of Latent Social Roles—I, II," *Administrative Science Quarterly,* 2 (1958), 281–306, 444–480. B. G. Glaser, in "The Local-Cosmopolitan Scientist," *American Journal of Sociology,* 69 (1963), showed that these two career orientations can be compatible in organizational environments that support scientific values; and E. H. Schein et al., "Career Orientations and Perceptions of Rewarded Activity in a Research Organization," *Administrative Science Quarterly,* showed that scientists' orientations toward a managerial or nonmanagerial career can be independent of whether they have an institutional or noninstitutional orientation. Note here that many basic research scientists actually become temporary technical managers of graduate students and other assistants on scientific projects—indeed they may seek this. Yet they tend to shun the idea of more permanent administrative responsibilities, and may criticize colleagues who become deans or college presidents for "deserting their scientific profession."

[16] Several studies have shown the importance of freedom in project selection among scientists, including J. W. Reigel, *Administration of Salaries and Intangible Rewards for Engineers and Scientists* Univ. of Michigan, Bureau of Industrial Relations, Ann Arbor, 1958, pp. 26–28; and L. Meltzer, "Scientific Productivity in Organizational Settings," *Journal of Social Issues,* 22 (1956). However, D. C. Pelz and F. M. Andrews, *Scientists in Organizations* Wiley, New York, 1966, pp. 8–34 have shown that it is generally not those scientists who have complete freedom to select their research projects, but rather those who have a moderate amount of freedom, who are most productive.

[17] For discussions on the values of publication among scientists, and on pressures to

more commonly viewed as intrinsic to the culture of universities because basic research is the predominant kind of research activity in the university, yet these values also occur among those engaged in basic research in industrial setings. However, those engaged in applied research—in the university or outside—are likely to begin to adopt a different set of values.

We see the values of applied researchers reflected in the fact that larger proportions of those engaged in applied research, both in universities and in industry, are more likely to identify themselves more closely with their employing organization—even though the majority of doctoral-level scientists in all categories still see members of their scientific profession as their more significant reference group (Table 5).

Table 5

Identify More Closely with	Engaged in		
	Basic Research	Mixed Research	Applied Research
Scientists in universities	1518	116	73
Scientific profession	82%	72%	63%
Employing organization	17%	26%	37%
Scientists in industry	144	240	248
Scientific profession	88%	67%	55%
Employing organization	13%	32%	45%

These data for scientists showing a shift toward identification with the employing organization among those engaged in applied research become even more significant when they are compared to the answers of over 2000 engineers in industrial companies across the nation when they were asked the same question in another survey conducted by the author. Fifty-eight percent of the engineers said that they identified themselves more closely with their employing organization, while the remaining 42 percent remained identified primarily with their engineering profession. In other words, in the terminology used in studies by Gouldner and others, those in more applied, problem-oriented activities are more likely to be "locals" in their value orientations; those who are more oriented toward the advancement of general knowledge in their scientific fields are more likely to be "cosmopolitan" in their most important reference group.[18]

"publish or perish," see R. K. Merton, "Priorities in Scientific Discovery," *American Sociological Review*, 22 (October 1956), 635–669; F. Reif, "The Competitive World of the Pure Scientist," *Science*, 134 (December 1961), 1957–1962; and T. Caplow and R. J. McGee, *The Academic Marketplace*, Basic Books, New York, 1958, pp. 81–93.

[18] A. W. Gouldner, "Cosmopolitans and Locals: Toward an Analysis of Latent Social Roles—I, II."

To the latter, the practical, day-to-day concerns of their employing organization are not likely to be in the forefront of their attention.

Since those who are engaged in basic research are more likely to be concerned with their status vis-à-vis their scientific colleagues rather than their coemployees in a particular organization, it is not surprising that those in basic research are much less likely to be interested in movement into managerial positions than is the case among those in mixed or applied research, as the survey data in Table 6 generally show (excluding those with ambiguous responses on ths question).

Table 6

| | Engaged in | | |
Prefer a Career in	Basic Research	Mixed Research	Applied Research
Scientists in universities	1518	116	73
Nonmanagerial positions	82%	70%	73%
Managerial positions	8%	21%	15%
Scientists in industry	144	240	248
Nonmanagerial positions	71%	58%	51%
Managerial positions	23%	32%	36%

Again our other survey of engineers gave further evidence of the career values of an even more applications-oriented group. Only 24 percent of the engineers said that they preferred a career in nonmanagerial positions; 75 percent said that they hoped to move into management some time in the future.

As mentioned previously, freedom to select the research projects that one undertakes and opportunity to publish the results of one's research are conditions that are highly valued by most scientists engaged in basic research and that distinguish these scientists from those in applied research, both in universities and in industry. Thus our survey data indicate that the proportions of scientists who said that freedom to select research projects is "extremely important" or "quite important" was as follows for those in the different categories of research activity in universities: in basic research, 75 percent; in mixed research, 44 percent; and in applied research, 40 percent. The comparable proportions of scientists in industry giving these same responses were: in basic research, 51 percent; in mixed research, 33 percent; and in applied research, 18 percent. On the question of the opportunity to publish one's research findings, the following proportions of scientists in universities indicated that it is "extremely important" or "quite important": in basic research, 69 percent; in mixed research, 58 percent; and in applied research, 49 percent. On the same question among scientists in industry, the replies were: in basic research, 68 percent; in mixed research, 43 percent; and in applied research, 18 percent.

A further generalization can be drawn from a closer examination of the previously cited data on the attitudes of scientists in various kinds of research in industry compared to those in similar kinds of research in universities. The proportions of those in basic research in industry who hold to certain values—for example, identification with their scientific profession, interest in remaining in nonmanagerial positions, a desire for freedom in selecting research projects, and a desire for opportunity to publish—are more similar to the proportions of those in basic research in universities who adhere to these same values than is the case among those in applied research in industry compared to those in applied research in universities. In other words, it is likely that a scientist who continues to perform basic research in industry will remain faithful to the same values held by his colleagues in universities, whereas a scientist who engages in applied research in industry is more likely to depart from the values held by his colleagues in universities.[19] Applied researchers are more likely to become socialized into industrial values with increasing amounts of industrial experience;[20] basic researchers are more likely to be insulated from the effects of industrial socialization.

What do all the "facts" presented so far mean in terms of the general problem under discussion in this chapter, namely, how to bring the talents of scientists to bear more effectively on the solution of the social and economic problems of the modern age? To this point, several tentative conclusions are suggested by the available data on scientists' values and attitudes:

[19] It is therefore those who retain a basic research orientation in industry, but who are required to do applied research that contradicts the value system of basic research, who are also most likely to feel alienated in the manner described by Opinion Research Corporation, *The Conflict Between the Scientific Mind and the Management Mind*, Opinion Research Corporation, Princeton, N.J., 1959; S. Marcson, *The Scientist in American Industry*, Princeton, N.J., Princeton Univ. Industrial Relations Section, 1960; and W. Kornhauser, *Scientists in Industry* Univ. of California Press, Berkeley and Los Angeles, 1962.

[20] On the socialization of scientists in industry into the values of applied research, see R. W. Avery, "Enculturation in Industrial Research," *IRE Transactions on Engineering Management*, **EM-7** (March 1960); R. G. Krohn, "The Institutional Location of the Scientist and His Scientific Values," *IRE Transactions on Engineering Management*, **EM-8** (September 1961), 133–138; M. Abrahamson, "The Integration of Industrial Scientists," *Administrative Science Quarterly*, **9** (1964), 208–218; and H. M. Vollmer, *Adaptations of Scientists and Organizations*, Chapter VIII, "Organizational Socialization."

1. By their initial socialization in the process of graduate education in universities, scientists tend to be strongly committed to the value system of basic research and, conversely, to reject values that are more compatible with applied research. In order to become effective applied researchers, scientists must undergo a process of reeducation and resocialization into a new pattern of industrial values.

2. Because many universities are essentially dominated by those engaged in basic research, the university culture usually is not likely to be a favorable environment for the socialization of individuals into a value system compatible with developing skills in applied research. Indeed, there are institutional pressures to expel applied research activities from the environment of many universities.

3. Conversely, because most industrial (and other nonacademic) organizations are essentially dominated by those with interests in the more immediate applications of science and technology to current problems, the culture of industry is not likely to be a favorite environment to support basic research. Indeed, there are continuous pressures in nonacademic organizations to force scientists into activities with more immediate payoff (i.e., applied research).

If these general hypotheses are correct, we might be led to the direct conclusion that basic research "really belongs" in universities and applied research "belongs" in industry and other nonacademic settings. However, this would be a superficial conclusion. It ignores the very important problems of how to educate more students to become skillful applied researchers in response to demands from many quarters for this, how to maintain a reasonable amount of both public and private support for basic research as the ultimate wellspring for applied technology, and to increase the understanding of those in nonacademic institutions for those in the academy and vice versa—in other words, how to maintain and strengthen the "unity in diversity" that is the keystone of a free pluralistic society. We cannot maintain such a society by completely relegating one set of values to one set of institutions, and another set of values to other institutions. We must seek for an interpenetration of value systems among different institutions, while at the same time maintaining the fundamental institutional capabilities and integrity of different institutions.

How to do this is an organizational matter as well as an educational matter. We must seek a better understanding of the form of organization that is compatible with the value system of basic research, on the one hand, while also seeking a better understanding of the form of organization that is compatible with the value system of applied research, on the other hand.

THE ORGANIZATION OF BASIC AND APPLIED RESEARCH

To understand the way in which applied research is characteristically organized and managed in contrast to basic research, and vice versa, it is useful first to consider certain important differences in the way these two kinds of research are ordinarily funded. In research funding there are important differences between prevailing practices in universities and in industry. For example, the majority of basic research activities in United States universities is funded by project *grants* from agencies of the federal government, while the larger proportion of applied research activities in universities is funded by project *contracts* from federal agencies. In contrast, the overwhelming majority of research of all types in private industry is funded from in-house allocations. At least this is the way the industrial scientists who do the research perceive the situation—even though a considerable proportion of these "in-house" funds in industry may have its ultimate source in federal government contracts held by companies whose managements may then reallocate certain proportions of these contract funds for research activities within their companies.

The perceptions of university and industrial scientists on the source of the funds that support their research is shown in Table 7, again drawing upon data from our national surveys.

Table 7

Report that Most of Their Funds for Research Are from	Engaged in		
	Basic Research	Mixed Research	Applied Research
Scientists in universities	1518	116	73
In-house allocations	19%	16%	22%
Federal project contracts	12%	36%	44%
Federal project grants	60%	39%	25%
Federal institutional grants	4%	3%	1%
Private foundation grants	3%	4%	4%
Other source	2%	2%	2%
Scientists in industry	144	240	248
In-house allocations	71%	77%	80%
Federal project contracts	23%	21%	17%
Federal project grants	3%	1%	1%
Federal institutional grants	1%	1%	1%
Private foundation grants	2%	0%	1%
Other source	1%	1%	1%

There are of course marked differences in the overall purpose and rationale that underlies the use of these different mechanisms in disbursing research funds. The research *grant* is essentially a mechanism designed to support the work of a particular individual (or group of individuals) to conduct research in a general topic area which is specified quite loosely in the grant. In contrast, a research *contract* is an agreement for the performance of certain work (in this case, research work) which is expected to produce a specified product, for example, a report on research done in terms of the statement of work specified formally in the contractual agreement. Thus, in the simplest terms, *grants* support *people* so that they can do certain kinds of work; *contracts* support *work* done according to agreed-upon specifications—which specifications may (or may not) include the identification of who is to do the work.

It seems more compatible with the value system that surrounds basic research for it to be sponsored by means of grants rather than contracts, because the grant format allows the maximum degree of freedom for individual researchers. Conversely, it seems more compatible with the purpose of applied research to support this kind of research either through research contracts or through in-house allocations of funds under the general control of management; the purpose of applied research, by definition, is to bring the skills of scientists to bear upon some practical problems of a contracting organization or of corporate management in the case of applied research conducted within the corporation. Managers and contractors for research are both aware of the common preference of scientists to drift off into the pursuit of topics of purely scientific interest. Therefore they use either the contract mechanism, or the comparable mechanism of specified work assignments and schedules for in-house work, to provide some reasonable assurance that the more immediate problem-solving interests of these kinds of research sponsors will be attended to by scientists.

The primary reliance upon individual grants in universities and upon in-house funding in industry is associated with certain important differences in the mode of initiation, mode of control, and mode of interpersonal interaction that occur in the two institutional environments.

First, university scientists are much more likely to feel a responsibility for going out on their own and seeking funding for their research work. They do not expect, nor do they receive, much assistance from their managers or academic administrators in this regard. The burden for writing a research proposal that is acceptable to a sponsoring agency rests squarely upon the shoulders of the scientist himself. At least, this is the way it usually is for university scientists engaged in basic research. Larger minorities of those in applied research are more likely to see the obtaining of research grants or contracts as a research management or administration responsibility, but the majority of university scientists in all categories of research assume that obtaining research funds is up to the individual scientist.[21]

The picture is quite different among scientists in industry. Here the large majority of scientists in all categories of research sees the obtaining of research funds as primarily a responsibility of research managers, or those managers directly involved in the research part of the corporation. This perception is compatible with the previous point that most industrial scientists see their research funding as coming from in-house sources. However, we can also note that a larger proportion (although still a minority) of the industrial scientists in basic research says that they assume primary responsibility for obtaining their funding themselves.

How scientists in industry and those in universities see differences in responsibilities to obtain research funds is detailed in Table 8 from our national survey.

Table 8

Say That the Financial Support for Most Research Projects Is Obtained by	Engaged in		
	Basic Research	Mixed Research	Applied Research
Scientists in universities	1518	116	73
Research scientists	89%	66%	62%
Research managers	5%	27%	23%
Managers not in research	2%	7%	11%
Other persons	3%	1%	4%
Scientists in industry	144	240	248
Research scientists	22%	15%	12%
Research managers	68%	73%	67%
Managers not in research	7%	9%	17%
Other persons	3%	3%	2%

Since most funds for research—and even funds for basic research—are perceived as coming from in-house sources in industrial settings, scientists in industry are more likely to submit to more direction from management in their project work than are scientists in universities. However, the kind of direction that they accept is more likely to be expressed as a form of "occasional consultation" with their research managers, more character-

---

21 For a more complete discussion of entrepreneurship among scientists in seeking reserch funding, see H. M. Vollmer and D. L. Mills, *Professionalization*, Prentice-Hall, Englewood Cliffs, N.J., 1966, pp. 276–282.

istic of a participative style of management, rather than "close direction" of their research work. Furthermore, a somewhat larger minority of industrial scientists engaged in basic research say that they "rarely discuss" their research work with their managers; they seem to be rather on their own in their research activities.

In universities, a large majority of scientists engaged in basic research insist that they are essentially independent of any direct supervision over their research work. In contrast, a sizable proportion of those in mixed basic and applied research, and an even larger proportion of those in applied research activities admit to "occasional consultation" on their work activities with their administrative superiors. The data supporting these statements both for university scientists and those in industry are shown in Table 9.

Table 9

Report That Their Immediate Supervisor or Manager	Engaged in		
	Basic Research	Mixed Research	Applied Research
Scientists in universities	1518	116	73
Closely directs research work	2%	4%	7%
Occasionally consults on work	29%	44%	49%
Rarely discusses research work	61%	48%	38%
Scientists in industry	144	240	248
Closely directs research work	2%	3%	10%
Occasionally consults on work	66%	70%	70%
Rarely discusses research work	32%	25%	19%

Finally, since basic research both in universities and in industry is likely to be an individually initiated, independent kind of activity for scientists, it is also more likely to be conducted by scientists working alone than is the case for applied research. Applied research in university settings often involves collaboration between scientists from the same discipline. In industry, however, our data (Table 10) show that applied research is about equally as likely to be done solo as by either monodisciplinary or interdisciplinary collaboration.[22]

---

22 For a further discussion of the tendency of applied research to be a team activity and for basic research to be a solo activity, see L. Kowarski, "Team Work and Individual Work in Research," in N. Kaplan, *Science and Society*, N. Kaplan, Ed., Rand McNally, Chicago, 1965, pp. 247–255. However, A. H. Cottrell, in "Scientists: Solo or Concerted," in *The Sociology of Science*, B. Barber and W. Hirsch, Eds., Free Press, New York, 1963, pp. 388–393, points out that even basic science is never entirely a solitary activity.

Table 10

In Most of Present Research Are	Engaged in		
	Basic Research	Mixed Research	Applied Research
Scientists in universities	1518	116	73
Working mostly alone	52%	27%	22%
Collaborating—same discipline	32%	41%	42%
Collaborating—different disciplines	15%	32%	36%
Scientists in industry	144	240	248
Working mostly alone	40%	36%	34%
Collaborating—same discipline	38%	30%	31%
Collaborating—different disciplines	22%	33%	35%

At this point we may pause for a moment to recapitulate several conclusions on the organization of basic and applied research that are suggested by the data presented herein:

1. Basic research requires a form of organization that emphasizes (a) a considerable degree of freedom for the individual scientist to select his research topics and to solicit funding for them; (b) a high degree of freedom in the day-to-day conduct of research work; and (c) special opportunities for insulation of the scientist from daily interruptions of his work so that he can concentrate upon the solo processes of investigation and analysis that seem to be especially characteristic of basic research.

2. Applied research requires a form of organization that emphasizes (a) relatively more direction for the individual scientist in selecting research topics and more assistance in obtaining funding for them; (b) more consultative direction and assistance from management in the day-to-day conduct of research work; and (c) more encouragement for the scientist to engage in monodisciplinary collaboration with other scientists (especially in universities) and in interdisciplinary collaboraton (especially in industrial or other nonacademic settings), as well as opportunities for doing some solo work.

3. Furthermore, the organizational requirements listed above for basic research are essentially compatible with the way in which most universities are organized and managed in the scientific disciplines today. Therefore few, if any, changes are needed to make universities more compatible with the organizational requirements of basic research.

4. Conversely, the organizational requirements listed above for applied research are essentially compatible with the way in which most successful high technology companies, government agencies, and similar nonacademic institutions are organized today. Therefore few, if any, changes

are needed to make nonacademic institutions compatible with the organizational requirements of applied research.

5. Nevertheless—and here is where the rub comes—many universities are not only culturally inappropriate settings for applied research, they are also generally incapable of including applied research within their purview of activities without major organizational readjustments. They must become capable in some parts of their organizational structure to provide more consultative direction for the individual scientist in selecting research topics and more assistance in obtaining funding for them, more consultative direction and assistance from management in the day-to-day conduct of work, and perhaps more opportunity for scientists to engage in interdisciplinary collaboration than has sometimes been the case in the past. In short, to support effective applied research in university contexts, universities must also provide organizational structures that are simultaneously part of the university (e.g., participating in the education of students), and yet are *insulated* from the effects of a basic research-oriented value system that would otherwise destroy or expel applied research.

6. Similarly, most industrial organizations and other "mission-oriented" or "production-oriented" nonacademic institutions are not only culturally inappropriate settings for basic research, they are also incapable of including basic research within their purview of activities without major organizational readjustments. They must become capable in some parts of their organizational structure to provide a greater degree of freedom for individual scientists to select their research topics and to move out on their own to obtain funding for their work, more freedom of operation in the day-to-day conduct of their work, and more opportunity to closet themselves in individual study and contemplation than has sometimes been the case in the past. Thus to support effective basic research in nonacademic settings, organizations must provide departments or divisions that are simultaneously contributors to the goals of the parent organization (e.g., where basic research is conducted in areas relevant to the present and future technology of the parent organization) and yet are *insulated* from the effects of a more immediate payoff-oriented value system that would otherwise destroy or expel basic research.

These conclusions are not all original in this chapter. They simply summarize what has been found in practice in many leading university, industrial, and government organizations. Thus, for example, beginning mostly after World War II, leading universities began to set up a variety of on-campus laboratories, institutes, and centers to conduct interdisciplinary research and to provide educational facilities essentially oriented toward interdisciplinary, applied research types of activity—the kinds of activities not ordinarily congruent with discipline-oriented departmental structures within these universities. What must be noted here, however, is the inevitable backlash against these kinds of applied research centers from the more basic research-oriented community that predominates in most universities. The Stanford Electronics Laboratories and Stanford Research Institute cases cited earlier are examples of this kind of reaction.

In contrast, federal government agencies primarily mission-oriented in character have also set up basic research-oriented laboratories and research contracting institutions within their structures. The Office of Naval Research (ONR), a principal forerunner of the National Science Foundation, is a prime example of an organizational adaptation to develop a strong basic research capability. The Office of Aerospace Research (OAR) of the U.S. Air Force, with its component in-house research laboratories and its grants and contracts agency, the Air Force Office of Scientific Research, represents a later organizational adaptation for the same general purposes. Both ONR and OAR activities have sponsored scientific work in their in-house laboratories and by grant or contract to outside scientists. Their work has made major contributions to scientific knowledge, as well as advancing knowledge in particular areas relevant to defense technology. The Army Research Office and the Advanced Research Projects Agency have served similar functions in other parts of the Department of Defense, as have the Bureau of Research of the U.S. Office of Education, the National Institutes of Health, the National Bureau of Standards, and other units within other federal agencies.[23] Nevertheless, throughout the periods of their existence almost all of these organizations have had to defend themselves from reoccurring attacks from some individuals who feel that "immediate payoff" should be the primary criteria for judging the merits of these kinds of oragnizations in their present settings.

Some industrial firms have also been bold in experimenting with the concept of establishing a corporate laboratory or central research organization devoted essentially to basic research. These include firms as diverse as North American Aviation, the Boeing Company, the Ford Motor Company, and the Bell Telephone Laboratories. In these kinds of corporations, however, there has also been controversy as to the value of basic research activities with only long-term payoffs, if any at all.

23 For a discussion of the functions of research organizations of this type, especially in the Department of Defense, see W. J. Price, "The Case for Agency Research," *Bulletin of the Atomic Scientists* (April 1969), 34–36.

The predominant organizational arrangement in these kinds of "mission-oriented" or "production-oriented" institutions is to have basic research *insulated* from other functions such as applied research and development but not *isolated* from other functions. In other words, a theory of bonds and barriers" is applied in which there is an organizational barrier between basic research and other functions, but at the same time there is a spatial bond between basic research and other functions colocated at the same site. Thus Dr. J. E. Goldman, Director of the Scientific Laboratory at the Ford Motor Company has written:

> Good research has to be cushioned. Perhaps I phrase it best if I say that good research must be insulated, but not isolated. It has to be insulated, or cushioned, because once people learn that they can utilize this talent to put out fires, to help solve immediate problems, then the research is crippled. It is for this reason that we are set up as we are—with basic research separated organizationally, but not geographically, from applied and product research.[24]

Jack Morton of the Bell Telephone Laboratories has pointed out that his organization has a similar organizational barrier between basic research on the one hand, and applied research and engineering on the other:

> . . . we want some feedback, so let us see how we get it from, say, applied to basic (research): We get it in one way with a space bond—people in applied and basic live in the same building. And we get it through a common language. But at the same time, we see that if applied people or engineering people can dictate what the research people do, they will kill the long range basic research. So we need an organizational barrier: One man—Bill Baker—is head of all basic research; other men head up applied research and engineering. Our people are free to sell, to stimulate and motivate all they like. But my engineers, for example, cannot tell the basic researchers what to do. And conversely, the basic researcher who believes he has made an important discovery cannot order the applied research or engineering people to pursue it. So this organizational barrier provides freedom for basic research and freedom regarding what shall be developed.[25]

Our survey data show that the organizational separation of basic research from applied research and development is the most characteristic situation for scientists engaged in basic research in industry, while those

24 J. E. Goldman, "Basic Research in Industry," *International Science and Technology* (December 1964), 44.

25 J. A. Morton, "From Research to Technology," *International Science and Technology* (May 1964), 88–90.

in applied research most often find themselves in activities that are mixed with engineering and product development (Table 11).

Table 11

Relation between Their Research Department and Development in Their Employing Organization	Scientists in Industry Engaged in		
	Basic Research (144)	Mixed Research (240)	Applied Research (248)
R & D independent of each other	65%	51%	30%
R & D mixed together	31%	45%	64%
D is not a major function	4%	4%	6%

In universities, as would be expected, over three-fourths of the scientists reported that "development is not a major function." The emphasis is almost entirely on basic research in the majority of university settings.

Our survey data show further that in nonacademic settings in which basic research is organizationally independent of applied research, scientists are more likely to experience a large degree of freedom in selecting their research assignments, to work by themselves or in collaboration with others from their same discipline, to produce publications in scientific journals, and to report that their scientific publications have been cited frequently by others. In contrast, where research and development is mixed together in the same department or division of a larger organization, scientists are much less likely to report the above items, but they are more likely to say that they frequently have had job-related contacts with others in their organization who are responsible for product development, manufacturing, marketing, and so on, and that they have had opportunity to help translate research findings into useful applications. The publication of research findings in scientific journals and the citation of these findings by other scientists are the indicators of scientific productivity most characteristic of those who are in basic research; whereas interpersonal contact between scientists and appliers of science and the direct participation of scientists in the translation of research findings into useful applications appear to be the indicators of scientific productivity most characteristic of those in applied research, as the survey data in Table 12 suggest.

Thus, taken altogether, our data suggest that the organizational insulation between basic research and applied research and development that prevails in some leading corporations and also in basic research-oriented universtities where applied research and development often does not exist to any appreciable extent facilitates the primary goal of a basic

Table 12

	Scientists Engaged in		
	Basic Research	Mixed Research	Applied Research
In universities	1518	116	73
Have produced five or more publications in past five years	71%	72%	49%
Report publications cited "fairly frequently" or "very often" by other scientists	60%	57%	43%
Report job-related contacts with applications persons "several times a month" or more often	4%	13%	13%
Have had opportunities to translate research into useful applications	10%	28%	41%
In Industry	144	240	248
Have produced five or more publications in past five years	66%	45%	25%
Report publications cited fairly frequently or "very often" by other scientists	53%	35%	12%
Report job-related contacts with applications persons "several times a month" or more often	11%	27%	48%
Have had opportunities to translate research into useful applications	24%	40%	42%

research activity, namely, the production of scientific knowledge which is made available to other members of scientific communities. Conversely, the mixture of applied research and various applications functions in the same organizational units in nonacademic settings facilitates the primary goal of applied research, namely, to obtain immediate applications of scientific methods and knowledge to the solution of practical problems.[26]

The data in Tables 11 and 12 also reflect some ambivalence in the situation that surrounds much of the applied research currently conducted in university settings. Although a reasonable proportion (41 percent) of university scientists now in applied research activities feel that they have had opportunities to translate their research into useful applications, only a small minority (13 percent) say that they have had

[26] See H. M. Vollmer, Ed., *The Fundamental Research Activity in a Technology-Dependent Organization* Air Force Office of Scientific Research, Washington, D.C., 1965, pp. 93–100.

much contact with the kinds of people who are directly involved in making these applications, compared with 48 percent of the applied research scientists in industrial settings. A large proportion (49 percent) of the applied research scientists in universities still seem to feel constrained to conform to the typical university norms of "publish or perish." Thus the available evidence suggests that the very small minority (less than 5 percent) of the university scientists who try to concentrate on applied research are frequently diverted from this concentration by the pressures in the larger culture of the university, which were discussed earlier. There appears to be as much of a need for insulation of applied research centers and institutes from the control system of the surrounding university as there is a need for insulation of basic research laboratories and departments in business firms. Concepts of bonds and barriers must be applied appropriately in all organizational settings.

THE FUTURE OF BASIC AND APPLIED RESEARCH

A review of the history of science and technology in the Western world shows that the two were not always intimately related. Prior to the twentieth century, for example, basic research in scientific fields was almost entirely an academic enterprise in the United States. In contrast, innovations in technology came largely through trial-and-error experimentation in industrial laboratories.[27] However, the second half of the twentieth century has seen a much closer relationship between science and technology. Increasingly, advances in technology have been based upon prior discoveries in basic scientific research. Conversely, the argument may also be made that both social and technological needs have stimulated enquiry in many fields of basic science. In spite of counterreactions on both sides, the growth of basic research laboratories in industry and government agencies and the proliferation of interdisciplinary centers and institutes with more of an applied research emphasis on university campuses are institutional manifestations of the increasing interdependence of science and technology.

One can draw three major conclusions from this pattern of historical development in the technologically advancing countries.

1. Basic research and applied research (related to engineering and development) are both necessary for continuing technological advance.

---

[27] See for example, R. H. Shryock, "American Indifference to Basic Science during the Nineteenth Century," in *The Sociology of Science,* B. Barber and W. Hirsch, Eds.

One kind of activity cannot be supported at the expense of the other. Support for both must be increased simultaneously if a technologically advancing society is to be sustained.

2. Although they have some elements in common, basic research and applied research are fundamentally different in their purposes or objectives, in their culture or predominant value patterns, and in the style of management and organization they require. Therefore there is a need for organizational insulation between basic research and applied research activities.

3. Since they are different but increasingly interdependent activities, there is a need for the development and strengthening of mechanisms for crossfertilization between basic and applied research. The success of these mechanisms for crossfertilization will not only contribute directly to the continued growth of both basic and applied research but also to the continued growth of technologically based societies and to the solution of major problems in these societies.

Because we live in a technologically based society and because we assume that the majority of our population desires this society to be strengthened and for scientific and technical skills to be brought to bear on the solution of major problems, we can expect that in the remaining decades of this century both public and private support for basic and applied research will increase; that there will be increased recognition in management theory and practice for the need to insulate basic and applied research activities; and that there will be increased emphasis on the identification, development, and application of mechanisms for cross-fertilization between the two kinds of research.

Here we discuss certain major considerations associated with each of these three anticipated developments.

Societal support for different kinds of research implies commitment of both financial resources and manpower skills. Two barriers must be overcome if support for basic research and support for applied research are to be increased simultaneously in the future. On the one hand, the attitude of depreciation among many scientists involved in basic research in universities toward applied research and its associated pattern of values must become modified if the supply of the more talented students going into applied research activities in their future careers is to increase markedly. The quality of applied research could be less than desirable if applied researchers continue to be considered "second-class citizens" in academic environments. On the other hand, the lack of understanding of many managers, administrators, legislators, and others toward basic research because of its inability to show immediate payoffs in cost/effectiveness terms must also become modified if the funding of basic research is to increase by any substantial amounts in the future. "Big basic research," which requires substantial investment in expensive equipment, especially requires a better understanding of the long-range and unpredictable nature of basic research on the part of the general public.[28]

To overcome both kinds of barriers requires education—education of scientists in universities so that they develop a more sympathetic appreciation of the values of applied research than many have at present, and education of leaders of business and government so that they better appreciate the special kinds of environments required by basic research. How these kinds of education could best be achieved is a special topic that requires fuller analysis and discussion. Here, however, it seems appropriate to point out that education of scientists and administrators to appreciate better the values, purposes, and modes of organization of the other group certainly needs to include interpersonal contact and dialogue between members of the two groups. This kind of interchange of views, along with a growing appreciation of the point of view of the other group, can begin to take place in conferences and seminars but would ultimately require scientists concerned with basic research and others concerned with applications of science to work together on joint task force or project team assignments from time to time. Working together to try to bring multidisciplinary skills, as well as different points of view, to bear on a common problem could force an understanding of other points of view in a way that looser discussions are not likely to accomplish. Such opportunities for scientists and applications-oriented administrators to work together occasionally on common assignments are likely to diminish if applied research activities are driven off campuses or if basic research activities are abolished in industrial firms and government agencies in the future.

While there is a need for more education of both scientists and applications-oriented administrators in their appreciation of the values of the other group, the point has also been emphasized repeatedly in this chapter that basic research on the one hand, and applied research on the other hand, are sufficiently different to require organizational insulation from each other if both are to flourish. *Insulation,* but not *isolation,* is the correct descriptive term for what we are talking about here.

There appear to be two principal means to achieve organizational insulation. One is to recognize in institutional charters or statements of goals that an institution will specialize in a particular function, and that

28 See A. M. Weinberg, "Impact of Large-Scale Science on the United States," *Science,* **134** (July 1961), 161–164.

the majority of basic research activities are more appropriately housed in one kind of institution, and vice versa for applied research. Such is the case already where it is recognized that the fundamental goals of a university are defined in terms of education and basic research, and those of a business firm or government agency in terms of applying technology for producing particular kinds of products or services for a market or clientele. These definitions of specialized institutional purpose are not likely to change very much in the future because they have definite utilitarian value. They allow the institution to concentrate its resources and energies and to develop specialized institutional competence in ways that would not be effective if their purposes became too diffuse.[29]

At the same time, however, it could be argued that within these commonly accepted definitions of institutional purpose there is considerable room to include what might appear at first to be somewhat deviant functions. Indeed, it could be argued further that some functions that at first appear to be deviant to the overall purposes of the institution will in the long run turn out to be essential to the achievement of these purposes. Such might be the rationale, for example, for recognizing that applied research activities have a place in the educational process along with basic research, in response to the demands of students who are asking for more relevance in university education today. Likewise, as large diversified corporations and government agencies with complex responsibilities become more future oriented in planning the products and services they provide for the larger society, there is likely to be an increasing need for them to devote more attention to sponsoring basic research in scientific topics related to the fields of technology that are most pertinent to areas of corporate activity ten or more years hence.

Where such deviant functions are included within the institutional framework of an organization primarily oriented toward a different purpose, there is a need for a further mechanism of insulation, namely, departmental separation between the function of either basic or applied research and other functions that vary markedly within the larger organization. Thus *within* organizations departmental separation serves to provide the kind of insulation that deviant functions require, much as institutional specialization serves the same end *between* institutions.

This brings us finally to consider some of the mechanisms that aid in crossfertilization between basic and applied research, either within institutions or between them.

Several of these have been mentioned already. There are formal

---

[29] The concept of specialized institutional competence is central in P. Selznick, *Leadership in Administration,* Row, Peterson, Evanston, Ill., 1957.

mechanisms for interpersonal communication, such as seminars and conferences; and there are organizational arrangements that encourage concentration on a common problem, such as interdisciplinary task force or temporary project assignments. Another that has been mentioned is colocation of organizationally separated basic and applied research activities at the same side—with lounges, meeting rooms, cafeterias, and other facilities provided in a way that encourages informal contacts between scientists and applications people.

Still another mechanism that assists the crossfertilization of basic and applied research is to identify and develop certain persons to perform what might be described as *bridging roles*. These may be "management generalists" at a second or higher level of management in technologically based organizations, who are educated both in a scientific and an operational field and whose main responsibility is to couple basic scientific activities and outputs to the applications interests of the larger organization.[30] Those who are designated "scientific and engineering" officers in certain military services essentially perform this role. Students trained in professional principles of management in schools of business administration after having received another degree in a scientific or technical field can also be expected to perform this kind of bridging role in many cases. Such is the kind of role that is performed by "tech reps" or technically trained salesmen in many companies, and also increasingly by corporate planners with a technical background.

The movement of personnel from one field of scientific specialty to another, the increasing recognition of "second careers" in new fields of research and application among many scientists, and the growth of new fields of scientific specialization out of combinations of persons with backgrounds in the older disciplines also suggest roles that many scientists themselves may perform in the future as "bridge persons" who assist in the development of better communication and understanding between different fields of science and between scientific and applications interests.[31]

Besides these kinds of bridging roles, there are also an increasing number of what might be described as "bridging institutions," whose primary goal is to link basic research skills to the applications interests of client organizations. These include private corporations such as A. D.

---

30 For a further discussion of "management generalists" as a bridging role, see H. M. Vollmer, *Adaptations of Scientists and Organizations,* Chapter III, "Scientists in Technology Management Organizations.

31 See J. J. Bosley and A. Shapero, *A Preliminary Analysis of Inter-Specialty Mobility of Technical/Professional Manpower Resources,* R & D Studies Series, Stanford Research Institute, Menlo Park, Calif., 1967.

Little, and nonprofit research organizations such as Battelle Memorial Institute and Stanford Research Institute. While seeking to preserve appropriate basic research capabilities within their structures, these kinds of organizations have also sought to excel in interdisciplinary research addressed to client concerns. Since the largest of these institutions continue to grow in size and smaller competing institutions are proliferating in number, it appears that they are successfully meeting, and perhaps in some instances serving to create, a market demand for the kinds of bridging services these kinds of institutions provide.

All in all, both basic and applied research generally appear to have an expanding future as long as the roles and institutional arrangements that support that future can be recognized and developed, and as long as scientists and administrators can be educated to understand and appreciate the values appropriate to each.

CHAPTER FOUR

Politics and Research

Don E. Kash, University of Oklahoma

It is useful in understanding the relationship of politics to research to think of each as a system. The political system of interest here is what we commonly call the federal government or "Washington." Easton proposes that political systems authoritatively allocate values, and the output of that process for our purposes is national policy.[1] Of particular interest in understanding the linkages between the political system and the research system is that portion of national policy called science policy. The most tangible starting point for an investigation such as this is the output in terms of the organizations and mechanisms that spend the system's research money and how they spend that money. My approach, then, is to focus primarily on the outputs of the political system.

Students of the political system have suggested numerous definitions of the phenomena they study, but they consistently return to the concept of power as one key to understanding. Although the pure political man who makes every decision solely in terms of its contribution to his

[1] David Easton, *A Framework of Political Analysis,* Prentice-Hall, Englewood Cliffs, N.J., 1965, p. 96. Although I use Easton's definition of politics, there is no intention to use his notion of the characteristics of a political system.

power is rare, the politician's concern for power is consistently present regardless of the substance of the issue with which he is dealing. As Price suggests, "In government, the politician is apt to make every decision both to accomplish its ostensible purpose and to maintain or increase his power. . . ."[2] Conceived in its pure form, the political system ". . . is concerned with power and action."[3]

When one looks at politics from a policy point of view, it becomes clear that there is no pure politics. There may be agricultural policy, foreign policy, or science policy, but there is no political policy. Politics takes place around issues that are a part of other systems that have a perceived empirical base. In this sense, politics is always parasitical. Politics may then help the actors in another system achieve common values if they exist; or as is more often the case, it may mediate among actors in another system who seek competing values, or it may mediate among competing systems. A political system may be said to be successful when it helps other systems maximize their values while protecting or enhancing its own power. It cannot maximize power independent of other systems. Politics in a pure form can be conceived of in the abstract, but political action must always take place in some substantive area or system.

Policy is the primary output of the political system and therefore involves action. Such action requires linkages with other systems. Politicians are then correctly perceived as having multiple motives and goals, since by definition they must respond to the values of more than one system. This is, I suspect, the basis of the traditional American suspicion of politicians.

Compare now the political system, with its inevitable demands on its participants, with the research system. "When a scientist says something, his colleagues must ask themselves only whether it is true. When a politician says something, his colleagues must first of all ask, "Why does he say it?"[4] In its pure form the research system is concerned with truth. An abstract formulation of the research system presents a relatively clear-cut picture of its values. The motives of its participants are curiosity and a desire to find truth, and its practictioners can do their work within the confines of the system. When one moves from discussing the research system in the abstract to a discussion of specific issues, the differences between it and the political system become apparent. The

2 Don Price, *The Scientific Estate,* Belknap Press of Harvard Univ. Press, Cambridge, Mass., 1965, p. 134.
3 *Ibid.,* p. 135.
4 *Ibid.,* p. 9.

substantive issues of research are not taken from other systems, but are rather issues internal to the research system.

As one begins to look at the actual operation of the two systems, it is of course clear that both are dependent for their operation on establishing linkages with other systems. The degree to which each system is dependent on other systems, however, has been vastly different. Political issues are always dependent on other systems, while research issues, until recent times, have been much less dependent on other systems. It is precisely the growing dependence of research on other systems that has made the study of science policy increasingly important.

As long as research was characterized by the notion of "little research" carried on in universities by a single researcher or a small informal group needing few facilities, research made few demands on other systems. World War II, however, saw a major change in the direction of "big research." As research questions called for larger groups and more expensive facilities, the research system came inceasingly to be dependent on other systems for the achievement of its goals. It was through the use of the political system that research obtained the desired support from other systems. Support for research was provided from the very beginning because it was perceived that research could contribute to the achievement of other national policy goals. That is, the federal government took on the support of research because it was seen as being instrumental to the achievement of substantive policy goals in such areas as defense, the economy, and foreign relations. To the extent that the political system took on the promotion of the goals dear to the research system it was because these goals were seen as instrumental to the achievement of other policy goals. Put in more concrete terms, the political system has supported research in this country as a means interest, whereas economic growth and military security have been end interests. The goals of federal research policy are those defined by the research system only as long as they seem to contribute to other more important policy goals.

Until the contemporary period it appears that the federal government has followed a research policy predicated on the assumption that what was good for research was good for the country at large. Therefore research policy could be made substantially by researchers. It is the thesis of this chapter that that assumption is undergoing modification.

It is my purpose in this chapter to look at the nature of the linkages that have been established between the political system and the research system in the United States. I propose, however, to go one step further and project into the future the continuing evolution of the relationship of the two systems. For the past 30 years, the research system has been supported in the pursuit of its own goals because those goals were seen as being instrumental to other national goals. There is growing evidence to indicate this will not hold into the future.

It is helpful to set some parameters for this study. The main focus is on relations between the federal government and the universities and particularly on the support for basic research. As we will see shortly, federal research policy is such a seamless web that it is necessary to violate those parameters almost immediately; but where I do this I will make it clear. A convenient way to handle the evolution of the politics-research relationship is to divide the last 30 years into the three periods suggested by Seitz and add a fourth period for the prognosis.[5] Before doing that, however, it is necessary to look at the way in which the federal government divides up its research money.

CATEGORIES OF RESEARCH

The National Science Foundation (NSF) estimated federal obligations for research and development (R & D) and R & D plant to be $15.6 billion in fiscal 1971. Of that total $5.9 billion was classified as paying for research and the rest for development. The research portion was divided $2.2 billion for basic research and $3.7 billion for applied research.[6] These figures suggest that the various categories are subject to precise delimitation and that one should look primarily at the activities covered only by the research category in a chapter concerned with politics and research. Quite the contrary is the case, for one can grasp some notion of the linkages between politics and research only by recognizing the lack of clear-cut boundaries between the research and development categories. The lack of a clear-cut distinction between the categories in the federal budget is only a mirror of the fuzziness on this question in the minds of congressmen, laymen, and even researchers. In fact, one of the dominant characteristics of our technological society is the continuous interaction between research and development. Historically, the roots of development are in the technology of the craftsman, and the roots of research are in the science of the scholar. Today those distinctions no longer exist because they both use the common methodology of science.

The boundaries separating one activity from another are rarely distinct in terms

5 Frederick Seitz, "The University: Independent Institution or Federal Satellite," in *Science and the University*, Boyd R. Kennan, Ed., Columbia Univ. Press, New York, 1966, p. 150.
6 *Federal Funds For Research, Development, and Other Scientific Activities, Fiscal Years 1969, 1970, and 1971*, NSF 70–38, p. 2.

of either the motives of the individuals involved or the consequences that flow from their work. Perhaps, however, the term "scientific technology," in contrast to the "empirical technologies" of the past, conveys best the notion of the increasing dependence of technological innovation on scientific theory today.[7]

Certainly, research must rate with democracy and religion in difficulty of precise definition. Lay usage of the term appears to include everything from working on subatomic particles to building a better toothpaste tube. Federal research policy, then, is partly the result of the political system's perception of the package of activities bought by the $15.6 billion. If the cynics are correct, this may make sense, for they argue that university researchers frequently have little difficulty in characterizing their research as either basic or applied depending upon the preferences of the agency from which they are seeking funding. Nonetheless, there are operational definitions which are used in the federal budget, and they are defined by NSF as follows.

Research is systematic, intensive study directed toward fuller scientific knowledge of the subject studied. Such study covers both basic and applied research.

Basic research is that type of research which is directed toward increase of knowledge in science. It is research where the basic aim of the investigator is fuller knowledge or understanding of the subject under study without regard to the practical application thereof.

Applied research is that type of research which is concerned with practical application of the knowledge or understanding gained (sometimes defined as all research except basic research).

Development is the systematic use of scientific knowledge directed toward the production of useful materials, devices, systems, or methods, including design, and development of prototypes and processes.[8]

Although the distinctions involved in NSF's definitions hinge on the motives of the researchers, they are probably as operational as any available distinctions.[9] It should be noted of course that the definitions used by the federal government have used the natural sciences as the frame of reference. In the social sciences there is the advantage of not having to deal with development, but the difficulty associated with drawing the

[7] Robert Gilpin, *France in the Age of the Scientific State,* Princeton Univ. Press, Princeton, N.J., 1968, p. 23.

[8] U.S. Congress, House, Subcommittee on Science, Research, and Development of the Committee on Science and Astronautics, *Government and Science,* 88th Congress, 2d Session, p. 3.

[9] Michael D. Reagan, "Basic and Applied Research: A Meaningful Distinction?," *Science* (March 17 1967), 1383–1386.

boundary between basic and applied research is nearly impossible. The relatively primitive stage of social science theory denies the reference points that exist by now in the natural sciences. We in the social sciences have not reached what Kuhn would call the paradigm stage:

> In the absence of a paradigm or some candidate for a paradigm, all the facts that could possibly pertain to the development of a given science are likely to seem equally relevant. As a result, early fact-gathering is a far more nearly random activity than the one that subsequent scientific development makes familiar.[10]

Given the preparadigm condition, Weinberg suggests an intelligent research strategy which could be applied to the social sciences. Such a strategy requires something analogous to that followed by his basketball coach: "In setting up a good shot at the basket, by all means keep the ball moving. It doesn't matter so much where the ball moves as long as it does not remain in one place; only in this way are openings created."[11] The lack of a paradigm, however, precludes the possibility of distinguishing between basic and applied research. The particular problem in the social sciences is in defining what is basic. One might well be able to operationalize a definition of applied research as the collection and collation of those data necessary or helpful in meeting contemporary social problems. However, we certainly do not want to reverse the NSF definition and say that "all research that is not applied is basic." Having recognized the difficulties involved in defining research with precision, I now discuss the substantive issues involved in the politics-research relationship.

ESTABLISHING THE POLITICS-RESEARCH LINKAGE

World War II forged the major linkages between the two systems, and in substantial part the "ad hoc" arrangements of that period still provide the major mechanisms for interaction between them. The war period saw the establishment of a very important monetary tie between politics and research, but this was possible primarily because of a significant modi-

[10] Thomas S. Kuhn, *The Structure of Scientific Revolutions,* Phoenix Books of the Univ. of Chicago Press, Chicago, 1962, p. 15.
[11] Alvin M. Weinberg, "Prospects for Big Biology," in the U.S. Congress, Senate, Subcommittee on Government Research of the Committee on Government Operations, *Research in The Service of Man: Biomedical Knowledge, Development, and Use,* 90th Congress, 1st Session, p. 34.

fication in the psychological dimension. Had it not been for the impact of the war on the psychology of the actors in both systems, the present monetary linkages would not exist. Doubtless, the greatest psychological distance was traveled by the academic members of the research system and by the congressmen and the military administrators of the political system.

Prior to the war, research in this country was small-scale and with a few exceptions dominated by university scientists. There was no general pattern of the government acting as a patron of the sciences as had existed in Europe. On the contrary, it was an integral part of the American belief system that support from the federal government would mean unwanted control of the university. In short, there was neither any expectation nor desire for federal support for university research from the university community—agriculture being the one exception. From the government point of view, the expectations and desires were the same. This pattern of expectation was violated in any substantial degree only by support for mission-oriented applied research in the areas of agriculture and natural resources. Most of this research was done in-house by civil service employees, the one variation being the support system for land grant schools. In summary, then, the political system and the research system had few linkages prior to World War II, and there was little desire on the part of actors in either of the systems to change this.

That intimate linkages were established quickly was the result of several reinforcing conditions. Not the least of these was that the American scientific community was prepared to make a contribution since it had come of age in the preceding decade.[12] This was only a necessary but not a sufficient reason for the rapid development of the linkages. Normal patriotism doubtless contributed greatly to the eagerness of the scientific community to make a contribution to the war effort. However, it should be added that this war was also perceived by the research community as especially threatening to its values. As Brooks suggests ". . . the Hitler menace appeared uniquely directed at the traditions and ideals which seemed most important to the academic scientific community, both European and American, while the flow of prominent scientist refugees from Germany had given the threat an immediacy and reality which was a powerful stimulus to action."[13]

Finally, a remarkable group of men were available to build the linkages between the two systems. Vannevar Bush and those who worked

12 Harvey Brooks, *The Government of Science,* M.I.T. Press, Cambridge, Mass., 1968, pp. 21–22.
13 *Ibid.*

with him in the wartime Office of Scientific Research and Development (OSRD) had the unique ability, on the one hand, to communicate the needs of the political system to the research community and, on the other hand, to communicate the possible contributions of the research system to the political community. Additionally, and of great long-run importance, they also made it clear to the government that the most effective way to obtain the contributions of research was through new organizational and legal arrangements. "Their objective was to establish an administrative framework that would enable the scientific community to avoid the doleful experiences of World War I, when scientists who wished to contribute to the war effort usually found themselves in uniform and subordinate to scientifically illiterate military men."[14] The oft-repeated stories of the atomic bomb, radar, and penicillin make it unnecessary to recount the successes of an approach that used flexible contracting arrangements to convert the universities into a part of the national arsenal.

From the viewpoint of this paper, the critical elements of this success story

. . . were the psychological consequences, for the American scientific community emerged from the war with the conviction that its contributions to victory were, first of all, indispensable. But even more important, in terms of planning how the pre-war orphan [research] was to be treated in the post-war period, the scientific community held that its contributions would have been unattainable if the management of the most significant wartime science and technology had not been left to scientists.[15]

Much the same set of psychological consequences was evident among federal administrators, particularly those in military agencies, and some congressmen. That science had the ability to produce in times of need, when given freedom to do so, was taken as a lesson of supreme importance by many of the federal administrators and many members of Congress.

Based on the changed attitudes of both the research community and political community wrought by the demands of the war, Bush and his colleagues at OSRD forged, on an "ad hoc" basis, a new set of monetary linkages between the two systems. These new linkages took the form of the research and development contract and the research grant. Prior to the war government purchasing was generally done according to rigid rules usually involving competitive bidding. Research could hardly be

---

[14] Daniel S. Greenberg, *The Politics of Pure Science*, New American Library, New York, 1967, p. 78.
[15] *Ibid.*, p. 82.

purchased in that way. It is only a slight overstatement to say that during World War II the flexible arrangements for purchasing research involved the government defining the goals in very broad terms and committing itself to provide all the money necessary to achieve them—and the researchers filled in the rest.

The favorable experiences of World War II permanently modified the attitudes of participants in both systems toward each other. Nonetheless, it came as something of a surprise for many, especially in the academic research community, when the political system continued to provide support after the war was over.[16] That the support was continued was a result of two circumstances. "First, the executive and legislative branches of the government felt that the scientific community deserved some form of continuing support as a reward for its effective work during the war. . . ."[17] Second, many people in the government were convinced that the various applied missions of several agencies would be furthered if the effective partnership between them and science could be maintained and expanded in the postwar period.[18] In pursuit of a continued partnership with the research community, the government was quite willing to let the researchers define their own goals and operate their own system with little outside interference.

Dominant in the value structure of the research community has been the search for truth. In operational terms this had meant placing basic research above all else. Part of the prewar tradition of suspicion that government support would lead to control was associated with the notion that such control would move the research system in the direction of applied research. The academic's ideal in research has been an image of the individual researcher pursuing his own goals motivated primarily by the simple but virtuous desire to understand for the sake of understanding rather than for more utilitarian reasons. Government support had called up images of controlling the direction of research and sullying the motives behind it, which would surely result from the inevitable growth of big research and its accompanying bureaucracy as the government became involved. The war changed all this as it became clear ". . . not only that big organization, big equipment, and generous funding were compatible with the creative process, but that with war-born instruments and technology ready to be applied to basic research, bigness had become indispensable in many fields of research, especially physics."[19]

---

16 Seitz, p. 151.
17 *Ibid.*
18 *Ibid.;* Bruce L. R. Smith, *The RAND Corporation,* Harvard Univ. Press, Cambridge, Mass., 1966, p. 38.
19 Greenberg, pp. 97–98.

Further, basic researchers began to perceive, along with those in government, that there was a payoff to be had from the interaction of basic and applied research. It was an article of faith that basic research was the source of technology, but it became clear that technology could also serve to produce new fundamental knowledge. As we shall see, this assumption would be questioned in a serious manner only after two decades had passed.

In summary, then, the temporary cooperation between the two systems caused by the war proved to be so satisfactory that a marriage of a permanent kind followed. A more ideal relationship could hardly be imagined since each system was allowed to define and vigorously pursue its own goals. It was in the interest of the research system for the political system to pursue security and prosperity because those goals seemed to require vigorous and growing support of research. It was in the interest of the political system for the research system to pursue its goal of more and better fundamental research because from that came security and prosperity. This happy state of affairs was, however, always dependent on the political system's viewing the research system's goals as means to national policy goals. Any change in national policy goals or in the perception of the instrumental value of basic research would rapidly create tension between the two systems.

CEMENTING THE POLITICS-RESEARCH LINKAGE

The linkages established between politics and research during World War II were "ad hoc" and formed around specific problems such as the atomic bomb project or the radar project. During the decade and a half following the end of the war, there evolved a complex set of arrangements for the support of research. By the 1960s a highly decentralized but nonetheless well-established and smoothly functioning set of mechanisms existed for the management of the politics-research linkages. Much of the decision making and operation of federal research policy was handled by the research system itself. As Price states:

. . . in the research and development programs, the scientists have brought to its most complete development an improvised system of federalism that makes use of private institutions for the conduct of federal programs. To those who argued that you cannot divide sovereignty, as to those who believed you could not divide the atom, the answer of the scientists was simply to divide it.[20]

[20] Don K. Price, *Government and Science*, Oxford Univ. Press, Oxford, 1962, p. 66.

This appears to have happened for several reasons. First, the growing complexity of scientific technology seems to have required the evolution of something similar to that which Galbraith calls the technostructure.[21] This is an interesting form of what Braybrooke and Lindblom call disjointed incrementalism, which requires the merging of political and technical decisions.[22] Some critics of the technological society contend that complex technology requires a group decision-making process which filters out any capricious personal prejudices. Ellul suggests that there is less and less opportunity in this system for choice ". . . among several means which are potentially applicable. It is really a question of finding the best means in the absolute sense, on the basis of numerical calculation."[23] If there is a kernel of truth in Ellul's view, it is not hard to understand why decision making has taken place increasingly in the boundary area where the political system and the research system overlap.

It is useful to look at how federal research policy has handled development carried on by industry, as opposed to university research. Particularly in the areas of major military and space technologies, the postwar period saw the growing use of the prime R & D contract. Under this arrangement, while the industrial contractor has primary responsibility for developing the new technological system, he can, in effect, let subcontracts on a cost-plus basis with other firms.[24] Therefore these prime contractors can play much the same role as a government agency in decision making and policy implementation.

Thus large prime contractors will invite design competition, establish source selection boards, send out industrial survey teams, make subcontract awards on a competitive or negotiated basis, appoint small business administrators, designate plant resident representatives, develop reporting systems to spot bottlenecks, make cost analyses of subcontractor operations, and request monthly progress and cost reports from subcontractors.[25]

The pattern of diffusing program authority in the R & D area was in part a response to the short time constants placed on new technological

---

[21] John Kenneth Galbraith, *The New Industrial State,* Houghton Mifflin, Boston, 1967, pp. 11–12, 60–71.

[22] David Braybrooke and Charles E. Lindblom, *A Strategy of Decision,* Free Press, New York, 1963, pp. 81–110.

[23] Jacques Ellul, *The Technological Society,* Random House, New York, 1964, p. 21.

[24] For a detailed review of R & D contracting, see Clarence H. Danhof, *Government Contracting and Technological Change,* Brookings Institution, Washington, D.C., 1968.

[25] U.S. Congress, House, Committee on Government Operations, *Eleventh Report, Organization and Management of Missile Programs,* House Report No. 1121, 86th Congress, 1st Session, p. 49.

systems and also a way to compensate for the shortage of the necessary skills within the governmental system. This was particularly true of the Air Force, which had major program responsibilities in the 1950s but little in-house research competence. Whether intentional or not, this diffusion of decision making turned out to be politically efficacious, for it soon built a very influential constituency among those organizations acting as Air Force contractors. As Nieburg suggests: "The Army learned an important lesson in its struggle with the Air Force during the Thor-Jupiter controversy—that its extensive in-house engineering-management capability was a positive disadvantage in mobilizing Congressional and public influence to support military missions and budgets."[26]

The pattern of operation evolved in government-industry R & D relations is consistent with the notion discussed earlier, the need for giving nongovernment organizations their head in doing research. With regard to basic research in the area of government-university relations, the pattern of decentralized operation was also established. Based on the tacit agreement between the two systems that control of research ought to be in the hands of researchers, the research system had great freedom in designing and implementing its own support programs. This should not imply, however, that there was any centralized grand design involved in the development of government-university linkages. To the contrary, the one effort at a grand design outlined in Bush's now famous *Science, the Endless Frontier* was significantly modified before it was finally institutionalized in the form of the NSF. Although there was general agreement within the political system that research ought to be in the hands of researchers, a design that put that research formally beyond the control of the political system as Bush had recommended was going too far. The political system might be willing to let researchers define research policy at any given time, but it was not willing to give this right to the researchers in perpetuity. President Truman's veto message for the bill that would have incorporated Bush's recommendations said: "It would, in effect, vest the determination of vital national policies, the expenditure of large public funds, and the administration of important governmental functions in a group of individuals who would be essentially private citizens."[27]

That Bush and other leaders of the research system should have pursued such a course doubtless reflected their recognition that the ultimate goals of the research system and the policy goals of the

---

[26] H. L. Nieburg, *In the Name of Science*, Quadrangle Books, Chicago, 1966, p. 189.
[27] The veto message is reprinted in U.S. Congress, House, Committee on Interstate and Foreign Commerce, *National Science Foundation, Hearings*, 80th Congress, 2d Session, p. 24.

political system might well at any point in time be different. It probably also reflects a certain naiveté on the part of what were at that time the most politically sophisticated leaders of the research system. Had the Bush recommendations been adopted, NSF would quite likely have been as politically impotent as the Smithsonian Institution. NSF has done as well as other federal agencies supporting research during the 1960s.[28] It should be noted, however, that in the mid-1960s, when the political system began to modify its view that basic research automatically contributed to important national policy goals, it became necessary to provide NSF with the political advantages to be gained from an applied mission and from authorization hearings before its own sympathetic congressional committees.[29] However, even during the period when NSF's charge was solely the support of basic research and its appropriations were growing most rapidly, it was always supported by the appropriations committees because of the perception that there would be an eventual practical payoff; it would ultimately contribute to other policy goals.[30]

Although the research community failed in its effort to formalize a grand design for the support of basic research, in substance it obtained what it wanted during the period following the war. Organizationally, the support mechanisms that developed for academic research were heterogeneous and pluralistic, but they shared a common pattern of operation that was everything the research community could have hoped for. To illustrate the degree to which the political system accepted the research system's definition of goals, it was the military agencies that turned out to be the initial patrons of basic research. Particularly, the most tradition bound and hierarchical of the services, the Navy, became the chief subsidizer and pattern setter for postwar government-university relations.

Under the aegis of the Office of Naval Research, the notion of project support came to dominate the whole support system. Its precise form was to vary a bit among the numerous federal agencies involved in supporting academic research, but the overall pattern was remarkably consistent. Seitz has pointed out the dominant characteristics of this period:

1. Almost all good scientists in universities were able to obtain with reasonable speed either contracts or grants with one or more agencies for research close to their own interests.

[28] Michael D. Reagan, "Congress Meets Science: The Appropriations Process," *Science* (May 23, 1969), 929–930.
[29] "Key NSF Hearings Open with Handler," *Science* (March 29, 1969), 1433.
[30] Reagan, "Congress Meets Science: The Appropriations Process," p. 930.

2. Although the funds involved in the contracts and grants passed through the administrative offices of the university, they were usually directed very specifically to the working scientist who generated the proposals for his support and maintained close liaison with governmental agencies.

3. Although the typical competent university scientist or engineer has had relatively free access to research money in the period between 1945 and 1960, the same cannot be said of the scholars in the social sciences and humanities, particularly the latter.

4. Since Congress has, in general, treated the mission-oriented agencies somewhat more generously over the years than it has the National Science Foundation, certain fields of science have advanced at the expense of others at various times.

5. The geometric growth with time of governmental funds available for universities, when coupled with the fact that a fraction of such funds are used for faculty salaries by some universities has transformed the academic hiring hall into an employees' market.

6. It is very important to emphasize that the money that has been channeled into the university system since the war through the government pattern of contracts and grants has incidentally given the universities much of the vitality that they have needed in order to prepare to handle the enormous demand for higher education that is now emerging so clearly in our society.[31]

It should be reemphasized at this point that the operative goal of both systems during this period was the support of the very best research; what was good for research was good for the United States. Given that assumption and the evolution of the project system of support, the academic disciplines became the unquestioned loci of power in the allocation of support for research. The academic system is designed so that one's disciplinary peers are the important judgment makers in determining his rewards; at the lowest level promotions and salary increases are, at least ideally, reflections of one's quality as judged by his peers. When one asks what is the best research, the question cannot be answered by just anyone claiming to be a researcher; it must be answered by members of a single discipline and generally by members of a subdisciplinary group. It comes as no surprise, then, that the shared commitment of the two systems to the support of the best research resulted in the creation of mechanisms that allowed one's disciplinary peers to award support. The best known organizational mechanisms for this purpose are the NSF review panels and the National Institutes of Health (NIH) study sections. The idea of calling on a researcher's peers to judge the quality of his ideas, his professional competence, and the adequacy of his facilities is patently obvious. This support pattern was designed and operated by a remarkably able group of scientist-politicians, most

31 Seitz, pp. 151–154.

of whom came out of the great research projects of World War II. That the programs they designed and implemented have provided billions of dollars for research with little scandal and remarkable scientific payoff is testimony to their integrity and skill.

A final point needs to be made with regard to the support of research as it developed during this period. Although support for research flowed to the able researchers, it also provided support for graduate education. In the American research system, graduate education is inextricably intertwined with research. That ". . . graduate education and the process of basic research belong together at every possible level. . . ."[32] is an article of faith in the research system. This interaction, initiated by the Germans but brought to full bloom in the American university,[33] was reinforced by the project support arrangements just described. In terms of the willingness of the political system to support research, this interdependence has always been supportive, for if nothing else practical can be seen, there is always the production of researchers with graduate degrees.[34] And in a society that has continuous economic growth as a goal and believes that highly trained manpower is a major contributor to that growth, it would be hard to find a better argument for the support of research.

In summary, then, the immediate postwar period saw the evolution of a research policy that transferred a great deal of the initiative for and control of research into the hands of nongovernmental institutions that were substantive operators within the research system. The style of decentralized control set by academic researchers also became the style that predominated in the area of development handled by industrial organizations. This pattern was based upon the belief that the most effective way to pursue national policy goals was to let the members of the research system pursue their own goals under R & D contracts or grants.

FRAYING THE LINKAGES BETWEEN THE SYSTEMS

By 1960 the basic elements of federal research policy had evolved, and the mechanism necessary for its management had been tested and found

---

[32] President's Science Advisory Committee, *Scientific Progress, the Universities, and the Federal Government,* Washington, D.C., 1960, p. 5, quoted in Michael D. Reagan, *Science and the Federal Patron,* Oxford Univ. Press, Oxford, 1969, p. 47.

[33] Joseph Ben-David and Abraham Zloczower, "Universities and Academic Systems in Modern Societies," in *Science and Society,* Norm Kaplan, Ed., Rand McNally, Chicago, 1965, pp. 62–85.

[34] Reagan, "Congress Meets Science: The Appropriations Process," pp. 929–930.

to be satisfactory by actors in both systems. If the political system had come out of World War II recognizing the importance of research to the achievement of national policy goals, by 1960 this had become an article of faith unquestioned by right-thinking men. Alternatively, whatever concerns may have existed in the research system at the end of the war had been completely allayed. Linked together, the two systems were willing to take on any challenge. The challenge turned out to be space. Largely as a result of Sputnik, in the initial 4 years of the 1960s the federal R & D budget jumped by $7 billion, doubling in total size.[35] Massive increases in funding came in each of the government's R & D categories, and the research system was able to absorb the new monies and use them effectively. The new demands for federal R & D funds required the government to commit 15 percent of its budget for these purposes. Suddenly, some congressmen, fearing that the appetite of the research system was voracious, began to raise questions about the utility of putting 15 percent of the budget into a system that was as little known as that of research.

The linkages between the two systems had been shaped in a climate in which it was possible for each to pursue its own goals and at the same time provide support for each other. They were also forged with each system understanding little about either the motives or the modes of operation of the other. By the mid-1960s two things began to change; the costs of research were now very large, and the nature of national problems began to be perceived differently by the political system. In the years between 1956 and 1964, the average annual increase for R & D obligations was 22 percent.[36] Further, in the mid-1960s leaders of the research community were stating that basic research would continue to need a 15-percent average annual increase in support to maintain its vitality.[37] This kind of growth starting from the dollar base existing in the mid 1960s was unacceptable to the political system. Throughout the postwar period the research system had been able to follow a policy of pursuing all good research. Now the monetary limitations were going to force choices among good research. As Weinberg argued in 1963, "If those actively engaged in science do not make choices, they will be made anyhow by the congressional appropriations committees and the Bureau

35 *Federal Funds for Research, Development, and Other Scientific Activities: Fiscal Years 1967, 1968, and 1969*, p. 3.
36 *Ibid.*
37 *Basic Research and National Goals* (1964), p. 13, a report by the Committee on Science and Public Policy of the National Academy of Sciences and issued as a Committee Print by the House Committee on Science and Astronautics.

of the Budget, or corresponding bodies in other governments."[38] The difficulties posed for the research system by the withdrawal of continued open-ended support are clear when it is recognized that the system has not ". . . been able to provide clear priorities criteria or to suggest a mechanism through which comparative allocations determinations might be made. . . ."[39]

The level of stress within the research system and the fraying of the linkages with the political system has been increased much more, however, by the changing nature of our national problems. Here the predominant concern has moved from external threats to domestic threats. Stated differently, growing national attention has been focused on the goals of economic and social progress. Translated into more specific concerns, these goals include at least the following:

1. Protecting the natural environment
2. Providing new sources of energy
3. Applications of cybernetics
4. Strengthening information management
5. Induction of industrial R & D
6. Stimulating transportation
7. Diminishing urban congestion
8. Enhancing adequate housing
9. Improving food production
10. Alleviation of crime
11. Upgrading the quality of education
12. Protecting the national health[40]

With regard to the portion of the research system that has handled the development of military and space technology, the modification of our national goals led to growing attacks on a military-industrial complex. The skeleton of that military-industrial relationship has been R & D contracts. Modern scientific technology of the kind demanded in our military and space programs has required large bureaucratic organizations. Such organizations, once in existence, become important supports for the continued pursuit of the goals for which they were created or, alternatively, for the creation of new goals that they can pursue. In more specific terms, "while many critics of American so-

38 Alvin M. Weinberg, "Criteria for Scientific Choice," *Minerva*, 1, No. 1 (1963), 161.
39 Reagan, *Science and the Federal Patron*, p. 278.
40 U.S. Congress, House, Subcommittee on Science, Research and Development of the Committee on Science and Astronautics, *Inquiries, Legislation, Policy Studies Re: Science and Technology*, 2nd Progress Report, 89th Congress, 2d Session, pp. 21–23.

ciety could see the ICBM and the sub-sonic jet as legitimate social goals, they see the ABM and the SST as responses to the survival goals of the involved organizations."[41]

Much the same kinds of critiques are being made of the big science projects of a basic kind. The most frequently cited example is the 200 billion-electron-volt accelerator being built west of Chicago for the pursuit of bigger and better high-entry physics. Even as early as 1963 questions were being asked about the utility of supporting expensive high-energy physics in terms of its contribution to national goals.[42]

It is important to note here that federal R & D policy is being questioned in two ways. First, that part of the research system oriented toward applied problems (particularly industrial concerns) is under attack because it is focused on the wrong problems. Second, that part of the research system oriented toward the system's own goals of basic research is under attack because it is no longer as widely accepted that the research system's goals actually represent the means to the achievement of national goals. Stated differently, there is growing concern that much research may be substantially irrelevant to the achievement of national policy goals; and the questions about the 200 billion-electron-volt accelerator fall into this category. The desire now is to allocate both the monetary and manpower resources more directly to the alleviation of major national problems. Some critics take the more extreme position that some research is leading to undesirable goals. The cardinal example here is the ABM debate, but the debate in Congress goes much deeper than an argument over the big military technologies. In a sense, the opposition to the ABM is based upon the belief that its first-order consequences are negative, but the much wider base of doubt being raised about the present operation of the political-research linkage is concerned with the less tangible second-order consequences.

The growing interest in a council of Social Advisors or in technology assessment is based upon the belief that ". . . technical changes have proved historically to be particularly explosive sources of second-order social, economic, and political changes that were never envisioned."[43] A growing concern in Congress over the condition of our natural environment has led to studies which are convincing growing numbers of

41 Don E. Kash, "Forces Affecting Science Policy," *Bulletin of the Atomic Scientists* (April 1969), 14.

42 Weinberg, "Criteria for Scientific Choice," p. 168.

43 Raymond A. Bauer, "Detection and Anticipation of Impact: The Nature of the Task," in Raymond A. Bauer, Ed., *Social Indicators*, M.I.T. Press, Cambridge, Mass., 1966, p. 4.

Congressmen that the research system and its output are partially responsible.[44] That output of the research system called technology has become both the God word and the Devil word of our time. It is this paradoxical perception of research that is generating increasing pressures in the political system for adjustments in its linkages with the research system. For if research is seen as the source of many social problems, it is also seen as the solution to those problems. There is then no inclination within the political system to cut its linkages with the research system, but there is a very real pressure calling for modification of the linkages. The research system is being asked to do more applied or programmatic research concerned with the achievement of national policy goals. Additionally, there is the request that research be used to identify the problems. Few demands are heard for an end to federal support of research, but many demands are heard that the research system take a larger share of responsibility for applying its basic work to the solution of practical problems.[45] In terms of the linkages between the two systems, this seems to mean adjustments that allow the political system to define in greater detail the goals of the research system.

It would be stressful enough for those of us in the research system if these changes involved only a reallocation of existing resources, but there are evidences that they will mean fundamental changes in the nature of the linkages. As an increasing number of congressmen are sensitized to a growing cultural lag which has its source in research, the pressure for action builds.[46] The area of research policy became the major center for action once it was perceived that "federal R & D expenditure, functioning both manifestly and latently, has been the fuel energizing the changes that have taken place in our society since the end of World War II."[47] That is, increasingly the area of federal research policy is seen as the point at which intervention can take place both to protect against the further development of the "accidental century"[48] and to correct some of the existing problems.

44 For a partial list of these studies see U.S. Congress, Senate, Committee on Interior and Insular Affairs, *A National Policy for the Environment*, 90th Congress, 2d Session, pp. 25–29.
45 This demand took on new dimensions with President Johnson's call for more application of biomedical research; quoted in *Science* (July 8, 1966), 149–150.
46 U.S. Congress, House, Committee on Science and Astronautics, *Technology Assessment: Statement of Emilio Q. Daddario,* 90th Congress, 1st Session, p. 13.
47 Kash, "Forces Affecting Science Policy," p. 11.
48 This is the apt title of Michael Harrington's insightful book which looks into the development of technology, Penguin Books, Baltimore, 1965.

THE PRESSURE FOR MODIFICATION IN THE LINKAGES

Looking ahead at the pressures on the politics-research relationship, there appear to be two kinds of demands developing. First, and most obvious, is the demand that the research system do more to help society meet its contemporary problems. Second, there is the growing demand that the research system do more to perceive and correct any negative consequences that may flow from its activities. As previously indicated, the demand for modifications in the linkages between the systems is a consequence of two interrelated developments. One is the growing importance of the goals of domestic social and economic progress as opposed to international security and prestige. The other is the growing body of thought that the pursuit of internally defined goals by the research system may not be the most efficient way to the achievement of national policy goals.

Serious concern within Congress on how better to use research to achieve national goals can be dated from 1964 and the Select Committee on Government Research (Elliott Committee). In the period since then, the House Science and Astronautics Committee's Subcommittee on Science, Research, and Development (Davis); the Senate Government Operations Committee's Subcommittee on Government Research (Harris); and the House Government Operations Committee's Subcommittee on Research and Technical Programs (Reuss) have looked at federal R & D. Numerous other committees and subcommittees have examined specific problems. The drive of most of these efforts has been concerned at least in part with how better to use research to achieve the new national goals. Put slightly differently, the drive has been to find ways to deal with our growing domestic problems.

Out of this complex of hearings, certain assumptions seem to be developing which provide much of the basis for the political system's efforts to modify its linkages with the research system. One of these is that our most pressing domestic social problems require new and innovative approaches. A second is that the people most likely to provide these new approaches are members of the research system, and within that system many of these new approaches will be devised by university researchers. A third and almost mystical assumption is that the methodology that must be used to find these new approaches is something called systems analysis.

In connection with the first assumption, there is a growing belief in Congress that the source of many of our pressing social problems is the rapidly advancing technology, which is the output of research that has immediate and massive impact.

Technology means change—change to the natural environment, change in personal habits and behavior, change in social and economic patterns, and not infrequently change in the legal and political processes. While many of these changes are beneficial, many are disruptive and dislocative. They change situations more rapidly than the pace at which individuals can adjust. The well-known cultural lag finds its logical beginnings in this phenomenon.[49]

Congressman Daddario frames the issue concisely in his letter of submittal for his statement on technology assessment: "I have forwarded to you separately a significant report on public policy issues involving science and technology during the past several years. That report shows beyond all doubt that Science and Technology, as a force to be dealt with by the Congress, has attained a stature comparable to national security, agriculture, commerce or any other continuing major national interest."[50] It was clearly not Daddario's intention that support for research be cut off or even reduced. Quite the contrary, his concern was that research support continue to grow. However, as his authorship of the legislation amending the National Science Foundation Act indicates, he was in favor of more applied research dealing with major problems.[51] The research Daddario was calling for concerned both new ways of dealing with the problems of the technological society and new ways of sensing and protecting against the negative consequences of technologies that are likely to flow from present research.

The second assumption, that the research system has the necessary talent to find new answers to problems, has both a positive and a negative impetus. Successful responses to the challenges of World War II and the cold was have created the expectation that research can make major contributions to domestic problems. In general, the political system seems to reflect the belief that tax funds have paid for the creation of a large pool of research talent and a great deal of basic research, and now the research system should be ready and able to provide tangible payoffs. Although it is recognized that such problems as crime and pollution are more complex because of the larger number of social variables, for many congressmen that is not sufficient explanation for

49 U.S. Congress, *Technology Assessment: Statement of Emilio Q. Daddario*, p. 12.
50 *Ibid.*
51 U.S. Congress, House, *Amending the National Science Foundation Act of 1950 to Make Improvements in the Organization and Operation of the Foundation*, Report No. 1650, 89th Congress, 2d Session, pp. 16–17.

the inability of the research system to respond. A growing tendency is to see the failure as attributable to the internal values and organization of the research system. President Johnson's statement calling for more utilization of the biomedical research paid for by taxes characterizes this view.[52] It is based on a fundamental faith in the problem-solving abilities of the research system; and, no matter what level of naiveté it may reflect, it is important in influencing the modification of the linkages between the two systems.

The faith in the research system as a potential problem solver is reinforced by a negative condition. In interviewing congressmen one finds considerable skepticism about the ability of the research system to respond effectively to contemporary problems. Much of this skepticism is based on the much larger role of social factors in domestic problems, and following from that the belief that the social sciences will have to play a role comparable to the natural sciences and engineering. Suffice it to say at this point that the social sciences do not generate widespread confidence in the applied problems context. Nonetheless, even the skeptics arrive at a position of support for efforts by the research system. They arrive there by a process of elimination after finding they have no other place to go. Take the single yet very complex problem of overpopulation. In such problem areas the appeal of a potential technological fix, such as Weinberg suggests, is powerful. In this case the technological fix is the intrauterine device.

Before the IUD was invented, birth control demanded very strong motivation of countless individuals. Even with the pill, the individual's motivation has to be sustained day in and day out; should it flag even temporarily, the strong motivation of the previous month might go for naught. But the IUD, being a one-shot method, greatly reduces the individual motivation required to induce social change. The IUD does not completely replace social engineering by technology; and indeed, in some Spanish-American cultures where the husband's virility is measured by the number of children he has, the IUD attacks only part of the problem. Yet in many other situations, as in India, the IUD so reduces the social component of the problem as to make an impossibly difficult social problem much less hopeless.[53]

A combination of the limited number of other options and the hope of such possibilities as that just suggested project on the research system ever-growing demands for help in problem solving.

[52] Quoted in *Science* (July 8, 1969), 149–150.
[53] Alvin Weinberg, "Can Technology Stabilize World Order?," presented as the United Nations Day after-dinner speech in Oak Ridge, Tennessee, October 11, 1966.

The third assumption underlying the pressure for modification in the linkages is the belief that systems analysis provides the necessary methodology for finding new ways to achieve national goals. Doubtless, the ultimate intellectual achievement of man would be a theory capable of explaining and predicting all phenomena both natural and human. Systems as a notion has been powerfully attractive to the research community because it seems to offer a slight opening in that direction. As Easton has stated:

. . . systems have made their appearance as a possible focus, beginning with the smallest cell in the human body as a system and working up through ever more inclusive systems such as the human being as an organism, the human personality, small groups, broader institutions, societies, and collections of societies, such as the international system. The assumption is that behavior in these systems may be governed by analogous if not homologous processes. General systems analysis is perhaps an even more ambitious effort than action theory to draw disciplines into a common framework, for it spreads its net over all of the sciences, physical and biological as well as social, and views them all as behaving systems.[54]

Researchers now propose that something called the systems approach is the way to do everything from teaching language arts to public school students to redesigning our urban environment. The appeal of the notion is also pervasive in government. What the operations research groups of World War II did in designing a response to the submarine threat is now called systems analysis. Such work as RAND's Strategic Bases Study and the government's Planning, Programming, Budgeting System (PPBS) are generally perceived as being covered by the label systems analysis. Further, these are perceived as concrete examples of the powerful contribution that systems analysis can make to the solution of important national problems. The lack of precise definition of the concept, the fact that it means many different things to many different researchers, and the fact that its methodology looses its power as the data becomes increasingly qualitative is less widely recognized. Rather, federal research policy is increasingly influenced by the belief that if able researchers would focus on pressing problems using systems analytic techniques they could make major contributions to problem solving. As an illustration, the Clark subcommittee made the following recommendation.

The subcommittee finds the systems approach to be a promising way to meet and solve some of the complex social and economic problems confronting state

54 Easton, p. 16.

and local governments. The subcommittee recommends Federal support to further explore and demonstrate the potentialities of the systems approach. In particular, legislation is needed to authorize studies and undertakings by the Federal Government to develop and demonstrate the systems approach, and to authorize grants to the states so that they can experiment with and demonstrate application of the systems approach by State and local government.[55]

Given the existence in the political system of the above assumptions and a growing dissatisfaction with the nature of the social contributions being made by the research system, it is no surprise that efforts are already under way to modify the linkages between the systems. If the linkages are modified as it appears the assumptions of the political system require, then adjustments will be necessary in both the value structure and the organization of the research system. Stated more precisely, the status of applied research will be elevated vis-á-vis basic research, and interdisciplinary research will be elevated vis-á-vis disciplinary research. It is important to emphasize that this does not mean a dismantling of the support system for basic disciplinary research. Rather, a more accurate prognosis is that an increasingly larger share of new research monies will be used to underwrite applied interdisciplinary research.

BASIC RESEARCH

What many critics call an excessive emphasis on basic research has come under increasing attack. Teller has argued that one consequence of this is the production of researchers by our universities who are unwilling to do applied work.[56] Such studies as Project Hindsight, which attempted to assess the payoff of the basic research supported by the military agencies since World War II, provided further support for those who questioned the emphasis of the research system on basic work. Nonetheless, the emphasis on more applied work never became a problem and never seriously threatened the research system's emphasis on basic research as long as the highest priority national goals were associated with external threats. The complex of arrangements that

---

[55] U.S. Congress, Senate, Subcommittee on Employment, Manpower, and Poverty of the Committee on Labor and Public Welfare, *The Impact of Federal Research and Development Policies upon Scientific and Technical Manpower,* 89th Congress, 2d Session, pp. 58–59.
[56] Edward Teller, "The Role of Applied Science" in *Basic Research and National Goals,* pp. 257–266.

has developed over the years to meet the needs for military and space technology has consistently demonstrated a capacity for transferring the results of basic research into useful items or processes in ever-shorter periods of time.[57] In general, foreign and military policy goals made demands on the research system in the physical sciences sector. It is the well-developed theory in the physical sciences that is the model of what ought to be in the life sciences and the social sciences. An applied research and development establishment stands ready to transfer new physical science theory into usable products.

No such complete theory exists in the life sciences, and we are in the preparadigm stage in the social sciences. Of equal importance, however, there is no highly efficient set of arrangements for applying the theory that does exist. Yet the new domestic goals being set by the political system are generally perceived as being heavily dependent on the life sciences and the social sciences. President Johnson's statement on biomedical research caused great concern in the life sciences community because it so explicitly called for a modification of the linkages between the two systems. It was an announcement that the political system no longer believed the most efficient way to achieve its goals was to let the research system define its own priorities. The basic value conflict was effectively framed by Surgeon General Stewart:

To what extent is "the future of medicine" the concern of the researcher in biomedical science? Is the future of medicine the primary reason for his professional being? A secondary reason? Or should he be totally involved in the search for knowledge, with no strings attached and no holds barred?

Most scientists would tend to give an affirmative answer to the last of these questions. So far as inner motivation is concerned, they are seekers after truth.

On the other hand, most of the people who directly or indirectly furnish support to the biomedical scientist would be inclined to say that "the future of medicine" is what they are paying for.[58]

What seems clear is that the life sciences will never have the opportunity that existed in the physical sciences for a long gestation period before social payoff demands are made.

In the social sciences the picture is much less clear. Studies and hearings abound in the last several years on the relationship of social science research to national goals. The social sciences have received increasing support recently even though in absolute dollars it remains

---

57 Chart taken from Pierre Lelong, "L'Évolution de la Science et la Planification de la Research," *Reveue Economique*, No. 1 (January 1964), p. 19, reproduced in Gilpin, p. 24.
58 Quoted in *Science* (July 8, 1966), p. 151.

a miniscule part of the R & D budget.[59] Two things are perfectly clear, however. First, there is absolutely no consensus among the members of either of the systems on whether, how, or how much the social sciences should be supported. Second, there is absolutely no question but that the reason for the support of the social sciences is the hope that they will be relevant to national policies. Certainly, the social sciences will never have the opportunity to delude themselves that the support coming from the federal treasury is for the pursuit of truth unrelated to social utility. Stated differently, if the life sciences have been allowed only a short gestation period to do their basic work, we in the social sciences can expect none.

In a sense, then, linkages between the political system and the social science component of the research system are just now being formed, and those linkages are likely to reflect the modifications that appear on the horizon in the other areas of the research system. These linkages are being formed at a time when anything but a smooth relationship between social science research and the political system seems assured. On the one hand, many congressmen will await the failure of social science to confirm their beliefs. On the other hand, some of the proponents of support for social science may have unrealistic expectations and become disillusioned when they are not fulfilled. In the social science community, a split exists between those who fear the corruption of their fields by externally generated demands and others who look forward to substantial breakthroughs with the availability of substantial federal funds. Perhaps the most optimistic view is stated by Reagan:

To be basic and to be policy-relevant are not antithetical when applied to the social sciences as they would be for, say high-energy physics. Very fundamental data and theory-building are needed in such areas as education and learning processes, human relationships in urban neighborhoods, or political attitudes among the electorate. Yet the basic work will have clear areas of application right from the start.[60]

DISCIPLINARY RESEARCH

The assumptions that have come to dominate much of the political system's approach to the support of research also pose something of a challenge to the power of the research disciplines. It is the growing

---

[59] *The Behavioral Sciences and the Federal Government* (National Academy of Sciences, Washington, D.C., 1968), pp. 40–41.
[60] Reagan, *Science and the Federal Patron*, p. 180.

focus on the need for interdisciplinary research that calls for modification in the disciplinary organization. As long as the pursuit of basic research was seen as an effective way to achieve national goals, the power of the disciplines over their own activities was unchallenged. As domestic concerns came to the fore, problem definition and resolution were seen as requiring a mix of disciplinary skills. The requirements of systems analysis as a methodology reinforces the growing belief that organizational modifications are necessary.

Leland Haworth, former director of NSF, previously the citadel of disciplinary support, has frequently stated the case as follows.

. . . I think that the solution of many of the most crucial problems that the country faces, in fact, the world faces, are going to depend very substantially on the social sciences and on their integration with the natural sciences and engineering.[61]

In its fiscal 1970 budget, NSF requested $10 million for this kind of research.[62] Despite its obvious enthusiasm for such research, the Daddario subcommittee expressed reservations about the NSF request.[63] The concern of many of the proponents of interdisciplinary attacks on social problems, particularly by universities, is that the money ends up being divided into parts which support perfectly fine disciplinary research that is only very indirectly related to the problem. In explaining why the requested $10 million was cut to $6 million, Congressman Daddario said: "They [the universities] are groping; you are groping; and you are kind of groping together."[64] Part of the groping he referred to is for new organizational arrangements.

The mechanisms through which the government has provided support for research are being modified so that the research system will have less complete control over its own destiny. As discussed earlier, the project grant system provided disciplinary control of much of the basic research money through a process that used review panels composed of consultants from the universities. Two things appear to be happening. First, there is a movement in the direction of providing support for universities through block institutional grants which allow the administrators more control and presumably more power vis-à-vis the researchers.

61 U.S. Congress, House, Subcommittee on Government Research of the Committee on Government Operations, *Hearings: National Foundation for the Social Sciences*, 90th Congress, 1st Session, p. 64.
62 *Science* (May 9, 1969), p. 656.
63 *Ibid.*
64 *Ibid.*

Second, there is growing pressure for some form of modification in the review mechanism itself.

Institutional grants, it is hoped, will modify the balance of power between the disciplines and the administrators, generate greater institutional versus professional loyalty and, with that, provide greater opportunity for organizational flexibility.[65] The modification of the review panel system, it is hoped, will protect against disciplinary myopia[66] and make the research system more responsive to political needs.[67] These movements, not surprisingly, parallel efforts to develop within the agencies a higher-quality management capability for applied research on domestic problems.[68]

In summary, then, the new assumptions regarding federal research policy seem to be leading to a modification in the disciplinary orientation of research and an emphasis on interdisciplinary research. The perception reflected here is that the major impediment to greater use of research in meeting domestic social problems is organizational, and it follows that the efforts to modify the linkages between the two systems will be designed to bring about changes in the organization of the research system.

CHARACTERISTICS OF THE LINKAGES IN THE FUTURE

If one projects the trends in federal research policy that have been isolated up to this point, what are likely to be the nature of the linkages between the two systems in the next decade? In the section titled "Cementing the Politics-Research Linkages," we presented six characteristics of the initial linkages as described by Seitz. What follows is an effort to project those characteristics and see how they are likely to be modified.

1. The initial set of linkages allowed almost all good scientists to receive support for research close to their own interests. That condition is not the case at present and is likely to be even less the case in the future. Several factors are influential here. Most obvious is the leveling off of general R & D monies provided by the federal government. This is happening at a time when the number of researchers being turned

---

65 Seitz, p. 157.
66 Weinberg, "Criteria for Scientific Choice," pp. 161–162.
67 *Science* (May 16, 1969), pp. 813–814.
68 *Report of the Secretary's Advisory Committee on the Management of NIH Research Contracts and Grants;* quoted in *Science* (July 8, 1966), p. 150.

out by graduate institutions continues to grow and with that is a growing demand for research support. It should be noted in this connection that the graduate education socialization process imbues young researchers with a value system that views basic research as the best kind. Many people have observed that this is true in engineering as well as the natural and social sciences. If this is true, then the traditional training ground of the applied researchers is just now moving in the opposite direction from the demands being made by the political system. For it seems likely that the linkages between the systems will be modified in a direction designed to induce ever larger numbers of good scientists to do research believed to be more immediately relevant to the achievement of the increasingly emphasized domestic goals. Reformulated, then, characteristic one is stated as follows. Most good researchers will be able to obtain support for applied research that is seen as relevant to the national interest.

2. The second set of linkages had support flow through the administrative offices of the universities to researchers who themselves maintained close liaison with the supporting agencies. That pattern is undergoing modification at present with the growing role of institutional support. As organizational flexibility is seen as being necessary for researchers to grapple effectively with social problems, and as the disciplines are viewed as the major impediments to change, this pattern of institutional support is likely to grow. Doubtless, student activists' opposition to certain kinds of federally supported research, when combined with the necessity for continued federal funds in universities, will reinforce this trend, since it is one way for university administrators to achieve some flexibility. As university administrators become the generators of research funds and maintain the liaison with the funding agencies, their leverage vis-á-vis the disciplines will increase. Since this pattern will by-pass the disciplinary review panels, it will result in reducing the influence of the research system in government as well as the universities. Characteristic two, redrafted, is as follows. Funds for the support of research will go directly to the administrators of universities who will exercise greater control over who and what will be supported, and those administrators will maintain close liason with governmental agencies.

3. The third characteristic of the linkages was that there was little support available for research in the social sciences and humanities, particularly the latter. This characteristic is in the early stages of change. Although its funding is still only a piddling amount, a National Foundation for the Arts and Humanities (NFAH) has been established; and in percentage terms the support for the social sciences has been growing

rapidly. Additionally, NSF now has specific legal authorization to support the social sciences. The most rapid growth of the support for social science research will likely be in those areas where research is inter-disciplinary and perceived as being policy-relevant. It seems unlikely that the social sciences will ever have the degree of control over their own destiny enjoyed by the physical sciences and to a lesser extent by the life sciences. Since the humanities are not perceived as being policy-relevant, they are likely to remain poorly supported although to a much greater extent masters of their own destiny. Characteristic three reformulated is as follows. Growing support for social science research will be forth-coming for work that is interdisciplinary and applied in nature, while support for the humanities will remain small but will have fewer strings attached.

4. The fourth characteristic of the linkages was that since Congress had treated the mission-oriented agencies more generously, certain fields of science have advanced at the expense of others. This pattern is likely to continue indefinitely with those fields that seem to be more relevant to domestic policy goals gaining on those that have seemed most relevant to foreign policy goals. Additionally, the focus on problem-oriented research is likely to generate the creation of certain new fields of research and some reorganization of the research system. Characteristic four requires no reformulation for the future.

5. The fifth characteristic of the linkages was that federal research funds had created an employees' market in the academic research system. A leveling-off of the general research support and a focus on applied problems is likely to result in less of an employees' market. The excep-tions will be in certain problem areas for researchers willing to do applied interdisciplinary work. On balance, then, the employees' market is likely to be much more selective than it has been. Reformulated, this characteristic is as follows. While a research support-sustained employees' market will undergo a general decline in selected problem areas, an employees' market condition will accelerate.

6. The sixth characteristic of the linkages was that federal research support had contributed to the ability of the universities to meet the growing demand for higher education. This pattern is unlikely to con-tinue into the future. Much of the support for education that previously came under the guise of research support is now likely to come as direct support for education from such sources as the Office of Education. The new pattern of research support will probably result in the creation of new patterns of graduate education designed to create applied re-searchers. In terms of its importance to the support of the general higher education system, research support will play a declining role. Reformu-

lated, this characteristic is as follows. Viewed broadly, research support will play a declining role in the support of higher education, although in certain specialized problem areas, it will generate new graduate and professional training programs.

CONCLUSIONS

The six points just made involve an admittedly hazardous effort at a prognosis of the relationship between politics and research in the next decade. All of the qualifications and uncertainties involved in such a prognosis are so obvious they do not need to be stated. What can be stated with more confidence is that the linkages between the systems are in the early stages of being modified. At a minimum the absolute cost of R & D support is now so great that the very best the research system can hope for is that it be allowed to set its own priorities. From the early days of the linkages, the political system provided support for instrumental reasons. In general, the members of the research system were less cognizant of this than might have been desirable. An equal lack of understanding seems to have characterized the political system's perception of research. Based on these low levels of mutual understanding, it was easy for both systems to accept on faith the idea that research automatically resulted in movement toward desirable social goals. As funding for R & D has leveled off and national goals have changed in this decade, this faith has been shaken. It is a time for both systems carefully to reevaluate the linkages, for without this the linkages that were previously based on low levels of mutual understanding may in the future be based on high levels of misunderstanding.

CHAPTER FIVE

Economics of Research

Richard A. Tybout, The Ohio State University

Over the past 50 years, there has been a major shift in the social process of technological invention. The shift had been toward formally organized research and development (R & D) and away from the self-employed independent inventor. The latter is by no means an extinct species; his ranks include diverse persons from the untrained to the college professor. But the new commitment of society is to the R & D organization.

The value of American resources funneled into R & D increased 37-fold in the 25 years from 1940 to 1965, or from 0.6 to 3.0 percent of GNP.[1] R & D employment and value added (measured at cost) are of the same magnitude as in the steel industry and the automobile industry. But the utility of R & D output is considerably greater. This follows from the fact that new knowledge intrinsically has utility beyond that which its originator generally finds sufficient to justify its production. In contrast, normal consumer goods have utility only to the consumers for whom they were produced. If new knowledge were reckoned at its commodity value (an impossible task), R & D output would exceed by a large factor the cost value on which the above comparisons were made. Steel

[1] See Table 3.

and automobiles would not, since value added in conventional industries is already based on market value of output.

For the scholar and the gadgeteer, knowledge and invention may be ends in themselves. For most other people they are means to other goals, such as increased productivity, improved consumer goods, or military efficiency. The question is then: By what means and to what ends is invention directed? Is invention an autonomous or a market-directed process? We shall find that it is market directed. Cause and effect in the rate and direction of R & D is not unlike cause and effect in conventional supply and demand analysis.

It is reasonable to expect a high correlation (lagged in time) between R & D expenditures and growth of the economy, but the chain of events is far from deterministic. Research is neither a necessary nor a sufficient condition for invention. Invention may be a necessary condition for technological change, but is not sufficient over any arbitrary time period because of social lags in adoption of best practice technologies. Moreover, economic growth and productivity gains can arise from many nontechnological sources, including work force education, market structure, and economic stability, to name a few.

The linkages from R & D to economic growth are explored in inverse sequence. It is necessary first to set technological change in the context of economic growth, then invention in the context of technological change, and finally R & D in the context of invention. On the basis of this analysis, certain policy considerations for R & D are evaluated.

Public support for R & D can be justified where, as noted above, the utility of new knowledge extends beyond the range from which a private financier can expect to receive a return for creating that knowledge. This test gives different results in different cases. It is the object of policy formulation to apply it skillfully and with due regard for at least two additional considerations: the efficiency of the R & D process itself and the implications of public policy for the competitive structure of industries in which the new knowledge is used. New products and productivity gains exert a major influence on the competitive standing of business firms. It is essential that public policy take account of competitive effects as well as the immediate efficiency of selected programs if long-term productivity gain of the economy is the ultimate goal.

The influence of social cause and effect will be apparent in all that follows. Indeed, R & D is conceived and explained herein as a socially directed process. That social science research itself has productivity significance is implied by the conclusion that R & D is socially directed; knowledge of society makes possible the improvement of social direction. Yet, we are not ready to assess the productivity of the latter. The economics of physical science R & D is but imperfectly understood. The economics of social science research is virgin territory, involving as it does more knowledge of the economic consequences of social science than is generally conceded to exist. As a matter of practical necessity, therefore, the focus of attention in this chapter is on physical and industrial productivity through R & D, itself a topic at the frontiers of economics knowledge.

ECONOMIC GROWTH AND TECHNOLOGY

Productivity

Productivity advance has been characteristic of Western civilization for the last millennium, but our measures of economic growth and their relevance to R & D are limited to recent history. The important points can be made on the basis of trends from the end of the nineteenth century in the United States.

In the period 1889–1919, real output per man-hour rose at an average annual rate of 1.6 percent; from 1920 to 1957, the gain was an average of 2.3 percent per year; for the entire range 1889–1957, the average was 2 percent.[2] Causes for the differential between these two periods include the increase in the percent of GNP that has been directed into R & D, but also such diverse causes as improved worker education, industrial health, and the shortened work week. Mansfield cites the difference in immigration policy between the two periods.[3] Some of the productivity gain came from more than proportional growth of capital stock and other phenomena unrelated to the labor force as such, although productivity may be expressed on a per man-hour basis.

Gains per man-hour translate into smaller gains in material welfare when the improved standard of living means increased leisure. The above average gain of 2 percent annually would give a 4-fold increase of GNP per capita if working hours had been maintained at the same level over the entire 70 years since 1900 (and if keeping a 60-hour work week would not have itself prevented some of the productivity gain). Instead, the United States experienced roughly a one-third reduction in the working hours per week and roughly a 2.5 -fold gain in real GNP per capita.

2 Edwin Mansfield, *The Economics of Technological Change* (1968) New York: W. W. Norton, p. 23.
3 *Ibid.*

Productivity gain has been uneven among industries. Some, such as agriculture, with high productivity gain and relatively inelastic demand, have experienced marked declines in employment. In other cases, for example, automobiles, chemicals, and electrical equipment, new products have been the result of invention. Transportation, communication, and other basic human needs are served in different ways today than they were in 1900, and the result of technological progress has been the creation and considerable expansion of new industries. The affluent American today spends his 2.5-fold increase in real purchasing power on many goods that were unavailable in 1900.

Whether the quality of life is greater or less than the expansion of purchasing power cannot be unequivocally answered except by the individual consumer. To make the comparison it is necessary for the individual to decide whether he would prefer to have an average income today to spend on today's products, or 2.5 times the average income of 1900 to spend on products available at that time.

Whatever the outcome of this comparison, it is important to note that adverse effects of the quality of life in the form of deterioration of the physical environment are not the simple product of technology, but of technology in conjunction with institutions that give priority to marketable products of the private sector and less attention to public amenities. The creation of new knowledge for environmental quality improvement is an example of R & D that will be very little conducted by the private sector unless the responsibilities of that sector are extended beyond their present boundaries. This point is different from the previously noted general case for public support of R & D, and it is important to note the distinction. Here we add to the case for R & D assistance along conventional lines the need for a social reorientation of priorities which, of course, would necessitate R & D in new directions.

Imputation

The problem of imputing productivity gains among their various causes continues to occupy a major position in economics literature. It is informative to consider here some of the difficulties.

As previously noted, productivity gains accrue to both labor and capital although they have been expressed per man-hour. An elementary step beyond this approach is to express productivity using a combined index. Thus Mansfield reports a total productivity index of the form $q/(bL + cK)$, where q is output given as a percent of some base period, L and K are labor and capital inputs as percents of their corresponding amounts in the same base period, and b and c are the respective shares of labor and capital, again, in the base period.[4] By using this approach a lower percentage gain in productivity is derived, 1.7 percent per year from 1889 to 1957, because capital has grown even more rapidly than labor. A more frequently used approach is to employ an aggregate production function with or without substitutability of labor and capital. Such a method was exemplified in Solow's original work based on a Cobb–Douglas production function. Solow found an annual growth rate of 1.5 percent.[5]

The above are aggregate measures of productivity. As such, they are based on the performance of all producers, those producers operating old equipment as well as those producers operating new equipment. A conceptual refinement would distinguish new from old capital and would consider only the gains in productivity of the new. A further conceptual refinement would distinguish capital-embodied from organizational productivity gains. The capital-embodied gains are limited by the vintage of the capital; the organizational gains have no such limits but can be considered to influence output as soon as they are assimilated. These distinctions made, the decks are cleared for further analysis of imputation.

Another difficulty is that technological progress more often than not takes the form of a new product rather than a new process. This introduces ambiguity in the measurement of welfare gains when the product is a consumer good, as previously noted. When the new product is an industrial good, it becomes the basis for technological advance, often of processes, in industries at the next stage of production. Interrelationships of this sort are impossible to separate between industries. Yet detailed studies at the industry level afford the best way of avoiding problems of aggregation described in the preceding paragraph.

A number of other causes of productivity increase should be mentioned. Larger-scale production, in and of itself, is responsible for improved combination and integration of processes and specialization of function, both of capital and labor.[6] Simple expansion of either or both capital and labor can and usually does bring more specialization. The same can be said of geographic specialization. Add to these effects the already mentioned causes of productivity gains, such as improved education and

---

4 *Ibid.*, pp. 27ff.

5 R. Solow, "Technical Change and the Aggregate Production Function," *Review of Economics and Statisics* **39** (1957).

6 Two alternative approaches to distinguishing scale effects from technological change are exemplified by R. Komiya, "Technological Progress and the Production Function in the United States Steam Power Industry," *Review of Economics and Statistics,* **44** (May 1962); and F. M. Westfield, "Technical Progress and Returns to Scale," *Review of Economics and Statistics,* **48** (November 1966).

health of the work force.[7] Technological change is embedded in overall economic change. The need for widespread sustained economic analysis is recognized, but the problems are pervasive and complex. Satisfactory answers to the imputation problem are only piecemeal today and will wait some time for a grand synthesis.

Employment[8]

One commonly centers his reservations about technological change on employment effects. Yet, the American economy has experienced no difficulty in making rather impressive shifts of employment among industries. The case of agriculture was cited above. Agricultural employment was cut by more than half in the 25-year period 1940–1965, from 9.5 to 4.5 million.[9] Mining employment went from 0.9 to 0.6 million over the same period of time.[10] Resounding increases in employment were experienced in other industries. The shift has taken place largely through attrition. In a declining industry older workers are not replaced as they retire. New workers enter expanding industries. Some times the introduction of innovations is retarded because of the bargaining power of those already in the industry but not to the long-run benefit of the industry itself. Individual hardship can result in individual cases and when a region such as Appalachia is committed to dying industries, the adjustment process is more painful than when the region is diversified. A regional change in residence and not merely a change in occupation is involved.

The ability of the economy to sustain radical shifts in employment was dramatically demonstrated at the end of World War II. From 1945 to 1948, defense expenditures were cut from 44 to 6 percent of GNP. The economy substituted civilian for defense production in corresponding degree with less than 4 percent unemployment throughout. Private consumption and investment replaced defense demand but labor markets accommodated the monumental change.

Technological unemployment for another reason was forecast by Weiner at the beginning of the computer revolution:

[7] For an example of a relatively comprehensive imputation, see Zvi Griliches, "Research Expenditures, Education and the Aggregate Agricultural Production Function," *American Economic Review,* **54** (1964).

[8] Several of the points made under this heading originated with Richard R. Nelson et al., *Technology, Economic Growth and Public Policy* (1967), Chap. 6 and 7. Washington, D.C.: Brookings Institute.

[9] U.S. Bureau of Labor Statistics, *Employment and Earnings Statistics for the United States, 1909–1968* (1968), p. xvi.

[10] U.S. Bureau of the Census, *Statistical Abstract, 1966* (1966), p. 218.

There is no rate of pay at which a United States pick-and-shovel laborer can live which is low enough to compete with the work of a steam shovel as an excavator. The modern (computer) revolution is similarly bound to devalue the human brain at least in its simpler and more routine decisions. Of course, just as the skilled carpenter, the skilled mechanic, the skilled dressmaker have in some degree survived the first industrial revolution, so the skilled scientist and the skilled administrator may survive the second. However, taking the second revolution as accomplished, the average human being of mediocre attainments or less has nothing to sell that it is worth anyone's money to buy.[11]

Weiner's second (computer) revolution appears now to be sufficiently advanced to allay his pessimism. Computer applications are widespread and, indeed, have given rise to many jobs for those of "mediocre attainment." Ph.D mathematicians were prominent among early programmers. More recently, the Ph.D's have moved with the frontier, leaving behind more routine tasks for those who make the bulk line applications of computers today and who often enter their professional training from the vantage point of a high school education. So it is with other aspects of technological change. Nuclear reactors were first operated on an experimental basis but are now routinized for power production. Agricultural extension agents instruct farmers in practical applications of complex laboratory-developed operations. New jobs, once complex, become simplified so that unskilled or low skilled workers can do them.

This is not to say that all is well and there are no problems. Individual cases of a lifetime skill rendered obsolete by technological change or of inability to find permanent employment remain. The point is only that by and large American society has accommodated technological change without major economic upheaval. Whether there has been upheaval of other kinds is another question. Patterns of living in an advanced technological society may well create significant stresses. However, discussion of their nature is best deferred to other chapters in this volume.

TECHNOLOGY AND INVENTION

Social Causation

Traditional practice is to consider technological change the result of a three-stage process, invention, innovation, and diffusion, dealing respectively with the origin, initial economic adoption, and succeeding

11 Norbert Wiener, *Cybernetics* (1948), pp. 37–38, New York: John Wiley & Sons. Material in parentheses added.

adoptions of a new technology. All three must be completed before any given technological change has a significant impact on aggregate productivity. Attention here centers on the relationship of invention to the three-stage process, or to aggregate technological change.

The functional distinction between invention and innovation is clear, but the implied distinction between cause and effect leading to each is often overdrawn. The weight of evidence suggests that both are governed by common supply and demand phenomena. Innovation is avowedly an economic process. To the extent that invention is the outcome of economic forces, the two are but different steps in a single process.

A social causation theory of invention is strongly suggested by parallel inventions at the same point in history in distinct civilizations isolated from one another. Examples are found in writing and number systems. Usher traces the decimal system of numeration to three independent sources.[12] Similarly, through analysis of textiles, it can be shown that several parallel systems of weaving developed in antiquity.[13] Thirty-five steamboats were built before Fulton pulled his across the dividing line of commerical success and then largely because of his legal monopoly of steamboat traffic on the Hudson River.[14] Gilfillan refers to 20,000 duplicate cases every year in the U.S. Patent Office.[15] Would knowledge have evolved in the same direction so often were it not for the drive of utilitarianism?

The supply of invention takes the form of ideas generated from received basic knowledge. The demand for invention (and innovation) takes the form of profitable opportunities for new functional means. In a functional interpretation of invention, supply adjusts to the opportunities manifest in demand. This is in contrast to the notion of autonomous inventions in search of markets. The latter postulates that once the basic science is out inventions automatically follow. Applied science is then viewed as the product of intellectual curiosity.

Schmookler has devoted considerable effort to distinguishing cause and effect implied by historic evidence. His evidence consists of case studies of the historic record for the important inventions in petroleum refining, paper making, railroading, and farming. In no single instance did he find an invention that could clearly be shown to have been pro-

[12] A. P. Usher, *A History of Mechanical Inventions* (1954), Cambridge, Mass.: Harvard University Press, pp. 49–50.

[13] *Ibid.*, pp. 50–55.

[14] S. C. Gilfillan, *Inventing the Ship*, Chicago, Ill.: Follett Publishing Co. (1935).

[15] S. C. Gilfillan, "Invention as a Factor in Economic History," *Journal of Economic History*, 5 (December 1945), p. 70.

duced as a sole result of the appearance of new basic knowledge.[16] On the contrary, there were hundreds of instances in which the stimulus for invention was unambiguously identified as a profitable opportunity recognized.[17] Many of the inventions used no scientific base; many others used scientific knowledge that had been established long in advance of the invention.

Basic Research and Invention

The conventional classification of R & D into basic research, applied research, and development established a framework of analysis of social causation. Basic research is concerned with laws of nature and generally leads to results too broad in significance to be patentable. Development, at the other extreme, is concerned with very specific applications of received knowledge. Applied research falls between the two. Applied research and development usually produce patentable results. The process from basic research to development should be expected to shade from least to most significance of economic forces in the process of invention.

Existing scientific knowledge, of course, establishes limits beyond which applications cannot go, at least insofar as they are based on general scientific principles. Efficient invention is based on a knowledge of general laws of nature. To some extent, basic research is undertaken by industrial concerns to augment known laws of nature. Thus the transistor was an outgrowth of basic science work on semiconductors at RCA Laboratories undertaken with the expectation that commercially significant results would result.[18] The study was of basic science and the hunches of the RCA research executives were validated. However, this case and others like it (for example, the development of nylon by duPont[19]) do not refute Schmookler's findings. On the contrary, they extend them back from applied to basic research. Schmookler's point is that invention does not arise from a dynamism of its own but in response to social wants. The cases cited above suggest that this is true not only of applied research and development, but also of basic research, at least in particular cases. Indeed,

16 Jacob Schmookler, *Invention and Economic Growth*, Cambridge, Mass.: Harvard University Press (1966), Chaps. 3 and 4.
17 *Ibid.*
18 See account by Richard R. Nelson, "The Link between Science and Invention: The Case of the Transistor" in National Bureau of Economic Research, *The Rate and Direction of Economic Activity* (1962).
19 Summarized in Frederic M. Scherer, *Patents and the Corporation*, Greenville, S. C.: Patents & the Corporation (1958), pp. 29–31.

telling arguments can be made for the application of economic causation in a more general way to the history of basic research.[20]

In the development of invention from basic knowledge, two characteristics of the process are relevant. First, it is the entire body of knowledge that establishes the domain for invention, not merely a particular recent discovery. Second, and more to the point, inventors do not wander aimlessly over this domain but search in specific directions dictated by the social utility of expected outcomes. They may be motivated to do this by their own ideas of social relevance or by the financial returns they expect, either as salaried researchers or as independent inventors. The hero-inventor of grade school textbooks may have been a disinterested gadgeteer, but if so, he was atypical of his peers. And whatever his motivation, his opportunities were conditioned by the views of his financiers.

Demand Pull Theory of Invention

A second line of evidence in support of a demand pull theory of invention is found in the correlation of periods of rapid technological change with high investment and low unemployment. Schumpeter developed a business cycle theory based on the observed clustering of inventions at times of economic expansion over the nineteenth and early twentieth centuries.[21] Schmookler found still more convincing evidence in a correlation (with time lag) between the number of capital goods patents and the sales of the same capital goods for selected industries that he studied.[22] The relation is evident in time series for the same industry and in cross sections across industries, the latter analyzed in such a way as to take account of differences in size among the industries.

The most reasonable interpretation of these results seems to be that invention is an economic activity pursued for gain. The prospects for gain are in turn highest when sales of the products to which the inventions apply are highest. The time lag between the peaks and troughs of capital goods sales and the peaks and troughs of invention is then the result of the latter reacting to the former. This is the essence of a demand pull situation.

[20] See Jacob Schmookler, "Catastrophe and Utilitarianism in the Development of Basic Science" in Richard A. Tybout, Ed., *Economics of Research and Development,* Columbus, Ohio: Ohio State University Press (1965). See also comments by Mendelsohn and Krantzberg on the Schmookler paper in the same volume.

[21] Joseph A. Schumpeter, *Business Cycles,* New York & London: McGraw-Hill Book Co., Inc. (1939). Schumpeter used the term "innovation" to include most of what is here termed "invention." The latter term was then reserved for processes more like basic research, which he regarded as autonomous.

[22] Schmookler, *op. cit.* (see footnote 16), Chap. 6 and 7.

It is important to note that nothing in the above logic prevents supply considerations from exercising their usual constraining effect. Additional knowledge opens new doors. No matter how many doors were already opened by prior knowledge, the advent of the new knowledge makes possible additional routes through the labyrinth of technology to the prize of invention. The new doors may offer short cuts (reduce costs) or they may make possible the achievement of the heretofore impossible. President Kennedy could announce almost a decade in advance that we would put a man on the moon before 1970. And this astonishing feat was accomplished. President Coolidge could have made no such announcement. The cost of and the possibility of invention are determined by the science base, in combination with available technological talent. It is in this connection that supply considerations enter.

Diffusion

The final link between invention and technological change, diffusion, introduces a range of social considerations which are digressionary to the focus of this chapter. Nevertheless, it is important to note some of the problems in this area.

Diffusion is, of course, not automatic, even after the qualities of an invention have been established. There is the problem of cognition. What is well established for some is not always obvious to others. The seemingly simple straightforward process of substituting hybrid corn for conventional seed took many years. In Iowa, where gains from the change were substantial, it took 5 years for 50 percent of the farmers to make the change.[23] In Alabama, where gains were smaller, it took 10 years for half the farmers to switch over.[24] In normal industrial situations there is the additional complication that capital committed to outmoded technologies is a sunk cost. The least-cost strategy is often to continue to use outmoded equipment until maintenance and repair costs rise too high, then to substitute the superior equipment. Thus Mansfield found that the average time between first use and use by 50 percent of the ultimate users of twelve industrial inventions was 12 years.[25]

Two kinds of economic considerations are apparent. First, the rate of adoption of an invention depends on the expected gain. New processes and products introduce uncertainties. The observed more rapid diffusion

23 Zvi Griliches, "Hybrid Corn: An Exploration of the Economics of Technological Change," *Econometrica,* **25** (1957).
24 *Ibid.*
25 Edwin Mansfield, "Technical Change and the Rate of Imitation," *Econometrica,* **29** (1961).

of hybrid corn with a high return than with a lower return implies a trade-off between the expected benefits and the uncertainties of a new technology. Second, other things equal, the longer-lived the capital to be replaced by a new technology, the lower will be the rate of diffusion. Again, the result is consistent with economic cause and effect. Superimposed on economic phenomena in these two categories are various influences of cognition and social acceptability of change.

INVENTION AND RESEARCH

Sources of Invention

Invention is the intended product of formal R & D programs. However, it is also the intended product of a large number of part-time and self-employed persons, some of them without college training. Others are faculty members at major universities working on their own or under contract. We know very little of the economic value of their inventions, but we do know that their inventions are important numerically.

A study of domestic patents granted as recently as 1953 revealed that 39.4 percent were assigned to individuals;[26] 58.4 percent were assigned to corporations and the remaining 1.8 percent to the federal government. From a field investigation of a random sample of the same group, it was discovered that about 40 percent of the inventions were made by persons who were *not* technologists (defined as engineers, chemists, metalurgists, and research directors). Moreover, half or more of the inventors (including some hired inventors) were not college graduates.

Granted that patents are not homogeneous in value, the sheer quantitative significance of the output from untrained persons is impressive. The invention industry is changing, but it has not changed so far that we can ignore the untrained independent. And it seems unlikely to this observer that it ever will. The wellsprings of creativity are too diverse.

Succeeding analysis is limited by necessity to formally organized R & D work, for it is only this component of research that is described by available data. National R & D efforts are larger than included in the formal component by the unreported and apparently significant volume of individual inventions.

R & D As an Economic Activity

R & D accounted in 1966 (the latest year for which fairly accurate data on intersectoral flows were available) for an estimated expenditure of

[26] Schmookler, *op. cit.* (see footnote 23); Appendix B is the source of information in this paragraph.

Table 1 Intersectoral Transfers of Funds for Research and Development, 1966 (million $)[a]

| | Performers of R & D Work | | | | | |
Sources of R & D Funds	Federal Government	Industry	Colleges and Universities	Other Nonprofit Institutions	Total	Percent
Federal government	3,260	8,300	1,990[b]	520	14,070	63
Industry	—	7,100	50	60	7,210	33
Colleges and universities	—	—	700	—	700	3
Other nonprofit institutions	—	—	90	150	240	1
Total	3,260	15,400	2,830	730	22,220	100
Percent	14	69	13	4	100	—

Source. National Science Foundation, "National Patterns of R & D Resources" (1967), Table B-la.

[a] Estimates, based on reports by performers. Figures represent different fiscal years for different agencies.

[b] Includes expenditures for associated federal contract research centers.

$22.2 billion, most of which should be considered as value added to GNP.[27] Sources of funds and performers of R & D making up this total are shown in Table 1. In comparison, primary metals (ferrous plus non-ferrous metals) made a value-added contribution of $16.1 billion to GNP in 1966.[28] The same figures for other industries were: fabricated metals, $13.1 billion; motor vehicles, $15.2 billion; food and kindred products, $15.6 billion.[29]

Industrial R & D employed 354,700 full-time equivalent scientists and engineers in January 1966.[30] During the same year industrial R & D expenditures accounted for about 70 percent of all R & D expenditures. (See bottom line of Table 1.) If the same industrial professional worker to expenditure ratio holds for nonindustrial R & D (the remaining 30 percent of all R & D), then about 500,000 full-time equivalent scientists and engineers were involved in all R & D in the economy. The number of supporting lab technicians and clerks is not known, but if taken into account would probably raise total R & D employment severalfold, or to the range of 1 or 2 million workers.

Compare employment in the previously mentioned industries. The averages in 1966 were: primary metals, 1,350,700; fabricated metal products, 1,351,300; motor vehicles, 861,600; food and kindred products, 1,777,200.[31] There is of course some overlap since industrial employment includes persons within each industry engaged in R & D, but if that overlap were eliminated by subtracting the same number of R & D employees from both the R & D total and each industry total, for pairwise comparisons, the results would still be of the same order of magnitude. As an economic activity, R & D is clearly comparable in size to our largest industries.

The principal purpose of Table 1 is to show the flow of R & D among major sectors. Programmatic objectives of R & D are determined by the

---

[27] The estimate here is made on a cost basis, as previously noted, rather than a market value basis. The latter is unavailable for R & D, as it is for government services.

To get contribution to GNP, two kinds of adjustments would need to be made. First, materials purchased for R & D would have to be subtracted out. Second, annual investment in R & D facilities and equipment would need to be subtracted out and annual depreciation on the same added in. Data are not available for either correction, but the first is judged to be small. The second could be net positive but is more likely net negative because R & D is still a growing activity, though since 1963, not growing as a percent of GNP. See Table 3.

[28] U.S. Department of Commerce, *Statistical Abstract of the United States* (1969), Table 465.

[29] *Ibid.*

[30] U.S. National Science Foundation, "Review of Data on Science Resources" (January 1968), Table 6.

[31] U.S. Bureau of Labor Statistics, *Monthly Labor Review* (December 1968).

source of funds; capabilities and means are determined by the performing groups. The dominant role of the federal government in funding and the dominant role of industry in conducting R & D are noted. In-house industrial projects account for the largest single source of nonfederal funds. Universities and other nonprofit institutions account for only 4 percent of the funds by source, but 16 percent by performance.

Federal Funding and National Trends

Table 2 implies the programmatic objectives of federal funds by associating them with sponsoring agencies. The data are for fiscal year

Table 2   Federal Expenditures for Total Research and Development, by Agency, Fiscal Year 1967

	Amount (million $)	Percent (cumulative)
Total, all Agencies	16,049.1	100.0
Department of Defense	7,606.5	47.4
National Aeronautics and Space Administration	5,130.5	79.4
Atomic Energy Commission	1,257.3	87.2
Department of Health, Education, and Welfare	993.5	93.4
Department of Agriculture	253.5	95.0
Department of Transportation	230.5	96.4
National Science Foundation	207.0	97.7
Department of the Interior	147.1	98.6
Department of Commerce	68.7	99.0
Veterans Administration	41.3	99.3
Office of Economic Opportunity	36.7	99.5
Other agencies	76.5	100.0

Source. National Science Foundation, "Federal Funds for Research Development, and Other Scientific Activities, Fiscal Years 1967, 1968, and 1969" (1968), Table C-3.

1967, hence do not correspond to those shown in Table 1. Table 2 shows that for a representative recent fiscal year over 85 percent of federal R & D money went for the programs of three agencies: Department of Defense, National Aeronautics and Space Administration, and the Atomic Energy Commission. These programs are similar in many essential respects. Next in importance is the Department of Health, Education and Welfare, which is concerned with quite different matters. Agriculture, transporta-

Table 3   Growth in Funds for Research and Development, United States Selected Years 1921–1968[a]

	Total R & D Expenditures (million $) (1)	Percent of GNP (2)	Percent of R & D Expenditures Federally Financed (3)	Federal R & D Expenditures (million $) (4)	Nonfederal R & D Expenditures as Percent of GNP (5)
1921	150	0.2	17	25	0.2
1931	300	0.4	13	40	0.3
1940	570	0.6	21	120	0.5
1953	5,150	1.4	53	2,740	0.7
1957	10,100	2.3	63	6,390	0.8
1961	14,500	2.8	64	9,215	1.0
1963	17,350	3.0	65	11,220	1.0
1965	20,470	3.0	64	13,070	1.1
1966[b]	22,200	3.0	63	14,070	1.1
1967[b]	23,800	3.0	63	14,930	1.1
1968[b]	25,000	2.9	62	15,560	1.1

Source. Years 1957 and earlier, Richard R. Nelson, et al., *Technology, Economic Growth and Public Policy* (1967), p. 46. Years 1921 through 1940 were estimated by Nelson from partial data. Years 1961 and later, U.S. National Science Foundation, "National Patterns of R & D Resources" (1967), Table B-1a.

[a] Figures are for different fiscal years by performing agency.

[b] Estimates by performing agency.

tion and the National Science Foundation (NSF) participate almost equally and support their own special programs. NSF, as we shall note, is vested with responsibility for basic research over a wide range of sciences. All remaining federal R & D accounts for 2.3 percent of the total.

A contrast with the pre-World War II pattern is informative. Dupree reports Department of Agriculture expenditures on research at approximately $21 million in 1931.[32] Nelson estimates that federal expenditures on R & D in 1931 were $40 million. (See Table 3.) Thus within the accuracy of the figures, agriculture accounted for about half of all federal expenditures on R & D that year. Since 1931 agriculture's absolute share has increased more than tenfold (in current dollars), but its relative share is only about 1.5 percent. (See Table 2.) Herein lies the contrast. Federal

[32] A. Hunter Dupree, *Science in the Federal Government,* Cambridge, Mass.: Belknap Press of Harvard University Press (1957), p. 345.

attention to civilian R & D has increased manyfold. But that is nothing compared to the astronomical increase in federal R & D for defense and related programs.

The growth of the federal government and of the total national effort in R & D is shown in Table 3. In large part, the federal growth reflects the increased importance of defense-related programs. The previously mentioned 37-fold increase in total national R & D from 1940 to 1965 can be observed in Table 3. Even more spectacular is the over 100-fold increase in federal R & D during the same period. Consistent with this is, of course, an increase in the fraction of R & D that is federally financed from about one-fifth in 1940 to almost two-thirds in 1965. The private sector of the economy was also expanding relative to GNP, as shown in column 5.

Structure of R & D

Functional Structure

The structure of R & D applicable to sources and performing sectors is shown in Table 4 according to the conventional division into basic research, applied research, and development. The very definition of these terms, as previously given, suggests a natural division of labor reflected in Table 4. The net shift of basic research from the federal government as a source is predominantly to the universities as performers. The net shift for applied research and development is primarily to industry.

The absolute volume of basic research conducted by industry is large, and that part funded by industry is also large, as indicated by comparison with university research in both the source and performance classifications. However, as compared with all R & D funded and performed by industry, basic research is quite small. Applied research and development is quite large. The data indicate that industry is predominantly concerned with projects most narrowly oriented to particular applications.

The relative importance of development has been established by direct studies. Thus Rubenstein and Hannenberg conducted a survey of industrial research characteristics of nonfederal projects. For a representative sample of 91 projects, they found a median time to complete of 6 months and a median project size of 12 man-months.[33] A McGraw-Hill survey conducted in 1958 found that 39 percent of the industrial respon-

[33] A. H. Rubenstein and R. C. Hannenberg, "Idea Flow and Project Selection in Several Industrial Research and Development Laboratories," in Tybout, *op. cit.* (see footnote 20).

Table 4   Transfers of Funds Expended for Performance of Basic Research, and Applied Research and Development, by Sector and Source, 1966 (estimate)[a]
(Million $)

	Basic Research	Applied Research and Development	Total
Sources of funds			
Federal government	2,049	12,021	14,070
Industry	497	6,713	7,210
Colleges and universities	530	170	700
Other nonprofit institutions	157	83	240
Total	3,233	18,987	22,220
Performers of work			
Federal government	459	2,801	3,260
Industry	650	14,750	15,400
Colleges and universities	1,899[b]	931	2,830
Other nonprofit institutions	225	505	730
Total	3,233	18,987	22,220

Source. National Science Foundation, "National Patterns of R & D Resources" (1967), Tables B-la, B-2a.

[a] Estimates, based on reports by performers. Figures represent different fiscal years for different agencies.

[b] Includes expenditures for associated federal contract research centers.

dents expected a payoff in 3 years and over 90 percent expected a payoff in 5 years or less for R & D then being conducted.[34] The term "payoff" in this context meant full recovery of the cost of conducting the R & D.

There are a priori reasons for expecting an industrial emphasis on development. Uncertainties about the outcome of an R & D effort are smaller the less ambitious the extension of received knowledge. Since profits are to be made from specific applications, it is to be expected that development, which deals with specific applications, will get the greater attention. Applied and basic research shift in degree the emphasis of a research program. If the program leads to useful knowledge, that knowledge will be relevant over a broader area the more fundamental the knowledge is. Most business firms cannot expect to obtain all the benefits from knowledge that is relevant over a broader industrial area, although how broad an area it is depends on the business interests of the firm. This line of reasoning suggests that the larger the firm the more likely it is to

[34] Dexter M. Keezer, "The Outlook for Expenditures on Research and Development during the Next Decade," *American Economic Review*, 50 (May 1960), 365–366.

have more fundamental science programs. And the evidence is that such is in fact the case.[35]

Industrial Structure

Differences among industries in the volume of R & D performed are shown in Table 5. One-third of all industrial R & D is performed in the

Table 5   Research and Development Performance, by Industry, 1967

Industry	Amount (million $)	Percent of Total Industry R & D	Industry R & D as Percent of Net Sales
All	16,420	100.0	4.2
Aircraft and missiles	5,568	33.9	21.5
Electrical equipment and communication	3,806	23.2	8.5
Chemicals and allied products	1,565	9.5	4.3
Machinery	1,478	9.0	4.3
Motor vehicles	1,377	8.4	3.4
Petroleum refining and extraction	469	2.8	1.0
Professional and scientific instruments	464	2.8	5.4
Primary metals	245	1.5	0.8
Rubber products	195	1.2	2.1
Food and kindred products	168	1.0	0.4
Fabricated metal products	165	1.0	1.3
Stone, clay, and glass products	152	0.9	1.9
Paper and allied products	94	0.6	0.7
Lumber and wood, textiles, and apparel	66	0.4	0.5
Other manufacturing industries	70	0.4	0.6
Nonmanufacturing industries	540	3.3	—

Source. National Science Foundation, "Research and Development in Industry, 1967" (1969), Tables 2 and 38.

aerospace industry and over one-half is in aerospace plus communications. These results are not surprising in view of the well-known emphasis of federal interest in the same areas. Chemicals, machinery, and motor vehicles make up the remaining industrial leaders. The top five industries accounted for 84 percent of the nation's industrial R & D in 1967.

[35] Concentration of research is discussed under the subheading "Size Structure."

Column 3 of Table 5 shows R & D as a percent of net sales revenue. In the top five industries, R & D intensity correlates with the absolute magnitude of R & D performed, but this is not true for the remainder of the industries. In fact, the professional and scientific instruments industry would rank third on a scale of R & D intensity but comes out seventh in the Table 5 ranking based on absolute amounts of R & D expenditures.

Apart from defense considerations, there are certain reasons to expect some industries to be more R & D intensive than others. Problems more amenable to solution by systematic search are those for which an adequate science base has been developed. The science base may be complex, but for systematic inquiry must also be tractable. The example of chemicals and electronics come to mind. Second, consumer demand places a high value on some forms of invention. This is the case for aerospace and medicine. The latter accounts for the drugs component of the chemical industry and for a part of the development in scientific instruments.

Size Structure

Table 6 deals with all industrial R & D in relation to firm size. Only firms conducting R & D are included. The most important comparison is between the 274 firms with over 10,000 employees and all other firms. The former group is the industrial giants. As a reference point, note that according to *Fortune*'s 500, only 320 manufacturing firms in the country had 10,000 or more employees in 1967.[36] The 274 of these firms represented in Table 6 put twice as much money into R & D per dollar of sales revenue as all smaller firms. Moreover, if we consider all firms, R & D concentration becomes much greater. Thus 274, or roughly 85 percent, of the nation's 320 largest firms conducted R & D in 1967. However, it is obvious that a very much smaller fraction of firms having less than 10,000 employees conducted R & D. The total number of manufacturing companies in the United States is not known with any precision, but appears to fall within the range 200,000 to 300,000.[37] Clearly, only a small fraction

---

36 *Fortune Directory* (Time, 1968).

37 This range was obtained as follows: At the upper end, the U.S. Bureau of the Census, *1963 Census of Manufacturers*, Chap. 2, Table 1, reported that there were 306,617 total manufacturers "establishments." For purposes of the present discussion, an "establishment" can be interpreted as a plant producing a certain line of products, as defined in the Census Standard Industrial Classification code. Now, it is well known that a given firm may own many plants and produce many different kinds of products. The evidence is, however, that multiplant firms are relatively limited in number. A compilation of firms operating all establishments with over 100 employees and a large fraction of the establishments with 50 through 99 employees showed that 23,507 companies operated 37,979 establishments in 1954. "Economic Concentration," *Hearings before the Sub-*

Table 6 Funds for Industry Research and Development Performance, by Size of Company, 1967

	Companies with Total Employment of				
	Less Than 1,000	1,000–4,999	5,000–9,999	10,000 and Over	Total
Number of companies conducting research	10,000 (est.)	858	223	274	—
Percent	88.1	7.6	2.0	2.4	100.0
Federal funds (million $)	251	393	216	7,528	8,388
Percent	3.0	4.7	2.6	89.7	100.0
Company funds (million $)	437	718	653	6,224	8,032
Percent	5.4	8.9	8.1	77.5	100.0
Total funds (million $)	688	1,111	869	13,752	16,420
Percent	4.2	6.8	5.3	83.7	100.0
R & D as percent of net sales	2.7	2.3	1.9	5.3	4.2

Source. National Science Foundation, "Research and Development in Industry, 1967" (1969), Tables 3, 8, 10, 13, 38.

149

of the firms with less than 10,000 employees are conducting any R & D at all.

Table 6 shows a reversal of R & D per sales dollar in the smaller sales classes. The explanation of this is not known, but might be obtained by further disaggregation of the figures among industries. Thus industries strong on research might be more heavily represented in the smallest and largest groups, those weak on research more heavily represented in the middle two groups. For reasons of this sort, it seems best not to attribute very much significance to the relatively small differences among the three smaller groups. Remember, also, that only firms doing research appear in Table 6 and these are but a small fraction of the small firms.

In an industry-by-industry study, Scherer found that for some industries there is a continual increase in R & D conducted as a function of company size measured as sales.[38] Chemicals was an example. In other cases R & D went through a maximum and declined. This pattern fitted machinery and food and tobacco. Despite such industry-by-industry variation, the aggregate data in Table 6 show the dominant importance of the largest firms.

A final observation from Table 6 is that the federal expenditure of funds for industrial R & D work is slightly more concentrated than the sponsorship of in-house R & D by business firms themselves. Compare percentage figures across the rows for company funds and federal funds. The explanation is to be found in the institutional patterns for R & D in defense and space research.

It is the large industrial organization that typically has the special management and technological skills in a sufficiently broad subject matter area to successfully supervise weapons systems development. An integrated weapons system approach is necessary, with attention given to

committee on Antitrust and Monopoly Pursuant to Senate Resolution 262, 88th Congress, 2nd Session, Part 1 (1964), p. 380. There was a small amount of double counting in the total number of companies, as indicated in the source. But it is also clear that the large firms most likely to have multiple plants are included. If all firms having multiple plants were included, if we ignore the small amount of double counting among firms, and if we also ignore the fact that the data apply to different years, then it would be necessary to subtract from the 306,617 total manufacturing establishments the difference between 37,979 and 23,507 to get the total number of manufacturing firms. The result would be closer to 300,000 than 200,000. We have allowed a wider range to take account of the certainty that there are more, although probably not many more, cases in which more than one plant is operated by the same firm and have rounded the estimate to allow for differences in data between the years to which the estimates apply.

38 Frederic M. Scherer, "Size of Firm, Oligopoly and Research: A Comment," Canadian Journal of Economics and Political Science, 31 (May 1965).

tradeoffs among many components. As a means of retaining all options in such tradeoffs, it is almost necessary for the government to engage a principal large contractor.[39] Other considerations leading to cost-plus-fixed-fee contracting also dispose the case toward large contractors.[40] Finally, we have noted in previous discussion a logical presumption that basic research is more likely to be carried out by the largest R & D performing firms. The evidence bears out our expectations on this point.[41] Now, defense R & D is often directed to ambitious technological change,[42] thus shifting the comparative advantage to the giant R & D contractors.

The confluence of these various circumstances is to bring the military-industrial coalescense of which so much has been said. On the one hand is the imperative of the arms race and the organizational advantage to rely on the giants of American industry. On the other hand are various problems to which this gives rise, in the direction of defense efforts and in the development of commercial by-products of defense-sponsored research. The former problems have been given adequate attention elsewhere.[43] Commercial by-products are important in selected cases, although numerically the instances in which they have been important are limited.[44] The difficulties in bringing noncontractors to a par with contractors where commercial by-products are significant is discussed at a later point in connection with the growth of the civil atomic power industry.

RESEARCH AND PUBLIC POLICY

The major issues of public policy center around federal support of research and methods of achieving effective adoption of the results in the private sector. There are two goals: (1) the stimulation of invention and (2) the fostering of a competitive structure for its adoption. Social problems of achieving these goals are interrelated. They are considered in

[39] See discussion by Merton J. Peck and Frederic M. Scherer, *The Weapons Acquisition Process: An Economic Analysis*, Boston, Mass.: Division of Research, Graduate School of Business Administration (1962), Chaps. 11–13.

[40] The need for cost-plus-fixed-fee contracting and its tendency to fall to large firms is the principal topic in Richard A. Tybout, *Government Contracting in Atomic Energy*, Ann Arbor, Mich.: University of Michigan Press (1956).

[41] U.S. National Science Foundation, "Research and Development in Industry, 1966" (1968), Table 72.

[42] Burton H. Klein, "The Decision Making Problem in Development," in National Bureau of Economic Research, *op. cit.* (see footnote 18).

[43] The classic reference is C. Wright Mills, *The Power Elite*, New York: Oxford University Press (1956).

[44] Nelson et al., *op. cit.* (see footnote 8), pp. 83–85.

sequence, with special attention to their meeting ground in the dissemination of technological know-how.

Public Support of Research

The case for increased public support of research is better the greater the divergence between public and private benefits expected from a given research dollar. The more fundamental the knowledge generated, the more likely it is to find uses beyond those anticipated. Even the results anticipated typically transcend the interests of a single industry or a single business firm. With applied research, this is less true, and for development, still less. Development in turn merges with design and the accumulation of know-how, which may have precious little significance beyond the immediate objective of a project.

If private benefits are expected in sufficient amount, these will justify private commitment to an R & D project. Indeed, some benefits beyond those experienced by the sponsoring firm may be taken into account if patent licensing of others is expected to yield revenue. The use of patents, however, has declined in the post-World War II period. The decline is the result of several related phenomena, including especially judicial requirements of compulsory patent licensing.[45] Consistent with the reduced importance of patents has been greater reliance on the headstart that know-how affords. This trend does not increase the breadth of social payoff that a given business firm is likely to take into account.

The spectrum from broad to narrow social relevance corresponds, of course, to the historic division of labor between publicly supported university research and industrial applied research. A federal commitment "To promote the progress of science . . ." was made in the National Science Foundation Act of 1950,[46] which authorized and directed NSF "to initiate and support basic scientific research in the mathematical, physical, medical, biological, engineering and other sciences" and to undertake various supporting programs.[47] The current magnitude of NSF efforts was noted in Table 2.

More radical programs have been proposed to fill the gap between basic research and whatever level of research is privately conducted. Thus the Kennedy administration in 1963 tried to launch an ambitious program for public support of technological progress. The principal object was to support with federal funds the actual conduct of industrial R & D for

---

45 Scherer, *op. cit.* (see footnote 19).
46 Public Law 807, 81st Congress. Quotation is from the preamble.
47 Section 3(a).

selected industries that have not been research oriented.[48] Among the latter, textiles, building, lumber, leather, and railroading were cited. Several programs were also proposed for disseminating research results. Two years later, the State Technical Services Act was passed.[49] The Act provides for federal matching of state funds used in programs to "enable business, commerce and industrial establishments to acquire and use scientific and engineering information more effectively."[50]

An agenda for considering the various aspects of public policy has been drawn up by Nelson and his associates, based, at least in part, on the body of opinion among scholars concerned with the economics of technology. The program extends from the creation of a National Institute of Technology, through in-depth applied research for certain technologies and industries, to the use of government procurement to support early growth of a new technology, and finally to extension services and like means of disseminating results.[51] The Nelson agenda is used here as a guide to discussion of various facets of the subject.

The National Institute of Technology would do for other industries what government research has done for agriculture, atomic power, civil aviation, and public health. It would relate the industrial technology to basic science, generally at the engineering level. The focus would be on problems of the industry, not on classes of phenomena, as characterize basic research, and not on particular products and processes, as characterize most industrial applied research and development. It would be directed to a gap that exists in the area between basic research and company-specific applied research, where scientists are not as interested in working and businesses are not as able to justify the work from the standpoint of the profits they would receive as a direct result of it. Generally speaking, the resulting knowledge would be in the public domain. Further development would be necessary to apply it within particular business firms.

In agriculture and atomic power, government generally conducts research down to the level of specific applications so that the commercial user of the technology can obtain from public agencies results, designs, and data that are specific to his needs. The National Institute of Tech-

---

[48] See Statement by J. H. Hollomon, Assistant Secretary for Science and Technology, in "Departments of State, Justice and Commerce, the Judiciary, and Related Appropriations for 1964," Hearings before a Subcommittee of the Committee on Appropriations, House of Representatives, 88th Congress, 1st Session (February 25, 1963), pp. 747ff., especially p. 755.

[49] Public Law 182, 89th Congress (1965).

[50] 79 Stat. 697.

[51] Nelson et al., *op. cit.* (see footnote 8), Chap. 9.

nology would not concern itself at this level as a general rule but might undertake development projects in selected cases. For example, where systems are involved, such as urban transit systems, no one manufacturer in its own R & D program is in a position to consider all the possible trade-offs among components.[52] In such cases there is a logical possibility of gain from public conduct of systemwide R & D. Another possible case for public conduct of development-level R & D might be in deficient industries such as cited above as targets for the Kennedy Administration's plans. There are built-in dangers to industry-specific development by the federal government in that the public agency can easily become committed to the fortunes of the industry, as opposed to the public welfare. Thus R & D for highway development to accommodate heavier axle loads is well and good as long as it is not designed merely to shift traffic from rail transport where service on the latter could be improved at less R & D cost. The example is hypothetical but the problem is not.

The suggestion by Nelson and associates for the use of government procurement to support the early introduction of worthwhile technologies would require a good deal more of federal procurement systems than they are now expected to provide and perhaps can provide. Detailed physical specifications are used in procurement to narrow the range in which subjective judgements must be made by procurement officers. It may well be desirable to broaden this range by giving more attention to objective tests of performance, but this recommendation can stand on its own and does not need to be applied in the procurement of novel products only.

Moreover, the out-of-pocket costs of using procurement as a proving ground may not be small. For example, ballpoint pens sold for $12.00 when first introduced in the mid-1940s. If new products can be obtained off the shelf, that is one thing. If some form of cost reimbursement contract is necessary for product development, that is another matter. The latter involve their own cost. There are no absolutes here, but it is well not to underestimate the costs of the proposal.

Dissemination of Technological Knowledge

Granted that a case can be made on deductive grounds for public support of R & D, especially for the development of the scientific underpinning of an industry, the way in which this is done will determine the competitive standing of individual members of the industry.

The problem of disseminating technological information is inherent in

[52] This is the same kind of situation as has led to principal weapons systems contractors, as previously noted.

any situation in which one party (a public agency or its contractor) creates the information and another (the private receiver) is expected to use the information. The importance of this link in the process is not always recognized.

Agricultural extension services have been a vital link in moving information from the laboratory to the field. Whether the agricultural example has broader significance is open to question. Contrary to the situation in agriculture, the industrial users of any research results from a hypothetical National Institute of Technology have rather differentiated and specific needs. Whether at the general industry level or the applied level, government industrial research programs can hardly be neutral among users to anything like the degree of neutrality possible in agriculture. In addition to the obvious point that technologies and products differ, there is the often overlooked point that capacities to receive information differ.

The point refers to institutional capacities of industrial firms. A firm with an R & D program of its own is better off than a firm without one. The firm whose R & D program deals with the specific subject area in which results are disseminated is best off. Agricultural extension does not operate at the same level. Information disseminated by the county agent is prestructured for direct application in an operational situation. As in the evolution of computer technology, complex research results have been sifted down to manageable codes for practitioners. Time is spent in the process, and this is not the situation generally encountered in disseminating industrial technological knowledge.

Industrial R & D should be thought of as a continuum from the general research result to the specific profitable application. Experience at one level is relevant for experience at the next level. This includes all intermediate stages through pilot plants, demonstration plants, and the accumulation of "know-how" in its various possible forms. Know-how is easiest to build from a background of experience with the technology at an earlier research stage. The point is illustrated by the results of a study conducted by the author in the early years of the shift of the atomic energy industry from the public into the private sector.

The study was made in the summer of 1957, 3 years after passage of the Atomic Energy Act of 1954, which was intended especially to bring private participation into atomic energy applications. In the 3 years the Atomic Energy Commission (AEC) had conducted a number of programs to disseminate information on atomic technologies. At least one such program had preceded the 1954 legislation but was selective and limited because of security restrictions. The object of the study was to evaluate the AEC programs as compared with other sources of information on atomic technologies, particularly information in the form of know-how gained by AEC contractors and subcontractors.

The study was conducted by mail survey with the assistance of the Congressional Joint Economic Committee. Relatively complete returns were received. Respondents were asked to identify their "single most important" source of technological knowledge in each of twelve named product-classes of commercial atomic energy products—reactor components, radiation-measuring instruments, and various special devices. One-hundred-thirty-four respondents answered in 229 product-classes, as shown in Table 7. In a few cases respondents indicated more than one "single most important" source and, for these, multiple votes were prorated, thus explaining the appearance of noninteger values in the table.

Consider first the totals for each column. The three most important sources of information were subcontracts, hiring of key personnel, and prime contracts, in the same order. Prime and subcontractors were the beneficiaries of know-how. When combined, they accounted for the largest single group. Otherwise, the way to get knowledge was to enter the market for technological manpower. The latter may be assumed to have received knowledge in proportion to the importance of all other sources, excluding itself.

The three AEC programs appear in columns 3, 4, and 5. Columns 3 and 5 were deliberate education efforts made by AEC. Access permits, represented in column 4, were simply rights to study, observe, and raise questions. Interestingly enough, column 4 was the best of the three. Even more important, all three put together did not get as many votes as the single outside source, periodicals, column 6.

A final interesting observation is that there were as many big firms, by product-classes represented, as there were small firms. Typically, the small firms, even in a concentrated industry, are far greater in number than the large firms. Compare, for example, our previous discussion in connection with Table 6.

In the atomic products industry, Table 7 shows no such heavy population at the small end of the scale. On the contrary, the single largest number of product-classes is found for the super giants, those that employ 25,000 and over. The disparity is not accounted for by the difference between product-classes and firms. The average number of product-classes per firm was 1.7. Large firms, roughly speaking, produced in two or three product-classes, small firms, usually in only one. Hence use of the product-class as a unit could not possibly have accounted for the difference between the distribution by size of firms in Tables 6 and 7. Only the outside sources, columns 6, 7, and 8 (not AEC programs), show a heavier number of votes at the small-firm end of the scale.

Table 7 Most Important Sources of Business Information about Atomic Technologies, June 30, 1957 (Number of votes as "single most important" source of information; duplicate votes prorated)

Size of Firm (Number of Employees)	AEC Prime Contracts (1)	Subcontracts (2)	AEC Study Groups (3)	AEC Access Permits (4)	AEC Training Programs (5)	Periodicals (6)	Private Consultants (7)	Hiring of Key Personnel (8)	Other (9)	Total[a] (10)
Under 10	2.0	2.8	0	0	0	4.2	4.3	6.1	1.5	20.9
10–24	1.0	3.5	0.4	0	0	3.1	1.7	4.3	1.0	15.0
25–49	1.2	7.5	1.0	0.2	0.2	6.2	0	2.7	2.0	21.0
50–99	2.3	6.0	0.5	0.7	0	0.7	0	11.7	1.0	23.1
100–249	5.9	6.8	0	0	0	1.0	0.3	5.0	0	19.0
250–499	0	4.5	0.3	2.4	1.0	4.8	0	5.0	2.0	20.0
500–999	2.0	2.0	0	0	0	1.0	1.0	7.0	2.0	15.0
1,000–2,499	3.1	0.5	0	0.1	1.1	0.5	0.1	0.5	0	5.9
2,500–4,999	4.0	3.8	0	0.8	0.3	2.0	0.3	1.0	0	12.2
5,000–9,999	3.5	3.0	0	1.0	0	0	1.0	2.5	1.0	12.0
10,000–24,999	3.5	5.0	0	8.2	1.6	0	0	3.7	0	22.0
25,000 and over	12.0	17.3	0	4.3	1.2	3.8	0.2	4.1	0	42.9
Total	40.7	62.7	2.2	17.7	5.4	27.3	8.9	53.6	10.5	229.0
Percent	17.8	27.4	1.0	7.6	2.4	11.9	3.9	23.4	4.6	100.0

Source. Richard A. Tybout, The Reactor Supply Industry, Ohio State University Bureau of Business Research, Monograph 97 (1960), Table 13.

[a] Slight differences between the figures in this column and the same data reported in earlier columns are due to rounding fractional votes to the nearest one-tenth.

157

A possible interpretation of the results is that small firms do not have the technological base from which to build and for this reason remain largely behind the technological frontier, except as they can graft new technology into their organizations by hiring special talents. This interpretation is consistent with Baldwin's finding that nonprofit and profit-making contract research agencies get most of their business from large firms who want to supplement their own in-house capabilities, not from small firms who could logically be expected to buy services they might not be able to keep a permanent staff to provide.[53] If small firms, or business firms of any size, are not in a position to develop their own technological knowledge, then neither are they in a position to assimilate technological knowledge developed for them by others.

Granted this problem, the proportional representation of small firms in atomic technologies was far short of their representation in economywide R & D, as shown in Table 6. Know-how was not effectively conveyed to this group, nor to the outsiders as a whole.

Competitive Structure

The problem of developing federal R & D programs is best considered as a tradeoff between short-term efficiency and the creation of know-how in a broad competitive base. Short-term efficiency seeks to get the R & D done and the results applied at lowest immediate cost. Long-term efficiency takes account of effects on competitive structure. To the extent that competition is fostered, the long-term prospects of adopting new technologies are improved. Competition provides the market incentive for invention and innovation. Without such incentive public funding of R & D will not achieve its long-run potential.

Short-term efficiency is promoted by the AEC pattern. AEC research is conducted by contract with private firms and universities, usually in AEC-owned facilities. For industrial applications members of the affected private industry do the work, and gain the know-how; hence they are in a position to apply the results expeditiously. Long-term efficiency would temper the advantages of the insiders and increase the capabilities of the outsiders, possibly at the cost of short-term delays in the R & D process. The question is just how much delay and how the know-how is to be imparted to outsiders.

At the opposite extreme from AEC is the purely public conduct of R & D. It has already been suggested that the agricultural example cannot

---

[53] William Baldwin, "Contracted Research and the Case for Big Business," *Journal of Political Economy*, **70** (June 1962).

be applied in a neutral way for industrial R & D, that somehow public policy should seek to cultivate a broader base of know-how than would normally exist. This need, of course, transcends the need for public control of any resulting patent rights, with nonexclusive royalty-free licensing. The latter we take for granted in public programs.

Intermediate possibilities would involve various forms of public-private cooperation, always a dangerous process if we want to keep open the doors to newcomers and if we want to keep alive a primary concern for consumers. Several considerations are relevant, although the state of the art in the design of such cooperatives hardly affords the basis for drawing up an optimal blueprint at the present time.

First, as previously noted, it is best if the research is conducted mainly on the science base for an industry, as opposed to specific applications.

Second, the undertaking of parallel, seemingly duplicating projects, should not be ruled out. This would open opportunities for a greater number of private organizations to participate. A good deal of attention has been given to the logic of parallel R & D efforts.[54] Briefly, there is much to gain in the learning process if search is undertaken by more than one research team independently but with communication at review points.[55]

Third, public decision makers should dominate, both in the selection of projects and to inhibit the extension of cooperation from R & D projects into the market for applications. The need here is important enough and the circumstances of competition difficult enough to warrant some limitation on what might otherwise be the optimal number of review points, as described above.

Fourth, de facto mutual funding through taxes, such as value-added taxes, would generate the necessary intense interest on the part of all members of an industry. The magnitude of industry-benefiting programs would be determined by the amount of such taxes derived from an industry. The level of the taxes should be determined by the expected benefits and costs of worthwhile industrywide R & D.

Fifth, tests of the effectiveness of any public-private cooperative should include a review of results along several lines: (1) whether the R & D conducted would have otherwise been carried out privately; (2) whether newcomers to the industry can effectively participate in the programs (from which know-how will inevitably be generated as a byproduct);

---

54 For some of the important considerations, see Richard R. Nelson, "Uncertainty, Learning and the Economics of Parallel Research and Development Efforts," *Review of Economics and Statistics*, **43** (November 1961).

55 The formal logic of research organization is discussed by Thomas Marschak et al., *Strategy for R & D*, New York: Springer-Verlag (1967), Chap. 5.

and (3) whether restrictive practices in the application of new technologies are fostered in the process of cooperation.

Whatever the cooperative arrangement, there is at least one respect in which institutional rigidities can be offset. This is through the market for professional manpower. The importance of this alternative was made clear in the atomic energy case. There are, of course, certain emoluments usually necessary to attract a highly valued researcher to a firm that has not been strong in R & D. These include base salary but are not usually limited to it. The problem is familiar to those who buy and sell services in the academic marketplace.

The suggestions made here for various attributes of public-private cooperative efforts are intended to illuminate certain problems inherent in the concept of a public responsibility for R & D. They are not thought to be exhaustive, merely because the subject has not received that much attention, here or elsewhere. Above all, a broad concept of public interest is imperative. The history of technology suggests that creativity is where you find it. Public policy should seek to ensure an open field for the search.

CHAPTER SIX

Research Settings

Simon Marcson, Rutgers University

Research organizations develop an atmosphere or climate within which the individual functions.[1] The vast number of research organizations that have emerged evolve differing types of research settings for the conduct of their work. In order to consider the variety of research settings within which research scientists work, it is necessary to categorize the types and codify the characteristics.

TYPES OF RESEARCH SETTINGS

There are eight types of research settings in which research is conducted: four types of organizations (university, government, industry, and non-profit) engaged in two types of activities (basic and applied). The university is the oldest research setting and remains the largest and most

---

[1] See Simon Marcson, *Scientists in Government*, Chap. X, "The Work Atmosphere," Rutgers Univ., New Brunswick, N.J., 1966; and "Research Environment: A Factorial Analysis of a Government Laboratory," a paper presented to the Seventh World Congress of Sociology, Varna, Bulgaria, September, 1970.

prestigeful employer of scientists in basic research. Ever since the end of World War I, however, the number of scientists in applied research has grown to fairly large proportions. Government provides the largest number of research laboratories (over 4000) for the conduct of research, with a preponderance of scientists in applied research. Industry is the most recent sector of the economy to enter into research with a high preponderance of its scientific manpower engaged in applied research. The fourth type[2] is the nonprofit one, a recent innovation, which has a relatively small number of scientists about evenly distributed between basic and applied research.

Table 1   Types of Research Settings by Number of Doctorate Scientists, 1968[a]

| Type of Organ- | Type of Research Activity | | | | |
| | Basic | | Applied | | |
ization	Number	Percent	Number	Percent	Total
University	28,818	75.5	9,447	24.6	38,265
Government	6,669	47.0	7,554	53.1	14,223
Industry	6,675	27.1	18.034	73.0	24,709
Nonprofit	2,315	49.0	2,425	51.4	4,740

[a] For number of scientists, National Science Foundation, *American Science Manpower, 1968,* Washington, D.C., p. 69.

These research settings[3] differ not only in type of research activity but in styles of administration, in tradition, and in types of authority

[2] This chapter considers only the first three of these research setings; the university, government, and industry. The fourth, nonprofit research, employs only a small portion of research scientists in the United States, and few data are available on them, although Vollmer points out that ". . . they are a significant type or organization for study." See Howard M. Vollmer, Todd R. Laporte, William C. Peterson, Phyllis A. Langton, *Adaptations of Scientists in Five Organizations: A Comparative Analysis,* Stanford Research Series, Stanford Research Institute, Menlo Park, Calif., May, 1964, p. 48.

[3] See Richard H. Hall, "Some organizational Considerations in the Professional-Organizational Relationship," *Administrative Science Quarterly* (December, 1967), 462–463. Hall's typology of research settings is as follows:

The work of professionals is carried out in three basic settings. The first is the solo practitioner setting, which has served as the basis for the analysis of professionalism in general. Although an interesting, if increasingly less common case, this setting is not excluded from the analysis. The second basic setting is the professional organization, such as the law or accounting firm, medical clinic, or social work agency. Scott has made a very useful distinction between types of professional organizations. One subtype is the "autonomous" professional organization, as exemplified by the medical clinic or law firm. In this setting, the work of the professional is subject to his own systems. In short, they differ in their cultural attributes to such an extent that in themselves they constitute subcultures with their own organizational work environment characteristics, their own standards of performance, their own norms of autonomy, their own criteria of creativity, their own incentive systems, their own patterns of conflict, and their own definition of innovation. It is the concern of this chapter to examine research settings in terms of some of the above factors.

While Table I indicates that the university is the largest employer of research scientists, it does not present the whole picture with respect to the distribution of scientists by employer. Educational institutions as employers also employ teaching scientists and therefore have a total of 117,746 or 40 percent of the nation's scientists in their employ. Industry employed 32 percent of the scientists in the National Register in 1968, while 10 percent were in the federal government. This scientific manpower is engaged in R & D primarily, and in management or administration secondarily. Twenty-one percent of all scientists are engaged in

Table 2 Total Number of Scientists by Type of Employer

Type of Employer	Number	Percent
Educational institutions	117,746	40
Federal government	29,666	10
Other government	10,031	3
Nonprofit organizations	11,204	4
Industry and business	95,776	32
Self-employed	6,462	2
Military	7,155	2
Other	1,729	1
Not employed	12,707	4
No report	5,466	2

Source. National Register of Scientific and Technical Personnel, 1968, *American Science Manpower, 1968,* National Science Foundation, Washington, D.C., 1969, p. 49.

rather than administrative jurisdiction, since professional tasks rather than administrative tasks provide the basis for the formal structuring of the organization. The second subtype is the "heteronomous" organization, in which the professional employees are subordinated to an administrative framework. Scott suggested that the degree of professional autonomy is less in this setting. Examples of this type of organization are public schools, libraries, and social work agencies, all of which are subject to externally (often legislatively) derived structuring. This distinction between the two subtypes of professionals organizations is used in the present analysis. The third setting is in the larger organization, in which the professional department is merely one part of the organization.

Table 3   Primary Work Activity

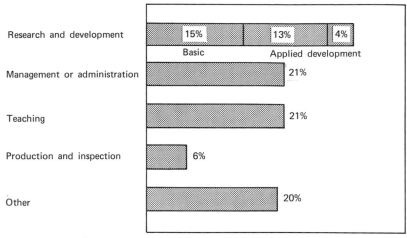

Source. National Register of Scientific and Technical Personnel, 1968, *American Science Manpower, 1968,* National Science Foundation, Washington, D.C., 1969, p. 14.

teaching. Another 6 percent of United States scientific manpower is occupied in production and inspection activities.[4]

These factors raise further questions about research settings. For instance: What are the differentials in emphasis on research for differing types of research settings? What type of organizational[5] model does the research setting tend to, and how does the particular type of

[4] See National Science Foundation, *American Science Manpower, 1968,* 1969, p. 48

Primary work activity	Number	Percent
Research and development	96,036	32
Basic research	46,177	15
Applied research	38,841	13
Management or administration	62,870	21
Management or administration of research and development	28,568	10
Teaching	62,087	21
Production and inspection	16,847	6
Consulting	12,334	4
Exploration, forecasting, reporting	14,365	5
Other	8,416	3
Not employed	12,707	4
No report	12,280	4

[5] S. Z. Nagi and R. G. Corwin, *The Social Contexts of Research,* Wiley-Interscience, New York, 1972, Chap. 1.

model influence research? Does the model tend to the bureaucratic type, the entrepreneurial, or some other? How do the reward and control systems function in differing types or research settings?[6] Do particular types or research settings develop organizational climates that differentially socialize the individual? What models of organization have been adopted by different settings for research, and how have they influenced research? The various research settings differ in pace and predictability of research consequences.

THE UNIVERSITY AS RESEARCH SETTING

The university's major function remains teaching, with 51 percent of its scientific manpower being engaged in teaching.[7] The early beginning of university research was entirely devoted to full-time basic research and scholarship by scientists devoted to the entrepreneurial approach to research. The university remains the major organizational setting emphasizing research and especially, basic research. In recent years, and especially since World War II, the university has increasingly adopted bureaucratic patterns.

The university adopted a pattern in which most of its scientific manpower engaged in research and also devoted often up to 50 percent of its time to teaching. However, because of the university's utilization patterns the university scientist can devote all his energies to his own basic scientific interests through research and teaching. This is markedly different from such research settings as are to be found in industry and government. In the latter two organizations, the usual pattern is that of full-time employment in research, or a combination of research and administration. The university scientist can fruitfully combine teaching and research in many cases by pursuing his own scientific interests and obtaining his own funding for his research activities. Thus the scientist can enhance his role as an independent entrepreneur at the expense of his own time and energy, thus modifying his status as an employee. The scientist in industry and government cannot similarly modify his role.

Colleges versus Universities

The university as a research setting is not a clear-cut, single homogeneous model. As a matter of fact, a sharp distinction must be drawn

[6] See Norman Storer's penetrating and illuminating analysis of these issues in *The Social System of Science*, Holt, New York, 1966, Chap. 5.
[7] National Science Foundation, *American Science Manpower, 1968*, Washington, D.C., 1969, p. 69.

between colleges and universities as employers. Folger et al., in a staff report of the "Commission on Human Resources and Advanced Education" points out that "college employment virtually eliminates the opportunity to pursue research for most scientists in this setting."[8] However, university scientists "generally had the highest citation rates."[9] However, the differences do not end there, for within the university system there are differentials. "Those in the better universities had considerably higher citation rates than those in the lower quality universities."[10] The determinants of scientific productivity do not seem to depend on the amount of time available for research for scientists in these various organizations of higher learning, but on strong motivation and a high-quality educational experience.[11]

Colleague Authority

The scientist's working environment includes an ingredient which may be characterized as "colleague authority." The organizational environment of the research laboratory includes the authority, ranking, and goal systems.[12] The research laboratory in the university as well, as the university as a whole, utilizes professionals within an organizational context in which an authority system is present. Parsons[13] points out that the concept of authority is not a central issue in the ideology of the professional. The member of a profession expects to defer only to superior professional knowledge and competence. For example, Parsons observes that ". . . the university is in some respects a peculiarly 'anti-authoritarian' type of organization. Its 'top management' is ordinarily subjected to a conspicuous set of limitations on its authority to intervene in the spheres of competence of faculty members who in one sense are subordinated."[14] Marcson has described the well-delineated authority system of the university as "colleague authority"[15] in which professionals do stress, as Parsons has noted, superior professional knowledge and competence. Colleague authority refers to a system of control in which

[8] J. K. Folger, et al., *Human Resources and Higher Education*, Russell Sage Foundation, New York, 1970, p. 267.
[9] *Ibid.*
[10] *Ibid.*
[11] *Ibid.*, p. 268.
[12] Simon Marcson, *The Scientist in American Industry*, Harper, New York, 1960, p. 12.
[13] Talcott Parsons, "Suggestions For A Sociological Approach to the Theory of Organizations," *Administrative Science Quarterly* 1 (September 1956), 237.
[14] *Ibid.*
[15] Marcson, *The Scientist in American Industry*, p. 130.

authority is shared by all the members of the working group rather than in an individual. In colleague authority decision-making authority is delegated to individuals, but the members view such authority as orginating in the colleague membership. The term "colleague" has its origin in professional working groups. It emphasizes a relationship of association, alliance, and working together, while as the same time accepting whatever inequality in status may be present.

In the university organization faculty self-rule within a parliamentary framework has emphasized the expected value system of a democracy and modified (although not necessarily eliminated) the occurrence of arbitrary despotic behavior.[16] The prevailing system of faculty organization has emphasized the mechanisms of persuasion and indirect control. Faculty self-rule has tended, too, to emphasize the notion that the source of authority is within the faculty, notwithstanding the fact that it functions within the framework of administrative controls.[17]

While collegial authority may positively affect the organization's working environment in terms of the individual scientist's self-esteem, Kornhauser points out that in terms of Weber's emphasis colleague control reduces the efficiency of the organization. "Collegiality invariably obstructs the promptness of decisions, the consistency of policy, the clear responsibility of the individual, and ruthlessness to outsiders in combination with the maintenance of discipline within the group."[18] One of the reasons for this is that the scientist's training does not prepare him to be an employee.[19] He is trained to be a member of a profession who engages in research. The scientist has internalized the values of his profession as to the importance of its scientific and professional ethos regardless of the goals of his employer.[20]

The inefficiency Weber saw in collegial organizations is to some degree expressed in the university scientist's antipathy to the term "management," and the practices associated with "management." As a matter of fact, few in the university would accept the concept of "management" as applicable to the university situation.[21] The term is never used. Certainly, as far as senior faculty members are concerned, they see themselves

16 Simon Marcson, "Decision-Making in a University Physics Department," *The American Behavioral Scientist*, **6**, No. 4 (December 1962) 38.

17 *Ibid.*

18 William Kornhauser, *Scientists in Industry: Conflict and Accommodation*, Univ. of California Press, Berkeley, 1962, p. 43.

19 Simon Marcson, "The Professional Commitments of Scientists in Industry," *Research Management*, **6**, No. 4 (Winter 1961), 271–275.

20 F. Reif, "The Competitive World of the Pure Scientist," *Science*, **134**, No. 3494 (December 15, 1961), 1959.

21 Marcson, *American Behavioral Scientist*, **6**, No. 4, 37.

as the real "managerial" group of a given discipline. In their decisions about the "management" of their discipline, they see themselves as autonomous and without peers. The scientist in the university is, then, not trained to be an employee, and eventually acquires a position in which he defines himself not as an employee but as a member with managerial authority both in his department and in the university.

Under the circumstances, how does the university achieve its working goals, or what mechanisms does it utilize that are substitutes for the unacceptable term "management." How does the department proceed to direct, staff, evaluate, and communicate with the department members? The major organizational mechanism indulged in by this management is the committee. There may be as many as sixteen committees and twelve subcommittees in a department consisting of only 26 senior faculty members.[22]

The departmental committees, as well as university committees, function throughout the year and manage the variety of activities involved in teaching and research. The managerial decisions the orgaization makes are made in these committees and involve almost every professorial member. This type of committee management, while it does not contribute to efficiency, spreads decision making and engulfs all professorial members in many time-consuming committee activities. This is possible in university organizations since faculty, in general, work without regard to time checks. To a large extent, and because of the participative management system, they are their own taskmasters and, as a result, frequently drive themselves beyond endurance. In industry, this amount of committee activity would gravely cut into a 35- or 40-hour work schedule. In a sense, then, the "management system" of colleague participation is made possible by the heavy working schedule of the faculty members. However, the acceptance of a heavy working schedule on the part of faculty members is dependent upon the system of participative management.

Bureaucratic Authority in the University

However, the university is not a case any more, if it ever was, of pure colleague authority. As bureaucratization has increased, "executive authority"[23] has grown as an admixture to colleague authority. In this respect, Kornhauser points out that "organizations are increasingly governed by professional standards, and professionals are increasingly subject

[22] *Ibid.*, p. 38.
[23] Marcson, *The Scientist in American Industry,* p. 121.

to bureaucratic controls".[24] As this occurs, colleague authority is modified more and more with executive authority and the university scientist becomes more and more a staff employee and less and less an independent member of participative managerial scientific entrepreneur. Kornhauser adds, "professional work requires considerable independence, but complex organizations require the coordination of professional work with other functions of the total enterprise."

Authority may be said to be organized in two ways in the university. The first type has already been referred to as colleague authority. The second type is inherent in the hierarchical organization present in academic departments. Professorial ranks confer power and authority on each ascending rank, especially in the area of appointments and promotions. How do these hierarchical ranks function as managers in such areas? Since the junior ranks of assistant professors and instructors are often excluded from participating in decisions involving appointments and promotions, consideration is confined to senior faculty. After an assistant professor has served two consecutive 3-year appointments, he necessarily must be considered for a promotion by his department. If he is not promoted, he must leave and seek a position elsewhere. The assistant professor can, however, be considered and be promoted at some earlier point. Under either condition he is evaluated by the senior faculty acting as a committee of the whole. His work as a teacher and as a research scientist is discussed. Since in the university, in most if not all instances his appointment is one of half teaching and half research, "his publications receive particular attention both as to quantity and quality with quantity being a factor of sizeable importance."[25] However, the basic assumption is always present that the man with the highest qualifications is being selected. His characteristics as a person are examined, and if there is some division of opinion, they are thoroughly examined. Preferential attitudes toward the candidate by senior faculty members are expressed and questions asked about his scholarship with, however, the frequent implications of these comments which can best be summarized in the phrase, "Will he fit in?" The individual's record of competence, then, is only one factor taken into account in the evaluation of the individual.

How does this research setting influence the scientist in the conduct of his research? How do the professional norms, commitments, and bureaucratic characteristics influence research? For junior level academic

24 William Kornhauser, *Scientists in Industry: Conflict and Accommodation*, Univ. of California Press, Berkeley, 1962, p. 7.
25 Marcson, *American Behavioral Scientist*, 6, No. 4, 38.

scientists, the consequences are clear-cut. In the university the starting salaries are lower than those in industry. The junior faculty member's position is insecure and uncertain. The existence of a clear-cut differentiation between tenure and nontenure positions contributes to strain among the nontenure members. The junior faculty member must be entrepreneurial to some extent while at the same time under the most extensive bureaucratic control experienced by any faculty member. He is the repository of a professional orientation toward research and teaching, and at the same time a member of an organization with bureaucratic[26] orientations toward a disciplined compliance with procedures. His compliance is obtained not only through his essential insecurity, but also through the manipulation of sanctions and the administration of rewards and expectations of rewards in terms of status rather than economic needs. Under these circumstances the junior faculty research environment is competitive, tension-bearing, insecure, striving, adaptive, entrepreneurial, compliant, and self-aggrandizing, demanding modesty, selflessness, involvement, recognition, and self-realization. To describe it as a research environment fostering strain would be an understatement. To describe it as a tense laboratory in which the mature professional is formed and out of which some emerge as creative scientists comes closer to the facts.

Once junior faculty have obtained senior faculty tenure positions, the academic scientist has greater security of position and a more assured sense of self-esteem. His salary rewards, while reducing the economic pressures experienced by junior faculty, remain somewhat less than those found in industry or government. Many other pressures are also reduced in his new senior faculty scientist status. He can now subject the organization's bureaucratic influences to some control. He can exercise more initiative in his entrepreneurial research ventures. He can now settle down to a long-term plan respecting his research activities. He can now begin to focus attention on the next generation of scientists and train graduate students in his field of specialization. The strains become less

Table 4 Median Salaries for Doctorate Scientists by Type of Employer, 1968

	Educational Institutions		Federal Government	Industry
	Academic	Calendar		
All scientists	$12,000	$14,800	$15,800	$17,500

Source. National Science Foundation, American Science Manpower, 1968, Washington, D.C., 1969, p. 232.

26 Peter M. Blau, "The Hierarchy of Authority in Organizations," *American Journal of Sociology*, **73**, No. 4, (January 1968), 456–457.

organizational and more in terms of professional performance, creativity, achievement, and continuity.

Limits on Autonomy

As in other research settings, the scientist enters university employment at first on trial. As in civil service, the trial period has a limited duration, and then the scientist has tenure or lifetime employment conferred on him. However, there is a difference. During the trial period the scientist in the university has a degree of autonomy that is rare for an individual in a similar status in government or industry. During his six-year trial period, the university scientist has a fairly wide latitude within which to choose research problems, pursue his teaching and research, and exercise initiative.

However, as the university has become involved in large-scale research, a certain amount of bureaucratic rigidity has crept into the university which affects the junior faculty especially. Their own autonomy is limited not only by their inherent status but also by the "managerial" powers of tenure senior faculty who constitute the two upper ranks of the associate and full professors. This status confers on senior faculty members the right to participate in promotion of junior faculty to the senior group of the department and a voice in two fundamental aspects of the department; that of the composition and the direction of the department.

This is not to say that junior faculty members[27] have no voice in the parliamentary democracy of university departmental organization. It is, however, a dependent role. Influence can be exercised to a large extent by aligning themselves with senior faculty members, which involves making a choice in terms of the senior faculty member's intellectual and research interests as well as his hoped for influence in departmental affairs. It would be difficult for a junior faculty member to accept a senior faculty member's patronage and, at the same time, for him to be antagonistic to the senior man's research and field of interest. The junior faculty member's dependency role also rests on the fact that there are usually more junior faculty staff members than there are openings in senior ranks for any one given department, although nationally demand has kept up with supply.[28] The consequences of this de-

[27] In recent years in some university departments, junior faculty participated in decision making involving voting on new appointments and chairmanships. However, it is questionable as to how "independent" such voting actually is.

[28] J. K. Folger et al., *Human Resources and Higher Education,* p. 68. While this is the most recent publication on supply and demand of scientific manpower, the picture seems to be rapidly changing in 1970 with a decreasing demand.

pendency influence the composition and the direction of the university department.

In essence, senior faculty members decide who enters the department, and therefore who their colleagues will be. The chairman of the university department can play both a subtle positive initiating influence, or a less subtle role based on the naked power of his political position and liaison role with the university administration. The chairman presides at departmental meetings and can, if he wishes, exercise a veto power; in this way he very frequently exerts a kind of negative influence on the composition of the department and in this way also limits the autonomy of faculty members—an autonomy that often has been exaggerated.[29]

The crucial factors in the issues of department composition and research and intellectual direction of the department are that they touch in a most fundameintal manner on the security and working environment of the scientist. As a matter of fact, they touch on the very survival of the scientist in that particular research setting. If the department should acquire several or a majority of scientists hostile to a particular individual, they can deny him rewards, recommendations, working space, students, and funds. In doing so they are of course destroying his working environment for productivity and creativity. In a sense, control of departmental composition can take on the character of the building of a protected sanctuary or a mutual admiration society. It is a disease that many weak college and even university departments fall prey to, saved sometimes only by the presence of one or two strong individualists who succeed in breaking the labored steps to departmental conformity.

In acquiring the status of senior faculty, the individual faculty member has ordinarily conferred on him the crucial right of participating as a voting member in all decisions of the department. "This is the real significance of the importance of tenure. Tenure, in itself, while it confers security and academic freedom on the faculty members, is not as important to him in his daily working environment as his role in the participative management of the department. As a trained professional scientist, he needs an authority system which allows him to search, discover, analyze, and publish his findings subject only to the pre-established impersonal criteria of science. He needs an authority system which permits autonomy and protects his self-esteem."[30] By participating in the management of the department, the scientist can try and often succeed in providing this, thus permitting the presence of that most important ingredient in his conception of a "climate of discovery." The distinguish-

[29] The chairman, in some universities, cannot exercise such powers.
[30] Simon Marcson, *American Behavioral Scientist,* **6,** No. 4, 37.

ing characteristic of the university as a research setting seems to be that it provides the strongest motivation and the highest quality educational experience as over and against industrial and governmental research settings.

GOVERNMENT AS A RESEARCH SETTING

Of the three major research settings in the United States, government is the smallest in scientific manpower although it is the major source of research and development funds. The federal government employed 10 percent of the total number of scientists in 1968, or a total of 29,666.[31] The National Science Foundation estimates the R & D spending by all sectors of the economy in 1970 is expected to be at a level of $27.2 billion, and the federal government expects to perform $3.6 billion of R & D in its own laboratories.[32] These research and development activities are conducted in a large number of settings. The total number of laboratory field stations, part of installations where R & D is conducted, networks of monitoring stations with perhaps an R & D nucleus, and possibly facilities of other types, all owned and operated by the federal government, may lie in the thousands. "There does not appear to exist anywhere a full and accurate compilation."[33] The total number of employees in all of these installations is "more than 300,000 scientists, engineers, and technicians who perform research and development in these laboratories . . ."[34]

The professional scientific personnel are to be found almost entirely distributed between R & D activities and management and administration. A little over 12,000 are in R & D, and somewhat over 10,000 in management and administration. *A little more than half of the scientists* in research and development were in applied research and the remainder in basic research. The total number of doctorate scientists in government

31 National Science Foundation, *American Science Manpower, 1968*, Washington, D.C., 1969, p. 69.

32 National Science Foundation, "National Patterns of R & D Resources," Washington D.C., 1969, pp. 7–8. The federal government financed more than 60 percent of all R & D conducted within the United States during 1967.

33 Committee on Government Operations, "A Case Study of the Utilization of Federal Laboratory Resources," November, 1966, U.S. Government Printing Office, Washington, D.C., 1966, p. 4. The difference between this figure and the figure of 29,666 rests on the fact that the smaller figure is based on the National Register of Scientific Technical Personnel, 1968, and therefore presumably denotes professional staff only.

34 National Science Foundation, *American Science Manpower, 1968*, Washington, D.C., 1969, p. 69.

Table 5   Number of Scientists by Primary Work Activity in Federal Government Employment, 1968

Scientific and Technical Field	Number
R & D	12,249
Basic research	5,664
Applied research	6,060
Management or administration of R & D	10,680
Teaching	294
Production and inspection	1,087
Consulting	866
Exploration, forecasting, and reporting	2,333
Other	1,362
Not employed	—
No report	795
Total	29,666

Source. National Science Foundation, *American Science Manpower, 1968,* Washington, D.C., 1969, p. 69.

employment equaled exactly the number in basic research 6669, and constituted a little less (47%) than half the total number of doctorate scientists in the government research setting.

Civil Service

Utilization of scientists by government differs from employment in the industrial and university research settings.[35] Employment in the federal government is regulated by an established system of rules and regulations of the Civil Service Commission functioning under congressional legislation. Industry and the university, however, have greater latitude than government in developing rules and regulations covering employment conditions. Industry can be and is sensitive to the labor market, while the university is influenced by its own conditions, customs, and traditions. At the same time, it should be noted that government, industry, and university are not homogeneous and conforming entities. As a matter of fact, Vollmer points out that "there appear to be more differences in employment conditions for research personnel within the federal government and within private industry than between industry and government."[36] Vollmer also states that the general thrust of the government

[35] Vollmer, p. 47.
[36] *Ibid.*

research laboratory is in expanding fundamental scientific research, while industry has tended to devote more attention to applied R & D.[37]

The Civil Service Act of 1883 created a Civil Service Commission whose function it was to recruit government employees on the basis of the merit system and to act as a policeman of this system. Since that time the Commission has increased its duties but has ceased to function as the executive branch's centralized personnel agent charged with recruiting, hiring, and dismissing. It does retain the overall concern of maintaining a high level of talent in government laboratories and modifying the bureaucratic barriers to such goals. The rules governing the civil service system in general, and the commission in particular, are those enacted by Congress. These regulations and those that cover almost all other aspects of the system are codified in the Federal Personnel Manual. At the same time, the Commission argues that its regulations allow the necessary flexibility, but that the personnel staffs of the various agencies do not make use of this flexibility in the rules. Two sources of flexibility are inherent in the system: (1) the fact that agencies can create or eliminate a position, or expand or reduce its duties and responsibilities before it is classified, and in this way custom-tailor the man to the job or vice-versa, and (2) the existence of certain alloted "excepted positions" outside the civil service schedule. However, whatever flexibility there is, it is unevenly utilized by the great variety of agency personnel officers and directors of research laboratories.

The government research organization is not troubled by the type of pressures that afflict the industrial or university research laboratories. The government laboratory is not concerned with either seeking to contribute to corporate profits or contributing to fundamental knowledge in a highly competitive publication race. However, while the government laboratory's activities are not for the most part devoted to the development of products, there is pressure on for the development of "useful hardware" within a limited time span.

The underlying problems for the government are not of the type faced by the industry scientist of a conflict between corporate goals and scientific goals. While the problems do include to some extent conflict of individual sicentist goals and organizational goals, the major problems arise out of the attempt to function within a well-equipped and well-supported laboratory enmeshed within a vast organizational apparatus with a multiplicity of goals that are not always clear or stable. The researcher's problem is more one of pursuing his career within a rigid social system without being forced into the mold of passive acceptance of

[37] *Ibid.,* pp. 43–44.

the bureaucracy of the given government agency or the rigidities of civil service. The problem for the scientist in the government research setting is one of remaining an effective professional scientist and engineer and not succumbing to the norms of low utilization so often present in vast, intricate scientific bureaucracies.[38]

The professional in a government laboratory, more so than in a large university, functions essentially within a bureaucratic setting. Bureaucracy in the government research setting constitutes a social system that, through its own rigidities, impersonality, hierarchical stratification, close personal controls, and inability to readily modify its characteristics, creates a series of conflicts for the professional employee. The training of the professional employee has instilled in him career concerns of autonomy, recognitions, and self-realization. These are for him the bases of creativity and the foundations for unique contributions. Organization concerns are rules, procedures, and the maintenance of organizational norms and minor accomplishments. The consequences of these organizational traits for the individual are pressures for conformity and compatability. For the scientist the dilemma is one of whether to move in the direction of an autonomous scientific environment, or toward that of compatability and acceptance of the organization's norms.

Research Administration

As in the industrial organization, career choice is between research as a bench scientist and development work or climbing the administration ladder. Since about 80 percent[39] of the government's R & D money is contracted out to industry and the university, the R & D system has a high proportion of administrative positions and the work environment provides for this type of career line. The result is that many government scientists find that they are actually contract officers instead of researchers. They are faced with the frustrating job of riding herd on an interesting research project instead of actually doing the work themselves. Of course, there are some areas where the research and publication opportunities for scientists are good, but the fact is the publication rate for government scientists is low, but not as low as that for industry.

Some government scientists do remain in research and rise to higher civil service salary levels in spite of the limitations. The number, however, is relatively small. The reason for this is that if a scientist wants to reach

---

[38] Marcson, *Scientists in Government,* p. 3.
[39] Simon Marcson, "Technical Men in Government," *Science and Technology* (January 1968) 64.

high professional salary levels he must assume increasing administrative responsibilities. It seems therefore that it is difficult for a scientist to rise to the top grades without assuming heavy administrative responsibilties which severely limit his opportunity for research work.

For many in government research, administration is a natural outgrowth of their work. Both scientists and engineers in government service quickly become aware of the complex hierarchical structures they are working in and learn that the most recognized form of status advancement is the administration ladder.[40] In the course of the scientist's work, he may develop a line of research which shows fruitful results, and he acquires several assistants. This new supervisory activity is legitimized with the rank of "section head." As a supervisor, the scientist devotes more and more time to administrative paper work, meetings, and being assimilated into the laboratory's power structure. New administrative aspirations emerge, and the next higher position of "branch head" becomes important. The position of branch head has more power and prestige, and it also has more of a part in the decision-making process, budgeting, and manpower assignments. Increasingly, the scientist becomes identified with the organization rather than his own professional work.

While there are a limited number of avenues to higher formal status in any organization, the government laboratory's table of organization and budgetary controls are usually tighter than those in industry and university, which raises special problems of career mobility. As a result, the procedure for conferring formal status consists of two systems:[41] ascription-oriented and achievement-oriented procedures. On the one hand, within the ascription framework, rank is automatically conferred on an individual without reference to significant tests of performance or competence but rather on the basis of such characteristics as age, seniority, or length of government service. On the other hand, within the achievement framework, rank sometimes is left open to be filled by competition, and individual effort is subjected to a variety of objective tests.

There are essentially three ways of attaining high formal status in the government hierarchy.[42] One channel to higher status involves starting as a government employee early in one's career, achieving tenure, and gradually progressing to higher position by means of promotions based on seniority. A second method of attaining higher rank is by beginning at a high civil service salary level by virtue of previous professional

40 *Ibid.,* p. 66.

41 Simon Marcson, "Government Bureaucracy and The Scientist," paper presented at ASA meetings, September 1966, p. 15.

42 Simon Marcson, "Career Development of Scientists in Government," paper presented at ASA meetings, September 1967, p. 3.

experience or an advanced educational level. Finally, a third method of attaining high rank represents an institutionalized evasion of the official promotional system. This is accomplished by transfers within government to a higher civil service level without suffering the disadvantage of losing seniority.

The Federal Personnel System, Civil Service Commission rules, and individual agency procedures stress security and tenure. Scientists in acknowledging the advantages of government employment emphasize the values of security and tenure. They stress the point of job security in the face of cyclical economic fluctuations. In addition, after they have served a 3-year probationary period, members of a government research organization, or as a matter of fact any government employee, cannot be dismissed unless the agency gives "sufficient reason" to the Civil Service Commission. In instances of declared reductions in force, government employees with tenure may be separated from their positions without the "sufficient reason" demanded under the rules of the Civil Service Commission. The tenure rules have "the function of enhancing job security and protecting the civil service employee from political interference; it also has the unintended effect of reinforcing the time-on-the-job aspects of advancement.[43]

The civil service system, however, is not without some of the characteristics of an achievement system. The U. S. Civil Service has attempted to infuse the concept of achievement into government employment and has stressed the introduction of merit awards. This is especially important in basic research areas where individuals can do autonomous work and can make scientific contributions with which they can become identified. The government research organization, then, has two competing systems which impinge on the individual employee: the one of ascription and the other of achievement. A traditionally organized research agency emphasizes ascription, a dynamic and changing one emphasizes achievement.

Scientists in government, especially engineers, besides placing great emphasis on security and tenure,[44] have a higher rate of dissatisfaction[45]

[43] Marcson, *Science and Technology* (January 1968) 68.

[44] Vollmer points out, in *Applications of the Behavioral Sciences to Research Management: An Initial Study in the Office of Aerospace Research*, pp. 70–71, ". . . a comprehensive study by Kilpatrick, Cummings, and Jennings has shown that among those outside federal government service, the image of what government employment has to offer most closely parallels the occupational values of those of lower educational and occupational attainments, i.e., job security and fringe benefits, rather than opportunities for advancement and self-development. However, those in federal service offer opportunities for challenging work self-determination, self-development, worthwhile service, and a sense of accomplishment."

[45] The study by the Committee on Scientists and Engineers for Federal Governmental

about salary prospects than do their colleagues in industry.[46] "Two-thirds of the government scientists and engineers are dissatisfied with their prospects for salary advancement; in industry, only one-fourth are dissatisfied. There is no other area of major importance in this survey in which the satisfaction level of government respondents is so far below that in industry."[47] The values of security and tenure of which salary is an intrinsic part are of crucial importance in bureaucracies in which position and office is emphasized. The social system that engenders such values stimulates attitudes of conformity to the organization, acceptance of authority and its implied policies and goals, and compliance with the organization's career boundary lines.[48] The highly talented scientist who finds the government bureaucracy distasteful can do one of two things: move to a position in the industrial or the university research setting, or become so essential through his talents to his government research agency that none of the bureaucratic or organizational problems are inflicted upon him, leaving him free to pursue his professional scientific interests and goals.

Value Climates

An attempt to measure the underlying reasons for the actions and perceptions of scientists and engineers in a government "space center laboratory" was undertaken by Marcson.[49] A factorial analysis was made indicating that four factors accounted for most of the variance involved in the correlation between the 20 adjectives the laboratory scientists responded to. The four factors were labeled as follows: factor 1—brisk; factor 2—anxiety; factor 3—sociable; and factor 4—overorganized. The first factor, brisk, pertains primarily to instrumental relationships at the center and to its formal organization. Factor 2, anxiety, represents criticism of the organization in both instrumental (formal) and expressive

Programs, "Survey of Attitudes of Scientists and Engineers in Government and Industry," Washington, D.C., 1957, reports that "government scientists and engineers clearly have some feelings of embarassment about their choice of a career in public service."

46 Committee on Scientists and Engineers for Federal Government Programs, "Survey of Attitudes of Scientists and Engineers in Government and Industry," U.S. Government Printing Office, Washington, D.C., 1957, p. 8.

47 *Ibid.* Another type of high dissatisfaction reported was "half the government respondents and two-thirds of those in industry thought that the overall competence of top management is better in industry than in government."

48 Marcson, *Science and Technology* (January 1968) 68.

49 Marcson, "Research Environment: A Factorial Analysis of a Government Laboratory," paper presented at the Seventh World Congress of Sociology, September 1970, p. 7.

regards (informal), and it focuses upon the formal and informal social organization. Factor 3, sociable, is primarily an expressive factor, dealing with the formal organization. Factor 4, overorganized, expresses criticism of the formal organization.

It is quite possible for these factors of experience structures to seem quite contradictory in nature. However, what must be understood is that each factor represents a different sphere of life at the space center laboratory.[50] When, however, the four factors are combined after the detailed analysis has been made, a total view of a government space center is possible.

The work environment at the space center induced on the part of the scientist a perceptive system by which he evaluated his contributions to the work and productivity of the organization. At the space center the staff members' perceptive system produced a low utilization rating.

This rating occurs within an *organizational social system* of rigidities and frustrations. Governmental organization is too massive and cumbersome for one to try to change it. In time, when the staff member's socialization is complete, he becomes inured and passively accepts the laboratory's way of doing things. He becomes part of the work and the character of the organization. The scientist's motivational levels for performance become adjusted to the workings of the organizational system.[51] The scientist's job becomes one of guiding industry contractors who are more visible when successes are achieved.

This does not mean that the organization is not productive. As a matter of fact, governmental research organizations are often very productive. What is of interest is the consequences of the staff members' self-definition for their own behavior and the motivational levels at which they perform. The results are fairly clear. A passive acceptance of low utilization is productive of low levels of striving. The anxieties and frustrations are motivating factors, but the overorganization and the rigidities in the structure induce passivity and a low level of striving; the strong motivation of the university research setting and its quality educational experience is, for the most part, missing.

INDUSTRY AS A RESEARCH SETTING

With the acceleration of innovation in modern society, industry has gradually become more involved in large-scale research activities. Today

[50] *Ibid.*, p. 15.
[51] Marcson, *Scientists in Government,* p. 501.

Table 6 Total Number of Scientists, by Field, Primary Work Activity, and Type of Employer, 1968

Scientific and Technical Field and Primary Work Activity	Total	Type of Employer							
		Educational Institutions	Federal Government	Other Government	Non-profit Organizations	Industry and Business	Self-Employed	Military	Other
All fields	297,942	117,766	29,666	10,081	11,204	95,776	6,462	7,155	1,729
R & D (A)	96,036	38,668	12,249	2,538	4,970	34,271	472	1,492	556
Basic research	46,171	28,818	5,664	1,005	2,315	6,675	132	739	309
Applied research	38,841	9,467	6,060	1,494	2,425	18,034	286	671	201
Management or administration (B)	62,370	10,270	10,680	4,044	2,921	30,910	792	2,506	437
Management or administration R & D	28,568	3,680	4,668	1,175	1,517	16,321	209	683	171
Teaching	62,087	60,230	294	291	218	254	39	366	167
Production and inspection	16,847	250	1,087	548	209	14,057	332	205	92
Consulting	12,334	2,181	866	955	1,642	3,222	2,952	249	124
Exploration, forecasting, and reporting	14,365	791	2,333	630	456	7,637	1,210	1,164	99
Other	8,416	1,854	1,362	657	425	2,361	272	751	161
Not employed	12,707	—	—	—	—	—	—	—	—
No report	12,280	3,494	795	318	363	2,564	373	422	93

Source. National Science Foundation, *American Science Manpower, 1668,* Washington, D.C., 1969, p. 69.

there are more than 5,500 firms engaged in company-owned research laboratories.[52] In addition, there are more than 500 independent commercial laboratories. Industrial research laboratories are the second largest employers of doctorate scientists, utilizing in 1968, 24,099 employees.[53] The median salary for these doctorate scientists, however, is higher than for any other sector of United States research activities. In 1968 industry paid its scientists a median salary of $17,500.[54]

The total number of scientists employed by industry was 95,776 in 1968. This constitutes nearly one-third of all scientists engaged in scientific and technical work as primary work. About one-third or 34,271 of the total number employed in industry were in R & D in 1968.[55] Industry utilized 73 percent or 18,034 of manpower in R & D in applied research, and the remaining 27 percent or 6,675 in basic research.

The industrial sector accounts for about 70 percent of the total United States expenditures in 1967.[56] The total funds invested by industry in research and development in 1967 was $16.4 billion; this included the federal support industry received. Four percent of industrial expenditures on R & D was for basic research ($655 million).[57] The remaining industrial R & D funds were allocated in 1967 to applied research ($3.0 billion) and to development (12.8 billion). The aircraft and missiles industry accounted for 35 percent of all industrial R & D spending in 1967:[58] "the industry that accounted for the second largest dollar (3.7 billion) volume of applied research and development in 1967."[59]

While industrial research had its beginnings at the turn of the century, research laboratories devoted to basic research did not begin to emerge in significant numbers until World War II. Since then, both doctorates in science and well-equipped laboratories devoted to both basic and applied research in industry have become precedent. Industrial managers' caution about the extent of their investment in basic research which may benefit the entire industry but which does not necessarily improve the competitive position of a particular firm, has led to a rather limited activity in

[52] William Mayhall, *Corporate R & D Administration*, American Management Association, New York, 1970, p. 12.
[53] National Science Foundation, *American Science Manpower, 1968*, Washington, D.C., 1969, p. 213.
[54] *Ibid.*, p. 232.
[55] *Ibid.*, p. 69.
[56] National Science Foundation, "Research and Development in Industry, 1967," Washington, D.C., 1969, p. 5.
[57] *Ibid.*, p. 11.
[58] *Ibid.*
[59] *Ibid.*, p. 12.

basic research. Industrial scientists engaged in basic research constitute about 15 percent of the total number of doctorate scientists.[60]

Bureaucratic Settings

With most of its scientists in applied research, the industrial research laboratory's environment has quite a different character and climate than that of the university. Entrepreneurial opportunities for the laboratory's staff are at a minimum. Bureaucratic organizational influences predominate. A structured system exists to integrate the work of many for solution of a limited number of specific projects. In most such organizations large-scale research is conducted by teams of technical specialists. In some cases this results in the concentration of hundreds, even thousands, of research people in one location. Under these circumstances there is need for a large administrative body and a highly structured hierarchy modeled after the parent company.

Industry managers rely on strict accountability to prevent wasted time and to reduce the number of poorly conceived projects and to motivate and lead resarch scientists toward company-oriented research. The result is a continuous effort on the part of the industrial laboratory to achieve accountability, control, direction, productivity, and market sensitivity.

Hall believes that organizations utilizing professionals need to move in the direction of less bureaucratization.[61] He notes that professionals tend to emphasize performance-based criteria of technical competence, while bureaucracy often depends on other criteria. "Since this is such an important value for the individual, it can be a source for such professional-organizational conflict as does exist."[62] It is at the same time important to realize that not all segments of the same research organization experience the same degree of bureaucratization or professionalism and therefore "may not present the professional with a work environment that is necessarily a source of conflict."[63] Industrial research laboratories have basic sections which have many, if not most, of the characteristics of the university as a research setting. At the same time, the bureau-

[60] National Science Foundation, *American Science Manpower, 1968*, Washington, D.C., p. 69.
[61] Richard H. Hall, "Some Organizational Considerations in the Professional Organizational Relationship," *Administrative Science Quarterly* 12, No. 3 (December 1967), 478.
[62] *Ibid.*
[63] Hall, *Administrative Science Quarterly*, 12, No. 3 (December 1967), 463.

cratic orientation of industry develops a demand for disciplined compliance with procedures that often create conflict.[64]

Bureaucratic forms of organization in industry are buttressed by the fact that research managers have ties to industrial management. Some management research studies have also endorsed it. Likert finds, for instance, that "a tightly knit effectively functioning social system"[65] enhances productivity. Thompson points out that "the present common practice of annual performance ratings by supervisors would probably have to be dropped. . . . It is clearly inconsistent with increasing professionalism, since professional standing is not determined by a hierarchial superior."[66] It is Thompson's view that the bureaucratic organizational approach which utilizes job descriptions does not readily accommodate professional work, rather peer evaluation will tend to be the practice in the innovative organization. A recent survey of research management assumptions and practices that prevail in industry is effectively summarized in the following conclusion.

As these statements indicate, the management of research and development is subject to many variables, one of which is the research managers themselves. These men are usually called from industry to campus and the laboratory to assume managerial responsibility, often with little management training. As a consequence, to perform their managerial duties they have to rely on their general observations, native intelligence, and intuition. Since these men are usually fully occupied with technical matters they should be provided with as much training, guidance, and assistance as the company can afford.[67]

Pelz[68] studied the consequences of organizational environment for R & D among scientists in universities, government, and industry. While the data are based on a large number of individuals and a variety of organizations, the study is not represented as a sample of research organizations or of individual scientists. Pelz comes to the following general conclusions about the environments of the most productive scientists and engineers.[69]

Effective scientists were self-directed by their own ideas, and valued freedom.

[64] Blau, *American Journal of Sociology* **73**, No. 4 (January 1968), p. 456.
[65] Likert, R., *New Patterns of Management,* McGraw-Hill, New York, 1961, p. 99.
[66] Victor A. Thompson, "Bureaucracy and Innovation," *Administrative Science Quarterly* (June 1965), 18.
[67] Mayhall, p. 26.
[68] D. C. Pelz and Frank M. Andrews, *Scientists in Organizations: Productive Climates for Research and Development,* Wiley, New York, 1966, p. 7.
[69] *Ibid.*

But at the same time they allowed several other people a voice in shaping their directions; they interacted vigorously with colleagues.

Effective scientists did not limit their activities either to the world of "application" or to the world of "pure science" but maintained an interest in both; their work was diversified.

Effective scientists were not fully in agreement with their organizations in terms of their interests; what they personally enjoyed did not necessarily help them advance in the structure.

Effective scientists tended to be motivated by the same kinds of things as their colleagues. At the same time, however, they differed from their colleagues in the styles and strategies with which they approach their work.

In effective older groups, the members interacted vigorously and preferred each other as collaborators, yet they held each other at an emotional distance and felt free to disagree on technical strategies.

The study design, however, is of such a character that it minimizes the generalizability of any findings concerning organizational impact on performance.

Career Ladders

The industrial research organization in its definition of tasks, chain of command, and span of control places its members in a dependent and subordinate employee relationship. The result is a hierarchical structure with a status system providing rank and reward satisfactions to its organization members. Both the ranking system and the system of satisfactions differ for scientific personnel and for its administrative staff in the industrial research organization. The ranking systems for scientists in basic and applied research is a simple one which moves the scientist from staff member to associate scientist and senior scientist. The administrative research ladder is more complex and can carry a scientist to the presidency of the entire company. The ladder begins with group leader and goes on to section head, department research manager, laboratory research director, laboratory vice-president of research, company vice-president of research, and company executive vice-president of research.

Autonomy versus Integration

Central in industrial research settings, as in government and universities, is the theme of conflict between autonomy and the integration of the professional in the research of the industrial laboratory.[70] The utiliza-

---

70 Kornhauser, p. 195.

tion of the professional scientist in industry reveals the strain between autonomy and integration. Large-scale industrial research tends to demand an organization involving work groups rather than individual effort. The result is that most of the industrial laboratory staff are members of work groups, but by no means all are.[71] The occurrence of assigned research modifies the autonomy of the scientist. However, feelings of resentment about the limitations in autonomy depend upon the type of supervision.[72] In addition, the occurrence of work groups does not necessarily force the scientist into a subordinate relationship in a team. The structure of the team or work group in research is of such a character that it permits its members latitude for independent work.[73] At the same time, the absence of autonomy, that is, being dependent on others according to Hagstrom[74] is "terrifying." If the research laboratory does not choose to recognize the professional scientist's autonomy, or "his" choice of problem, then the organization runs the risk of undermining the motivation of the organization's scientists.[75]

Accommodations

As management seeks to incorporate the scientists in its organization, it is faced with the task of satisfying their main needs and wants. In so doing the organization can release the potential for productivity in the sciences. The key to this objective is an interlinked syndrome of recognition–autonomy–motivation. In turn, autonomy can provide the impetus and high productivity as long as the work situation provides some impetus.[76] The work situation has this impetus within it when there is a possibility of seeing the consequences of one's research. The resulting impact of interlinking of recognition, autonomy, and visibility of results is high motivation for the professional scientist. According to Gordon,[77] these processes can be undermined as the goals of the scientist are delimited and his freedom decreased by the organizations engaged in applied research that threaten the scientist's autonomy.

[71] Marcson, *The Scientist in American Industry,* p. 96.
[72] Likert, p. 97; Pelz, p. 97; Marcson, *The Scientist in American Industry,* p. 97.
[73] Marcson, *The Scientist in American Industry,* p. 97.
[74] Warren O. Hagstrom, *The Scientific Community,* Basic Books, New York, 1965, p. 22.
[75] Kornhauser, p. 56.
[76] Simon Marcson, "The Utilization of Scientific and Engineering Manpower in Industry," *California Management Review* 12, No. 4 (Summer 1970), 38; Barney G. Glaser, *Organizational Scientists: Their Professional Careers,* Bobbs-Merrill, New York, 1964, p. 8.
[77] G. Gordon and Sue Marquis, "Freedom and Control in Four Types of Scientific Settings," *American Behavioral Scientist,* 6 (December 1962), 37–42.

Hagstrom advances the view that industry as well as government is developing accommodations to the tensions between the autonomy of the professional and the organizational control of the professions. "The strains between professional autonomy and the control of professions lead to the development of organizational forms that can accommodate both. Industrial and governmental organizations have found forms capable of accommodating both their own interests and those of their science employees; and American society through forms such as the contract system, appears to be finding ways of accommodating science institutions to government."[78]

Kornhauser defines industry's accommodation as one of balancing the pressures toward the achievement of immediate advantages as over against protecting the integrity of the research function. "Where research is turned into a mere search operation for manufacturing or sales, its distinctive competence to contribute to large-range goals will be rendered ineffective. Much depends on the opportunity for research to free itself from immediate control by other parts of the organization. The central process generating this autonomy is the social differentiation of the research function."[79] It is necessary, according to Kornhauser, to clearly separate research from the other organizational operations, resulting in the protection of the integrity of research goals. It is in this way that the tensions between the goals of science and the goals of industry can be accommodated, states Kornhauser.

Another type of accommodation is pointed out by Laporte in the tendency of research organizations to modify traditional structural arrangements. Laporte states, "The dependence of managers on scientists for achieving technical goals leads to a modification of traditional bureaucratic devices in operating large organizations."[80] Insofar as the research organization responds to the scientist's working values, the organization changes away from control of subordinates toward individual autonomy. In doing so the industrial research organization undergoes not only accommodation, but acculturative[81] change.

According to Marcson, the scientist in industry in the course of changing and adapting to the research setting "develops four types of career goals: (a) the scientist who is dedicated to scientific research although his conceptions of scientific research may change; (b) the scientist who is administratively oriented and proceeds to build his career within the

---

[78] Hagstrom, p. 296.
[79] Kornhauser, p. 42.
[80] Todd R. LaPorte, "Conditions of Strain and Accommodation in Industrial Research Organizations," *Administrative Science Quarterly,* **10,** No. 1 (June 1965), 37.
[81] Marcson, *The Scientist in American Industry,* p. 62.

confines of the industrial research organization; (c) the scientist who after years of successful achievement comes to realize the financial and prestige ceiling in research and becomes interested in moving into administration; (d) the scientist who after years of achievement comes to feel that he can no longer compete and becomes interested in moving into administration.[82] Type a, the largest number of scientists in the industrial research laboratory changes eventually from having a major interest in basic research to one in applied research. The change in research goals expresses industry's research management's concern in motivating its scientists toward effective industry-oriented research.

The two different ladders for scientists and administrators gradually came into being to enable distinguished scientists and specialists to advance in rank and salary without taking on managerial or supervisory functions. A professional promotion ladder also provides the additional advantage of greater freedom for the research staff and greater opportunities for purely scientific rewards. Industrial firms have also supported and expanded the professional ranking system by including time off for attendance at professional meetings sponsored not only by professional associations but by the company itself. Industrial research organizations provide payment for professional dues, tuition refunds for further professional training, and opportunities for publication of research findings. By and large, however, Kornhauser points out that "industry tends to slight professional incentives and rewards, even for its research scientists and engineers."[83]

The Authority System

The industrial organization, because of its bureaucratic character, rests on a high concern with the legitimacy of power of command and designated office holders functioning within organizationally defined rules. The ensuing policies, sanctions, and goals constitute the organization's authority system. In industry the company's authority system, because of its hierarchical and bureaucratic command structure, permeates the research setting.

In the transfer of its industrial practices to the research laboratory in the company, there appear such practices as frequent detailed reports and the extensive use of review and accounting controls.[84] The industrial firm's inherent tendency is to develop procedures and policies which

82 Ibid., p. 71.
83 Kornhauser, p. 135.
84 Mayhall, p. 23.

are more amenable to routinization and standardization of its work. In its interest in research or developing new research concepts which will ultimately aid corporate product development whether in basic or applied research, industrial research management must foster an environment that meets the conflicting demands of scientific independence and integration.[85] Industrial research organizations alternately swing from attempts at integration to programs of independence on the part of the research manager. The industrial research organization frequently fails to see that adequate research direction does not necessarily destroy independence, while it does help maintain an integrated organization.[86]

Marcson has described the organizational authority system prevailing in industry as executive authority.[87] Executive authority has particular relevance to the business corporation. The traditional executive system found in all areas of industry places decision making in the hands of a "chief executive officer and his appointed staff and, to a certain extent, a board of directors. The chief executive is responsible for the performance of his immediate subordinates, the top executives. These in turn assume responsibility for their subordinate officers, and so on down the line. Within prescribed limits responsibility may be delegated, but the ultimate control or authority rests with the chief executive. The chief executive or the executive in the traditional industrial organization functions without recourse to significant considerations of the views of subordinates. Within prescribed limits he issues directives and orders. In the eyes of his subordinates, he holds the position of "boss." The traditional industrial organization that is tied to this type of authority system tends to resist the emergence of any authority system for professional employees.

The transference of this system of authority to industrial research evokes not only resentment, but resistance. Arbitrary authority on the part of laboratory directors or research managers runs contrary to the scientist's self-conception of his status and professional ethos. Research management positions involve full-time duties requiring expertness in managerial decision making. It is as a result presumed, that since the executive occupies a managerial position and fills this function, he is now expert in this area. The executive office holder now occupies a dominant

85 Clayton P. Alderfer, in "The Organizational Syndrome," *Administrative Science Quarterly* (December 1967), p. 441, points out, "If the concept of organizational climate is a valid one, then the longer a person stays with an organization, the more he experiences and becomes a part of the climate. At first he is socialized by the system; later he becomes an agent of the socialization process."

86 Marcson, *California Management Review*, 12, No. 4 (Summer 1970), p. 33.

87 Marcson, *The Scientist in American Industry*, p. 121.

position in both fields of science and management, and his authority is based on his being an incumbent of a particular position.

The professional scientist is resentful of this type of authority because its origins and legitimacy come from outside the professional unit.[88] Whether or not immediate supervisory officers are professionals, quite often professionals find themselves subordinate to top level nonprofessional management personnel. The result is that the professional scientist views and accepts his nonprofessional supervisor with some reservations and resentment.

It is for the above reasons that Likert[89] points out that this type of management approach involves the critical weakness of overlooking motivation. Likert states that the underlying assumptions of industrial management depend on management textbooks which emphasize authority and control as the basis of effective administration. Motivation for the professional scientist cannot be encompassed in a contractual system command, duty, and obedience. The scientist's motivation is tied more effectively to an authority system based on persuasion and indirect control.

Orth[90] defines the scientist's need for a creative industial research climate as depending on management's recognition of

. . . the respect accorded to professional status in the academic world; the traditional aversion of scientists to any discipline except its own; the scientists' need for and appreciation of first-class facilities; colleagues of high professional status; and work assignments of real interest; the value of opportunities for mobility; and the importance of reseach.[91]

Orth further advances the view that "companies should not try to change professionals into "organization men" and expect them to be creative."[92]

Industrial research management in recent years has come to recognize that executive authority need not be arbitrary. Many research organi-

[88] W. F. Whyte, *Organizational Behavior*, R. D. Irwin, and Dorsey Press, Homewood, Ill., 1969, p. 597.

[89] Rensis Likert, "Developing Patterns of Management," American Management Association, General Management Series, Number 182, 1956, p. 16.

[90] Charles D. Orth, 3rd, "The Optimum Climate for Industrial Research," *Harvard Business Review* (March–April 1959) 57–64. In Charles D. Orth, 3rd, Joseph C. Bailey, and Francis W. Wolek, *Administering Research and Development: The Behavior of Scientists and Engineers in Organizations*, R. D. Irwin and Dorsey Press, Homewood, Ill., 1964, p. 59, D. G. Moore and R. Renck point out, ". . . there are indications of a relationship between productivity in research and professional employee morale."

[91] *Ibid.*

[92] Mayhall, p. 23.

zation managements seek to gain the consent and participation of their subordinates in the decision-making process. The spread of some "participative" involvement of scientists in decision making has not modified the authority hierarchy. The trend in many cases is therefore to develop a working environment based on a mixture of executive authority and colleague authority. As a new model of authority emerges in the industrial research setting, however, the two differing authority systems are not always compatible, leading to a certain amount of strain. The dynamics of the industrial research setting do not permit stagnation or the encrustation of any one tradition. The industrial research setting is exploring new pathways to research achievement and excellence. In its restlessness to attain greater prestige and performance levels, it is in strong competition with the university research setting in the organization and administration of research.

CHAPTER SEVEN

Agencies of Research Support: Some Sociological Perspectives[1]

Robert L. Hall, University of Illinois at Chicago Circle

Agencies of research support are human organizations, and they share many characteristics with other organizations which have been more extensively studied, such as industrial, medical, and educational organizations. There are also important differences among these agencies which systematically mediate their effects upon their environment. The purposes of this chapter are to describe the morphology and characteristic behavior of the genus, research supporting agency; to examine some important differences among species and individual variants within the genus; to describe the ways in which agencies of research support in the contemporary United States relate to their environment.

Hard data are rarely available on these matters, and this chapter is

1 Much in this chapter has benefited from discussions with academic colleagues and with staff members in granting agencies. Earlier drafts were read by Steven Alger, Ronald Corwin, Boyd Keenan, Saad Nagi, James Norr, Henry Riecken, Norman Storer, and Gerald Swatez, and their comments have improved this chapter. However, I have ignored their advice often enough so that I must accept full responsibility for the chapter's weaknesses.

based largely upon informal interviewing and observation, including participant observation. The chapter is intended to be suggestive, not definitive; to provide a perspective and some hypotheses, not to give answers; to stimulate research, not substitute for it. It would be helpful to have comparative information from other nations, but such comparisons are outside the scope of this chapter. It would be helpful to have many systematic studies of granting agencies so that the following analysis could be less speculative. Such studies are not available. Before proceeding to an analysis of the functioning of agencies of research support in the United States, it is useful to provide some background in a broad description of the principal sources and types of research support.

MAJOR SOURCES AND DESTINATIONS OF UNITED STATES RE-SEARCH SUPPORT

The sources of financial support for research in the United States are numerous and varied. The system of support (if it can be called a system) is a chaotic and pluralistic one in which some classes of research can receive support from a great variety of sources and some classes find no available source. Scientists, always suspicious of any centralization of authority in research, have generally praised and defended this untidy pluralistic system of support. President Kennedy's science advisor, Jerome Wiesner, is reputed to have said that one of his functions was to protect the anarchy of science (Greenberg, 1967, p. 115).

The overwhelming portion of recent financial support for research and development (R & D) has been provided by agencies of the federal government, and those agencies receive most attention in this chapter. Reports of support are usually divided into three categories: basic research, applied research, and development. These distinctions become important in understanding agencies of research support and the way in which they relate to their environment.[2]

In order to convey briefly the division among major sources of support, let us consider five sectors which are distinguished in many statistics: federal government, state and local governments, industry, universities and colleges (including research centers administered by universities), and other nonprofit organizations (including private foundations). Each of these sectors may be viewed both as a source of research funds and as

---

[2] For valuable discussions of the problems and limitations of such classifications, see Brooks (1968), Kidd (1959b), and Shepard (1956).

a performer of research, as shown in Table 1. Of all funds for R & D in 1970, the federal government provided 55 percent and industry provided 40 percent, other sectors being only minor contributors (see columns X and Z, Table 1). However, if we focus on *transfers* of funds among sectors for the conduct of R & D, the dominance of the federal government becomes even clearer. That is, if we omit funds spent within a sector for its own research (e.g., money spent by industry for research within industry, by universities for research within universities, etc.), we find that of all funds transferred among sectors, 94 percent originate within the federal government, 4 percent within state and local government, 1 percent in industry, and 1 percent in nonprofit organizations such as private foundations (see columns W and Y, Table 1). Hence the federal government is clearly dominant as a supporter of research performed by others, and private nongovernmental sources, including both private foundations and industry, account for only about 2 percent of such support.

There has been a very substantial growth in federal support for research in recent years. Over the 14 fiscal years from 1956 through 1969, the total federal support for basic research increased from $206 million to $2146 million. This represents an average annual increase on the order of 20 percent (the median is 18 percent, and the mean 20.5 percent). Over the same period the increase for applied research was from $646 million to $3301 million, which represents a median annual percentage increase of about 9 percent, and a mean of about 14 percent. The most recent increases have been smaller; for the period 1964–1969, the mean annual increase was less than 7 percent for basic research, and less than 3 percent for applied research.

Over the 18 years, 1952–1969, in which there have been systematic reports[3] about federal support, support for research has been dominated by six major agencies of government—the Department of Defense (DOD), the National Aeronautics and Space Administration (NASA),[4] the Atomic Energy Commission (AEC), the Department of Health, Education, and Welfare (HEW), the Department of Agriculture (USDA), and the National Science Foundation (NSF). Up through fiscal year 1960, DOD was the single dominant research-supporting agency by any criterion: largest dollar obligations for total research; largest for basic re-

[3] The National Science Foundation has been the major source of data since NSF was created and assigned the function of systematic recording of federal expenditures in this area. Many data in this chapter are drawn from NSF publications, and I am grateful to Benjamin Olsen and Joseph Schuster of NSF for assistance in locating needed information.

[4] Prior to 1958, the National Advisory Committee for Aeronautics.

Table 1 Funds for Research and Development in 1970 (estimated), by Sector Providing Funds and Performing Sector (million $)[a]

Sources of Funds	Performers					Total ($)		Distribution of Sources (%)	
	Federal Government	State and Local Government	Industry[b]	Universities and Colleges[b]	Other Nonprofit Institutions[b]	Intersector Transfers Only[c] (W)	All Funds (X)	Intersector Transfers Only[c] (Y)	All Funds (Z)
Federal government	(3,650)	53	8,500	2,250	600	11,403	15,053	94	55
State and local government	—	(77)	12	380	34	426	503	4	2
Industry	—	2	(10,738)	60	85	147	10,885	1	40
Universities and Colleges	—	1	—	(570)	—	1	571	0	2
Other nonprofit institutions	—	2	—	140	(231)	142	373	1	1
Total, intersector transfers[e]	0	58	8,512	2,830	719	12,119	—	100	—
Total, all funds	3,650	135	19,250	3,400	950	—	27,385	—	100

[a] Source. National Science Foundation (1969b, p. 14, Table 3).
[b] Includes federally funded centers administered by this sector.
[c] Omits parenthetical figures in main diagonal.

search; largest for applied research; largest for development. However, rapid increases of the NASA budget in the post-Sputnik era resulted in NASA's exceeding DOD's obligations for basic research beginning in 1961, and approximately equaling DOD's obligations for total research by the late 1960s, although DOD remained the largest spender for development (National Science Foundation, 1969a, Tables C-93, C-94, C-95, and C-96).

Although DOD was the single clearly dominant agency during the 1940s and 1950s, there were at least three dominant agencies during the 1960s—DOD, NASA, and HEW. A fourth agency—AEC—would be added to this list if we considered R & D combined. A fifth agency—NSF —would be added if we considered importance in basic research only. Over the last 20 years, the importance of nonmilitary agencies of research support has steadily increased relative to that of DOD. It is too early to estimate the effect in the 1970s of recent legislation which broadened NSF's authority to enable it to support applied research.

During the 1950s and 1960s, support by private foundations for scientific research grew in parallel to federal support, although at a very much lower level (NSF, 1969c, Chap. 6). Over the period from 1953 to 1966, support provided by private foundations grew from $36 million to $92 million, an average annual increase of 7.5 percent. The rate of increase declined in the mid-1960s, so that in 1964–1966 the increase was only 3 percent.

Just as a few major federal agencies dominated federal support, a few major foundations dominated support by private foundations (NSF, 1969c, Chap. 6). There are thousands of private foundations in the United States. However, three large foundations—Ford Foundation, Rockefeller Foundation, and John A. Hartford Foundation—with combined assets in excess of $4 billion, gave $56 million in 1966, about 60 percent of that year's total support by private foundations. Of the $45 million in extramural research funds provided by private foundations to universities and colleges in 1966, the three large foundations provided about 60 percent. The 100 foundations with largest R & D expenditures provided about 93 percent of the funds given by all private foundations.

MAJOR DIFFERENCES AMONG RESEARCH-SUPPORTING ORGANIZATIONS

Agencies that support research can be usefully classified in terms of several significant characteristics. Several of these characteristics concern the type of support provided by the agency and correspond roughly to the classifications of scientific activities suggested by Brooks (1968, pp. 55–56). They can be characterized by the way their support is distributed over the three categories, basic research, applied research, and development. They can be characterized in terms of the way that their support is distributed among categories of performers (i.e., who actually conducts the research), such as university, industry, government laboratory, non-profit research institute. They can be characterized in terms of what Brooks called "the social purpose or function of the research," such as health, defense, natural resources, space exploration. They can be characterized in terms of the way that their support is distributed among scientific disciplines.

For each federal agency and their major subdivisions, information on most of the above characteristics is available in NSF's published statistics (1969a). We can illustrate by examining some important differences among several agencies which currently have a major role in supporting at least one of the three major areas—basic research, applied research, and development.

Many differences among agencies are illustrated in Table 2. DOD and NASA are development-oriented agencies whose R & D programs are dominated by hardware development and its associated technological problems. Of the total budget they obligate for R & D, the lion's share goes into development and the secondary share into applied research.[5] Within these agencies a small *proportion* of R & D resources goes into basic research, but they are both major contributors to the support of basic research simply because of the magnitude of their total programs. HEW devotes the largest share of its R & D resources to applied research, with basic research second. AEC is a large supporter of development activities (surpassed only by DOD and NASA) and an important supporter of basic research; but AEC gives relatively little to applied research. NSF has supported almost exclusively basic research; in recent years it has been the only agency spending more on basic research than on either applied research or development. NSF and AEC are the only two that spend more on basic than on applied research.

If we turn our attention to the performer, we find that 90–95 percent of federal research support can be classified in one of three major categories: intramural research (i.e., research within government research organizations), industrial research (including research in industry and in industrially managed centers), and academic research (including research in universities and in university-managed centers). In recent years these three sectors have been about equal in dollar obligations for total re-

[5] See also NSF (1969a, Table 17).

Table 2 Federal Obligations for Research and Development, Classified by Agency, Performer, and Character of Work, Fiscal Year 1969 Estimate (million $)

Performers	Agencies							
	NASA	DOD	HEW	AEC	NSF	USDA	Other	Totals
Basic Research								
Intramural	187.8	87.7	78.5	4.4	11.9	72.5	104.1	546.9
Industrial[a]	329.4	26.0	0	32.8	1.0	0.1	1.4	390.7
University[b]	120.4	158.1	264.0	272.7	216.3	23.3	18.8	1,073.6
Other	7.2	18.8	70.6	13.8	11.6	6.0	6.9	134.9
Subtotal	644.8	290.6	413.1	323.7	240.8	101.9	131.2	2,146.1
Applied Research								
Intramural	270.5	580.2	137.0	0.8	0.3	107.0	174.3	1,270.1
Industrial[a]	256.0	593.2	44.1	33.1	0	0.9	51.0	978.3
University[b]	65.0	120.0	420.7	59.1	4.6	35.8	45.0	750.2
Other	9.0	49.1	192.7	3.4	1.0	1.3	46.0	302.6
Subtotal	600.5	1,342.6	794.6	96.4	5.9	144.9	316.3	3,301.2
Subtotal all research	1,245.3	1,533.1	1,207.7	420.2	246.7	246.8	447.5	5,447.3
Development								
Intramural	358.8	1,337.2	30.7	11.4	0.7	14.1	76.8	1,829.7
Industrial[a]	2,184.9	4,639.9	18.0	735.9	0.2	0	226.0	7,804.9
University[b]	23.6	147.4	27.7	217.8	6.5	0.3	14.8	438.1
Other	3.4	186.2	42.4	50.3	10.8	0.1	34.2	327.4
Subtotal	2,570.7	6,310.7	118.8	1,015.5	18.2	14.5	351.7	10,400.1
Grand total, R & D	3,815.9	7,943.8	1,326.5	1,435.7	264.9	261.3	799.2	15,847.4

[a] Includes federally funded research centers managed by industry.
[b] Includes federally funded research centers managed by universities.

199

search (basic and applied combined). However, development is performed primarily by industry (about 75–80 percent) and secondarily as intramural research (about 15–20 percent), with very little development work in universities. Outside the three major categories of performers, there is a small but sometimes significant category of nonprofit research organizations and, in rare cases, federally funded centers administered by such nonprofit organizations. The total dollar support to these organizations has grown fairly steadily, but in the last 6 or 8 years the proportion of all research support to them has been stable at about 6 percent.[6]

Against this background concerning the distribution of federal support among categories of research performers, we can now examine agencies for their differences as to who are the performers of their research. Some of these differences are illustrated in Table 2. NASA and DOD are industrially oriented, while HEW, AEC, and NSF are university oriented. NASA's and DOD's orientation to industry appears to be associated with their orientation to hardware development but seems to carry over into other areas. For example, they are virtually the only agencies that grant any basic research support to industry, although AEC grants a substantial amount to industrially administered research centers (NSF, 1969a, Tables C-29, C-30, C-31). As another illustration, note in Table 2 that DOD and NASA put about 40–50 percent of their applied research support into industry and only 10–15 percent into universities and university-managed centers, while HEW does almost the opposite, putting about 10 percent into industry and about 50 percent into universities. The Department of Agriculture and the Veterans Administration are examples of agencies oriented primarily to intramural research (NSF, 1969a, Tables 17 and C-12).

Research-supporting agencies differ also with respect to the fields of science for which they provide support. To illustrate, DOD's research support goes primarily into engineering and physical sciences, while the major part of HEW's support goes into the life sciences and social and psychological sciences. Also, NASA's main support goes into engineering and physical sciences, but a substantial secondary portion goes into environmental sciences (NSF, 1969a, Table 17).

The above broad sketch of the relative size and orientation of major federal agencies points up some important characteristics of the agencies, but for many purposes the level of analysis is too gross. For example, HEW is a massive organization with a wide range of different bureaus and offices which support research, including the National Institutes of Health (NIH), the National Institute of Mental Health (NIMH), the Office of

[6] Data in this paragraph come from NSF (1969a, Tables C-98 and C-101).

Education, the Social and Rehabilitation Service, and several others. These separate portions of HEW differ in many of the above characteristics, sometimes strikingly. NIH and NIMH (both parts of the Public Health Service) are alike in supporting essentially no development activity, in supporting somewhat more applied than basic research, and in having universities as their major performers. NIH invests the overwhelming portion of its research money in the life sciences. NIMH also invests heavily in the life sciences but has very substantial support for the social and psychological sciences. The Office of Education has over half of its R & D money in development and far more in applied than basic research, and its support is almost exclusively for the social and psychological sciences. Universities and nonprofit organizations are the principal performers for the Office of Education, and also for the Social and Rehabilitation Service. However, the Social and Rehabilitation Service invests almost exclusively in applied research, divided almost equally between the social sciences and life sciences. Much detail on such matters is available in NSF statistics concerning federal support for research (NSF, 1969a, Table 17 *et passim*). Not only are there important differences among the different bureaus and offices of HEW, but even within one as large as NIMH there can be substantial differences between different programs within the organization.

It should be clear from the above that there are risks in using aggregative statistics to characterize federal research-supporting organizations. In studying these agencies we first have to decide on the size of organization that will be treated as an independent organization, and some generalizations depend heavily on this decision.

The fields of science particularly supported by the private foundations included especially the life sciences and social sciences (NSF, 1969c, Chap. 6). Of the $74 million provided in 1966 for current research support (as distinguished from buildings, endowment, etc.), $40 million went to life sciences (mostly medical and health related), $21 million to social sciences, $10 million to mathematical and physical sciences, and $2 million to psychological sciences. The major foundations specialized to some degree. Ford Foundation gave $12 million for social science (some 60 percent of the total for social science), and John A. Hartford Foundation gave $14 million for life sciences (about 35 percent of the total for that area).

COMMON FEATURES OF EXTRAMURAL SUPPORTING AGENCIES

The following analysis concentrates on federal agencies of extramural support, which provide the bulk of research support. These organizations have some important characteristics in common, and we try to sketch, in broad brush strokes, some common features of the way they function as organizations. In this analysis we ignore intramural research and we ignore nongovernmental sources of support. To impose some order and establish a frame of reference for this analysis, we make some use of the terminology of Cyert and MacCrimmon (1968). Consequently, we describe first the major types of roles, participants, and goals in these organizations, and major features of their environments.

Roles

Within a typical research granting or contracting agency, we can distinguish four major classes of roles which are considered in subsequent analyses: the governing boards (such as the councils at NIH and NIMH, the National Science Board at NSF, and the AEC); the top administrators; the professional staff employed full-time by the agency, consisting largely of scientists in the fields in which grants are made; and the advisory groups (such as study sections at NIH and NIMH, and advisory panels at NSF), which consist of "outside" scientists employed part-time as consultants (paid or unpaid).

Participants

The participants who fill these roles are drawn to some extent from civil service personnel in other federal agencies and to some extent from the organization's client environment (universities or industrial laboratories, for example). Of course, recruitment practices and turnover vary among agencies, but there is usually a quite evident flow of personnel back and forth between the research-supporting agency and the class of organizations to which it provides research support.

Goals

As Kidd has pointed out (1959a, p. 4), most federally financed research is administered by agencies whose primary function is not research. The primary goals of the larger research-supporting agencies are practical ones; they are mission oriented. For example, the goals of DOD center about the military security of the country and military support of its foreign policy; the goals of HEW, as indicated in its title, are to promote the health, education, and welfare of the United States citizens. Some of the participants in each such agency find that they cannot perform their roles satisfactorily, or that major organizational goals are blocked, because they lack either technological devices with certain capabilities or knowledge about how to bring about desired effects. This leads to secondary goals of seeking the development of devices or knowledge. Within a major department such as DOD, smaller units concerned with technological development exist. These units sometimes find that they lack knowledge needed to design hardware to bring about desired effects. Research becomes a goal in order to support development. In many cases mission-oriented agencies also provide basic research support (e.g., Office of Naval Research, Public Health Service, Air Force Office of Scientific Research), justified largely on the grounds that applied research and development falter for lack of basic knowledge in particular areas upon which they must build.

Given the existence of research units within a mission-oriented agency, there is a strong tendency for these units to establish secondary goals which take on overriding importance. For example, in university-oriented programs, the enhancement of organizational prestige becomes an important intermediate goal because a prestigeful research organization attracts more qualified applicants, and a large group of qualified applicants yields a better selection of projects to support. Also, prestige makes it easier to recruit quality staff members and to obtain some free services such as consultation from professionals outside the agency. This appears to be an illustration of the more general organizational process noted by Thompson (1967, p. 33), in which organizations seek prestige to enhance their power over their environment at very little cost.

Enlargement of the program also becomes an important secondary goal. In part, this occurs because program growth tends to become an informal criterion of the performance of the program administrators among the researchers with whom he deals. In part, it occurs because a growing program has more capability to bring about some change in its environment. A growing program has opportunity to experiment and innovate, while a stable or shrinking one tends to have its money tied up in continuing support of projects already begun. Most programs of research support have goals (whether explicit or not) that involve bringing about some kind of change outside the organization; for example, attracting more researchers into a particular class of research, raising the level of research experience available to graduate students, improving the technology applied to a particular problem, and so on. If all available money is tied up in continuing support, the professional staff can do rather little toward achieving such goals.

Roles and Goals

Goals characteristically differ somewhat among the major groups of roles in granting organizations. The governing boards appear to be drawn heavily from the high-ranking administrators of outside organizations—primarily university administrators in the case of university-oriented agencies. Their goals for the granting agency tend to emphasize satisfaction of the needs of the outside organization. For example, the governing boards of university-oriented granting agencies are especially likely to support institutional grants which tend to serve as general support for higher education. In other words, they define support of institutions of higher education as a major goal of the research-supporting organization and help to shape its programs so as to serve that goal. The advisory groups of the same agencies tend to be drawn mostly from among teaching and research faculty. They define support of faculty research projects as a major goal of the research-supporting organization and help to influence its programs so as to serve that goal.

Environment

We can distinguish several significant elements of the environment of a typical federal research-supporting agency. These elements include several classes of organizations that conduct research, especially universities, industrial laboratories, and nonprofit research organizations. Within each of these organizations there is a population of professional people capable of performing research, and there is also a group of administrators of the research-performing organizations. For federal agencies Congress is, of course, a particularly important aspect of the organization's environment because it controls the flow of resources and is therefore in a position to exert powerful influence on organizational goals. The higher executive office to which the agency reports and the Bureau of the Budget (more recently the Office of Budget and Management) are important for the same reasons. Other granting agencies and their personnel constitute another important part of the organizational environment. In addition to all of the above organizations in the agency's environment, there are several broad characteristics of the environment that are of particular importance, such as the level of knowledge and technology in each specific field, levels of knowledge and technology in other nations (e.g., space technology in the U.S.S.R.), and the levels of available professional manpower for serving on the staff and conducting research.

RELATION OF AGENCY TO ENVIRONMENT

Building upon the above broad description of the roles, goals, participants, and environment of a typical extramural granting agency, we can examine the social organization of research that has developed in the United States. The historical development of this system has been summarized briefly in a report of the Committee on Science and Public Policy of the National Academy of Sciences (1964), and the portion up to 1940 has been treated more comprehensively by Dupree (1957).

Institutional Symbiosis

Production of new knowledge in the United States seems to be organized largely in interdependent pairs of institutions which exist in a kind of mutualism. Usually, one of the partners is a federal agency, but it may also be a private foundation or an industrial organization. Each federal agency has some goals that are partially blocked by the need for improved knowledge or technology. The agency itself is typically not well equipped—in personnel, facilities, or mode of organization—to develop the needed knowledge itself. Hence it sets out to buy the knowledge from outside entrepreneurs who are willing to manufacture it. As a result, there is a tendency for each agency to establish especially close ties with a particular institutional sector or sectors determined largely by its principal goals (e.g., development of technological devices, improvement of applied knowledge in a specific area, etc.). Thus, for example, NIH relate closely to institutions of higher education and institutions of medical care; NASA relates particularly to the aerospace industry, and so on. Characteristically, a kind of institutional symbiosis appears to develop in which a granting agency and some particular institutional sector develop a wide range of mutual dependencies and exchanges of resources.

One important aspect of this institutional symbiosis is the process of goal setting through interaction between an organization and its environment, which has been described and analyzed by Thompson and McEwen (1958). Similarly Swatez (1966) has suggested that the activities of the Lawrence Radiation Laboratory are best understood by considering the interaction between the Laboratory and significant elements of its environment. In his analysis organizations ". . . are embedded in a pluralistic institutional context within which their goals and the means to pursue them are transactionally established." Just as sociologists have insisted that individual values, motives, and goals are usually generated and modified by interaction with other people, so also with organizations. "Organizational goals" should be viewed not only as a property of an organization but also a product of interaction of organizations in a larger institutional context and as an expression of the relations among organizations.

Illustration: Federal Support of Academic Research

The concept of institutional symbiosis can be illustrated by examining the relationship between agencies that engage in extramural support of basic research (such as NIH and NSF) and universities. Universities provide the agency with manpower for research in the form of released time of faculty and the availability of graduate students as research assistants. They provide the agency with research proposals which make it possible to establish a visible and prestigious portfolio of grants and to argue for increases in budget. Often they lend professional personnel to the agency to serve on the professional staff, and routinely they provide part-time services of faculty to serve on the advisory groups that participate in the decisions as to which proposals to support. In turn, the agency provides the universities with money (in research grants or contracts), which helps universities to supply the research needs of some of their more prestigious faculty, offer support for graduate students, and purchase expensive research equipment and facilities.

The two symbionts exercise much influence over performance evaluations of each other's personnel. In the universities persons in decision-making positions are always hard pressed to find good performance criteria for faculty. Judging from much informal observation and report, many deans and promotions committees make use of faculty success in obtaining grants or memberships on advisory groups as signs of the quality of their faculty when it is time for promotions and raises. Evidence presumably relevant to this point is presented by Orlans (1962, pp. 201–203), who found a widespread belief among faculty that a scientist who has obtained research grants is more esteemed than another of equal talent and productivity who has not obtained grants. Informally, a granting agency often relies heavily on its advisory groups (drawn from university faculty), its governing board (drawn largely from university administrators), and its grantees (mostly university faculty) in obtaining assessments of the performance of the agency's professional staff and in assessing the value and success of particular programs.

The close and extensive interaction involved in this relationship results in much mutual cultural influence as well. Storer (1962, 1966) has discussed the set of shared values and norms and the modes of reward, both of which are essential parts of the social system of science. These kinds of elements are diffused readily between academic institutions and granting agencies. Academic values, such as the development of knowledge for its own sake, are easily adopted as at least secondary goals in mission-oriented agencies which provide extramural research support. There is apparent mutual influence in the ways of categorizing research and researchers. One might argue that the natural tendency is for academic research to be classified in terms of scientific discipline and for the government research programs to be organized in terms of the social purpose of the knowledge (cf. Brooks, 1968, p. 59). However, the universities and the research agencies adopt (or adapt) one another's categories. In part this appears to result from academic efforts to organize research around areas that are currently well funded. In part, organizing into the same categories seems to simplify communication and exchange of resources between the two groups of organizations. It would be interesting for example, to study the reorganization of the fields of biological sciences in recent years (from categories such as botany, anatomy, zoology to categories such as microbiology, psychobiology, systematic biology) as related to the support programs of mission-oriented agencies and to the organization of the Biological Sciences Division of NSF.

Exchange of personnel between the symbionts and mutual assistance in finding suitable personnel help to assure similarity on many basic values. Procedures and standards of evaluating performance come to be very similar within the two kinds of organizations, and as minor innovations develop in one setting, they diffuse readily to the other. Evaluations of the relative importance of particular lines of research are also likely to be communicated between the two types of organizations, so that values of personnel in the two become more and more alike.

Finally, the universities and the agencies become important political supporters of one another. Congress feels the pressure from universities to enlarge budgets for granting agencies, and the agencies communicate many needs of higher education to Congress and seek funds for new programs aimed at these needs. Reports agree on the profound mutual dependence that has developed but differ in implicit or explicit evaluations of this phenomenon. Some analysts have commented on the scientific community as a remarkable establishment which has drawn massive federal funds while maintaining a maximum of control over these funds through the system of governing boards and advisory groups (e.g., Price, 1962; Greenberg, 1967). At the same time, a report by the Committee on Science and Public Policy of the National Academy of Sciences (1964) describes the "alliance between the Federal Government and institutions of higher education" and is lavish in praise of the alliance and outspoken about its significance. In the preface the report calls this mutual dependence, ". . . one of the most profound and significant developments of our time."

There appear to be closely analogous relationships between development-oriented agencies (such as NASA and DOD) and the sectors of industry with which they contract for research. Without extensive research it is difficult to determine how far the analogy may be valid and what significant differences may be present.

The NonProfits: A By-Product?

In recent years there appears to have been an increase in the number of independent, nonprofit research organizations. There are indications that in some cases the establishment of these organizations is motivated by a desire to break out of the rules established by the alliance of universities and granting agencies. That is, some scientists find the administration of research grants within universities too restrictive and believe that they can conduct the same research better in an independent organization. Rules generated by university administrators and agency administrators do not always please university faculty. In some cases, however, there may be university cooperation in establishing research organizations loosely affiliated with the university so as to bypass some agency rules about salary rates or other matters. The motivations for the establishment of nonprofit research organizations need careful study; those organizations may be, in part, an unintended by-product of the close alliance between universities and federal granting agencies.

Organizational Interaction and Decision Making

In summary, it appears that many important features of a research granting agency arise from the nature of its interaction with particular outside institutions. It is in the nature of an extramural program of research support that it must interest outside organizations in conducting research. To do so, the agency develops particular sensitivity to the needs of the research performers and does much to adapt programs so that they are attractive to the potential performers. In this process the agency and the performers develop a symbiotic relationship which spreads through many of the activities of both.[7]

[7] Henry Riecken has pointed out (personal communication) that this relationship appears functionally similar in many respects to relationships between other (non-research) federal agencies and "outside" organizations; for example, between regulatory

Any extramural granting agency tries to get outside persons or organizations to do something which the agency cannot do. The granting agency cannot accomplish its higher-level goals unless outside organizations can be induced to accept some of the agency's operational goals as its own. Hence there is much bargaining—both implicit and explicit—in the interaction between granting agency and performing organization as they define operational goals that are mutually acceptable and the levels and types of resources required. Kidd (1959a, pp. 34ff and Chap. 11) has described this process and labeled it the "reconciliation of goals and functions." He describes mechanisms through which this reconciliation is developed, such as study groups, commissions, and advisory groups, as well as some ways in which agencies and universities adapt to their mutual dependence (Kidd, 1959a, Chap. 9 and 10).

Thompson (1967, p. 28) has noted: "The relationship between an organization and its task environment is essentially one of exchange, and unless the organization is judged by those in contact with it as offering something desirable, it will not receive the inputs necessary for survival." The process of establishment and modification of organizational goals through interaction with significant elements of the organization's environment is illustrated in Selznick's (1949) study of the TVA, Swatez's (1966) study of a major research laboratory, and Zald's (1960, 1963) studies of correctional institutions.

In examining granting agencies and their interaction with their environments, we can distinguish a few systems of interaction and decision making which are analytically separable but certainly not independent of one another; for example, goal setting, evaluation of proposals, personnel actions (recruitment, evaluation, and reward), and flow of scientific information. Each of these is considered in a following section.

GOAL SETTING

Hierarchy of Goals

As in all complex organizations, there is a hierarchy of goals in a research-supporting agency. These range from high-level, rather abstract goals (e.g., expanding health-relevant knowledge), through intermediate goals (e.g., encouraging and supporting research in microbiology), to

commissions and the sectors they regulate, between the Veterans Administration and veterans organizations, between the Department of Commerce and various business groups.

low-level operational goals (e.g., providing adequate support for the continuation of Dr. X's research in microbiology; providing research experience for graduate students; justifying a specific grant; evaluating research proposals). As is usual in complex organizations, the levels are somewhat associated with levels of the organization, and low levels of the organization frequently lose sight of the high-level goals and displace them with clearer, more attainable goals. In the case of granting agencies, the levels of the organization are also associated with levels of an outside performing organization so that social interaction occurs primarily between operating professional staff of a particular program and faculty of universities, or between higher-level agency staff and administrators of universities. The mutual dependence between a granting agency and a performing organization, including emulation of procedures and values, appears to occur particularly between corresponding levels of the respective organizations. Hence differences of goals within a granting agency to some extent directly reflect corresponding differences within the performing organizations.

Boundaries and Priorities

One essential part of goal setting in a granting organization is the definition of boundaries of eligibility within a program of support. For example, the program may define certain fields of knowledge as outside its boundaries, such as solid-state physics, or social sciences. It may define certain performers as outside its boundaries, such as profit-making organizations or individual researchers unattached to an organization. It may define whole classes of activity as outside its boundaries, such as basic research, or predoctoral research. As an illustration, NSF in its early years defined the support of most social science as outside its goals, following the precedent set by the National Academy of Science which admitted physical anthropology, prehistoric archeology, and experimental psychology, while excluding most other areas. This was gradually modified until, by the 1960s, virtually all basic research in social science was eligible. Recently, there has been further modification which makes much applied research eligible. As another illustration, federal agencies generally defined research related to contraception and population control as outside their goals in the 1940s and 1950s, although this appears to have begun changing rapidly in the late 1960s.

There appears always to be substantial outside pressure on defined program boundaries. No matter how the rules of eligibility are defined, there is always someone whose research falls just outside the defined limits of eligibility. Understandably, they press for redefinition of boundaries.

At the same time, the advisory groups that evaluate proposals are generally drawn from fields that are defined as eligible. Sometimes they resist broadening of the program, either arguing self-interest (e.g., "If we allow support to go to industry, university research will be destroyed") or other grounds (e.g., the difficulty of judging quality unless a program is homogeneous).

Within the boundaries of a program, operational goals are further defined by specifying types of research that will receive priority or special emphasis. The decision to have no specific priorities is one possible decision, and such a laissez-faire (or "marketplace") program is especially likely to occur in an agency such as NSF which supports basic research largely for its own sake, rather than supporting research because of its contribution to a practical mission of the agency. Mission-oriented agencies often state and publicize research "requirements" which define areas in which research proposals are particularly desired.

Recurrent Issues of Goal Setting

In addition to simple eligibility and priority, there have been certain recurrent issues of goal definition in federal programs. Several are treated here.

Existing Quality versus Development

There has been much controversy on the issue of supporting quality where is exists, as against developing quality where it is lacking. Nearly all agencies rely upon the system of project grants awarded competitively on the basis of the quality of the proposal and its personnel, which tends to result in the concentration of research support in a relatively few institutions of highest quality (Arnold, 1968; Carnegie Report 1963; Kidd, 1959a, Chap. 3; Orlans, 1962, Part 2). This system has even tended to draw increasing numbers of highly qualified researchers into these few institutions rather than to second-rank institutions.[8] Both the governing boards and the advisory groups have tended to be drawn disproportionately from the same top institutions, thus adding to the risk that they might define goals in such a way as to continue the concentration of support.[9]

[8] The Department of Agriculture appears to be the only agency that has developed research activities that are organized to be entirely geographically dispersed. See Kidd (1959a, p. 56) and Shaw (1960).

[9] According to Greenberg (1966a) the composition of governing boards has been shifting away from the elite institutions.

Congressional pressures, however, have generally tended away from exclusive reliance on existing quality as a basis for granting funds and toward some criteria of geographical distribution and enhancement of quality. This is probably especially true in those cases in which influential committee chairmen come from states that lack institutions of high quality.

Project Grants versus Institutional Grants

Another recurrent issue of goal definition, closely related to the last, has been project support as against institutional support (Greenberg, 1966a; Kidd, 1959a, Chap. 6; Orlans, 1962, Chap. 18). The former concentrates on supporting the development of knowledge in small building blocks which are intended to accumulate into major advances in knowledge. The latter concentrates on building the general strength of knowledge-oriented institutions (chiefly universities) on the grounds that they can best advance knowledge if they are strong and healthy. This issue clearly becomes entangled in the stratified internal politics of both universities and granting agencies. The top administrators of research agencies tend to have especially close contact with the governing boards and must be especially responsive to them. These boards are drawn disproportionately from the ranks of high administrators in universities. The professional staff at the operating level of granting agencies tend to have especially close contact with the advisory groups, which are drawn from teaching and research faculty. As suggested above, much communication of values and problems occurs *between* agency and university but *within* levels. Up to the early 1960s, the system of project support seemed to have clear dominance, and then in the middle and late 1960s there was a shift of emphasis from project support toward institutional support.

One interpretation of this shift is as follows. The project system upset the internal balance of power in universities by making successful faculty entrepreneurs quite independent of their administrators. The administrators could exercise relatively little control over directions of development other than by their selection of faculty to be hired. Babbidge (1968), for example, has discussed this from the point of view of a university president, and other major academic administrators have often made similar remarks as they discuss problems of their universities. At the same time, the project system was less than satisfactory to Congress because of the geographical concentration of support and the resulting difficulty in building quality institutions in new areas. Both Congress and the governing boards (representing high university administrators) saw benefit in making more grants to institutions for broad institutional improvement rather than to individual faculty members for specific research projects

(Walsh, 1966; Greenberg, 1966a). Hence the high administrators in research agencies and those in universities were allied in opposition to the faculty of the universities and the operating level of professional staff in the agencies. As the amount of broad institutional grant money increased relative to that for projects, the university administrators gained some of the control over distribution of funds which had resided with the alliance of faculty and agency staff. The university administrators regained some of their lost power to set directions within the university.

Continuity of Support versus Innovation

Another recurrent issue of goal definition is initiation of innovative research versus support of sustained programs. Many programs of research support like to define themselves as innovators—a definition that implicitly altercasts some other agencies as sustaining established lines of research, because there is no point in initiating if no one will sustain. In a pluralistic, overlapping system of support such as that in the United States, there appears to be a tendency for small or shrinking programs to try to get enlarging programs to pick up support of established lines of research. This mechanism cushions some of the impact of shifting fashions in research support. There are always some programs of research that are eligible in more than one agency and can be shifted as money shifts.

The tendency of research-supporting agencies to prefer being innovators seems to reflect a free enterprise ideology in a curious way. The assumption seems to be that established lines of research should be able to draw support if they are any good, in just the same way that a product, once invented and tested, should sell sufficiently well to create its own support. In this instance, as in many others, knowledge seems to be viewed as a product subject to the same pragmatic tests of utility as more tangible products; if it is worthwhile, someone should be willing to pay for it. This pragmatic view of knowledge appears to militate against sustained support for lines of research that do not clearly show practical payoff. As indicated above, there is a tendency for competition within agency budgets between continuity of support for research in progress on the one hand, and support for new and innovative proposals on the other hand. If agencies favor new proposals over renewals to continue established lines of research, then the wise researcher will avoid undertaking any line of research that cannot be "completed" in a reasonable time. The pragmatic view of knowledge, combined with the tendency of many agencies to cast themselves as innovators, probably has the effect of discouraging some scientists from initiating lines of research which might be very important but slow to reach the point of clear application to a practical problem. (Cf. Kidd, 1959a, p. 113; Orlans, 1962, pp. 254–255).

Communication of Goals

Explanation of the goals and preferences of a research-supporting organization is always a problem and is a common area of misunderstanding (Orlans, 1962, Chap. 17). Program aims and boundaries necessarily leave some ambiguity. It is well known in sociology that ambiguity about an important matter begets improvisations of knowledge (e.g., Shibutani, 1966). That is, the development and modification of popular knowledge is a constant social process in which ideas about important matters, based on imperfect information, undergo constant reality testing, often in very imperfect tests. Gaps in imperfect knowledge must be filled as well as possible by consensus, and the ideas that survive imperfect tests are retained and reused (cf. Shibutani, 1966, Chap. 5). In universities, where research grants are of great importance, this is the kind of process that seems to occur and result in partially erroneous shared beliefs about granting programs. The image of the agency painted in such beliefs can, if the belief becomes widespread, become a self-fulfilling prophecy. For example, on occasion academic men in a particular specialty have examined grants lists and concluded that their specialty is outside the limits of a program. As a consequence they have not submitted proposals, and the agency could not make grants in the area in question because of an absence of proposals. This problem of an agency's image creates a built-in conservatism in a program. Similarly, if word spreads that an agency is unable to support much new research because of budget cuts, the academic community often cuts back on proposals to the agency. This weakens the agency's position in seeking budget and may make the predicted budget cut self-fulfilling or at least self-aggravating.

The problem of conveying an accurate image of the agency's goals and preferences is aggravated by the tendency of outsiders to personify a complex organization and overlook its internal differences. Thus an outsider may take the statements of one member of the professional staff as representing the position of the agency. A statement by a staff member, ignorant of other parts of his agency, has sometimes been taken as the basis for a simple belief about the whole agency. For example, one staff member might express lack of interest in a proposal on the physiology of contraception in ignorance of the fact that another program in the same agency is actually seeking such proposals. This way of overgeneralizing from the remarks of one staff member appears to be another instance of filling the ambiguity surrounding program objectives by building on shreds of available information.

Political Pressures on Goals

In interaction between the research agency and Congress, the agency often tries to sell the importance of its program on the basis of a few particularly successful past grants, and those congressmen who are opposed to the program often attack it on the basis of picking out a few vulnerable grants. Agencies have not usually succeeded in making the point attributed to John Wanamaker, who is supposed to have said that he knew that half of his advertising budget was wasted, but unfortunately did not know which half (Greenberg, 1966b). Any grant program that is not exceedingly conservative is certain to have a large proportion of grants that are failures, but it is impossible (with available techniques of evaluation of proposals) to predict which ones. Hence hostile critics can always point to failures in order to argue that the research budget is too large.

Organized pressure groups sometimes interject themselves into this interaction between granting agency and Congress, resulting in some pressures toward redefinition of agency goals. For example, the newsletters of conservative lobbying groups have sometimes printed lists of titles of research grants with their dollar costs, apparently selecting titles that sound silly to laymen in the absence of any clarifying information. In this way they apparently aim to demonstrate waste so as to justify budget reductions. The granting agency then receives many inquiries about the listed grants, often as letters of inquiry from constituents to congressmen, forwarded to the agency by the congressman for explanation. This creates a pressure on grants administrators to act so as to minimize failures rather than to maximize the ultimate payoff per unit cost, which would probably imply taking risks. Thus there is created a subtle pressure to play it safe, to bet on sure things, which constitutes some redefinition of agency goals.

Environmental Consequences of Goal Setting

The goal-setting activities of granting agencies have a number of systematic effects on the environment of the granting agencies, at least in the academic world. One of the most discussed has been the distortion of university programs that appears to result from constraints built into the programs of research support (Carnegie Report, 1963; Orlans, 1962,

Chap. 6; Walsh, 1966). While universities have very broad aims in the accumulation and dissemination of knowledge, each research granting agency must define narrower limits. Most of the dollar support is in mission-oriented agencies, and these missions conform only to rather small parts of the work of a comprehensive university. Even in an agency such as NSF, which is not mission oriented, there must be boundaries of eligibility much narrower than all university scholarship, and this has meant greater availability of money for research in science than in humanities, and more in basic scientific research than in applied research that did not chance to be relevant to the mission of an agency with research money.

The patchwork of federal support has often resulted in the over-development (from the university's point of view) of a particular specialty, relative to others, resulting from what Mack (1969) has called the reverse Midas effect (i.e., all that turns to gold, we touch). From the university's point of view, federal support often seems also to push universities toward greater emphasis on research instead of instruction or service, and to reinforce the tendency for evaluation of university faculty primarily on the basis of their research (cf. Orlans, 1962, Chap. 14).

There have been suggestions lately that some industries have also suffered from the reverse Midas effect. Many industrial organizations have invested heavily in developing expertise in an area that is heavily supported as a matter of national policy, such as defense or space-related technology. Some industries now appear to be self-consciously diversifying in order to counter the maladaptive effects of their dependence on this continued support.

There are many subtler effects of agency goal setting, which may be even more important in the long run. For example, as suggested above, in setting their goals about project versus institutional support, the agencies have important impact on the internal political balance of universities. Because of the symbiotic relationship between agency and university, this political effect is a by-product of agency decision-making processes.

In setting goals about the support of research facilities, the agencies have important effects in extending the range of feasible research. There are major classes of research that are not possible without investment by granting agencies in major facilities that are beyond the means of all or most single universities. Federal agencies have helped to provide expensive general-purpose facilities such as radiotelescopes in astronomy, particle accelerators in physics, and survey services and data archives in the social sciences. The creation of such facilities on a basis that is accessible to researchers from many institutions brings about much research that would not otherwise be possible.

PROPOSAL EVALUATION

The preceding discussion has concerned goal-setting processes of granting agencies and their effects. A second major process, often closely tied to goal setting, is that of proposal evaluation, which is crucial in determining the allocation of research support among outside applicants. The allocation of extramural support can be analyzed as a rather complex system of decisions involving interaction between the agency and its outside performers at many steps. (Kidd, 1959a, Chap. 11; Orlans, 1962, Chap. 18.)

The Peer-Merit System

In this process the advisory groups have their major function. Most agencies have institutionalized some form of the "peer-merit" system, in which groups of researchers pass judgment on the proposals of their peers. The details vary. Some advisory groups (e.g., many study sections at NIH and NIMH) make decisions about proposals by voting. The members may first vote "yes" or "no" as to whether a proposal meets minimal standards of acceptability, and then make a five-point rating which is averaged over all members to assign a priority in allocation of funds. The priorities so assigned can be (but rarely are) changed subsequently by action of a governing board. In the advisory groups each proposal is usually read by two or three members, one of whom has responsibility for presenting it and explaining it to the rest of the members before they vote.

However, some advisory groups (e.g., most advisory panels at NSF) do not make decisions by a formal vote on each proposal, and they make recommendations to the professional staff rather than decisions that bind the professional staff. At NSF the advisory panels also usually have some outside mail reviews available to help them when they meet. The NSF panels do not set a strict numerical priority for each proposal, although their advice generally conveys the panel's judgment as to which are the most important and valuable proposals.

Apparent Effects

We can make some plausible guesses as to how such differences affect the outcomes, based on small group research in other settings and on participant observation in advisory groups, although direct evidence from recorded interaction within advisory groups is not available. Most probably, assigning each proposal to two or three readers systematically increases the influence of those readers over the votes of nonreaders within the panel, thereby increasing the probability of an idiosyncratic judgment. However, the same effect may occur within an advisory panel that does not assign readers to proposals, provided that the proposals they handle are sufficiently diverse so that self-selection of readers occurs and the two or three most qualified influence the others.

In other words, the diversity of the proposals handled by an advisory group probably has a systematic effect upon decisions by the group. A wide-ranging and diverse program more often encounters a proposal that only one or two advisors feel qualified to judge, and they probably influence the others. Hence we would expect idiosyncratic judgments to be maximized in a broad, diverse program. However, if an agency has many narrow programs, each with an advisory group, this aggravates the problem of fund allocation and establishment of priorities among the various programs.

The peer-merit system is intended to assure the best possible judgment of scientific merit, relatively free from political pressures, and most observers seem to feel that it serves this purpose reasonably well. Certainly, organized science (such as NAS-NRC) supports the system strongly. As a rule, this system in its various forms is especially responsive to the academic system of prestige. For example, an advisory group finds it difficult to disapprove a proposal by a well-known and respected academic scientist, even if the proposal gives rather little information on which a detached judgment could be made, and even if he proposes a type of research in which he has not demonstrated his ability. The academic reputation tends to be accepted in lieu of other evidence about the probable success of the proposed research. A young, unknown scientist must present much more detailed evidence of having "done his homework"—that is, having thought through his research problems and planned for them in detail—than is the case for an established scientist, even though the established scientist is probably in a better position to do this without first receiving a grant.

A Model of Proposal Evaluation

In the process of evaluating proposals, it appears that principal bases of judgment are typically threefold: the probability of a visible research product, the probable scientific importance of that product, and the relevance of the product to specific goals or requirements of the granting agency. In many agencies the judgment of eligibility or relevance to goals is left to the professional staff or to the governing board, and the advisory groups of scientists concentrate on probable success and importance. While the stature of the scientist making the proposal clearly enters into the evaluation, we assume in this analysis that it has its effect by influencing estimates of probable success and probable importance.[10]

Some of the problems and likely effects of the peer-merit system of evaluation can be analyzed, in the absence of direct documentary evidence, by setting up a simple model of important aspects of the decision process based upon informal observation of its operation. Imagine that each qualified judge makes two independent judgments of each proposal—the probability of a successful outcome, and the probable scientific importance of the outcome if it is successful. When judges agree in placing a proposal high on both dimensions or low on both dimensions, proposal evaluation is a simple problem. However, two chief problems of indeterminancy arise—one in which judges agree in placing a proposal high on one dimension and low on the other, and one in which judges disagree in their judgments on one or both dimensions.

Consider the case of a proposal adjudged to have high risk of failure but high potential value if successful. For example, this might be a brilliant, novel proposal about a previously untried way to research a particular problem for which existing methods are less than adequate. If the novel method succeeds, the results would be of great significance, but there is a strong chance that the method will fail and produce no results.

In contrast, consider the case of a proposal that is adjudged a sure thing to produce some unexciting but publishable results. This might be a proposal from a scientist who has been a steady producer of sound but rather pedestrian research and proposes more of the same.

When the level of research support is high enough to permit the support of some proposals that are not high on both probable success and potential value, there is a decision problem in choosing between the two types of cases described above. Of course this problem would again be bypassed if the level of support were so high that all of both kinds

---

[10] Kidd (1959a, p. 106–108) makes the interesting and important point that in judging proposals reliance on the substance of the proposal, rather than the identity of the proposer, is a device to permit losers to accept the decisions. He suggests that even if the judgments are made partly on the basis of ability of the individuals involved, it is important for the operation of the system to maintain the fiction that the proposal is the sole basis of the judgment.

could be supported, but that is an unlikely event. As suggested above, congressional pressures, resulting from criticism of individual grants rather than whole programs of grants, tend to push decisions toward preferring the sound, plodding proposal to the high-risk, high-payoff proposal so as to minimize failures. If a major aim of the research program is to maximize the number of productive innovations, then it would seem that the high-risk, high-payoff proposals should be preferred.

Environmental Consequences of the Judgmental Process

In making judgments of the probability of success of a proposal, one important factor in the judgment is usually the past record of productivity of the person making the proposal. Hence early productivity of young scientists becomes especially important. Some young scientists, coming to understand this system, carefully avoid trying any very novel or risky kind of proposal. If it should fail, the failure would probably hamper future efforts to obtain research support. In grant-seeking, as in many other activities, success breeds success.

As was suggested above, research grants have become one important part of the process of evaluating university faculty for raises and promotions. In some fields of science, he who cannot raise outside research money may be considered a poor prospect for permanent tenure because (it seems) he is not well regarded by his colleagues in his discipline. This creates an added pressure to engage in "safe" research and especially in the kinds of research currently favored in granting agencies, thus exaggerating the reverse Midas effect. Within universities a research grant tends to be viewed as a sort of prize, indicating favorable evaluation by one's colleagues nationally. Sometimes, at least, the grant is awarded as a risky investment or as a marginally acceptable proposal on a problem viewed by the agency as especially crucial to its interests. These two conceptions of a grant fail to mesh.

It is clear that another major effect of the system of advisory groups within extramural granting organizations is the diffusion of responsibility for important decisions, thus minimizing the possibility of criticism for financial awards made by the decision of bureaucrats. Failures are inevitable in a granting program unless the program is so cautious that it takes no risks, and in that case major successes are also unlikely. If some decisions are inevitably going to be wrong, the only way to insulate the agency staff from difficult pressures, both from potential grantees and from Congress, is to show that the mistakes were made on the basis of the best available expert judgment.

PERSONNEL DECISIONS

The recruitment of professional staff to serve in granting agencies, similar to other decision processes of the agencies, is shaped by the agency's interaction with performing organizations. The major source—indeed, almost the only source—of professional staff for the university-oriented granting agencies is university faculties. The process of scouting for agency staff usually relies heavily upon the same advisory groups that evaluate proposals, and they are composed of university faculty.

For the most part, the positions in granting agencies are highly visible ones. The incumbents are constantly in contact with academic men from many different universities and deal with them about matters of research and education. Consequently, they become likely targets for recruiting to university positions. Hence there is a substantial flow of personnel back and forth between agencies and universities. Some university faculty, unhappy with their location, appear to use a Washington agency as a stepping stone to a different academic position. Some appear to use it as a route to academic administrative positions.

Some granting agencies have institutionalized the constant flow of personnel to and from universities by encouraging hiring on leave of absence from the university for a period of 1 or 2 years. This appears to have the effect of keeping the agency particularly sensitive to university needs and problems, although there is some cost in that a large share of the staff are always new to their jobs and learning how to perform in them. Constant turnover also appears to have the effect of introducing new ideas and new emphases into research programs, thus minimizing the possibility of perpetuating idiosyncratic features of programs. Turnover may, then, help to counteract the conservative effect, described above, of shared misunderstandings of program goals.

Agencies differ in the way they define the job of program administrators, as mentioned above in the discussion of proposal evaluation. These differences appear to have important consequences for the recruitment of professional staff. Those agencies that have a rather rigid set of decision rules about the evaluation of proposals, such as by averaging ratings of advisory groups, leave little discretion to the staff. As a result, the average quality of the staff they can hire is probably lowered, but they are more protected from mistakes by the staff. This aspect of the personnel system seems to contain a classic example of a self-fulfilling prophecy. If an agency is afraid that it may not be able to hire staff of high quality, the position to be filled is hedged in with formal decision rules so that the incumbent cannot make costly mistakes. This makes the position less attractive to quality staff, and the earlier expectation is fulfilled.

Budget changes also appear to have important consequences for personnel recruitment and retention. As an expanding program leaves more opportunity for innovative efforts by the staff than a stable or declining one, there appear to be flows of innovative staff members into expanding programs. Given the ebb and flow of federal budgeting, this kind of personnel movement seems to imply the hypothesis that the older agencies have accumulated many staff who are not innovatively inclined. This hypothesis seems consistent with the observation of some Washington observers that agencies become stodgier as they get older.

FLOW OF SCIENTIFIC INFORMATION

Informal linkages among scientists have become extremely important in determining the flow of scientific information, apparently increasingly so as the information explosion proceeds. Price (1963) has treated some important aspects of this, including the development of informal collegia within which research information about a specialized topic is exchanged. A program of research support, with its own advisory group and program staff, brings about many informal contacts among scientists who share a general area of research interest. An important by-product of the process of proposal evaluation is the informal exchange of much information.

As large numbers of proposals are received by a program, they must be read by the staff and assigned to reviewers—sometimes outside mail reviewers, sometimes a subset of the advisory group, or sometimes both. In choosing the reviewers the staff bases decisions largely on knowledge as to who is conducting related research. Clearly, these decisions in turn affect the flow of current research information to scientists with related interests. Quite commonly, a scientist first becomes aware of some research related to his own when he receives a proposal for review. Some of the ideas involved influence the reviewer's own research, and some are passed on to students and colleagues.

When the advisory group meets and discusses proposals, the discussion usually elicits comparisons of each proposal with similar research. Hence these discussions reinforce the substantial knowledge already present in the program staff and the advisory group as to who is conducting what research.

Both the program staff and the members of an advisory group generally acquire the reputation of being particularly knowledgeable about research in progress within the domain of the particular program. Consequently, they are often consulted informally even by scientists who are not submitting proposals. Consequently, they occupy a nodal position in the informal network of information flow.

When potential grantees inquire informally about the possibility of support for a particular kind of research, they often learn about related research elsewhere in the country because the agency staff are especially well informed. The time lag between funding and research completion and the time lag between completion and publication have become substantial in many areas of science. These lags increase the importance of informal channels of communication, including the channels through advisory groups and professional staff of granting agencies, as well as the collegia described by Derek Price (1963). Specialized knowledge within agency staff and advisors about research planned and in progress is far ahead of research published in journals, probably by at least 2 or 3 years in most instances, because of the two time lags mentioned above.

After the review of a proposal has been completed, it is quite common for the program staff to inform the author of the proposal of the major points that emerged in review of his proposal. Both in successful and in unsuccessful proposals, this feedback of information can be very important. It may contain information about similar research in progress but not yet published, procedures and techniques developed in other research that might be adapted to the proposed research, specific criticisms as to research design, and so on. Customarily, the anonymity of individual reviewers is preserved in providing this feedback. Although many journals review reports of *completed* research anonymously, this informal feedback from proposal review may often be the only anonymous and relatively candid criticism available before research is well under way.

It is clear that the process of reviewing and evaluating research proposals has by-products of substantial importance in shaping the informal flow of scientific information among scientists. Appointment to an advisory group is a recognition of specialized knowledge, but membership serves to reinforce and enhance the extent of current research knowledge possessed by members. This expertise becomes recognized among scientists, with the result that members occupy crucial positions for the informal flow of scientific information.

CONCLUSION

The support of research in the United States is organized in an untidy collection of overlapping agencies of support. It is characterized by a lack of centralized planning or constraint and by a spirit of entrepreneurship. Scientists act as entrepreneurs in seeking to obtain the resources they need in order to carry on their preferred lines of research and generate knowledge. Staff of research agencies act as financial entrepreneurs, seeking a portfolio of good investments of their grant money so that they can point to research products commensurate with their expenditures. Knowledge is treated as a commodity to be manufactured, and it can only be manufactured by investing in an organization to produce it.

The entrepreneurial approach to producing knowledge has some important implications. First, the granting agency that seeks to invest in producing knowledge must find qualified organizations and motivate them to carry on the needed research. Consequently, a close working relationship is established between the agency that seeks knowledge or technology and the organization (university or industry) that produces it.

There are many related linkages established between a granting agency and a set of outside organizations which are its research performers. Each link can be construed as an exchange of resources, often involving explicit or implicit bargaining. The performance of research is exchanged for the payment of money. Personnel are exchanged on temporary or long-range basis. The agency and the research performers exchange much advice, largely through elaborately institutionalized channels for advice, such as advisory groups of scientists and governing councils. They exchange political support. They exchange scientific information. Finally, there appears to be much exchange of norms and values—reflected in ways of organizing, ways of evaluating staff performance, and goals sought.

These many exchanges result in the establishment of a strong mutual dependence between granting agency and higher education, or between granting agency and a segment of industry. With so many linkages there is a massive amount of communication back and forth between the symbionts, resulting in sensitivity and responsiveness to needs of the other and perhaps also in a parochial viewpoint that is insensitive to other institutions. That is, the university-oriented agencies may be insensitive to industry and to nonprofit research organizations, for example.

One important feature of this symbiosis is that the agency and its research performers expend much energy on each other's administrative problems and bargain extensively to find working arrangements that serve both parties. Among recent issues illustrating this point are the issue of project versus institutional support, the issue of cost sharing and the nature and level of support for indirect costs (Carnegie Report, 1963; Kidd, 1959a, Chap. 5; Orlans, 1962, Chap. 16), and the issue of federal payment of faculty salaries (Orlans, 1962, Chap. 15).

The close mutual dependence results in some distortions of purpose so that goals are subtly altered. It results in some changed motivations of scientists. For example, some scientists seek money from a granting agency more as a sign of quality than as a means to knowledge. The meaning of a research grant is thus subtly distorted from being a purchase of knowledge to being a prize for individual accomplishment. The importance of this kind of recognition to some scientists is so great that their choice of areas and methods of research may be distorted to play it safe in obtaining recognition.

The system of interdependent institutions described above appears to be relatively responsive to shifts of national goals. Over the last 20–25 years, research priorities have shifted quite clearly from major attention to military defense to emphasis on health and space technology and, most recently, to contemporary societal problems, which promises to be the main thrust of the 1970s. Probably, the same amount of money invested in research in government intramural laboratories or in institutional support for higher education in the form of general-purpose grants would be more rigid and unresponsive to changes of goals.

In order to perform its main functions, a research granting agency must elicit the cooperation of performing organizations and must retain the confidence of those who provide resources (Congress and the Executive Branch in the case of federal agencies). In a sense, then, the research-supporting agency serves as a mediator, or communication link, between the knowledge-producing institutions on the one hand, and the legislative and executive branches of the federal government on the other hand. The agency communicates and explains to the federal government the needs and problems of knowledge-producing institutions, and it communicates to those institutions the national goals and priorities. From long experience the agency is sensitive to the needs and problems of its research performers and tries to translate national goals into programs that are helpful to the performers. It also tries to translate the needs of its research performers into programs that can gain support as contributing to national goals.

Many writers have commented on the "partnership" between segments of the federal government and higher education and on the partnership between other segments of the federal government and the defense industry or the aerospace industry. However, there is a lack of research to establish the nature of these linkages and their effects, and to trace possible parallels between the two types of partnership.

At the outset this chapter set the objective of suggesting hypotheses and stimulating research. Clearly, the empirical basis for many statements in the chapter is weak, and there is a wealth of opportunity for research. The chapter will do more for knowledge in this area if it stirs someone to prove the statements wrong than if it gains casual acceptance as a completely accurate and definitive account.

REFERENCES

Arnold, Christian K. (1968). "The Government and University Science: Purchase or Investment?" In *Science Policy and the University,* Harold Orlans, Ed. Washington, D.C.: Brookings Institution, pp. 89–100.

Babbidge, Homer D., Jr. (1968). "A View from the Campus." In *Science Policy and the University,* Harold Orlans, Ed. Washington, D.C.: Brookings Institution, pp. 323–330.

Brooks, Harvey (1968). "The Future Growth of Academic Research: Criteria and Needs." In *Science Policy and the University,* Harold Orlans, Ed., Washington, D.C.: Brookings Institution, pp. 53–76.

Carnegie Report (1963). "Twenty-Six Campuses and the Federal Government." *Educational Record,* **44,** 95–136.

Committee on Science and Public Policy, National Academy of Sciences (1964). *Federal Support of Basic Research in Institutions of Higher Learning.* Washington, D.C.: National Academy of Sciences.

Cyert, Richard M., and Kenneth P. MacCrimmon (1968). "Organizations." In *The Handbook of Social Psychology,* 2nd ed., Vol. 1, G. Lindzey and E. Aronson, Eds. Reading, Mass.: Addison-Wesley, pp. 568–611.

Dupree, A. Hunter (1957). *Science in the Federal Government: A History of Policies and Activities to 1940.* Cambridge, Mass.: Harvard Univ. Press.

Greenberg, D. S. (1966a). "Basic Research: The Political Tides are Shifting." *Science,* **152** 1724–1726.

Greenberg, D. S. (1966b). "Money for Science: The Community is Beginning to Hurt." *Science,* **152** 1485–1487.

Greenberg, D. S. (1967). *The Politics of Pure Science.* New York: New American Library.

Kidd, Charles V. (1959a). *American Universities and Federal Research.* Cambridge, Mass.: Harvard Univ. Press.

Kidd, Charles V. (1959b) "Basic Research, Description vs. Definition." *Science,* **129** (February 13), 368–371.

Mack, Raymond W. (1969). "Theoretical and Substantive Biases in Sociological Research." In *Interdisciplinary Relationships in the Social Sciences,* M. Sherif and C. Sherif, Eds. Chicago: Aldine, pp. 52–64.

National Science Foundation (1969a). *Federal Funds for Research, Development, and Other Scientific Activities,* Vol. XVIII, NSF 69-31. Washington, D.C.: Government Printing Office.

National Science Foundation (1969b). *National Patterns of R & D Resources: Funds and Manpower in the United States, 1953–1970,* NSF 69-30. Washington, D.C.: Government Printing Office.

National Science Foundation (1969c). *Scientific Activities of Nonprofit Institutions, 1966,* NSF 69-16. Washington, D.C.: Government Printing Office.

Orlans, Harold (1962). *The Effects of Federal Programs on Higher Education: A Study of 36 Universities and Colleges.* Washington, D.C.: Brookings Institution.

Price, Derek J. (1963). *Little Science, Big Science.* New York: Columbia Univ. Press.

Price, Don K. (1962). "The Scientific Establishment." *Proceedings of the American Philosophical Society,* **106,** pp. 235–245.

Selznick, Philip (1949). *TVA and the Grass Roots.* Berkeley: Univ. of California Press.

Shaw, Byron T. (1960). "Research Planning and Control in the United States Department of Agriculture: The Experience of an Old and Well Established Research Agency." *Annals of the American Academy of Political and Social Science,* **327** (January), 95–102.

Shepard, H. A. (1956). "Basic Research and the Social System of Pure Science." *Philosophy of Science,* **23** (January), 48–57.

Shibutani, Tamotsu (1966). *Improvised News: A Sociological Study of Rumor.* Indianapolis and New York: Bobbs-Merrill.

Storer, Norman W. (1966). *The Social System of Science.* New York: Holt.

Storer, Norman W. (1962). "Some Sociological Aspects of Federal Science Policy." *The American Behavioral Scientist,* **6** 27–30.

Swatez, Gerald (1966). *Social Organization of a University Laboratory.* Ph.D. Dissertation, Univ. of California (Berkeley).

Thompson, James D. (1967). *Organizations in Action.* New York: McGraw-Hill.

Thompson, J. D., and W. J. McEwen (1958). "Organizational Goals and Environment: Goal-Setting as an Interaction Process." *American Sociological Review,* **23,** 23–31.

Walsh, John (1966). "Demand for Institutional Support Attains the Form of Legislation." *Science,* **152,** 1041–1043.

Zald, Mayer N. (1963). "Comparative Analysis and Measurement of Organizational Goals: The Case of Correctional Institutions for Delinquents." *Sociological Quarterly,* **4,** 206–230.

Zald, Mayer N. (1960). "The Correctional Institution for Juvenile Offenders: An Analysis of Organizational 'Character,'" *Social Problems,* **8,** 57–67.

CHAPTER EIGHT

Relations Among Scientific Disciplines

Norman W. Storer, Baruch College, City University of New York

For certain purposes the scientific community may be treated as a
single entity, but its division into areas, disciplines, specialties, and
subspecialties means that it is quite heterogeneous and that the differences and relationships among its constituent parts are worthy of attention.
To add dimension to our understanding of the place of scientific research
in society, the fact that science is *not* an undifferentiated whole must be
examined and its implications explored.

Science is, in Parsons' words, a "culture-oriented" enterprise;[1] that is,
it is primarily concerned with the production of an "intangible"
cultural component—knowledge. This raises immediate problems for
any attempt to explore its infrastructure. Do we mean by discipline a
body of knowledge or a group of scientists? The two referents of the
term are not distinguished in ordinary usage, but since they represent
very different phenomena it is necessary that they be clearly recognized
here so that their mutual interdependence can be taken into account.

1 Talcott Parsons, "The Institutionalization of Scientific Investigation," in *The Sociology of Science,* Bernard Barber and Walter Hirsch, Eds., Free Press, New York, 1962,
pp. 7–15.

To be specific, it is obvious that "knowledge" cannot exist in any meaningful sense without men to "know" it, but it is also obvious that the factors that influence men's awareness of knowledge and their ability to extend it are quite different from those that influence the ways in which pieces of knowledge are fitted together to provide more comprehensive and accurate understanding of the phenomena to which they refer. Yet, as we shall see, the characteristics of a body of knowledge do influence the relationships that develop among those who "know" it, just as these relationships influence the rate and direction in which that knowledge develops.

To understand the relations among scientific disciplines, it is necessary first that we examine the various differences that exist among them, keeping in mind of course the dual meaning of the term *discipline*. This chapter focuses first upon the origins of the division of science into its component parts as we know them today, examining this process both in terms of knowledge (the cultural or intellectual aspect) and of organization (the social aspect). Then, with this critical distinction still in mind, we take up the problem of how differences among disciplines may be most usefully characterized. Finally, we consider the various possible relationships that might develop among disciplines and what we know of them now.

THE INFRASTRUCTURE OF THE SCIENTIFIC COMMUNITY: ORIGINS OF THE DISCIPLINES

The institutional goal of science is the extension of empirical knowledge. That is, its purpose is the construction of sets of symbols, descriptive of reality, which are increasingly more valid, more economical, and more comprehensive. (This implies, incidentally, that the translation of newly won knowledge into technological achievements is not ordinarily taken to be the scientist's direct responsibility, nor is it usually a major motivation in the conduct of his research. Ideally, increased knowledge of reality is an end in itself, even though it is obvious that basic scientific knowledge may well find practical application in the future through the work of others.)

Accepting this "pure" goal of science, we can see that activity directed toward it must rest ultimately on the assumption that there is only *one* reality "out there," even though there are many different ways to symbolize its parts and their relationships. The assumption rests upon logical as well as experiential grounds; not only is it reinforced by men's experience with the universe, it is logically necessary if they are to have faith that research is worthwhile.

If there were no "reality" beyond men's imaginations, or if the most fundamental aspects of reality were characterized by random, capricious change, there would be no possibility of building a trustworthy body of knowledge about it. Direct sensory experience, however, persuades us that there *is* an external reality which is both organized and stable in its fundamental characteristics. The sheer cussedness of the universe—its dogged refusal to act in accord with our wishes and beliefs unless *they* are in accord with the rules that govern *it*—is sufficient to establish this faith.

Repeated observations of spatial and temporal correlations among physical events, further, tell us that this external reality is organized into "clusters" of events and relationships. These clusters are distinguished from one another not only by differences in spatial and temporal location but also by the fact that change in one cluster seems to have little or no effect upon another. Placing a pot of water on the stove and bring-it to a boil, for instance, seems to have no effect upon the cat sleeping in the corner of the kitchen; conversely, the water boils at the same temperature regardless of whether the cat is asleep or awake.[2]

Systematic observation of empirical clusters of events leads to the identification of different categories of events, which are more abstract and economic descriptions of reality. This is not the place to go into the processes through which men develop symbolic categories. It is sufficient here to indicate that they do, and that the conceptual distinctions they make among different categories of natural events approximate the distinctions that exist among different parts of reality.

The "boundaries" separating different categories may not be immediately apparent, of course, and they may be drawn differently if different criteria of separateness are employed. Not only is it often difficult for men to agree on these criteria, to agree on *which* boundaries should be drawn and *where*, but it might be said that the history of science is in one sense the history of men's attempts to identify and analyze the major clusters and categories of events that make up reality. In this regard, Darwin's *Origin of Species* represents a creative and highly effective response to the problem of how to account for the boundaries we recognize among the various categories of plants and animals that are called species.

The process of identifying and analyzing clusters and categories of

2 It is interesting to note, though, that the cat awakens *immediately* when the refrigerator door opens; the author has tested this repeatedly.

natural events is called research. It is a painstaking and time-consuming activity. One man rarely has enough time in his life to concentrate on more than a few of these clusters. It is inevitable, therefore, that the major clusterings of natural events come to be matched by clusters of men engaged in their investigation. The scientific community is thus differentiated roughly in the same way that natural phenomena are separated into distinctive categories, so that at any given time the organization of science comes close to reflecting men's current understanding of the organization of nature.

The self-assignment of individuals to the study of different aspects of reality at any given time has depended upon the number of individuals available for such work and the number of natural phenomena that seem capable of successful exploration. The relatively small, undifferentiated body of "learned men" that existed in the sixteenth century has been growing and becoming more differentiated ever since. By 1800 the physical sciences (physics, chemistry, astronomy, geology) were clearly distinguished as special fields of research; it was roughly during the nineteenth century that the biological sciences emerged as distinctive fields; and since 1900, the social sciences have acquired legitimacy as separate disciplines.

Current Organization of the Scientific Community

The present division of science into the physical, mathematical, life, and social sciences represents the most general subdivision of the scientific community. Within each of these broad areas, more specific clusters of events and relationships have been singled out for attention and have become the foci of the major scientific disciplines. Each discipline is in turn composed of "smaller" and more specific foci of attention called specialities, and these may be further subdivided into what may be called subspecialties. It is ordinarily the last of these that commands the interest and energy of an individual scientist; his work obviously requires him to understand the broader range of phenomena of which his particular subject matter is a part, and for this reason he identifies himself with a discipline, but his own particular subspecialty is usually complex enough to command his full-time attention.

If there were only *one* "best" way to categorize and describe natural phenomena, we would have a scientific community whose organization was a nearly perfect reflection of our understanding of the organization of nature. There would be no doubt that a man whose major interest lies in the investigation of faster-than-light particles (at present, this seems only a theoretical possibility) is a member of the subspecialty called "high-energy phenomena," which in turn is part of the specialty of "elementary particles" within the discipline of physics.

Actually, however, the same man might also be classified as specializing in "relativity and gravitation," which belongs under a different category within physics—or he might even be identified primarily as a mathematician, which is another discipline entirely. Because there are so many different ways of approaching the same phenomenon, and because a given phenomenon can be assigned to many different categories (according to the criteria one uses in identifying a category), there *is* no "best" way to describe the organization of nature. Thus there is no single, universally accepted rule to be followed in laying out the infrastructure of the scientific community.

The assignment of scientists to areas, disciplines, specialties, and so on, is therefore by no means entirely logical. Instead, it might be described as the result of multiple compromises among several relevant factors: the overlapping criteria by which empirical categories are defined, historical precedents, the incompleteness of current scientific knowledge, and certain human needs and values (including both interest in solving practical problems and the need to organize scientists into effective groups). Like the species with which Darwin was concerned, the organizational components of the scientific community are neither absolute nor unchanging; their "survival" is never assured, nor can we say that they are the most effective possible "species" of scientific endeavor that might be devised.

Perhaps the most we can say is that the lines dividing the physical, mathematical, life, and social sciences are stronger (because they are more abstract and have been recognized over a longer period of time) than are those dividing the disciplines within each of these areas. These divisions in turn are stronger than those that divide a single discipline into specialties. Below this level the lines drawn between subspecialties tend to be informal and are continually changing.

Specialties acquire legitimacy as they are recognized in terms of "sections" of scientific societies, as topics graduate students may choose for intensive training within their disciplines, and as categories in abstracts of the literature and in the National Register of Scientific and Technical Personnel. At the university level, however, disciplines (including some that may be characterized as "interdisciplinary," such as biochemistry) are the most specific groupings of scientists that are formally recognized. To subdivide the faculty into smaller groups would require more administrative paperwork and additional problems of organizing and coordinating curricula, while to keep the faculty organized into fewer but larger groups would render more difficult the kind of informal collegial control that seems most effective for such groups.

It is apparent, then, that there are practical advantages in having the scientific community organized as it is—into "working groups" of sub-specialties, small enough to facilitate efficient communication and continuing flexibility, and yet fitted in turn into larger and more formal groups which are still meaningful in terms of shared research interests and afford administrative convenience as well. It would be impossible to give up *all* organization (as seems to be advocated by some scientsits because lower-level distinctions seem so arbitrary), and equally impossible to organize the scientific community so rigidly that boundaries between its different parts would never be breached. Illogical as it may be by any single criterion, then, the infrastructure of science apparently represents something close to an optimal compromise among several competing criteria, all of which are relevant to the real situation. Out of these compromises have emerged the social structure and conceptual structure of science that form the background against which we shall examine the relationships among scientific disciplines.

Before turning to these relationships, it is necessary first to develop a picture of the theoretically important ways in which disciplines may vary, and then to examine the empirical differences among disciplines that exist in America today.

DIMENSIONS OF VARIATION AMONG THE DISCIPLINES

If the only differences among scientific disciplines lay in the distinctions among the phenomena they investigate, it would be relatively easy to analyze their relationships. However, even though the intrinsic differences among these phenomena seem to be the logical place to start, it turns out that this is not a very productive approach to the problem. It may allow us to say that some forms of research cost more than others, or that some subjects are more amenable to team research than others, but our present state of knowledge does not allow us to go much farther along this line. Instead, we must turn to both the social and the cultural aspects of scientific disciplines in order to characterize their differences.

The Social Dynamics of Science

During the 15 years that have elapsed since Merton's presidential address to the American Sociological Society (now Association), "Priorities in Scientific Discovery: A Chapter in the Sociology of Science,"[3] there has

---

[3] Robert K. Merton, "Priorities in Scientific Discovery: A Chapter in the Sociology of Science," *American Sociological Review*, 22, No. 6 (December 1957), 635–669.

developed a reasonably solid conceptual model, or "paradigm" in the sense that Kuhn has used the term,[4] of the scientific community as a whole. From Merton's seminal work has flowed a substantial body of empirical research and theoretical development, nearly all of which has been based on the central assumption that the quest for professional recognition is the normatively appropriate motivation for scientific activity. Such recognition, of course, is obtained almost exclusively in return for the contribution of new knowledge to the scientific community.

The ethos of science—the norms or principles governing scientists' relations with their colleagues—was first described by Merton in 1942[5] and is generally taken to be compatible with his subsequent work on the "driving energy" within science. Thus the central model identifies both the energy that is "native" to science and the structure through which it is channeled so that scientists continue to be motivated to carry out research and bodies of empirical knowledge continue to be built up within the various disciplines. While there is not complete agreement that the norms discussed by Merton are essential to the maintenance of the scientific community, the fact that scientists *do* seek professional recognition has been documented beyond question. The revelations of Watson's *The Double Helix*[6] came as no surprise to the sociologists of science.

Others have derived questions from this paradigm that have led to research on many aspects of the scientific community: competition and collaboration in research,[7] the influence of nonscientific factors on the receipt of professional recognition,[8] the consequences of the receipt of recognition,[9] the structure of informal communication networks,[10] and

[4] Thomas S. Kuhn, *The Structure of Scientific Revolutions*, Univ. of Chicago Press, Chicago, 1962.
[5] Robert K. Merton, "Science and Democratic Social Structure," in *Social Theory and Social Structure*, Rev. ed., Free Press, New York, 1957, pp. 550–561.
[6] James D. Watson, *The Double Helix*, Atheneum, New York, 1968.
[7] Warren O. Hagstrom, *Competition and Teamwork in Science*, Univ. of Wisconsin Department of Sociology, Madison, Wisconsin, July 1967, mimeographed.
[8] Diana Crane, "Scientists at Major and Minor Universities: A Study of Productivity and Recognition," *American Sociological Review*, 30, No. 5 (October 1965), 699–714; Stephen Cole and Jonathan R. Cole, "Scientific Output and Recognition: A Study of the Operation of the Reward System in Science," *American Sociological Review*, 32, No. 3 (June 1967), 377–390.
[9] Harriet Zuckerman, "Nobel Laureates in Science: Patterns of Productivity, Collaboration, and Authorship," *American Sociological Review*, 32, No. 3 (June 1967), 391–403; "The Sociology of the Nobel Prize," *Scientific American*, 217 (November 1967), 25–33.
[10] Derek J. de Solla Price, "Networks of Scientific Papers," *Science*, 149, No. 3683, 510–515; Nicholas C. Mullins, "The Distribution of Social and Cultural Properties in Informal Communication Networks among Biological Scientists," *American Sociological Review*, 33, No. 5 (October 1968), 786–797; Diana Crane, "Social Structure in a Group

such topics as patterns of name-ordering in multiple-author papers[11] and the invidious distinction between basic and applied research.[12] Such studies, following out the various questions implicit in this paradigm, seem a good example of contemporary "normal" science in the Kuhnsian sense. To call this work "puzzle-solving" is correct in that it represents the exploration of questions derived from the paradigm, but this is not to say that the research is not creative or satisfying. It will be some time yet before the paradigm's major questions have been investigated and enough anomalies have been identified to raise the need for transition to a new paradigm through a miniature "scientific revolution."

For the present, the touchstone assumption of the centrality of the quest for professional recognition provides a useful starting point from which to examine certain important ways in which scientific disciplines differ from one another. It directs us to ask about the factors that influence the allocation of recognition and to examine the roles that both cultural and social factors play in this process.

Differences among Bodies of Knowledge

The desire for professional recognition requires that the scientist be sensitive to his colleagues' views and opinions, for it is they who must bestow this as response to his contributions to science. Very few scientists have the ego strength to ignore their colleagues altogether, and very few are so completely motivated by private curiosity that they have no interest in what their colleagues think of their work. Generally, a scientist is deeply interested in whether his colleagues think what he has done is valid and whether they think it is of importance in advancing the body of knowledge with which they are mutually concerned.

Imperfect as it often is, in terms of whatever absolute standards might exist, the judgment of his colleagues must represent for the scientist the criteria he is trying to satisfy in his research. His scientific peer group may be wrong in its judgment of validity (as illustrated in the case of the "N-rays" that were supposedly discovered in France around the turn of the century);[13] they may be wrong in determining the significance

of Scientists: A Test of the 'Invisible College' Hypothesis," *American Sociological Review*, 34, No. 3 (June 1969), 335–352.

11 Harriet Zuckerman, "Patterns of Name-Ordering among Authors of Scientific Papers: A Study of Social Symbolism and Its Ambiguity," *American Journal of Sociology*, 74, No. 3 (November 1968), 276–291.

12 Norman W. Storer, "Basic versus Applied Research: The Conflict between Means and Ends in Science," *Indian Sociological Bulletin*, 2, No. 1 (October 1964), 34–42.

13 Evon Z. Vogt and Ray Hyman, *Water Witching USA*, Univ. of Chicago Press, Chicago, 1959, pp. 50–53.

of someone's findings (as was the case in the initial rejection of Mendel's work); but the opinions of one's colleagues represent the only social validation that a scientist can find. As a result, the current consensus within a discipline on standards of validity and significance (based on the acceptance of a given paradigm) ordinarily has a great deal of influence upon what a man investigates, how he goes about it, how he presents his findings, and the amount of professional recognition he is likely to receive in return for his work.

The very existence of consensus within a discipline or a specialty is problematic, however, as is the relative precision of the standards involved. In the Kuhnsian scheme a field may be in the preparadigm state (in which case it is relatively new and has not yet achieved substantial consensus on the basic character of its focal interest), it may be in a "normal" state (meaning that its practitioners generally agree on the standards of validity and significance that should apply to research in the field), or it may be in a state of "revolution" (in which the old consensus has broken down and the field is seeking a new definition of its subject matter—a new paradigm).

Since each discipline is in a preparadigm state only once, and revolutions that pervade entire disciplines are relatively rare, it is clear that most of the mature sciences are "normal" most of the time. (It may be argued whether the social sciences have yet achieved consensus on basic disciplinary paradigms, but it seems reasonable to assume that most specialties with these disciplines have approximated a condition of normal science.) For our purposes, then, we may take for granted the existence of a satisfactory level of agreement among the practitioners of the various disciplines on the standards by which validity is determined and the relative significance of new findings to a field's development is assessed.

There remains the question of how tightly integrated a given body of knowledge is. Regardless of how widely a paradigm is accepted within a discipline, there can still be a good deal of variation in terms of the precision with which the different "bits" that make up its body of knowledge are related to each other. In a field that is highly quantified—in which central concepts are defined by measurement and their relationships to each other are expressed mathematically—the body of knowledge is organized with considerable precision. Precision of this sort is much lower when concepts are defined in words rather than numbers and when their relationships are described verbally rather than in quantified statements.

The importance of this kind of difference among disciplines lies in its consequences for the allocation of professional recognition. In a relatively "hard" discipline, one whose body of knowledge is cast largely in quantified terms, it is comparatively easy for a man's colleagues to determine just how valid and significant his contributions are. In a "softer" science, criteria for allocation of recognition are fuzzier and the relationship between contribution and recognition is less clear-cut.[14]

The position of a discipline on this "hard–soft" continuum thus has important implications for the interpersonal expectations held by its members. We can expect that competition for recognition will be more intense in a harder discipline, since the greater precision with which its knowledge is organized points more clearly to the most significant problems currently awaiting solution and also facilitates rapid recognition of the scientists who first solve them. It is doubtful, for instance, that there has ever been a race to solve a particular problem in a social science that could be compared to the race in molecular biology to identify the structure of DNA; none of the social sciences has yet developed a sufficiently "hard" body of knowledge to make possible such precise indentification of a crucial research problem.

At the same time, the bestowal of recognition on the scientist who first solves one of these significant problems is more readily accepted as "just" by his colleagues, and there is relatively little concern that it was gained illicitly through the exploitation of personal friendships, organizational position, or "influence."

The softer sciences, however, are more likely to be characterized by the existence of competing "schools," which are widely (and sometimes with good reason) accused of using weapons other than "truth" in their attempts to gain ascendance over other schools. Such schools tend to form around specific institutions or charismatic figures and to rise and fall in influence according to essentially nonscientific variables. This situation seems to be true of many of the social sciences today, and these are also the disciplines in which, because the relationship between contribution and reward is less dependable, there may be widespread feeling that scientific success is due more to having gone to the right graduate school and knowing the right people than to the objective merit of one's research.

In interpersonal atmosphere, then, as well as in terms of more directly measurable characteristics, the various disciplines may differ considerably from one another. The differences discussed above, it must be emphasized, spring directly from differences in the bodies of knowledge with which they are concerned. The relationships among their members are organized around knowledge, after all, and it should not be

---

14 Norman W. Storer, "The Hard Sciences and the Soft: Some Sociological Observations," *Bulletin of the Medical Library Association,* **55,** No. 1 (January 1967), 75–84.

surprising that the shape or condition of a discipline's knowledge has some influence upon its members' behavior.

Other factors as well, social rather than cultural in nature, operate independently to shape the disciplines in varying ways. Among these are demographic, occupational, and economic factors, which are taken up as they produce differences among the disciplines in America today, in a subsequent section. Data are virtually nonexistent on such things as variations in the (structure of different scientific associations and in the ways research projects are typically organized in different fields, but we may assume that they are not only symptomatic of other differences among disciplines but also contribute to them.

Differences in the Social Context of Research

Just as the distinction between hard and soft sciences has been proposed as the most powerful single variable in explaining disciplinary differences in the cultural realm, it is probably the distinction between basic and applied research that has the greatest explanatory power in the social structural realm.[15] This assertion is based on two major arguments.

First, the applied researcher has less prestige within science than the basic researcher. The scientist who is identified primarily with applied research is, at least by implication, less deeply engaged in the activities that are central to the scientific community. (The words "is identified," it should be noted, are of crucial importance here, for the importance of the distinction between basic and applied research lies more in what scientists tend to believe about the two types of research than in any intrinsic differences between them in terms of quality or procedure. Where scientists locate a colleague on the basic–applied continuum tends to be primarily a function of where he is employed; educational institutions are thought to be the natural home of basic research, government to cover the middle section of this continuum, and industry to be the site of most applied research.)

Because the applied researcher is not thought to be as free as the basic researcher to "follow his nose," or to select for his work those problems that other scientists define as most significant for the advancement of knowledge, he tends to be viewed as a "defector." He can neither contribute fully to the ongoing work of his discipline (because he is solving problems posed for him by nonscientists), nor can he expect to earn through his research the professional recognition that,

15 Storer, "Basic versus Applied Research," *op. cit.*

normatively, he should be seeking. By going into applied research, then, he has in effect indicated his lack of commitment to the central norms and goals of the scientific community. Because of the invidious distinction thus made between the two categories of researchers, there tends to be less communication between them and probably less sense of sharing a common professional identity.

Second, the applied researcher is more involved in the "practical," everyday world than is the basic researcher. He works on problems that are important in the everyday world and is in frequent, work-oriented contact with nonscientists because of this. To the extent that his research is expected to "pay for itself," he must be more concerned with organizational problems and with practical economic matters. We might expect, then, that the applied scientist finds it easier sometimes to think of himself as a businessman, an administrator, or even a politician, than does the basic researcher.

The important question, of course, is what percentage of a discipline's members are engaged in essentially applied research. If the preceding hypotheses are correct, this figure should have implications for certain ways in which the disciplines differ from each other; in how they tend to view the importance of "pure" knowledge, the kinds of careers their members think are desirable, their level of concern with salary and other aspects of their employment, and the ways in which their bodies of knowledge are developed (steadily along a broad front, or by intensive thrusts at a few points along the frontier).

Having proposed two basic dimensions along with scientific disciplines may vary, one concerned with the intellectual meaning of *discipline* and the other with the social or organizational aspects of the term, we turn now to a consideration of the empirical parameters of American science.

EMPIRICAL DIFFERENCES AMONG THE SCIENTIFIC DISCIPLINES IN AMERICA

The National Science Foundation's National Register of Scientific and Technical Personnel today lists twelve major categories of scientists, not including "engineering" and "other specialties." These are the following.

Anthropology
Astronomy

Atmospheric, lithospheric, and hydrospheric sciences (which include meteorology, geology, and oceanography)

Biology

Chemistry

Economics

Interdisciplinary specialties (which include biochemistry, biophysics, electronics, physical chemistry, psychometrics, and statistics)

Linguistic specialties

Mathematics

Physics

Psychology

Sociology

Within these major categories are listed close to 100 principal specialties and, within these, nearly 1000 specific subspecialties. The extent to which this sort of subcategorization is carried out is of course partly a function of the mechanics of coding such distinctions for the computer, and partly a function of the numbers of scientists who claim each one as a major interest. To list *sub*subspecialties would undoubtedly strain the coding system, and there is no point in listing subcategories which, although they might exist "on paper," do not command the concentrated attention of at least a few scientists.

Thus even the National Register, organized with the advice of experts in all branches of science, cannot serve as a completely accurate guide to how far the differentiation of the scientific community has proceeded. Indeed, changes in the scheme of categories from one year to the next, and the complaints of scientists for whose needs any given scheme is partly inadequate, emphasize the almost insurmountable difficulties that arise when one attempts to draw a comprehensive organizational chart of science.

Some of the present categories are obviously "finer" than others. Within linguistic specialties, for instance, we find the specialty referred to as "applications to language training," and under this heading such subspecialties as "linguistics in second-language pedagogy" and "linguistics in the teaching of native-language skills." It is hard to deny that these subspecialties command the attention of far fewer scientists than do "aerodynamics" and "plasma physics," which are accorded equivalent standing as subspecialties under the specialty "physics of fluids" in the discipline of physics.

Yet the National Register is about the best guide we have, and to the extent that it identifies socially meaningful divisions within the scientific community, we may use it as an acceptable list of the major components of this community. There are serious questions to be asked, too, about the varying extent to which the Register covers members of different disciplines. Data for the Register are collected mainly in cooperation with professional scientific associations, and it is not known how the percentage of nonrespondents varies from one discipline to another, or even what proportion of a discipline's total practicing membership is represented in its professional association. Despite these caveats, though, the Register provides virtually the only information we have on the demographic, occupational, and economic characteristics of American scientists, and we must make the best use of it we can.

Demographic Differences

The figures given in Table 1 serve primarily to indicate the considerable diversity that exists among the major scientific disciplines in terms of numbers, sex ratio, geographic distribution, and—if the percentage of scientists in a discipline who hold the doctorate can be used as a measure—quality. There are, for instance, nearly fourteen times as many chemists in America as there are sociologists, even though this ratio is sharply reduced if we compare only those holding the Ph.D. in the two fields (there are about nine times as many Ph.D. chemists as there are Ph.D. sociologists).

Even among the physical and life sciences—those ordinarily considered the "real" sciences by the public—we find extensive variation not only in absolute numbers but in the percentages who have earned the Ph.D. Nearly half of the biological scientists hold the doctorate, while less than one-third of the chemists and little more than one-tenth of the atmospheric and space scientists do. It is significant to note, too, that while none of the social sciences has fewer than 50 percent of its members holding the doctorate, not one of the physical, mathematical, or life sciences has this high a proportion. This may reflect only the fact that those fields that have relatively little promise of economic application tend to be supported mainly by universities (as may be seen in Table 2), at which the Ph.D. is of greater importance. It also suggests, however, that membership in a discipline that has little practical value is more difficult to establish without obtaining the formal accreditation symbolized by the Ph.D.

Where thorough acquaintance with only a small part of a discipline's body of knowledge is enough to assure one a full-time job (as in the case of a man whose B.A. in chemistry enables him to find employment running quality tests on insecticides), the percentage of those who lack the doctorate but still consider themselves members of that discipline is likely to be fairly high since it is easier here to consider oneself a professional even without a lot of advanced training.

Since it is those scientists who hold the doctorate who make up the professional core of a discipline, being the men and women who are most likely to make science a lifetime career, it has seemed most useful to consider the variation among disciplines in terms of age particularly for these people. Several independent variables probably account for the marked variation among the disciplines in this respect: differential rate of growth over the past two decades, the relative economic value of the disciplines (which should tempt people to delay earning the Ph.D. because it would be less essential in getting a job), and perhaps simply variations in the relative difficulty involved in earning the doctorate now as compared with 20 years ago and more.

Despite this, it is interesting to note that only one of the physical and mathematical sciences for which data are available has *fewer* than 45 percent of its Ph.D.'s under the age of 40 while none of the biological and social sciences have *more* than 45 percent in this younger age range. This may be simply because the former two categories have experienced greater growth (because of enhanced economic worth) in the years since World War II, but the other factors noted above have undoubtedly also played a role in producing some of this systematic variation.

In terms of sex ratio, the data in Table 1 suggest quite clearly that women are more attracted to (or perhaps meet fewer obstacles in entering) those disciplines that are less mathematical and less "practical." With the exception of the agricultural sciences, which are especially practical, and of economics, which is both practical and highly quantitative, the biological and social sciences have uniformly higher percentages of women than do the physical and mathematical sciences. In support of this contention, if we compare these figures with those given in Table 2 concerning the percentages of scientists employed in government and industry together, we find that there is a fairly strong negative correlation between the two; of the top seven disciplines in terms of female members, only one of these is also among the top seven ranked according to percentages employed in government and industry. Since both practicality and quantification have traditionally been identified in this country with masculine interests, perhaps the best conclusion to be drawn here is that society's values seem to exert an appreciable influence upon recruitment to science, even when their influence upon a scientist's later work is markedly lower.

Finally, we see that members of the various disciplines are by no means distributed equally about the country. For illustrative purposes, data

Table 1 Selected Demographic Characteristics of the Major Scientific Disciplines

Area and Discipline	Number of Scientists Registered[a]	Percentage of Total Scientists[a]	Percentage Holding the Ph.D.[a]	Percentage with Ph.D. under 40[b]	Percentage of All Who are Women[b]	Percentage of All Living in[b]	
						N.Y., N.J., and Pa.	Ark., La., Texas Okla., and
Physical							
Chemistry	93,788	31	31	49	8	28	4
Physics	32,491	11	44	59	3	23	4
Earth and marine	23,746	8	21	43[c]	3[c]	8[c]	25[c]
Atmosphere and space	5,745	2	10	46[d]	2[d]	10[d]	8[d]
Mathematical							
Mathematics	24,477	8	29	57	10	22	5
Computer sciences	6,972	2	1	[e]	[e]	[e]	[e]
Statistics	2,639	1	35	51	10	22	1
Life							
Biological	46,183	16	49	41	11	20	4
Agricultural	12,740	4	18	33	[f]	7	5

Social

Psychology	23,077	8	64	43	22	25	4
Economics	11,510	4	53	37	4	23	6
Sociology	6,638	2	51	34	16	20	3
Political science	5,176	2	59	e	e	e	e
Linguistics	1,541	1	62	43	21	19	4
Anthropology	1,219	f	93	34	19	19	3
Total	297,942	100%			Average	22%	8%

[a] From "Salaries and Selected Characteristics of U.S. Scientists, 1968," Reviews of Data on Science Resources, No. 16 (December 1968), National Science Foundation, Washington, D.C.

[b] From American Science Manpower 1966, National Science Foundation, Washington, D.C., 1968, pp. 19, 61, 102–103, 200.

[c] Figures for "earth sciences" in American Science Manpower 1966.

[d] Figures for "meteorology" in American Science Manpower 1966.

[e] Data not given in this source for this discipline.

[f] Less than one-half of 1 percent.

are given on the percentages of scientists in each discipline living in the Middle Atlantic region of the nation (New York, New Jersey, and Pennsylvania) and in the West South Central region (Oklahoma, Texas, Arkansas and Louisiana). The former region contains, on the whole, 22 percent of all American scientists, while the latter contains 8 percent. Scientists in the earth sciences, meterology, and agricultural sciences are clearly underrepresented in the Middle Atlantic region, and those in the earth sciences are markedly overrepresented in the West South Central area.

The fact that much of the nation's oil production is centered in the West South Central region must obviously account for the presence of so many earth scientists there, and thus indirectly for their underrepresentation in the Middle Atlantc states. By the same reasoning, we can understand why there are so few agricultural scientists in the latter region; indeed, if it were not for the presence of so many earth scientists in the West South Central states, the percentage of the nation's agricultural scientists located there would be appreciably higher than the overall average for that region.

Certain disciplines, then—those with value to specific economic interests—are distributed geographically in rather different ways than are those disciplines that tend to be centered in education institutions. Such differences tell us less, perhaps, that do those concerning relative size, the proportion of scientists in a discipline who hold the doctorate, or the proportion who are women, but they add weight to the conclusion that the American scientific community is highly heterogeneous.

"Psychological" Differences

The demographic differences among disciplines represented in Table 1 do not tell us anything about the differences in personal style or social atmosphere that may characterize the different disciplines. While we know relatively little about such differences, it is obvious that they exist. Both Roe[16] and Eiduson[17] found that social scientists tend to be more gregarious and people-oriented than are biological and physical scientists. Lipset and Ladd have reported recently that wide differences exist among teachers in various disciplines in terms of political preferences and associated attitudes. They find, for instance, that the percentages of professors who approve of student "activism" on campus ranges from 63 percent of the social scientists down to 19 percent of those in agricultural

16 Ann Roe, *The Making of a Scientist*, Dodd, Mead, New York, 1953.
17 Bernice T. Eiduson, *Scientists: Their Psychological World*, Basic Books, (New York, 1962).

sciences, with physical sciences (40 percent), biological sciences (40 percent), and engineering professors (26 percent) falling between these extremes.[18]

Variation along such dimensions seems to be influenced partly by the existence of a special attractiveness between certain disciplines and certain personality types, and also by such nonpsychological factors as the histories of the disciplines, the average age and class background of their practitioners, and so on. Even if modal personality types do have some influence in determining these sorts of differences, then, it is clear that social and cultural factors must also play a large role.

Occupational Differences

Table 2 gives us an overview of the range of variation among disciplines in terms of the occupational characteristics of their members, presenting data gathered by the National Science Foundation on where the members of the disciplines are employed and the kinds of "principal work activity" in which they are engaged.

The difference between two of the physical sciences, chemistry and physics, stands out immediately. The proportion of physicists (48 percent) employed in educational institutions, for instance, is twice as large as the proportion of chemists (22 percent) so employed, while the opposite relationship holds true for employment in industry. And while the majority of physicists (53 percent) is engaged primarily in basic research or teaching, less than one-third (29 percent) of the chemists are principally involved in these central scientific activities. However, the percentages of both disciplines' memberships engaged in applied research and development are equal, contrary to what we might expect; this accounted for, though, by the fact that nearly one-half of the chemists (42 percent) are employed in administration and production.

While these figures apparently give us good reason for supposing that physics as a discipline is much more in the mainstream of science *qua* science than is chemistry, it is likely that these differences would be considerably reduced if we were to look only at Ph.D.'s in the two fields. Data, unfortunately, are not available to test this assertion.

It is not surprising to find that the social sciences, almost without exception, have a higher percentage of their members employed in educational institutions than do the other areas of science. Relatively lacking in immediate economic utility and, with the exception of psychology, in

18 Seymour Martin Lipset and Everett Carll Ladd, Jr., ". . . And What Professors Think," *Psychology Today*, 4, No. 6 (November 1970), 49–51, 106.

Table 2 Selected Occupational Characteristics of the Major Scientific Disciplines[a]

Area and Discipline	Number of Scientists Registered	Percentage Employed in			Principal Work Activity of Those Reporting[c] in percentages				
		Education	Govern-ment[b]	Industry	Applied Research and Devel-opment	Basic Research	Teaching	Adminis-tration and Production	Miscel-laneous[d]
Physical									
Chemistry	93,788	22	7	57	24	17	12	42	6
Physics	32,491	48	12	29	25	30	23	18	4
Earth and marine	23,746	25	17	41	7	10	18	25	39
Atmosphere and space	5,745	13	33	9	11	9	5	29	46
Mathematical									
Mathematics	24,477	53	7	30	14	9	42	23	12
Computer sciences	6,972	13	1	65	38	2	3	25	32
Statistics	2,639	34	28	26	23	7	19	25	25
Life									
Biological	46,183	59	15	10	13	31	29	19	8
Agricultural	12,740	23	54	16	18	6	8	57	9

Social

Psychology	23,077	56	15	8	21	8	24	20	27
Economics	11,510	58	17	14	16	6	42	26	10
Sociology	6,638	73	7	e	10	15	55	15	6
Political science	5,176	76	10	e	4	9	62	18	7
Linguistics	1,541	73	5	e	6	12	62	12	8
Anthropology	1,219	81	4	e	3	20	62	12	4

[a] From "Salaries and Selected Characteristics of U.S. Scientists, 1968," *Reviews of Data on Science Resources*, No. 16 (December 1968); National Science Foundation, Washington, D.C.

[b] Includes "federal government" and "other government" but not "military."

[c] Those who gave no report of principal work activity, or who were unemployed, are not included in the base against which these percentages are calculated. These proportions ranged from 4 percent for the agricultural sciences to 14 percent for the linguistics.

[d] Includes consultation, exploration, forecasting, reporting, and "other."

[e] Less than one-half of 1 percent.

the ability to satisfy immediate individual needs, social scientists would be hard put to find employment in substantial numbers anywhere *but* in academic institutions.

Atmospheric and space scientists, however, as well as agricultural scientists, are most important to national programs (rather than to private industry or individual needs) and are therefore represented most prominently in government employment. The greatest single employer of the former group, however, (about 35 percent of them) is the military services—which are not included in Table 2 because they employ such small numbers of other scientists. If the military services are defined as "governmental" employers, however, then this field of science is the one most deeply engaged in governmental service; about two-thirds of all atmospheric and space scientists receive their salaries directly or indirectly from the federal government.

It is probably for the same reason that most social scientists are found in educational institutions—relative lack of immediate economic value— that we find such high percentages of their members reporting teaching as their principal work activity. It is likely, moreover, that the percentage of a discipline's members who fall into this category is the best single indicator of how little immediate economic or social value a field has (especially if we define the space program as having "social" value). Perhaps the rule should really be: "Those who cannot do (something of practical value) *must* teach."

Economic Differences

Table 3 presents data on salaries and on federal support of basic and applied research. Here we find some support for the contention that scientists would *like* to be at the center of the scientific community (that is, engaged in basic research). If educational institutions are most closely identified with basic research, government less closely, and industry hardly at all, then the general pattern of differences in median salaries paid to scientists by these broad categories of employers becomes intelligible. Higher salaries must be paid by those employers who are farther, occupationally, from the center of the scientific community, to offset the "deprivations" that their scientific employees sense in the situation.

With only two minor exceptions (mathematical sciences and agricultural sciences), the median salaries of those scientists who work for educational institutions are lower than those received by government employees, which in turn are lower than those received by scientists in industry. The fact that industry undoubtedly employs a larger proportion of non-Ph.D.'s than either the government or educational institutions only increases the significance of this relationship. In general, it appears that the more closely an employer is identified with basic research, the less it must pay in order to attract scientists to work there.

To be sure, differences in the average age of men working for each type of employer, in the scarcity of men in the various disciplines relative to present demand for their skills, and in the distribution of primary work activities within each employment category are all likely to play some part in determining the differences that appear in Table 3. The proposed relationship between median salary and type of employer as a function of the "closeness" of each to basic research can thus be no more than speculative at this point, and data are not available in such form now as to allow a more detailed test of this interpretation.

Finally, Table 3 indicates that there are marked differences among the disciplines in terms both of percentages of scientists receiving federal support and in per capita support received. While the former is greatly influenced by the percentage of scientists in a discipline who are employed by government (the atmospheric and space sciences, and agricultural sciences, are particularly prominent here, as shown in Table 2), the fact that research in some fields simply *costs* more undoubtedly influences the amount per capita that the federal government devotes to research in the various disciplines.

Obviously, a great deal remains to be learned about the meaning of these figures. It is not difficult to understand why, for instance, the per capita federal support for research in the mathematical sciences should be so low; in comparison to the experimental sciences, the cost of research equipment and supplies is virtually nil. It is not so easy, though, to understand why the per capita support for research in chemistry is almost identical to this figure.

It is quite likely that atmospheric and space scientists are not fully covered by the scientific manpower data since this category is relatively new. At the same time, the space program *has* been exceedingly expensive. Between an underrepresentation of space scientists and the costs of much research in this area, then, the figure of $122,197 average federal support for each scientist in this category receiving support does not surprise us. Why, though, the fields of economics, sociology, and anthropology should receive *more* support per capita than either the biological or agricultural sciences, is simply a puzzle now. At present, such economic data are useful more in displaying these differences than in testing hypotheses about them.

Table 3 Selected Financial Characteristics of the Major Scientific Disciplines

Area and Discipline	Number of Scientists Registered[a]	Median Salaries, Ph.D.'s (thousand $)[c]			Scientists Receiving Federal Support[a]		Total Federal Support (thousand $)[a]	Support per Capita[a] ($)
		Education	Government[b]	Industry	Number	Percent		
Physical								
Chemistry	93,877	12.0	13.9	15.0	25,967	28	$242,169	9,326
Physics	32,491	12.0	15.7	17.0	20,190	62	776,869	38,476
Earth and marine	23,746	12.8	13.8	14.4	6,910	29	385,858	55,840
Atmosphere and space	5,745	13.0	16.2	18.5	5,067	88	619,173	122,197
Mathematical								
Mathematics	24,477	13.6	18.2	18.0	8,757	36	130,021	9,308
Computer sciences	6,972	e	e	e	3,667	53	e	e
Statistics	2,639	13.5	17.0	17.0	1,545	59	e	e
Life								
Biological	46,183	13.0	13.4	15.0	27,356	59	434,270	15,875
Agricultural	12,740	13.0	12.9	13.8	8,856	70	113,533	12,820

Social

Psychology	23,077	12.5	13.8	17.5	10,024	44	108,042	10,778
Economics	11,510	14.0	16.2	20.0	4,353	38	69,692	16,010
Sociology	6,638	13.0	15.2	f	2,311	35	50,049	21,657
Political science	5,176	e	e	e	1,484	29	e	e
Linguistics	1,541	12.0	f	f	450	29	e	e
Anthropology	1,219	13.0	f	f	476	39	11,213	23,557

[a] From "Salaries and Selected Characteristics of U.S. Scientists, 1968," *Reviews of Data on Science Resources*, No. 16 (December 1968), National Science Foundation, Washington, D.C.

[b] Includes "federal government" and "other government" but not "military."

[c] From *American Science Manpower 1966*, National Science Foundation, Washington, D.C., 1968, pp. 91–92.

[d] Calculated from *Federal Funds for Research, Development, and Other Scientific Activities*, National Science Foundation, Washington D.C., 1968, pp. 152, 174. Actual 1967 federal obligations for basic and applied research are divided by the total number of scientists in each discipline given as receiving support in *Reviews of Data on Science Resources*, No. 16, as cited above, to yield "support per capita."

[e] Data not given in this source for this discipline.

[f] Less than one-half of 1 percent, or number of cases too small to calculate a median.

Organizational Differences

We lack systematic data that can tell us about the broad differences among the disciplines in terms of their internal organization: how much intradisciplinary cooperation there is, how patterns of both vertical and horizontal mobility may differ from one discipline to the next, and how much weight is given in different disciplines to informal as compared with formal channels of communication. There are, however, some scattered findings that bear on such questions.

Hagstrom, in a study of competition and teamwork in science focused entirely upon university scientists in physics, chemistry, mathematics, and biology, found that the level of "competitiveness" varied considerably from one of these fields to another. The proportion of scientists reporting that they "do not feel safe to discuss their work with all other persons doing similar work in other institutions" (a measure of how much they fear that others may try to "steal" their work in order to gain priority—and thus professional recognition—for themselves) varied from 45 percent in mathematics to 64 percent in chemistry. Physics (48 percent) and biology (52 percent) fell between these extremes.[19] It is likely that a much smaller proportion of social scientists would indicate such worries, since the race for priority is mush less intense in a soft science.

Hagstrom also found that while mathematicians average only 3.19 collaborators in their work (colleagues, postdoctoral fellows, graduate assistants, and technicians), chemists averaged 6.24 and experimental physicists averaged 8.40.[20] However, chemists were most likely to wish for more assistance (64 percent of them expressed this need), while 48 percent of the experimental physicists and only 25 percent of the mathematicians wanted more assistance. Nearly half of the mathematicians, in fact, said explicitly that they neither had nor wanted any assistance at all, in comparison to 20 percent of the theoretical physicists, 2 percent of the experimental biologists, and less than 0.5 percent of the experimental physicists.[21]

In their studies of scientific communication, Garvey, Lin, and Nelson have tentatively identified several interesting differences among scientific disciplines.[22] While research that resulted in a published article took about a year for both physical and social scientists to complete, the former

---

[19] Hagstrom, *op. cit.*, p. 8.
[20] Calculated from Hagstrom, *op. cit.*, p. 29.
[21] *Ibid.*, p. 35.
[22] William D. Garvey, Nan Lin, and Carnot E. Nelson, "Scientific Communication in the Physical and the Social Sciences," Johns Hopkins Univ. Center for Research in Scientific Communication, Baltimore, 1970, Baltimore, mimeographed.

took an average of 6 months to prepare and submit a report of their work, while the latter averaged 9 months between completion and submission. A further distinction appears in the finding that only about 7 months elapse between submission and publication for physical science papers; the equivalent average for social science papers is nearly 12 months.

The rate of rejection for submitted manuscripts is considerably higher in the social sciences than in the physical sciences. Garvey, Lin, and Nelson found that less than 15 percent of the physical science papers submitted to journals after presentation at a national meeting were rejected, while the comparable figure for the social sciences was 40 percent. Disciplinary differences in terms of overall rejection rates—the percentages of all submissions that are rejected—are even more striking. Zuckerman and Merton found that the mean rejection rates in 1967 for journals in sixteen fields, ranging from history, language and literature, and philosophy, down to physics, geology, and linguistics, varied from 90 percent for history to 20 percent for linguistics. The social sciences ranged from 47 percent (anthropology) to 84 percent (political science), while the physical sciences ranged from 31 percent (chemistry) down to 22 percent (geology).[23]

Compounding these differences is Garvey, Lin, and Nelson's finding that rejection of a physical science paper by one journal adds an average of 4 months to the period before it achieves publication in a second journal, while for the social sciences rejection adds an average of 8 months to the hiatus between oral report and publication.

Despite the greater delays experienced by social scientists in bringing their work formally to the attention of their colleagues through publication, they were less likely than physical scientists to make use of other channels of communication. Eighty-three percent of the physical scientists disseminated their work to others in some way (usually through preprints) before submitting it for publication, compared with 72 percent of the social scientists. Similarly, 75 percent of the physical scientists and 66 percent of the social scientists had made some report of their work to their colleagues through colloquia, preprints, or technical reports.

Such findings suggest that there is much less pressure in the social sciences to achieve publication than there is in the physical sciences, despite the fact that publication is usually an important criterion for academic promotion in both areas. We might interpret the relative slow-

23 Harriet Zuckerman and Robert K. Merton, "Patterns of Evaluation in Science: Institutionalization, Structure, and Functions of the Referee System," a paper presented at the 1968 Annual Meetings of the American Sociological Association, Boston.

ness of social scientists to get into print partly as the result of there being less competition for priority in softer disciplines and, at the same time, the higher rejection rate experienced by social scientists as evidence of the lack of consensus on standards of excellence in such fields. On the basis of the findings cited above, we might conclude that at least 85 percent of the physical scientists are in agreement on what constitutes publishable material, since roughly this proportion of manuscripts are accepted by the first journals to which they are submitted. The comparable figure for the social scientists is about 60 percent. It is interesting, further, to note that nearly twice as many physical scientists abandoned plans for publication after receiving a first rejection (63 percent) as did social scientists (38 percent).

Much of what we know about differences in communication practices and patterns in the different disciplines, then, seems to be traceable to the relative hardness or softness of their various bodies of knowledge. A soft science lacks rigorous standards of excellence, and thus is weak both in its ability to build a tightly cumulative body of knowledge and in its members' motivation to compete vigorously for priority.

We have virtually no systematic information on differences among the disciplines' professional societies or associations. There are presumably differences in the percentage of members who cast their ballots in electing officers, in how authors are selected to present papers at meetings, in the criteria by which scientists are deemed eligible for nomination to associational office, and so on. In some disciplines a man's contributions to knowledge seem to carry considerable weight in his winning an election, while in others his services to the association may be more important. The American Chemical Society tends to elect its presidents from academia one year and from industry the next;[24] comparable patterns can probably be found in other scientific societies.

The size of a discipline's membership, the distribution of its members among different types of employers, and its relative hardness should all play a part in determining how its professional association is organized. The large number of scientific societies in this country alone should afford opportunity for some highly interesting research on the subject.

Conclusions

In this section we have focused upon the ways in which scientific disciplines differ from one another. Taking explicit account of the dual

24 Anselm L. Strauss and Lee Rainwater, *The Professional Scientist: A Study of American Chemists,* Aldine, Chicago, 1962.

meaning of the term discipline, as it refers to both a collectivity of individuals and a body of knowledge, it has been suggested that most of the differences about which we have data can be traced to the position that different disciplines occupy on one or the other of two fundamental dimensions of variation. Whether a discipline's body of knowledge is "hard" or "soft" seems to have important implications for the relations among its practitioners, particularly in terms of communication practices. Whether its members are concerned principally with basic or applied research has consequences for their salaries, the conditions under which they work, and presumably also for the extent of their involvement in the central activities of the scientific community.

Differences in size, distribution among employers, concern with problems that are important to nonscientists, and communication practices seem so great in some instances, in fact, that the reader may seriously question the utility of trying to say anything at all that has empirical validity in terms of the "scientific community" as a whole. Only in the ideal sense, perhaps, referring to an ideal model of "the social system of science" against which this heterogeneous reality must be compared, does it seem possible to talk of *the* scientific community. In the following section, we shall see some of the ways in which the different parts of this community are related to each other so that the word "community" is not entirely a misnomer.

RELATIONS AMONG THE SCIENTIFIC DISCIPLINES

It is possible here to consider only two of the principal forms of relationship that may be found between groups of people: cooperation and competition. Neither of the other forms (consensus at one end of the continuum and conflict at the other) seems applicable in the case of scientific disciplines. Continuing with the distinction drawn between the cultural or intellectual and the social or organizational aspects of the disciplines, we examine cooperation and competition among them in terms of both their knowledge relationships and their organizational relationships.

It must be admitted at the outset that we know very little about these relationships. The study of science has not yet advanced to the point where the investigation of such things promises to have much theoretical payoff, and the number of social scientists interested in such research is only now reaching the level at which a cumulative flow of findings may be expected. What follows, then, must be largely a codification of the author's unsystematic observations rather than a review of research informed by a carefully constructed set of hypotheses. At best, it may provide a useful first approximation to a conceptual framework from which meaningful research questions can be drawn.

Intellectual Cooperation

Here our interest focuses on what we know of how the disciplines "help" each other in terms of knowledge. What use, in other words, do botanists make of knowledge developed by chemists? How might psychology be advanced by taking advantage of what geographers have learned? We are interested here in the extent to which instances of such cooperation actually occur, and in the factors that encourage or impede disciplinary cooperation at the level of knowledge.

It is agreed, by and large, that knowledge tends to flow from the harder to the softer disciplines, at least in substantive form, while theoretical analogies may apparently flow in either direction, depending on the apparent attractiveness or explanatory power ascribed to a particular paradigm. As long as one discipline is interested in a phenomenon whose component parts form the subject matter of another discipline (as chemistry focuses upon compounds, the components of which—atoms and the various particles of which they are composed—are the focus of physics), the former is certain to arrive sooner or later at a stage where further understanding of this subject matter requires more detailed knowledge of its parts. Just as the flow of knowledge from physics to chemistry has been institutionalized in the interdisciplinary field of physical chemistry, so the parallel relationship between chemistry and biology has produced the field of biochemistry and the interaction between physics and biology the field of molecular biology.

Until quite recently, and with the exception of physiological phychology, here has been a major gap between biology and the social sciences. The focus of the latter on man's use of symbols and the critical role they play in his relations with other men has presumably contributed to the conviction that biological knowledge is only minimally relevant to the understanding of social phenomena. Today, however, with intensified public interest in the population explosion and the pollution of the environment, as well as the asking of increasingly sophisticated questions about human and social behavior, it appears that the interface between the biological and social sciences is about to receive a substantial input of manpower and funds. In terms of basic knowledge, the flow is almost certain to be from the biological to the social sciences, even though in understanding concrete empirical "ecosystems" there is likely to be a more even exchange.

In the realm of theoretical models, metaphors, and paradigms, the history of the "survival of the fittest" idea is of interest here. In its barest form, almost without any elaboration, the idea first came to light at the beginning of the nineteenth century in the work of Thomas Malthus, who was an economist. The kernel of this idea is said to have been the inspiration, nearly half a century later, for the evolutionary theory of Charles Darwin (and of Alfred Russel Wallace). From biology, the idea was picked up again, this time with more details, by the social sciences (such as they were in the latter nineteenth century) and by the public in the form of "social Darwinism" and was used as an intellectual defense of laissez-faire capitalism.

Ordinarily, however, since the harder sciences have tended to be more advanced and thus more prolific in the production of abstract models, it is probably true here as well that the flow is primarily from hard to soft. It is likely, for instance, that the Newtonian model of the solar system, Mendelyeef's periodic table, and even Boyle's Law have served, implicitly if not explicitly, as models for various theories in the biological and social sciences. Certainly, functional analysis and systems theory in the social sciences can be traced back to earlier theoretical work in biology.

There are two principal obstacles to the transfer of substantive information from one discipline to another. The first is simply the difficulty that scientists in different disciplines have in understanding each other's technical language, even though with sufficient good faith and patience such communication barriers can be overcome. The second obstacle shows up most frequently in the form of pride—the feeling on the part of each scientist that *his* discipline faces the toughest intellectual problems, shows the greatest ingenuity in solving them, and has less to learn from other disciplines than they do from it. Such opinions are a natural concomitant of loyalty to one's own discipline, but in this case they may have a more understandable basis as well.

The need to communicate with one's disciplinary colleagues in terms that they can understand means that a scientist may often be reluctant to introduce materials with which they are unfamiliar. For instance, if a psychologist begins to make use of biological concepts and variables in his work, relatively few other psychologists will be able to appreciate this; the majority will be at least partly unable to respond to his work and, worse, may reject it on the grounds that it is irrelevant to their interests. Apparently, it is only when many people in one discipline come to recognize that their work might be aided by an input of knowledge from another discipline that this latter obstacle can be gradually overcome.

There have, of course, been attempts to pick up the other end of the stick—to wave the banner of "interdisciplinary research" as something good in its own right even before it has been tried. While this kind of enthusiasm tends to come in periodic waves, the experience has been almost universal that when scientists begin with only a "let's work together" ideal, they have great difficulty in finding a research topic that requires the whole-hearted cooperation of every discipline involved. Instead, interdisciplinary research turns out to be useful and mutually stimulating primarily when a *problem* has been first identified and *then* scientists with knowledge and skills relevant to its investigation are brought together to work on it. The dynamics of science are such, however, that even successful collaborations of this sort are rarely viable beyond the concrete research problem that initially gave them their start; oil and water may indeed be shaken together until they form a nearly homogeneous mixture, but without repeated shakings they tend to separate out again.

In the realm of research methodology and instrumentation, transfers from one discipline to another seem to have been quite common and to take place without particular difficulty. Statistics, for example, was first brought to a level of wide-ranging utility by agricultural scientists who needed it to help in interpreting their experiments in plant breeding and nutrition. By now, it is associated primarily with the social sciences. The measurement of radioactivity, a technique developed by nuclear physicists, is now used extensively by archaeologists and paleobotanists, as with carbon-14 dating. The list of cases in which a research technique originating in one discipline has been picked up by scientists in one or more other disciplines is endless.[25]

Perhaps, indeed, this may be the chief form of interdisciplinary cooperation, because fewer obstacles to the transfer of information exist at this level. For one thing, the data-generating advantages to be gained through using a new research technique are fairly obvious, whereas the theoretical utility of a concept borrowed from another discipline may not be. The question of *how* one obtains his data, in other words, is probably less important (if one's colleagues accept them as valid) than what one does with them. The use of a new research technique does not necessarily commit a scientist to writing about phenomena that lie outside his colleagues' common universe of discourse, and in this sense the scientist may tend to agree that the end justifies the means.

[25] In a personal communication to the author, Robert K. Merton has remarked on the intriguing difference here between scientific and national boundaries; in the case of the latter, it is generally ideas rather than technology that diffuse more easily—a fact that should have important implications for our understanding of why international technological cooperation is not always successful.

In applied research, cooperation among different disciplines probably occurs quite often. Here not only are disciplinary identities less important —the aim is to solve a practical problem, not to add to an organized body of "pure" knowledge—but success is measured by criteria other than those of logical "fit" with an established body of knowlege and acceptance by a particular group of scientists. Perhaps the only obstacle to such cooperation in applied research is that of the communication difficulties experienced by men trained in different disciplines, and this cannot long survive a concentrated attack by all parties involved in the research.

Finally, some mention should be made of the various attempts to integrate scientific knowledge without regard for disciplinary boundaries. The history of such attempts goes back at least to the *Philosophes* of eighteenth century France—a century when it seemed still possible for an individual to command all scientific knowledge. Since then, however, efforts to "unify" science have been directed primarily toward the construction of theories of such breadth and abstraction that the knowledge contained in many disciplines may be deduced from them, or may at least be viewed as representing the working-out of such theories in different areas of empirical phenomena.

Perhaps the best known example of such an effort in the physical sciences is Einstein's unfinished attempt to link gravitational and magnetic phenomena in a single comprehensive physical theory. In the biological and social sciences, which deal with "open systems," the leading example of an attempt to integrate these disciplines is general systems theory.

The more abstract such theories become, of course, the more they verge on becoming philosophies of science rather than substantive frameworks within which vast ranges of empirical knowledge can be integrated. However, the promise of more economical and far-reaching conceptual formulations that can help to bridge current gaps between disciplines continues to lure some of our brightest and most imaginative minds. It may not be too long before new generations of scientists are given enough training in such general vocabularies that disciplinary cooperation will become much more common than it seems to be today.

Intellectual Competition

Competition implies vested interests, which in turn imply connections between men and knowledge. The only types of connection that can engender competition would seem to be those of "ownership" (which discipline has the "right" to investigate or to interpret a particular empirical phenomenon?), and of relative value (which discipline's body of knowledge is more "valuable," either in terms of absolute goodness or vis-à-vis the interests of a third party?).

The existence of competition *within* disciplines is well known, centering as it does on the quest for priority in scientific discovery. Competition *between* disciplines, however, has received much less attention and we know little about its nature or extent. The simplest form of competition over ownership ought to be the case in which each of two disciplines claims that some newly discovered phenomenon should be investigated by *its* practitioners. The case is rarely so clear-cut, however, and ordinarily such contests focus instead upon the question of whose analytical apparatus or interpretive framework is better suited or will be more effective in the investigation of a particular topic. The problem of racial differences, for instance, can legitimately be studied from the perspectives of genetics, phychology, and sociology—but there does exist a kind of implicit competition over which of these disciplines can provide the most satisfactory explanation ("account for the most variance") of whatever differences may be found.

Competition over ownership of the "right of interpretation" thus shifts imperceptibly to competition over which discipline's body of knowledge is "more valuable." Within the scientific community as a whole, physics is generally agreed to be the "best," largely because it embodies the ideals of science: a focus on basic knowledge, rigorous theoretical organization and sophisticated research techniques, broad coverage of empirical phenomena, and so on. With respect to the public, though, the criteria of value may themselves be contested. Is relevance to human health more valuable than knowledge for its own sake? Is the ability to make a transistor perform better than knowledge of *why* it performs?

Competition for public esteem (and, indirectly, for support) is usually implicit rather than explicit, and its outcome is inevitably ambiguous except in the few cases in which a large program of governmental support for research on a particular topic is either initiated or phased out. Given the ordinary inability of science, however, to demonstrate the concrete worth of its "product" upon demand, the disciplines have for the most part found it more important to present a reasonably united front to the public, on the assumption that interdisciplinary squabbling will only hurt all parties. This is taken up in more detail in a subsequent section.

Competition is sharpened, of course, when it involves individuals rather than groups. Perhaps it is the sort of pride mentioned above that is responsible for resistance to (and thus a kind of competition with) particular scientists when they move from their original disciplines to other fields after having been successful in the former. There was the case a few years ago, for instance, of a young Nobel prize winner in physics who announced his intention of turning his attention to the specialized sub-field of virology. Intended or not, this was received as an insult by many virologists, who apparently felt that the scientist in question seemed to be offering his high-level talents to help them along with a job they could not master themselves. Similarly, Linus Pauling's efforts to "mathemat-icize" chemistry were criticized by some as a kind of unwelcome in-tellectual aggressiveness; although originally a chemist, Pauling had devoted a good deal of time to quantum physics and seemed to be "bringing it to chemistry" with an evangelical enthusiasm that did not sit well with his colleagues.

In both cases it is interesting to note that the flow was *to* a discipline that was relatively softer. The obvious explanation for this is that it is easier to move in this direction because less time is needed to master a softer science—its body of knowledge is not organized in a rigorously hierarchical fashion so that one need not study topics in rigid sequence in order to master it. The story has it, though, that the young physicist soon discovered that there was more to virology than he had supposed, so that he did not immediately produce any spectacular breakthroughs, and it is debatable how much influence Pauling's efforts had in redirecting the course of chemistry. In any case the factors that work to produce the hard-to-soft direction of intellectual migration among scientists deserve considerable study.

It should be remarked, in conclusion, that disciplinary competition in terms of knowledge is not usually an easily observable phenomenon. The fundamental belief that the validity of knowledge is unrelated to the characteristics of the man who produced it, and the complementary belief that a scientist should be free to investigate whatever he chooses, make it difficult for scientists to be open in attempting to deny others the right to work in "their" disciplines. If demonstrable validity is all that counts, it is clear that no one should be deprived of the opportunity to move from one field to another, even though the fact that an appreciable record of accomplishment in a given field is usually prerequisite to obtaining research support means that only the most energetic and persistent field changers ever acquire, finally, the wherewithal to implement their in-tentions.

Truth triumphs in the long run, we suppose, so that competition between disciplines in terms of any given intellectual matter must be a short-run problem. Yet the pace and direction of scientific advancement is obviously shaped by immediate events, so that to understand more of this the nature and dynamics of intellectual competition among scientific disciplines will require much more thorough investigation than it has yet received.

Organizational Cooperation

Having separated the intellectual aspects of disciplinary relationships from the social or organizational, we must conclude that cooperation among the disciplines in terms of the latter must be concerned primarily with their common professional or career interests. This in turn may be divided between two foci: concentration on internal problems (upgrading research standards, improving the training of graduate students) and concentration of the relations between science and the public.

Internal improvement seems to be the province of *areas* of science— the physical, mathematical, biological, and social sciences—rather than of the scientific community as a whole. Efforts in this vein are ordinarily handled through organizations, although they differ widely in character. The American Institute of Physics, the Federation of American Societies of Experimental Biology, and the Social Science Research Council all have important responsibilities in upgrading research and training in their particular areas of science but carry out their work through different organizational mechanisms. By means of publications, fellowship programs, conferences, training institutes, and other devices, they may attempt to help their "constituents" keep up with new developments relavant to their disciplines; they may cooperate in the development of new curricula for public school, undergraduate, and graduate students; and they may work to improve communications both within and among their supporting disciplines.

Such organizations may also take some responsibility for keeping tabs on the "health" of their disciplines by publishing reports on numbers of new degrees granted, average salaries, projecting future needs for scientists in various fields, and cooperating with the National Register of Scientific and Technical Personnel in compiling statistics on the American scientific community as a whole. They have also cooperated with the National Research Council in cosponsoring the production of comprehensive reports on the nature, achievements, and anticipated needs of various areas and disciplines.

However, this is not the place to go into detail about the acitivites of such organizations. For our purposes it suffices to say that in using them as principal mechanisms, the disciplines have been both active and successful in cooperation aimed at internal improvements.

Cooperation vis-à-vis the public and the federal government has not been as well organized, but there has been a great deal of it since the end of World War II. Concern with the handling of nuclear research, resulting in the establishment of a civilian Atomic Energy Commission, and with the establishment of the National Science Foundation, were the two major instances in the late 1940s when the scientific community moved to try to present a united front to the government. To be successful in such enterprises, of course, the competing interests of different disciplines must be mediated within the community before a genuinely coherent policy can be urged upon the President or Congress. Needless to say, this has not always been accomplished, so that in specific cases different groups of scientists have offered conflicting advice to policy makers. One might suggest here that since 1945 the more directly related to war or national defense a topic has been, the less scientific consensus there has been on what to do about it. Clearly, whenever nonscientific factors loom large, scientists find that "the facts" alone do not provide guidance and so must draw upon other values and attitudes to arrive at policy proposals.

The one thing the disciplines do agree on is that more funds for research are needed. They can unite, often with considerable effectiveness, at this level of generality, and until 1968 the continued rise in federal research spending attested to their success. Today, however, the scientific community is coming to be viewed by Congress as just one more pressure group competing with others for a share of the federal budget, and the likelihood that science will obtain even the 6 percent annual increase claimed necessary to offset rising costs is by no means certain.

Probably, the major organizations that undertake to speak for science to the public are the American Association for the Advancement of Science (AAAS) and the National Academy of Sciences, the latter being a quasi-governmental group in which membership is a high honor rather than simply a matter of paying dues. The Academy's membership, less than 1000, contrasts with the more than 120,000 members of the AAAS, but the eminence of the Academy's members and the Academy's traditional responsibility to provide scientific advice to the government have given it considerable authority.

However, these and other organizations have no monopoly on informing the public of what science is doing and what it needs. Any individual or group of scientists is free to make statements to the press and to offer advice on any issue. Often there is less than complete agreement on the implications of science for public policy, so the public is treated to conflicting advice from scientists; in the end, public attitudes may often be primarily shaped by nonscientific factors. The controversy over the hydrogen bomb, over the fluoridation of water,[26] and more recently over the possible hazards to health in birth control pills and various food additives—all have involved scientists speaking on both sides of the issues and attempts to forge scientific consensus have failed.

Is a 1 in 10,000 chance of developing cancer from a food additive sufficient risk to ask that its use be banned? Will the development of a new weapon persuade potential enemies to behave more peaceably or will it only make them more warlike? The scientific facts in the matter are rarely at issue; it is when scientists try to derive *prescriptions* from *descriptions* that disciplinary cooperation tends to fail. Perhaps it is understandable, then, that the great scientific organizations prefer to speak in more general terms to the public; scientific research is a good thing and a valuable national resource, it provides a satisfying career, and it deserves both public esteem and support.

Organizational Competition

Disciplines occasionally compete for manpower and research funds, and sometimes for public approval, but none of this seems to be very obvious or very bloody. Many outstanding undergraduates have enjoyed the flattery of having two or more departments trying to recruit them as majors, and in some cases this competition may extend to the point at which the student selects a field for graduate training. We know little, however, of how such competition is typically conducted, although it is probable that a spokesman for any discipline may well indulge in some mild denigration of other disciplines as he attempts to persuade the student that *his* discipline promises greater satisfactions and more attractive career opportunities.

Beyond this, there is always some departmental competition on the campus for new faculty positions, raises, research facilities, and so on, even though this generally takes place in terms of personalities or competing interest groups rather than as disciplines per se. At the local level it is difficult to view such interdepartmental competition as purely a form of disciplinary competition since there is so little to distinguish the behavior of science departments from that of any others. Their actions, in fact, resemble those of any group trying to maintain or improve its situation within a larger organization, be it a university, or a governmental agency.

26 Harvey M. Sapolsky, "The Fluoridation Controversy: An Alternative Explanation," *Public Opinion Quarterly*, 33, No. 2 (Summer 1969), 240–248.

To the extent that there is disciplinary competition for public prestige, it seems to involve vague efforts to persuade the public that a given discipline deserves the support and esteem of the public *just as much* as any other—rather than that other disciplines deserve less. The public's interest in a particular discipline is largely a function of its "press," and here the "hot" fields have an advantage. The rise in prestige of nuclear physicists between 1947 and 1963 seems to have been due entirely to increased public awareness of atomic weapons and atomic power;[27] very likely, the prestige of biologists is rising now as more important discoveries are being made in this area.

Competition among disciplines for research funds presents a much more complicated picture. The federal government provides the major portion of all research funds in the United States and these may be granted by agencies having responsibility for disciplinary interests (such as the Atomic Energy Commission and the National Science Foundation), or they may be granted by agencies having responsibility for particular problems such as education, pollution, urban redevelopment, and poverty. In the former case competition must focus at the higher policy making levels where funds are initially allocated among different discipline-oriented divisions; should the division of psychobiology receive more funds than the division of chemistry, or the division of oceanography more than the division of zoological sciences? After such allocations have been made, competition for research money tends to be intradisciplinary and to be settled on the basis of genuine scientific merit.

In the case of a problem-oriented agency, there is probably more competition among disciplines at the level of specific grants since there is nothing in its "charter" to prevent it from giving more money to an anthropologist and less to a geologist or vice-versa. Given the vagueness of pressures to increase funds for particular disciplines, however, it is likely that the interests of such agencies' staff members carry a good deal of weight in such decisions. The policies of problem-oriented agencies do not usually come to the attention of disciplinary associations in the same way that those with specifically disciplinary responsibilities do, and there is rarely any firm representation of particular disciplinary interests to their administrators. There thus seems to be relatively little direct competition among disciplines even in these more contestable situations.[28]

27 Robert W. Hodge, Paul M. Siegal, and Peter H. Rossi, "Occupational Prestige in the U.S., 1925–63," *American Journal of Sociology*, **70**, No. 6 (November 1964), 286–302.
28 This last statement may reflect the writer's naiveté more accurately than it reflects reality. A reviewer of a previous draft of this chapter noted here, "I believe that these

To repeat what was pointed out above, general lobbying for research funds tends to be a cooperative rather than a competitive effort. There may be some emphasis on "we need more for this discipline," but rarely is there any explicit claim that another discipline should receive *less*. The scientific community may try to persuade Congress or a specific agency to put less money into a *different* enterprise (as has been the case with the space program, which many scientists define as largely an engineering rather than a scientific enterprise), but rarely do the disciplines engage in internecine warfare.

CONCLUSIONS

If this review of the relationships among scientific disciplines has failed to turn up any startlingly new phenomena, it is primarily because these relationships are rarely intensive or of critical importance to the immediate work of scientists. Certainly, the overall identity of the scientific community is important to the position of research in society, and we know that in the long run disciplinary boundaries ebb and flow, emerge and disappear, according to principles that we do not yet understand. For the average working scientist, however, the relation between his discipline and others does not seem to be of major immediate interest or consequence.

We have seen that the disciplines vary tremendously in terms of size, level of development, and in their particular relationships to the rest of society. In some cases looking for relationships among them may be comparable to searching for the relationships between elephants and fleas. Yet because we know that knowledge does flow across disciplinary boundaries, that new research specialties do grow up and acquire identities, and that the community as a whole does share a common orientation to the natural universe, it is important that we be concerned with the internal dynamics of the scientific enterprise.

It is obvious that many potentially significant research questions lie in this area, awaiting only a more comprehensive theoretical framework to make them meaningful. With the development of such a framework, and perhaps with a more adequate historical perspective than has been employed here, it is certain that much more can be learned of the area of phenomena that has been only dimly sketched here, and that this knowledge will be of both basic and practical value.

comments underestimate the extent of inter-discipline competition, overt denigration, and 'internecine warfare.' (During some . . . years of observation of doings in Washington I have observed impressive ferocity in inter-discipline attacks.)"

CHAPTER NINE

Relations Between Researchers and Practitioners

James P. McNaul, The Ohio State University

Similar to science and technology, until recently, the roles of researchers and practitioners have followed largely independent courses of development and institutionalization. The increasingly closer relationships between science and technology have brought researchers and practitioners into much greater interaction. In this chapter we characterize the two roles, discuss the patterns of communication within and between the two categories, examine the interface between researchers and practitioners in situations of interdisciplinary problem solving, and identify some of the areas of potential conflict.

ROLE DIFFERENTIATION

"Science" is a logical point of departure which can serve as a reference to other terms.[1] Merton has delineated three aspects of science by suggesting

1 The following discussion draws on several sources. Particularly, Craig C. Lundberg,

that the word "is commonly used to denote [one or more of] (1) a set of characteristic methods by means of which knowledge is certified, (2) a stock of accumulated knowledge stemming from the application of these methods, [or] (3) a set of cultural values and mores governing the activities termed scientific. . . ."[2] Methods refer to how a person *does* his work; knowledge refers to the information he has received and the cognitive processes he applies, how he *thinks* while doing his work; and values and mores refer to the way a person *feels* about his work. These terms are all role oriented but differ in the degree to which they apply to each occupation. If we place science at one end of a continuum, then "nonscience" can be placed at the other end. The type of science we place at the end of the continuum is commonly referred to as "basic science" in which the goal is the pursuit of scientific knowledge for its own sake. Nonscience includes the uses of products that result from the application of science, while generating no new scientific knowledge in the process.[3] This implies that, at any other point along the continuum, there is, or or can be, contribution to knowledge, even as a by-product of activities oriented to other goals. Somewhere between these two extremes is the field of "applied science" in which the goal is applying scientific knowledge rather than creating it or consuming the product of its application.[4] These categories are illustrated in Figure 1. These continua indicate a close relationship between the applied researcher and the scientific practitioner, and that elements of the two may be embodied in certain occupations.

The three dimensions of science noted by Merton can be used to differentiate the activities involved in the various disciplines and fields of practice. These three dimensions can also be conceived as constituting continua that range from science to nonscience as illustrated in Figure 2.

"Middlemen in Science Utilization: Some Notes toward Clarifying Conversion Roles," *American Behavioral Scientist,* **9** (February 1966), 11–14; and Howard M. Vollmer and Donald L. Mills, Eds., *Professionalization,* Prentice-Hall, Englewood Cliffs, N.J., 1966, pp. vii–viii.

2 Robert K. Merton, *Social Theory and Social Structure,* Rev. ed., Free Press, New York, 1957, p. 551.

3 Since an individual can occupy many roles, he could at one time be in the field of nonscience (being operated on for some illness) and at another time be in the field of science (a researcher in nuclear physics). The key determinants of the particular role set are the individual's activity, the goal of the activity, and the knowledge content used. Thus the theologian may, or may not, use science in his vocational activities, but in many of his roles he is undoubtedly a user.

4 Here we deviate from Lundberg who includes practice in the realm of nonscience along with utilization. Lundberg, *op. cit.,* p. 12. We feel this moves the end point of the continuum to a point where it has no definitional base.

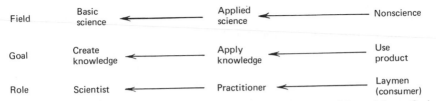

Field	Basic science ←	Applied science ←	Nonscience
Goal	Create knowledge ←	Apply knowledge ←	Use product
Role	Scientist ←	Practitioner ←	Laymen (consumer)

Figure 1. Conceptual relationships of "science" as a field. *Source.* Adapted from Craig C. Lundberg, "Middlemen in Science Utilization: Some Notes toward Clarifying Conversion Roles," *American Behavioral Scientist,* 9 (February 1966), 12.

Each occupational area or discipline can be mapped along methodological, knowledge, and value and norm dimensions.[5] When an occupational field ranks beyond a certain point on these scales, we can probably have some general acceptance on referring to it as science. For example,

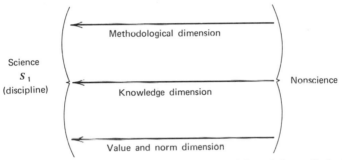

Figure 2. Dimensions of "science" as a field. *Source.* Adapted from Craig C. Lundberg, "Middlemen in Science Utilization: Some Notes toward Clarifying Conversion Roles," *American Behavioral Scientist,* 9 (February 1966), 12.

there is fair agreement that physics, chemistry, psychology, and sociology all fall beyond this point and rank as sciences. Yet there is also agreement that the "hard" sciences—physics and chemistry—rank higher (more scientific) than the "soft" sciences—psychology and sociology. A field such as administrative science would probably evoke much disagreement as to whether it actually meets the criteria for being considered scientific. Of course, operationalizing the criteria and establishing the weights and cutting points are highly problematic in themselves. However, the schema can help in comparing disciplines and practical fields, and in comparing the degree to which practices are oriented to and based on scientific foundations.

[5] It may be no mean task to obtain consensus on what constitutes a discipline or subdiscipline. We ignore that problem for the purposes of this discussion.

The roles and activities carried out by persons in given scientific disciplines or fields of practice are not homogeneous. Therefore the relative positions of the disciplines and fields themselves on the dimensions in Figure 2 can be only partly revealing. For greater specificity this conceptual diagram can be expanded to include another dimension that depicts the degree to which activities and commitments of persons within an area adhere to the three aspects of scientific orientation (Figure 3).

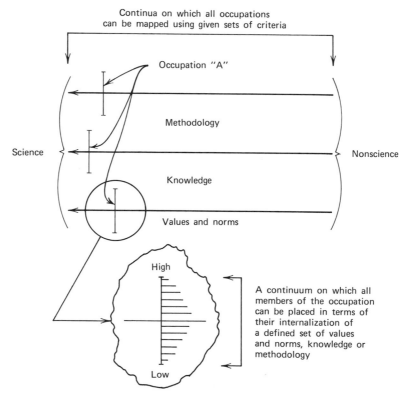

Figure 3. Science activity and role occupant differentiation.

Using a model such as this permits two important aspects of an individual's behavior to be examined. One element is the social pressure that results from being in a given occupational role. The other is the internal motivation caused by strongly held values and beliefs. The richness of the researcher and practitioner roles can be better understood with a model such as this than by using a simple unidimensional model. Each of the many potential roles along this continuum, that is, basic researcher, applied researcher, development engineer, laboratory technician, quality control supervisor, and so on, occupy relatively different positions along each dimension, and the relative weighting of the dimensions varies. In addition, the relative distribution of members along a high/low internalization scale varies for each occupation.

Lundberg summarized the potential of this conceptual scheme:

We hope to be able to systematically examine any known occupational role which tends to utilize science to find out how close or how far away it is from the pure scientific role and in fact what proportions and what dimensions of science it does exhibit. Such a systematic schemata would also permit us, if we first array known conversion roles, to identify roles which are as yet still to be developed.[6]

Such a framework permits us to better analyze, understand, and place in perspective the many new roles that are developing in research and technology. Some of these are research support roles and some are new knowledge conversion roles, but many of them have yet to become stabilized in terms of functions and status. For example, Swatez argues that the size and complexity of research instruments in high-energy physics has resulted in: (1) new roles for trained physicists in designing, building, maintaining, and sometimes operating equipment and gathering data; (2) growth in the relative number of technicians as opposed to Ph.D. research workers; and (3) development of elaborate administrative units and the resultant mixed roles.[7] As becomes more evident, the term researcher is used in reference to a role near the left end of the continua, while the term practitioner refers to roles falling in the middle.

The Researcher

The role of researchers has already been well delineated in other chapters of this volume. It suffices to say here that the goal of researchers is the extension of certified knowledge. This is one basic criterion that differentiates them from practitioners whose goals are typically the utilization of knowledge for applied ends. Another major difference is in the orientation of researchers to their peers in the scientific community and the orientation of practitioners to clients and consumers of services and products. The role of a basic researcher falls close to the left ends on the continua depicted in Figure 3. His activities and commitments are highly in accord with scientific values and approaches.

6 Lundberg, *op. cit.*, p. 13.
7 Gerald M. Swatez, "The Social Organization of a University Laboratory," *Minerva*, 8 (January 1970), 56–57.

The Practitioner

While the role of a "basic" researcher is fairly well defined in the literature, the role of the practitioner is far more diverse depending on the field, goal orientation, and work settings. A basic researcher can be referred to the left ends of the continua. The characteristics of a practitioner are varied and can range widely along all three dimensions. Two items are probably most important. For example, on the knowledge dimension, a practitioner may be committed to scientific knowledge, but his use of it is different. Instead of extending it, he attempts to apply it to the practical problems of a third group, that is, clients or consumers. Thus, unlike the cycle of activities in scientific research which begins with theory and feeds back to theory, the cycle of technology comprises exploratory development, advanced development, and production. The term practitioner extends beyond those involved in hardware technology to include others who apply knowledge to policy formulation, organizational planning, and therapeutic ends.

Concerning the methodological dimension, practitioners may utilize advanced methodologies, but it is apt to be different in many respects from those used by researchers. Tools or techniques may be the same (computers, instruments, and so on), but they are used in different ways or to different ends. Finally, practitioners can be expected to be less committed to scientific values and ethos and be highly committed to credos related to clients' interests and the provision of services. These differences are largely attributable to differences in goals.

An example of one source of the difference may be seen in the socialization process during graduate education. In most sciences the teacher/researcher roles are usually combined so that graduate students are heavily exposed to research values, theory, and methods. However, in the more client-centered medical sciences, this process appears to be reversed. At an early stage the medical student is exposed to research-oriented specialists (probably Ph.D.'s) as he takes basic courses that are not related to clinical medicine.[8] In later years, when the physical, biological, or social science student is heavily engaged in a research project, the medical student is primarily engaged in clinical effort as he works with patients under a particular staff doctor. This staff doctor is probably a practitioner first of all, a teacher second, and a researcher third, if at all. In a study of practicing physicians in solo practice, in a privately owned medical organization, and in a government medical organization,

[8] Howard S. Becker and Blanche Geer, "The Fate of Idealism in Medical School," *American Sociological Review,* 23 (February 1958), 52–54.

it was found that 30 percent or more physicians in all settings had part-time teaching affiliations.[9] Only in the government medical organization did a significant number engage in clinical research. Thus the medical student is subjected to a much stronger practitioner bias in his education than is the graduate student in nonmedical sciences. This is in keeping with the client service orientation of most medical education institutions.

PATTERNS OF COMMUNICATION

The knowledge-related functions of researchers and practitioners have already been defined as the creation of new knowledge and the application or utilization of existing knowledge, respectively. If one is to extend or use knowledge, one must "know." A vital question, then, is how information is transferred and communicated. Communication among researchers has been a major concern of the sociology of science, so that there is a relatively clear picture of the patterns in this area. Much less attention has been given to communication among practitioners. Our understanding of the communication patterns between researchers and practitioners is even less clear.

While the technical complexities of communication have been appreciated for some time in engineering circles, social models of communication have remained somewhat fragmented.[10] Scientific communication is particularly complex:

> But the comprehension, the understanding of scientific knowledge is a very different thing from being the recipient of a communication. I think there is an element of action inseparable from understanding: to question, to try, to apply, to adapt, to ask new questions, to see if one understands, and to test what has been told: action in the laboratory or the observatory, or on paper, or, at the very least, in the motions of the spirit.[11]

In the sciences many different communication channels with many send-

[9] Gloria V. Engel, "Professional Autonomy and Bureaucratic Organization," *Administrative Science Quarterly*, 15 (March 1970), 13–14.

[10] For a classic treatise on the mathematical aspects of communication theory, see C. Shannon and W. Weaver, *The Mathematical Theory of Communication*, Univ. of Illinois Press, Urbana, 1949. For a recent summary of research on social communication in formal organizations, see Harold Guetzkow, "Communications in Organizations," in *Handbook of Organizations*, James G. March, Ed., Rand McNally, Chicago, 1965, pp. 534–573.

[11] Robert Oppenheimer, "Communication and Comprehension of Scientific Knowledge," *Science*, 142 (29 November 1963), 1194.

ers and receivers may have to operate "synergistically" in order to complete effectively the transmission of a given message.[12] When complexities of communication are combined with complexities of role prescriptions of researchers and practitioners, it becomes very difficult to evolve a model of the entire communication and interaction process. To appreciate the communication patterns between researchers and practitioners, one must understand the communication processes within each group. Differences in these processes can help explain the relative isolation of the two groups from each other.

Communication among Researchers

A survey of 50 United States scientists revealed they obtained information: "from journals regularly scanned, 30.4 percent; from citations in other papers, 10.9 percent; from author reprints, 5.8 percent; from abstracting or indexing services, 6.4 percent; from compendia, 4.3 percent; from casual conversation, 22.6 percent; by asking colleagues, 8.1 percent; other methods, 11.5 percent."[13] This survey reveals that nearly 58 percent of technical data comes through written means, the majority of the rest through interpersonal communications. The magnitude of the problems of scientific communication for the average researcher is illustrated by estimates (in 1962) that "over a million scientific or technical papers are published each year in journals, bulletins and reports," and that this output is doubling every decade or so.[14]

Hagstrom agrees that "formal communication in the sciences is primarily carried on through articles appearing in scientific journals."[15] He also sees formal communications as part of the system of recognition that performs a fundamental function in the social control of science. Citations and acknowledgments of others' work constitute a form of recognition of its significance.

While the estimate of over a million articles a year being published can be overwhelming, one may be tempted to discount it by assuming that scientific journals and articles tend to be highly specific and highly

12 Herbert Menzel, "Scientific Communication: Five Themes from Social Science Research," *American Psychologist,* 21 (November 1966), pp. 1000–1001.

13 B. Glass and S. H. Norwood, "How Scientists Actually Learn of Work Important to Them," *Proceedings of International Conference on Scientific Information,* Vol. I, National Academy of Sciences—National Research Council, Washington, D.C., 1959, pp. 195–198.

14 C. P. Bourne, "The World's Technical Journal Literature," *American Documentation,* 13 (1962), 159–168.

15 Warren O. Hagstrom, *The Scientific Community,* Basic Books, New York, 1965, p. 23.

segmented, so that a researcher in a given area only has a limited number of sources to review and researchers to keep up with their work. Few data are available on this matter, but available evidence indicates a high rate of growth of information even in highly specific areas.[16] In February 1961, the Division of Research Grants of the National Institutes of Health (NIH) established an Information Exchange Group No. 1 (IEG 1) with membership open to researchers in the field upon request. The purpose of the group was to exchange relevant information through memos or working papers which were reproduced and distributed to all members of the group. Although the subject matter, "Oxidative Phosphorylation and Terminal Electron Transport," sounds highly esoteric and limited in scope, in a period slightly exceeding 4 years, the membership had grown from 32 members to 592 members. During this four-year period, 533 papers were distributed. These papers were authored by 555 different persons, of whom only 231 were among the 517-member group. This indicates that there were at least 286 researchers, nonmembers of IEG 1, who were also active in the area during that period.

Results of the same survey also show that collaboration, a very intensive form of communication, is conducive to scientific productivity.[17] It seems that in each area there is a very active core of researchers around whom revolves a large "floating population" of researchers who collaborate with the core members on multiauthored papers. "The most striking feature of . . . the investigation is the finding that separate groups [of authors related to each other by collaboration] exist in what would otherwise appear to be a single invisible college."[18] Indication was that each of the subgroups was generally centered on, but not necessarily confined to, the particular institution or location of its core members.

The fundamental importance of formal and planned communication channels in science should not obscure the significance of those of an informal and unplanned nature.[19] By informal communications we mean those that occur outside institutionalized channels such as journals, scientific conferences, professional meetings, and others within particular organizations (e.g., staff meetings). Informal communications primarily include interpersonal communications through letters and notes, and exchange of preprints and working papers. The last-mentioned forms tend

[16] The following information comes from Derek J. DeSolla Price and Donald DeB. Beaver, "Collaboration in an Invisible College," *American Psychologist,* 21 (November 1966), 1011–1018.

[17] This makes the reasonable assumption that collaboration in writing indicates collaboration in research activities.

[18] Price and Beaver, *op. cit.*, p. 1016.

[19] Menzel, *op. cit.*, pp. 1001–1002.

at times to become highly routinized such that over time the patterns of exchange stabilize into networks that include defined groups of individuals. However, inquiries that elicit working papers are often informal and unplanned. "While informal communication in the sciences is largely unplanned, and sometimes appears accidental, there is actually a good bit of regularity to it":[20]

1. There are certain individuals who tend to provide the channels for much of the informal communication, at least across organizational boundaries.[21] In some organizations there is evidence of a two-step flow of information using informal channels, in which the majority of the members of an organization have *few* contacts outside the organization and a minority have *extensive* contacts outside the organization and in effect act as sources and transmitters of information used by other organizational researchers. These few ". . . individuals act as technological gatekeepers for the rest of the laboratory."[22]

2. There is a limited number of places, occasions, and times in which informal communication takes place with a high degree of regularity. This regularity tends to be built around certain activities such as conferences, purposeful travel, luncheons, coffee breaks, and technical society meetings, but occurs as adjuncts to them.

3. There are shared expectations concerning the communications and responses to them. These expectations are guided by the forms of exchange in science that are based upon contribution-recognition. Usually, the initiation is in order to (*a*) obtain information on a specific point, (*b*) inform the other person of work in progress and get general information in return, (*c*) pass on specific information with or without anticipating anything in return, or (*d*) deliberately establish interaction in the hope of obtaining some unknown bit of information.[23] Often the response involves no conscious decisions on the part of a scientist.[24] How-

---

20 *Ibid.*, p. 1001.

21 Note that this emphasizes individuals who provide the transmission medium, not necessarily the information content.

22 Thomas J. Allen and Stephen I. Cohen, "Information Flow in Research and Development Laboratories," *Administrative Science Quarterly,* 14 (March 1969), 18.

23 For some other variations and elaboration, see Herbert Menzel, "Planned and Unplanned Scientific Communication," in *The Sociology of Science,* Bernard Barber and Walter Hirsch, Eds., Free Press, New York, 1962, pp. 421–423.

24 Chester I. Barnard, *The Functions of the Executive,* Harvard Univ. Press, Cambridge, Mass., 1938, pp. 168–169. Two important reasons why a communication attempt would fall outside the zone of indifference and require a conscious decision to participate in the interaction on the part of the respondee are (1) uncertainty or negative certainty regarding the colleagial status of the initiator and (2) a high-cost, low reward outcome anticipated from the interaction, perhaps based on past experience (nonreciprocity).

ever, researchers become reluctant to communicate information they believe is premature or for other reasons related to their work. In scientific circles knowledge is a source of influence.[25] Inquiries seeking information are a form of recognition of an individual's knowledge. Emitting responses to these inquiries is a validation of such recognition.

4. The content of the communication transmitted over informal channels has certain characteristics. As noted by Hagstrom:

> Formal channels of communication demand responsibility: the scientific article is expected to be a finished and polished piece of work. Informal channels of communication, on the other hand, often involve a great deal of permissiveness. People can make suggestions without committing themselves, and others can criticize the work without having to make any final decision with regard to its validity.[26]

Things such as preliminary and untried ideas, information on experimental (or organizational) procedures and techniques, and clarification requests on obtuse or particularly difficult published material are very apt to be transmitted through these kinds of channels. These channels are also used for information that might expose the solicitor to sanctions or ridicule. The new researcher who has to ask for information he knows he should know seldom puts the request in writing and is usually very careful *who* and *how* he asks.

Interpersonal relations and communication at the nontechnical level appear to influence the evaluation of scientific standing. The frequency of contacts with colleagues among researchers in laboratories was shown to be positively associated with peer evaluations of scientific productivity and overall usefulness to the organization.[27] Interestingly enough, there was no significant difference in performance when objectively measured by the numbers of papers published. It might also be expected that informal communication networks consist primarily of individuals with relatively similar scientific and/or professional orientations. Individuals with certain characteristics and values tend to recognize similar attributes in others and to associate with them more than with other peers.[28] In a study of an academically affiliated education research center, two groups of individual orientations were identified as organization men and re-

---

25 J. R. P. French, Jr., and B. Raven, "The Bases of Social Power," in *Studies in Social Power*, D. Cartwright, Ed., Univ. of Michigan, Institute for Social Research, Ann Arbor, Mich., 1959, pp. 150–167.
26 Hagstrom, *op. cit.*, p. 31.
27 Donald C. Pelz and Frank M. Andrews, *Scientists in Organizations*, Wiley, New York, 1966, p. 37.
28 L. Festinger, S. Schachter, and K. Back, *Social Pressures in Informal Groups*, Harper, New York, 1950.

search men. The study concludes that ". . . the organization man communicates with his own kind while the research man communicates with his own kind.[29] Gouldner reports similar findings in the study of a university faculty, in which locals tended to vote for locals in faculty elections and cosmopolitans tended to vote for those with a similar outlook.[30] There are no reasons to believe that these interpersonal factors do not exert as much influence on the patterns of informal communication among researchers.

Communication among Practitioners

Several factors limit the discussion of communication among practitioners. First, it has already been mentioned that the role of practitioner varies considerably because of its problem orientation and differences in organizational settings. There is also a lack of data and consensus on what patterns of communication exist in applied activities. Furthermore, there is an absence of conceptual models for the process of communication among practitioners analogous to contribution/recognition exchange in scientific communication.

Available data reveal many similarities as well as differences in patterns of communication in applied technology and in research. Probably the greatest difference between the two spheres is in sources of information. It was noted earlier that scientific journals, in various forms, provide the bulk (53.5 percent) of information to scientists. A comparison between seven engineering projects and two research projects in physics shows that 51 percent of the ideas in the research were reported to have come from the literature. Only 8 percent of the ideas in the engineering projects were attributed to the same sources. In these engineering projects, 33 percent of the ideas were reported to have come from vendors of potential equipment or subsystems for the projects or from the customers of the products being developed, in this case a government laboratory. The last-mentioned sources, to the extent they existed, were not mentioned as sources of ideas for the research projects. However, the research projects made relatively greater use of previous personal experience, while the engineering projects made considerably more use of analysis and experimentation. These data indicate the relative lack of use of journals in applied work. However, all engineering societies have tech-

29 Alfred G. Smith, *Communication and Status: The Dynamics of a Research Center,* Univ. of Oregon, Center for the Advanced Study of Educational Administration, Eugene, Oregon, 1966, p. 8.
30 Alvin Gouldner, "Cosmopolitans and Locals," *Administrative Science Quarterly,* **2** (December 1957; March 1958), 290, 456.

nical journals, and many have highly specialized journals tailored to specific interests and needs. Medical journals abound, many with very special interest groups in mind. Unfortunately, there is limited data on readership of these journals that would permit the identification of who reads what journals or journal articles. Based on available studies of information sources, one can only suggest that the closer the individual's role to that of the researcher, the more journals and formalized, documented information sources he uses. And the closer the role is to that of the practitioner, the more the use of sources internal to the organization or oriented to vendors and clients. This shift occurs because as one moves away from the ideal research role journals lose significance as factors in the social and organizational control of the occupation. Information related to the needs of consumers assumes greater significance for goal achievement. The practitioner is not being evaluated with regard to what he contributes to knowledge, but rather in terms of the utility to the user of his contribution to the product. Rewards in his organizational setting are structured on this basis. The same client centered analogy could be applied to the medical practitioner who gets his information from other practitioners who "tried it" on patients, from pharmaceutical detail men who are armed with user data, or medical equipment manufacturers.

Because of their greater dependence on informal channels, patterns of communication among practitioners are expected to be more influenced by interpersonal factors and forms of association. As pointed out in regard to researchers, practitioners can also recognize and associate themselves with others of similar characteristics. In a study of two engineering groups, it was concluded that

> Data suggest that Department A members identified with the same reference group as others who most closely resembled themselves. Reference group affiliation apparently reflected both status similarities and reference group values.[31]

Several important questions can be raised about identification and colleagueship among practitioners. What is a colleague to the practitioner? Is it someone in his discipline; in his work groups of his own educational and socioeconomic level; or simply someone engaged in technical activity who is similar to himself?

In a study of the personnel of an organization, a set of criteria was used to assess the degree of professionalism: (1) a claim to technical ex-

---

[31] Louis B. Barnes, *Organizational Systems and Engineering Groups: A Comparative Study of Two Technical Groups in Industry,* Harvard Business School, Boston, 1960, p. 78.

pertise in one's occupation, (2) a claim to autonomy over one's work efforts, (3) a commitment to one's profession as opposed to one's organization, and (4) a feeling of responsibility to society for the maintenance of professional standards. The questions of choices of colleagues and organizational communication were also considered in the study.

Each respondent was asked to list those individuals in the organization with whom he felt he had a colleague relationship and those with whom he felt he had a social relationship. Each was also asked to list those people with whom he had initiated communication over the past three workdays. Respondents were grouped into high (top 30 percent), intermediate, and low (lower 30 percent) professionalism category. The ranks of individuals making the selection and those of individuals selected were then compared. Significant relationships were found:

1. For all levels colleague choices tend to be made from one's own professionalism level.

2. There is a status bias in the choice of colleagues in that fewer low professionals are included in the choices of high professionals than high professionals are included in the choices of those in lower ranks on professionalism.

3. Individuals high on professionalism have a clearer concept (or a more stringent set of criteria) of what constitutes a colleagial relationship as opposed to a social relationship in that there is less overlap in their colleagial and social choices than in the choices of individuals low on professionalism.

4. Individuals high on professionalism are more apt to seek out people with like orientation outside their own organizational elements or levels than persons who are low on professionalism.

5. Individuals of high and low professionalism tend to communicate with others of the same professionalism level, despite organizational constraints.[32]

These data provide evidence that informal communication and interaction among practitioners are highly influenced by their value systems much the same way the scientific researcher is influenced, although the particular values may be different.[33] Because of the tendency for practitioners to depend more on communications within their organizational

---

[32] James P. McNaul, "Behavioral Patterns among Professionals in a Research and Development Environment," unpublished Ph.D. Dissertation, Stanford Univ., 1969, pp. 109–127.

[33] Of course, the generalization of these findings is limited by the few disciplines involved and the single, development-oriented organization.

elements for information, these patterns of informal communication assume added significance.[34]

Communication between Researchers and Practitioners

The number of studies dealing with the problems of communication between researchers and practitioners, in the process of conversion of knowledge to technology, is rather limited. Price argues that science and technology operate relatively independently of each other.[35] In science new knowledge is discovered on the basis of earlier scientific information. Technology builds upon its own prior developments, creates its own knowledge base, and often proceeds to its application without fully appreciating (or caring about) its relationships to basic sciences. Given the differing sources of information used by the two groups, and the widely differing goal orientations which tend to inhibit communication and interaction between researchers and practitioners, this argument assumes some face validity. There are no indications of the existence of institutionalized channels of communication between researchers and practitioners such as those that exist within each of the two groups. While some have suggested certain processes that are necessary for converting social science knowledge into a form suitable for application and have argued the need for a social engineer role that would parallel the physical engineering roles, no specifications were given as to the communication channels that could, or would, be used for this process.[36]

The current state of the art in scientific knowledge is transmitted from science to technology through the medium of the textbook used in the training of technologists.[37] This is hardly a short time lag communication medium when one considers the year or more it takes to get a journal article published, the several additional years it takes to get articles codified into published textbooks, and the multiple years from training to utilization. Despite the natural resistance to accept this as the primary source of information transfer, there is little evidence to suggest that any others play a major role. Occasionally, technology reaches a dead end in a particular area and becomes unable to move

[34] Donald G. Marquis and Thomas J. Allen, "Communication Patterns in Applied Technology," *American Psychologist*, 21 (November 1966), 1053.

[35] D. J. De. S. Price, "Is Technology Historically Independent of Science?," *Technology and Culture*, 6 (1965), 553–568.

[36] Harold Guetzkow, "Conversion Barriers in Using the Social Sciences," *Administrative Science Quarterly*, 4 (June 1959), 70, 76–77.

[37] Price, *op. cit.*, p. 564.

beyond a given state without new basic information.[38] In this sense, technology often defines problems for science. Many organizations with large applied science activities also support basic research laboratories as a source of scientific information. Scientists in these laboratories are called upon by practitioners when the needs arise. Kornhauser cites the use of frequent, formalized meetings between researchers and practitioners as a means of transferring information and stimulating problem identification on the part of researchers.[39] This pattern is more workable in industrial settings where organizational sanctions and rewards can be used to reinforce the process. No institutionalized process exists, however, to bring the general range of practitioners in contact with the general range of researchers. Motivations for this type of interaction do not seem to be present.

The transfer of information from science to technology can be expected, then, to occur most frequently where there are organizational forces, backed by rewards and sanctions, to that end through scheduled meetings, consultations, special reports, and so on. This of course assumes the presence of both researchers and practitioners within the same organization. In some cases research scientists may be encouraged to perform applied activities by handling specific practical problems. While this was quite successful during World War II because of the strong social justification and motivation connected with the war efforts, these conditions generally do not exist today.[40]

Some application-oriented fields are much closer to science than others. There is some evidence that the degree of relationships may be related to the rate of change in the basic science and the technological field. For example, Marquis and Allen show that the ratio of citations of technological journals to those of scientific journals ranges from 6:1 for articles in a journal in applied mechanics to 1:1 for a journal in nuclear science and engineering.[41] Since nuclear science and engineering is a rapidly changing technical area, it is apparently more closely related to its science base.

Despite these variations, we may conclude that in general there is a lack of articulation in the patterns of communication between science and technology. Variations from this seem to depend on organizational pressures, and on differences in the state of individual technological fields or areas of science.

38 J. A. Morton, "From Physics to Function," *IEEE Spectrum*, **2** (1965), 62–66.
39 William Kornhauser, *Scientists in Industry: Conflict and Accommodation*, Univ. of California Press, Berkeley and Los Angeles, 1963, p. 67.
40 A. P. Rowe, "From Scientific Idea to Practical Use," *Minerva*, **2** (Spring 1964), 310.
41 Marquis and Allen, *op. cit.*, p. 1059.

RESEARCHERS AND PRACTITIONERS AND
INTERDISCIPLINARY GROUPS

In recent years there has been increasing emphasis on the use of inter-disciplinary groups. In general, "applied research tends to be inter-disciplinary. . . . Interdisciplinary research is less common in basic science."[42] In fact, most development projects in engineering are at least multidisciplinary, since it is difficult to develop a product of any degree of complexity using only one technological base. There is always the question of differences between interdisciplinary and multidisciplinary efforts. We use the term interdisciplinary to refer to any problem-solving group in which members from more than one discipline must be involved. For many of the reasons cited for the lack of communication between researchers and practitioners, interdisciplinary groups have tended to be constituted of either of these two categories. Aside from industrial settings where collaboration between researchers and practitioners is at times required, few interdisciplinary problem-solving groups combine members of the two categories. In a report of interdisciplinary research teams, Stone observes that

. . . there are two basic considerations which are conducive to successful teamwork. The first is effective intrateam communication; the second is realistic, respectful division of labor, combining both assigned and achieved status for all members.[43]

It appears to be very difficult to satisfy these requirements because of variation in goals, value systems, levels and types of knowledge and methodology, and differences in the systems of social control that operate in science and in technology.

AREAS OF POTENTIAL CONFLICT

Differences between researchers and practitioners in perspectives, inter-ests, and approaches to problems give rise to conflicts that place many constraints on the fulfillment of the two roles. The significance of such conflicts can be expected to increase as the gap between science and technology is narrowed. Practitioners are often in the position of gate-

42 Hagstrom, *op. cit.,* p. 147.
43 Anthony R. Stone, "The Interdisciplinary Research Team," *The Journal of Applied Behavioral Science,* 5 (July, August, September 1969), 356.

keepers concerning researchers' access to data. And, scientific principles receive stringent testing when put to application.

In reviewing some of the areas of potential conflict we in effect summarize the differences between researchers and practitioners pointed out earlier.[44]

1. *Value system.* The value system of science is the increase of knowledge. The value system of technology is the use of knowledge. Although these sound deceptively simple, the internalization of these objectives by researchers and practitioners leads to wide differences in behavior. This differing value system is also reflected in the areas of study pursued, the type of social control exercised, and the ways of evaluating performance. In fact, these value systems underlie most of the differences noted below.

2. *Communication.* The communication patterns of researchers and practitioners differ widely in terms of sources of data and membership in the various communication networks. There seems to be a tendency for individuals to include others having similar values in their communication networks. Thus there is considerable segmentation in communication between the researcher and practitioner roles and even among various groups of practitioners.

3. *Time frame.* Time orientation among researchers is generally of a longer term than among practitioners. Basic researchers are not confronted with the dying patient, pressures for profit, social pressure for solutions to social and environmental problems, and so on. However, when in an open race for discoveries, researchers may be under considerable pressure which greatly limits their time frame.

4. *Uniqueness versus patterns.* While scientific researchers are usually in pursuit of discovery of the patterns that constitute principles and laws, and are interested in uniqueness primarily as they may explain the patterns, practitioners are more concerned about uniqueness in products, policies, or individuals to whom they render therapy or other services. To researchers abstract principles are the building blocks of science. To practitioners they can only provide segmental explanations of highly complex and concrete entities.

5. *Finality.* To researchers scientific knowledge is never final. For all knowledge is subject to further testing and modification. This of course does not negate the cumulative nature of such knowledge. Practitioners, however, accept knowledge with greater finality. This is particularly characteristic of nonexperimental practitioners in fields such as counseling, education, and psychotherapy. Skepticism, which is a general norm

[44] For a somewhat different approach, see Saad Z. Nagi, "The Practitioner as a Partner in Research," *Rehabilitation Record,* (July–August 1965), 3–4.

in science, would have negative effects in practices influenced by the practitioners' confidence in what they are doing.

6. *Environmental control.* Research often requires manipulating variables in the research settings. Experimental designs are built on control and manipulation. Practitioners, especially in areas related to social science research, tend to resent changes in operations required by research designs. The recent surge of emphasis on evaluative research has added to this resentment.

The roles of researchers and practitioners are complex in and of themselves. We understand only partially the many variables and relations involved in each. The picture becomes more complex when consideration is expanded to the interaction between the two role sets. Glatt gives a description of the problems inherent in this interaction:

It [lack of involvement of researchers in actual organizational change] also reflects the lack of trust and confidence between researcher and practitioner, and a mutual lack of understanding of what the researcher might contribute to the practitioner, and what the practitioner might contribute to the researcher. Typically, the researcher cannot imagine what a practitioner could contribute to his research design, and furthermore often feels that he cannot reveal all of his purposes for the sake of a "scientifically objective" result. This attitude goes a long way in creating a relationship of mutual suspicion between researcher and practitioner when, in many cases, the secrecy is simply the researcher's defensive measure against perceived threats from the organizationally more powerful practitioner. At the same time, the practitioner finds it uncomfortable to be "one-down" in the "one-upmanship" game he all too often correctly perceives, and cannot imagine what he can gain short of exposure of "weaknesses" of a kind that a practitioner cannot afford to have revealed. The practitioner sees the researcher much less as a helper in his efforts to understand and cope with his real and imagined problems than as a disinterested bystander in the process of organizational life or, at worst, a threat to his self-image.[45]

The problems of relationships between researchers and practitioners have been the object of more concern than systematic research and analysis. The spectacular success in the development of scientific technology in fields such as engineering, medicine, and agriculture has placed social science and related technology under pressure. Models and data on the ways these technologies have emerged in connection with the harder

45 Evelyn Glatt, "Research and Application: An Approach to Management Problems in an R & D Laboratory," *IEEE Transactions on Engineering Management,* Em-11 (September 1964), 92.

sciences, and the relations between researchers and practitioners in these fields, can be useful in evolving similar developments concerning social problems. By this we do not mean to convey that what happens in hardware technology is applicable to social problems, but that we can learn from differences as well as similarities.

CHAPTER TEN

Forbidden Knowledge

William Petersen, Ohio State University

In the spring of 1969 I sent out a form letter to the appropriate officer of every professional society I could identify in the physical, natural, social, and applied sciences, and to the administrator in charge of research at each major American university. After a brief statement of the purpose of my investigation, I posed the following questions:

1. Has your professional association or academic institution ever adopted a set of principles governing research? If so, would you please enclose a copy if one is readily available or, if not, give me a full reference?

2. Whether or not such a set of principles has been adopted, has there been a discussion of the issue among the researchers you can speak for, and can you refer me to key articles or letters?

3. In some instances the group especially concerned with the matter I am investigating is associated with a particular subgroup, such as the Federation of American Scientists in physics, or those in ethnology who define their field as applied anthropology. Is there such a group in your discipline or on your campus, and if so to whom should I write for information?

Most of those so addressed were kind enough to respond, and their replies make up part of this chapter's raw material.

No general norms designating what research is legitimate had been adopted by a number of universities (for example, Brandeis, Case Western Reserve, Duke, Missouri) and professional societies (for example, American Economics Association, American Society of Mechanical Engineers, American Society for Engineering Education, American Veterinary Medical Association, Genetics Society of America, Institute of Electrical and Electronics Engineers).

In a few instances the canon adopted by a professional society included the general approbation of knowledge that was once routine among scientists. For instance, "The Chemist's Creed," approved in 1965 by the Council of the American Chemical Society, reads in part: "As a chemist, I have a responsibility to my science—to search for its truths by use of the scientific method, and to enrich it by my own contributions for the good of humanity." Somewhat more vaguely, the "Canons of Ethics for Engineers," incorporated as part of the bylaws of the American Society of Agricultural Engineers, state: "The Engineer . . . will strive to increase the competence and prestige of the engineering profession, will use his knowledge and skill for the advancement of human welfare." In view of the general trend in American academia, these traditional statements must be regarded as exceptional, perhaps the consequence as much of bureaucratic dalliance as of true difference in principle.

It is typical now to hold that some limitation ought to be placed on the gathering of new knowledge. In the discussion that follows, these limitations are organized according to the value that is served (actually or supposedly) by such forbearance—the protection of a person's or animal's life or physical well-being, the protection of privacy, and the avoidance (or, on the contrary, support) of certain political goals. Paradoxically, the efficacy of the restrictions and the fervor with which they are imposed both increase through this list, contrary to what one might expect.

THE PHYSICAL PROTECTION OF EXPERIMENTAL SUBJECTS

The commonest limitation to research is one or another safeguard designed to protect the physical well-being of human subjects. Perhaps the broadest statement is the so-called "Helsinki Declaration" adopted in 1964 by the World Medical Association as a guide to physicians engaged in clinical research.[1] The code includes no legal or other sanctions;

[1] It has been published by the American Medical Association as a separate pamphlet

it is enforceable only by the moral pressure of the profession. In fact, the Helsinki Declaration suggests few deviations from the norms that had already been established in Western medicine. Its content can be classified as follows.

1. Moralistic clichés, empty of meaning since the key terms are not defined: "Clinical research must conform to the moral and scientific principles that justify medical research." "Special caution" should be exercised in the use of drugs or experimental procedures that can alter the subject's personality.

2. Apparent restrictions that in fact depend entirely on the physician's judgment: "If at all possible, consistent with patient psychology," the doctor should obtain the patient's consent for any therapy he prescribes. Research is legitimate only when the foreseeable benefits are greater than the inherent risks, according to a "careful assessment" by the physician.

3. A defense of the medical profession against what were deemed to be unwarranted restrictions: "In the treatment of the sick person, the doctor must be free to use a new therapeutic measure if in his judgment it offers hope of saving life, re-establishing health, or alleviating suffering."[2] All clinical research should be "under the supervision of a qualified medical man."

4. Possible innovations of no great importance: In nontherapeutic clinical research, "the nature, the purpose, and the risk" must be ex-

---

(undated). Among the American medical organizations, in addition to the AMA, that endorsed the Helsinki Declaration were: American Academy of Pediatrics, American College of Physicians, American College of Surgeons, American Federation for Clinical Research, American Heart Association, American Society for Clinical Investigation, Central Society for Clinical Research, Society for Pediatric Research. In 1966 the House of Delegates of the AMA adopted a statement on "Ethical Guidelines for Clinical Investigation," supplementing its earlier "Principles of Medical Ethics" with a paraphrase of the Helsinki Declaration (see American Medical Association, *Proceedings of the House of Delegates,* Las Vegas, Nevada, November 28–30, 1966, pp. 189–190).

2 An interesting application of this principle is to be found in the case of "Dr. Daniel Martin," a pediatrician of "Littletown, Connecticut," who was arrested on a morals charge (the facts are from an actual court case, with the names of the persons and town changed). Dr. Martin had an excellent reputation, with a record of remarkable success especially with disturbed or disoriented children. His mode of therapy, in which he claimed to be a pioneer, was to commit homosexual acts with his child patients. "In the management of disturbed children," he wrote, "many general approaches have been used, among them force, admonition, kindness, and traditional psychiatric medicine. None of these has been so successful that a further search for methods is not indicated. . . . I knew the law and knowingly violated it." According to at least some of the testimony, the "therapy" was successful. Martin was sentenced to 1 to 6 years in prison. See Richard C. Donnelly et al., *Criminal Law,* Free Press, New York, 1962, pp. 8–28, 61–62.

plained to the subject. Even after his consent is given, "the subject or his guardian should be free to withdraw permission" at any time.

The literature on the subject, of course, is not limited to commentaries on the Helsinki Declaration.[3] A recurrent theme is the especial difficulty in setting any guides to research combined with therapy. An occasional disease, identified by an unambiguous diagnosis, can be treated with a specific remedy that has no possible adverse side effects; and, at the other pole, healthy persons have sometimes been subjected to deliberate risk in a controlled experiment (a classic case in medical history was the identification of the mosquito as the carrier of yellow fever). By the nature of the art, however, most diagnoses are not wholly certain, most treatments can be effective only to a degree, and most experiments are on patients.

Seemingly, the law is in the process of linking therapy even more closely with experimentation, on the basis that the physician carries the same professional responsibility in either role. In the first legal suit (and to my knowledge the only one so far) resulting in an award for damages to a volunteer subject in medical research, the issue was the precise meaning of the "informed consent" that the physician-researchers obtained. The plaintiff, a student at the University of Saskatchewan, had been paid a stipulated fee to undergo tests with a new anesthetic. As a consequence, according to his allegation, he was unconscious for 4 days and hospitalized for 10 days, and he suffered a presumably permanent diminution of mental ability that forced him to withdraw from the university. In the first trial he was awarded $22,500 in damages. The university appealed, claiming that the judge had erred in his instructions to the jury by describing as a doctor-patient relation what in fact had been a contractual one. The appellate judge held, however, that the professional and legal duty of a physician to a subject of experimentation is at least as great as that of a physician or surgeon to his patient, and that, as the lower court had found, the plaintiff had not actually been informed fully of the risk he was taking. He had been told that the test was "safe," not that it involved a new drug about which little was known. "The subject of medical experimentation is entitled to a full and frank disclosure of all facts, probabilities, and opinions which a reasonable man might be expected to consider before giving his consent."[4]

---

3 For example, see Irving Ladimer, "Ethical and Legal Aspects of Medical Research on Human Beings," *Journal of Public Law,* 3 (1954), 467–511; Henry K. Beecher, "Human Studies," *Science,* 1964 (June 13, 1969), 1256–58; Paul S. Rhoads, "Medical Ethics and Morals in a New Age," *Journal of the American Medical Association,* 205 (1968), 517–522.

4 Halushka *v.* University of Saskatchewan et al. 1965, 53 D.L.R. (2d). The two deci-

Apart from the avoidance of fraud (which this case seemed to approach), physicians can do little more than consult with one another (one important reason, incidentally, for the rapid rise in the cost of medical services). Whether as therapist, experimenter, or therapist-experimenter, the doctor must carry full professional responsibility for his act. No one outside the profession is competent to set or administer controls, and the day-to-day scrutiny of his work that virtually all research physicians (as well as many in practice) continually seek from their colleagues cannot resolve the permanent dilemma: how to safeguard the welfare of the patient-subject without unduly impeding the advance of medicine.

That the effect of overall guiding principles may be slight is suggested by the crucial example of experimental transplants of human organs. The possibility of serious abuse is patent, in part because the medical and legal definitions of "death" have become ambiguous.[5] Yet in statements by the Board of Medicine of the National Academy of Sciences and the Judicial Council of the American Medical Association (AMA), the only meaningful safeguard against abuses connected with human transplants—in addition to admonitions about adequate training of the surgeon and the like—is that "an independent group of expert, mature physicians" (or, in the case of the AMA council, "at least one physician other than the recipient's physician") should declare the donor to be dead or on the point of death.[6] In short, the conclusion is the same as that cited earlier; control of research by the medical profession must be mainly internal, for no one else is competent to exercise appropriate restrictions.

Nonmedical scholars who do research involving human subjects are in a different position, since they usually make no claim to act as therapists.

sions were based in part on British and American precedents, and this case will undoubtedly be cited in American courts. Copies of the two judges' opinions can be obtained from the Institutional Relations Section, Division of Research Grants, National Institutes of Health.

5 With techniques now available it is possible in some cases to maintain "life" (as stipulated by the traditional criteria of persistent respiration and heart beat) even when there is not the remotest possibility that the patient will ever recover consciousness. According to a prestigious committee of the Harvard Medical School, thus, "responsible medical opinion is ready to adopt a new criterion for death to have occurred in an individual sustaining irreversible coma as a result of permanent brain damage." See Henry K. Beecher et al., "A Definition of Irreversible Coma: Report of the Ad Hoc Committee of the Harvard Medical School to Examine the Definition of Brain Death," *Journal of the American Medical Association*, 205 (1968), 337–340.

6 "Cardiac Transplantation in Man," *Journal of the American Medical Association*, 204 (1968), 147–148; "Ethical Guidelines for Organ Transplantation," 205 (1968), 341–342. See also Irvine H. Page, "The Ethics of Heart Transplantation: A Personal View," 207 (1969), 109–113; Emile Zola Berman, "The Legal Problems of Organ Transplantation," *Villanova Law Review*, 13 (1968), 751–758.

In 1966 the U.S. Public Health Service established a policy requiring all institutions receiving research, training, or other grants to file with it a statement either that no human subjects are involved or, if so, that the institution will accept responsibility to protect their rights.[7] In its formal statement of compliance, the institution must state its principles concerning the protection of human subjects, and this statement is one basis of the review committee's decision on whether or not the grant should be made.

With this stimulus all major institutions of higher learning have undertaken to establish canons of research involving human subjects and to adopt criteria for their enforcement. I received such statements from Harvard (separately from Harvard Medical School, Harvard University Health Services, and the Center for the Behavioral Sciences), Cornell, New York University, New School for Social Research, Princeton, Howard, Virginia, Ohio State, Iowa, Minnesota, and Washington. These differ in detail, but all are designed in the main to conform to the requirements of the U.S. Public Health Service and so follow its broad directives. As far as one can tell from such formal statements, to date this policy has impeded research very little if at all. The main purpose of the federal government, one can suppose, has been to evade legal responsibility for the misuse of grant funds; and in accepting that responsibility, universities have set up the bare mechanisms of control, making students who are doing research responsible to their professors, the professors responsible to a faculty research committee, and so on. If there are serious abuses, and particularly if these result in successful law suits parallel to the one against the University of Saskatchewan, these skeletal controls will undoubtedly become more restrictive; but that is now only a possibility.

That human subjects of research are afforded little protection is true also in the professional code of psychologists, whose research is—by its subject matter—perhaps most liable to abuse. According to an introductory statement, "a student of psychology who assumes the role of psychologist shall be considered a psychologist for the purpose of this code of ethics," with the same rights and responsibilities as full members of the profession. Apart from this important extension of those deemed to be qualified, the "research precautions" suggested are reminiscent of those recommended for the medical profession:

---

[7] U.S. Public Health Service, *Protection of the Individual as a Research Subject,* U.S. Government Printing Office, Washington, D.C., 1969; Eugene A. Confrey, "PHS Grant-Supported Research with Human Subjects," *Public Health Reports,* 83 (1968), 127–133; William J. Curran, "Governmental Regulation of the Use of Human Subjects in Medical Research: The Approach of Two Federal Agencies," *Daedalus,* 98 (Spring 1969), 542–594. This issue of *Daedalus,* on "Ethical Aspects of Experimentation with Human Subjects," contains several other articles pertinent to this discussion.

a. Only when a problem is of scientific significance and it is not practicable to investigate it in any other way is the psychologist justified in exposing research subjects, whether children or adults, to physical or emotional stress as part of an investigation.

b. When a reasonable possibility of injurious after-effects exists, research is conducted only when the subjects or their responsible agents are fully informed of this possibility and agree to participate nevertheless. . . .

c. Investigations of human subjects using experimental drugs (for example: hallucinogenic, psychotomimetic, psychedelic, or similar substances) should be conducted only in such settings as clinics, hospitals, or research facilities maintaining appropriate safeguards for the subjects.[8]

Thus in the worst case—from the subject's point of view—the professional society sanctions a psychology student who deliberately inflicts physical or emotional stress on subjects because he deems it useful for his research, or who uses experimental drugs in the vicinity of a therapeutic facility.

The American Sociological Association has not gone nearly so far. A preliminary set of ethical principles was drafted by a committee appointed in 1967, printed a year later, and voted on more than a year after that. The entire text of the relevant paragraph reads as follows: "All research should avoid causing personal harm to subjects used in research."[9] The parallel statement by the American Anthropological Association, concerned with such issues as defending the freedom of research and appropriate settings for support and sponsorship, does not so much as mention any professional responsibility of an ethnologist to the people he studies.[10]

The guidelines concerning the care of laboratory animals are similar though, as one would hardly expect, more stringent. A committee of the Institute of Laboratory Animal Resources has issued a "guide" to the

[8] American Psychological Association, *Ethical Standards of Psychologists*, Washington, D.C., 1963. This is featured prominently in all of the profession's discussion of ethical issues, and it has been reprinted in several appropriate places, for example, in Anne Anastasi, *Psychological Testing*, 3rd ed., Macmillan, New York, 1968. See also American Psychological Association, *Casebook on Ethical Standards of Psychologists*, Washington, D.C., 1967, and, for attempts to relate the general principles to particular fields in psychology, the following: Ad Hoc Committee on Ethical Practices in Industrial Psychology, "Ethical Practices in Industrial Psychology: A Review of One Committee's Deliberations," *American Psychologist*, **19** (1964), 174–182; A J. King and A. J. Spector, "Ethical and Legal Aspects of Survey Research," **18** (1963), 204–208; S. Messick, "Personality Measurement and the Ethics of Assessment," **20** (1965), 136–142; "APA Takes a Stand on Psychological Assessment," *A.P.A. Washington Report* (February 1970), 6–7.
[9] Text distributed to members by the American Sociological Association in December 1969. See also *American Sociologist* (November 1968).
[10] Fellows of the American Anthropological Association, *Statement on Problems of Anthropological Research and Ethics*, Washington, D.C., American Anthropological Association, n.d.

care of laboratory animals, with reasonable controls.[11] A board set up jointly by the veterinary profession and federal agencies has established board certification for animal technicians; at a junior level, the applicant must be 18 years old and a grammar school graduate, have a year's experience and a recommendation of his superior, and pass an appropriate examination. The prerequisites for certification at the senior and master levels are only slightly more selective.[12] The American Physiological Society established a set of "Guiding Principles in the Care and Use of Animals" used in research. They "must receive every consideration for their bodily comfort," including in particular anesthesia during operations.[13]

These regulations have been made partly obsolete by the Animal Welfare Act, passed originally in 1966 and amended in 1970 (Public Laws 89–544 and 91–579). Under the act the Secretary of Agriculture sets "minimum requirements with respect to handling, housing, feeding, watering, sanitation, ventilation, shelter from extremes of weather and temperatures, adequate veterinary care, including the appropriate use of anesthetic, analgesic or tranquilizing drugs . . . [in] research facilities" (Section 13). The act provides for inspections, the licensing of adequate handlers and facilities, and penalties for infractions of a year's imprisonment or a fine of $1,000, or both. Each year the Department of Agriculture issues a list of approved research facilities, and this accreditation is a prerequisite to having any grant or contract considered by any agency of the National Institutes of Health.[14]

In sum, the advance of knowledge concerning individuals, whether their physical bodies or their psyches, typically is made by testing hypotheses, and thus involves a risk to the experimental subjects. The usual escape from the dilemma, to experiment first on laboratory animals, can be only partial; for with different physiologies, the reactions to the test stimuli may also be different. In any case one would hope that knowledge could be increased without inflicting avoidable pain on any sentient being. Concerning both animals and humans, the general rule has been to depend on self-regulation by the professions. There are few statutory controls, and those are not well enforced. The one suit brought by an

[11] Committee on Revisions of the *Guide*, Institute of Laboratory Animal Resources, National Research Council, *Guide for Laboratory Animal Facilities and Care*, 3rd ed., U.S. Government Printing Office, Washington, D.C., 1968.

[12] *Ibid.*, Appendices III and IV.

[13] Quoted from a form the Society distributes to laboratories with the suggestion that the director sign it and post it for the guidance of the staff.

[14] National Institutes of Health, "Care and Treatment of Laboratory Animals (NIH 4206)," NIH Guide for Grants and Contracts, No. 7, June 14, 1971.

experimental subject focused on the fact that he had not been informed of the risk he was incurring. It can hardly be said, in short, that research is unduly hampered by unreasonable controls over either the use of human subjects or the handling of laboratory animals.

THE PROTECTION OF PRIVACY

The many books published during the past decade on the issue of privacy range from serious commentaries to a best-selling vulgarization.[15] Their common theme has excited organizations from the John Birch Society to the American Civil Liberties Union. Government agencies at various levels have investigated the matter and made recommendations.[16] The frequently paranoiac tone of many discussions can be illustrated with an editorial from the *New York Times* (August 6, 1966):

Can personal privacy survive the ceaseless advances of the technological juggernaut? . . . The Orwellian nightmare would be brought very close indeed if Congress permits the proposed computer National Data Center to come into being. . . . Perhaps in the long run the fight to preserve privacy is a vain one. But, like the struggle to preserve life, it must be continued while any shred of privacy remains.

Perhaps the most authoritative official statement on the issue is the one by a special committee assembled under the President's authority. According to this pamphlet, an inherent conflict exists between, on the one hand, "the right of the individual to decide for himself how much he will share with others his thoughts, his feelings, and the facts of his personal life" and, on the other hand, the right of society "to know anything that may be known or discovered about any part of the universe." The committee's statement is heavily weighted to favor the second of the rights, beginning with the disclaimer that "most current practices in [behavioral research] pose no significant threat to the privacy of research subjects." To reduce this threat as much as possible, the participation of subjects must be based

---

15 Ranging, thus, from Alan F. Westin, *Privacy and Freedom*, Atheneum, New York, 1967; Samuel Dash et al., *The Eavesdroppers*, Rutgers Univ. Press, New Brunswick, N.J., 1959; and Edward V. Long, *The Intruders*, Praeger, New York, 1966, through such works as Myron Brenton, *The Privacy Invaders*, Coward-McCann, New York, 1964, down to Vance Packard, *The Naked Society*, McKay, New York, 1964.

16 See, for example, "Special Inquiry on Invasion of Privacy," Hearings before a Subcommittee of the Committee on Government Operations, House of Representatives, 89th Congress, 1st Session, 1965, U.S. Government Printing Office, Washington, D.C., 1966.

on their informed consent "to the extent that it is consistent with the objectives of the research"; but "in the absence of full information, consent [may legitimately] be based on trust in the qualified investigator and the integrity of his institution." The scientist must design research so as to protect his subjects' privacy "to the fullest extent possible," considering whether "the benefits outweigh the costs"—that is, the benefits to society through the researcher as opposed to the costs borne by the subject.[17]

The analysis and proposed norms are reminiscent of those already discussed with respect to the physical protection of patients subject to therapeutic experimentation. Two important differences, however, should be noted. First, the authority of the medical profession, contrary to that in the social disciplines, is great enough to impose ethical standards on most of the individuals doing research. Second, the research done in medicine and allied sciences generally helps realize such universal goals as the extension of life or the reduction of pain; but there is seldom so clear a public benefit from, for example, sociologists' research on race relations, or political scientists' on "voting behavior," or even economists' on the causes and cure of inflation. If we grant that other values must sometimes be sacrificed to the furtherance of knowledge, we must also be careful to distinguish this from mere ideology.

The contrast between widespread popular distrust of data-gathering agencies and the sometimes bland, self-serving defense by their representatives obviously affects research in many ways. In this discussion the issue is *not* the allegedly widespread use of wiretaps, concealed microphones, and hidden cameras. Such supposed facts are here seen only as buttresses to the general lack of confidence that can, and often does, envelop any empirical work, especially one associated with a government institution. If any information that any research organization or official agency collects can (will?) be misused, one solution is to prevent its collection altogether. And that mood of suspicion thus seemingly warrants, however irrationally, an attack on the collection of data that are obviously useful and that, moreover, hardly threaten the privacy of anyone.

Two such instances are presented: the objections to **classifications by race** and the recent attacks on the census. Until the mid-1960s one important goal of civil rights organizations was to remove racial designations from public forms and the data compiled from them. They achieved a few notable—if sometimes temporary—successes.[18] The reasons for this

17 Office of Science and Technology, Executive Office of the President, *Privacy and Behavioral Research,* U.S. Government Printing Office, Washington, D.C., 1967.
18 New Jersey omitted race or color from its certificates of birth, death, and fetal death in 1962, restoring it again later that year or, in effect, the following year; see U.S. Public Health Service, *Vital Statistics of the United States, 1963,* Vol. II, Part A, Sec-

opposition to identifying a person's race on public documents can be usefully reduced to three main arguments:[19]

1. *It is morally wrong for a government to require a man to identify himself by race. It is an invasion of privacy.* It was mainly on this basis, for example, that the American Civil Liberties Union sought to have the question on race deleted from the 1960 census schedule. It would be difficult to maintain, however, that the color of one's skin is any less an element of one's persona than the colors of one's hair and eyes, which appear routinely on such documents as a driver's license or a passport—and excite no one's opposition. And in a period when consciousness of group identity is rising, when political programs to alleviate social problems are often linked to certain races (even if sometimes half-disguised as "the underprivileged," "the inner city," or the like), it is even harder to dissociate personal differentiation from the parallel subgroups of the population. Both at the individual and the social level, race significantly distinguishes one from another, and government programs of all kinds (for instance, both segregated schools and desegregation) operate in accordance with this differentiation. Is it reasonable or useful to draw an ethical line at a mere census enumeration, in order to preserve our ignorance of this important classification? I think not.

2. *Race identification on forms is often used to discriminate against the individual identified on the form.* Persons who defend this proposition typically do so on pure faith. Apart from a small number of lower-level positions in the federal bureaucracy, few jobs of any kind are filled without a personal interview. In the typical circumstances the lack of a racial designation on an initial form could hardly be much of an impediment to discrimination in either employment or the distribution of welfare, education, or any other social services. (And if the bare possibility of discrimination is taken to be a sufficient warrant to eliminate the designation of race, this need be done only on personal documents. For example, birth certificates issued in New York State carry no race identification, but confidential records that include this information are maintained so that group data can be compiled.)

3. *Statistical summaries by race are often used to reinforce stereotypes and prejudices—for example, racial breakdowns of crime, venereal disease,*

tion 6, U.S. Government Printing Office, Washington, D.C., 1965, pp. 6–9. In all of the national compilations by race, thus, this one state is omitted for 1962 and 1963. I wrote to several New Jersey officials for details on this interesting switch but received no responsive reply.

19 Albert Mindlin, "The Designation of Race or Color on Forms," *Public Administration Review,* **26** (1966), 110–118. See also Earl E. Huyck, "White-Nonwhite Differentials: Overview and Implications," *Demography,* **3** (1966), 548–565.

and dependency statistics. Thus, for example, according to a member of its national staff, "the NAACP opposes the compilation and publication of racially classified data on crime and illegitimate births because such information sheds no significant light on the causes, because it serves no useful purpose in curbing these offenses, because it is subject to distortion and misrepresentation, and because it is utilized to thwart the drive toward an egalitarian, pluralistic society."[20]

In the past the principled opposition to certain types of knowledge, the stance known during the last century as know-nothingism, was generally associated with reactionary politics. Liberals typically held that knowledge per se is valuable and, in particular since prejudice is fostered by igno-rance, that more and better data about the various ethnic groups generally helps to improve the relations among them. Indeed, according to the American credo the administration of justice should be color blind, as well as access to employment, public institutions, and all other services not reasonably designated as private. However, it was an aberration from this democratic norm to apply it to the gathering of knowledge, and some of the liberal organizations that in the 1950s expressed their own type of know-nothingism half-reversed this position during the 1960s. To develop social policies that would better the lot of racial minorities, in any case no easy task, was made more difficult by the resultant confusion.

The earlier policy of inhibiting the dissemination of certain types of knowledge was so general that it affected even newspapers. Following the example of such prestigious organs as the *New York Times,* many papers in the United States began to omit all racial identifications from persons in the news. Even so, the subsequent spectacular rise in the crime rate, especially among Negro youth in Northern cities, did not escape public attention; and the conscientious deletion of the offenders' race from news stories probably did more to reinforce the stereotype of the Negro crim-inal than the contrary. During the same period, moreover, many more Negroes were appointed or elected to places of honor, and as long as the policy was in effect, their race was often specified through a photograph. After several years the practice broke down—partly by such evasions, partly through newspapers' sympathetic reports about black militants, who shrilly demanded that they be identified by race.

More generally, statistics by race are crucial to these efforts to achieve the "egalitarian, pluralistic society" that the NAACP is working for. If the designation by race were to be deleted from the census schedule, as the ACLU advocated, one could still write philosophical essays on the virtues

[20] Henry Lee Moon, speaking before the 1962 meeting of the American Statistical As-sociation; quoted in Mindlin, *op. cit.*

of equality, but it would no longer be feasible to show that Negroes get less schooling and worse jobs, that their health is poorer and their lives are shorter, that in general the discrimination they suffer has measurable effects. Even more important, without such statistics it has been impossible either to compare the effects of the varied, often experimental, ameliorative programs, or to check on compliance with legislation designed to end discrimination. Since the passage of the Civil Rights Act of 1964, which stipulated that "no person shall, on the grounds of race, color, or national origin, be excluded from . . . any program or activity receiving federal financial assistance," the lack of group data on race has been of great assistance to bigots. For it is generally difficult, if not impossible, to prove that one particular person was denied benefits of any kind because of his race rather than a legitimate criterion of discrimination. However, if the distinctions so made reveal a pattern, then the burden of proof falls on the responsible administrator; he must try to show, contrary to the evidence, that racial discrimination was not practiced.

Colleges and universities that receive federal grants and contracts (hardly any do not) are now required not merely to enroll or employ qualified Negroes who apply to them but to take what is termed "affirmatve action"—that is, to seek out Negroes and invite them to apply. But the university administrators charged with carrying out this directive are plagued by the fact that, in accordance with the immediately prior norm, Negroes are often not identified as such in lists of high school graduates, college students, university faculty, and the like.

An even more striking contradiction exists in two parts of the Civil Rights Act of 1964. According to Title VIII, "no person shall be compelled to disclose his race, color, national origin, . . . nor shall any penalty be imposed for his failure or refusal to make such disclosure. Every person interrogated orally, by written survey or questionnaire, or by any other means with respect to such information shall be fully advised with respect to his right to fail or refuse to furnish such information." If this were applied to the census—and the wording of the act suggests no reason why it should not be[21]—answering the question on race would be stipulated to every respondent as voluntary, although under other laws replies to all items in the census schedule are mandatory. The very ambiguity, if it were to be exploited in litigation challenging either proviso, would damage the tabulations by race.

The sometimes hysterical opposition to the collection of data by race

21 The same title calls for a census "count of persons of voting age by race, color, and national origin"; there is no indication of how the implied contradiction should be resolved.

became more intense when it was proposed to include a question on **religious affiliation** in the 1960 census. Indeed, the proposal was met with indifference by the vast majority of the population, and it was actively supported by social scientists and many Catholic groups. However, the opposition of Jewish organizations, supported by one or two liberal associations, was sometimes offered by recalling, however irrelevantly, the genocide in Nazi Germany; and this emotionality has characterized much of the subsequent discussion.[22] In response to this largely irrational opposition from a minuscule portion of the population, the Census Bureau withdrew its proposal. It also rejected a renewed suggestion to include a question on religious affiliation in the 1970 schedule, partly because of the harm it would do to the Bureau's public relations, partly because its officials "were not sufficiently impressed with the stated need for the data to face the antagonism of those that are opposed to its collection."[23] Yet the issue is essentially parallel to that concerning race, even down to establishing accountability. A vast amount of public money is allocated by both criteria (in the case of religion, mainly by the facts that churches pay no taxes and that private donations to them may be deducted from taxable income), and with the religious statistics presently available there is no way of even estimating whether, by any criterion one chooses, the presumed public interest is served.

Undoubtedly, the main reason the **Census Bureau** did not choose to take on another dispute is that it was already **under general attack.** Although this was part of the general furor over the right to privacy, the issue of confidentiality is in fact irrelevant—except in the mouths of demagogues. However improbably, the Census Bureau has established a perfect record, never once accidentally or illegitimately revealing a single datum tied to an individual; but this has not inhibited those who say they are protecting the people's privacy.[24]

---

22 Cf. William Petersen, "Religious Statistics in the United States," *The Politics of Population,* Doubleday, Garden City, N.Y., 1964, pp. 248–270.

23 Herman P. Miller, "Considerations in Determining the Content of the 1970 Census," *Demography,* 4 (1967), 744–752.

24 The laws and administrative rulings guarding privacy are quoted in Conrad Taeuber, "Invasion of Privacy," *Eugenics Quarterly,* 14 (1967), 243–246; some of the court cases in which these rules have been upheld are discussed in Petersen, *op. cit.* A prime instance of the Census Bureau's probity, even under intense pressure from other government agencies and despite a prevailing mood of hysteria, was its refusal in 1941 to disclose the names and addresses of Japanese Americans. "To its everlasting credit, the Bureau of the Census demonstrated a higher devotion to the Constitution than did many of those who were responsible for the creation of detention camps for our fellow citizens who happened to be of Japanese ancestry" (Representative Cornelius E. Gallagher, Dem., N. Y., as quoted in the *New York Times,* May 9, 1969).

The first move in Congress against the census was in a bill offered by Congressman Jackson Betts (Rep., Ohio), which would have limited the mandatory questions to seven: name and address, relation to head of household, sex, date of birth, race or color, marital status, and visitors in the home at the time of the census. Many of the questions in the schedule, Mr. Betts argued, have no relation to the constitutional provision for a census, serve no public purpose, and violate the privacy of citizens; and such "probing of people's affairs is certainly unwanted and unnecessary." His stand catapulted him into national prominence, and the lesson was not lost on others in Congress. By mid-1968, 65 bills to limit the 1970 census, originating with Representatives of 43 states, had been introduced in the House, and nearly a third of the Representatives were on record as sponsors of one or another of these bills.[25]

This massive opposition, it must be emphasized, had nothing to do with any special features of the 1970 census. On the contrary, as compared with previous counts, it was planned to use sampling to relieve respondents of the duty of answering a larger portion of the schedule, so that in the 1970 census four-fifths of the household heads were asked only 24 out of the total of 89 questions. Nor did the questions differ in being unusually intrusive, in spite of nationwide propaganda to the contrary.[26]

A pretest of the 1970 census in Dane County, Wisconsin, was undercut by a mail campaign and advertisements in local newspapers, both organized by "The National Right to Privacy Committee," of which Vance Packard and William F. Rickenbacker were cochairmen. A pretest in Chesterfield and Sumpter Counties, South Carolina, was publicly attacked by Senator Strom Thurmond. At one time it seemed that there might be no enumeration in 1970. When the attacks reached a climax in 1969, the schedules were already printed; and if a new law had called for substantial changes, it would not have been possible to prepare and distribute new questionnaires before 1971. That may have been the main reason that the varous anticensus bills failed to pass. This does not mean, however, that the attack is over. On the opening day of the 91st Congress, Congressman Betts introduced H.R. 20, almost identical to the bill he

---

[25] "Census Programs Attacked as Invasions of Privacy," *American Statistician*, **22** (April 1968), 12–13; "Attacks on Census Increase," **22** (June 1968), 11; "The Census Inquisition," *Population Bulletin*, **25** (May 1969); John Kantner, "The Census under Attack," *American Sociologist*, **4** (1969), 256.

[26] One question (repeated virtually verbatim from the 1960 census) was, "Do you have a bathtub or shower?" with a choice among three answers: "Yes, for this household only"; "Yes, but shared with another household"; and "No bathtub or shower." In the publicity attacking the census, this effort to measure the quality of America's housing was paraphrased as "Do you take your shower with other persons?"

had sponsored in the previous Congress except that the mandatory questions were reduced to six, with "race or color" eliminated from his earlier list.

Even if the attacks were to cease immediately, some damage has been done. A census in a democratic country is more accurate than its counterpart in a totalitarian country simply because the count is based on the willing cooperation of the people, who are certain that the information they reveal for statistical purposes will not be used against them. Once irresponsible and false charges against the Census Bureau eroded this certainty, the accuracy and completeness of the returns were bound to suffer. Census Bureau officials, one should note, acclaimed the enumeration as the most accurate ever completed in this country—an assertion intended, one can assume, to undercut the hostility. However, officials of several areas that had been centers of opposition to the Bureau's activities were indignant because they would lose federal funds through what they termed, possibly correctly, a serious underenumeration.

To defend the mammoth, technically expert, politically neutral compendium of essential data that we know as the census would be unnecessary if a judgment were based only on accurate information and rational criteria.[27] No American institution—whether federal, state, or local government, business firm or trade union, church or school—could be competently administered without the guide to management furnished by census figures. The fact that everyone benefits from the enumeration means, however, that the census has no special constituency. Its main defenders against the attacks were various professional societies in the social sciences, almost all of which issued statements or even tried—not very successfully—to organize a countermovement. As one employee of the Census Bureau remarked following some positive testimony before a congressional committee, after a decade of issuing hundreds of manifestoes on almost every political issue, expressing ill-informed opinions in highly emotional language with the full authority of their academic standing, professors have opened up a vast credibility gap between themselves and Congress. In reply to Congressman Betts, when academia had something important and valid to offer, its genuine expertise was largely ignored.

27 One official of the Census Bureau asked me, if I were testifying before a congressional committee, fully aware that the allocation of sufficient funds depended in large part on its goodwill, how I would respond to this comment: One congressman admitted the justice of the witness's remarks that the collection of population data was useful but asked why the government had to be involved in it. When he wanted to know how many persons live in a certain city, he said, he looked up the fact in an almanac; why could not everyone else do the same and save the government many millions of dollars?

ACADEMIC FREEDOM

The absence of external impediments to the scholar's search for new knowledge and his communication of findings was not, in the traditional meaning of academic freedom, merely a specific instance of the civil rights generally guaranteed by a liberal society. The greater freedom granted to the academician was based on the premises that the "advancement of learning" (the title of Francis Bacon's eloquent call for the "instauration" of experimental inquiry) is greatest when not hampered by extraneous restraints, and that the consequent increase in knowledge benefits the whole community. In this perspective the freedom of academicians is not an absolute right but rather an institutional norm that, just as any other, must be weighed against others in order to find the balance that promotes maximum general welfare. This traditional denotation of the term has recently been both broadened and narrowed in scope. On the one hand, the range of those entitled to the special freedom has been extended to include both grade-school teachers, who make no claim to the advancement of scholarship, and graduate or even undergraduate students. Professors now claim absolute immunity not only within their fields of competence but for speeches and acts that express their nonprofessional, often uninformed, opinions as citizens. On the other hand, academic freedom has suffered during the past decade or so the most massive and successful attacks in the history of American higher education. Whether public or private, large and "anonymous" or liberal-arts, metropolitan or small-town, colleges and universities have undergone violent assaults that in the worst cases have institutionalized a gross deterioration of academic standards. Often it has been alleged that no defense was possible, that these institutions are—in part just because of the tradition of academic freedom—supremely vulnerable. Manifestly, the point has some validity. One can test its generality by asking how administrators and faculty would have reacted if the students (aided often by "nonstudents," in the common euphemism) attacking their universities had been associated with the Ku Klux Klan, Governor George Wallace, and similar reactionary symbols.

The rights to teach and to learn free from outside harassment barely existed in the United States before World War I. In 1918 the Committee on Academic Freedom of the American Association of University Professors (AAUP) held that faculty members unsympathetic to the conflict were obliged "to refrain from public discussion of the war and, in their private intercourse with neighbors, colleagues, and students, to avoid all hostile or offensive expressions concerning the United States or its government." Those who broke this rule could, in the view of the AAUP, be legitimately dismissed.[28] Very slowly and modestly before that time, much faster and more successfully in the following decades, the academic community joined battle with boards of trustees representing the views of corporate business; presidents subservient to conservative alumni, donors, or religious denominations in control of church-sponsored colleges; and congressional committees expressing "McCarthyism." By around 1960 the battle had been won, and *the* foe of academic freedom had been identified irremediably as the political right.

The response of liberal academia to the new attack from the left can be represented, *pars pro toto*, by a recent issue of *Daedalus*, the official organ of the American Academy of Arts and Sciences, on "Rights and Responsibilities: The University's Dilemma."[29] Its themes can be briefly—and therefore not entirely adequately—summarized as follows:

1. The nation is in the deepest crisis of its recent history. "Leadership is secretive, suspect, and uncertain; fears are deep and pervasive; resentments are powerful and insidious. . . . The university is at the center of the storm, and . . . how could it be otherwise?" (Stephen R. Graubard). In short, if academicians are dissatisfied with national, state, or local policies concerning Southeast Asia, race relations, inflation, pollution, and so on, they must acquiesce in the disruption, even the destruction, of the institutions for which they are responsible.

2. "The students" at Columbia established "communes," responding to a drive that is "at bottom religious" (Walter P. Metzger). However, in no major upheaval did "the students" act as a unit. Typically, a very small minority sought and finally achieved a violent confrontation with legitimate authority, and then a larger proportion, invariably encouraged

---

[28] Quoted in Sidney Hook, "The Strategy of Truth," *New Leader* (February 13, 1956). For more detailed evidence on how recently academic freedom has been established in this country, see John P. Roche, "We've Never Had More Freedom," *New Republic* (January 23, 1956); Richard Hofstadter and Walter P. Metzger, *The Development of Academic Freedom in the United States*, Columbia Univ. Press, New York, 1955.

[29] *Daedalus*, **99**, No. 3 (Summer 1970). The contributors to the issue, apart from the single instance of Walter P. Metzger, represent no greater competence to discuss academic freedom than whatever derives from some experience with revolting students. Their single point of view is not balanced by articles of such scholars as Sidney Hook, perhaps of all professors now alive the one who has devoted most effort to defending colleagues under attack, and presently associated with the University Centers for Rational Alternatives; Lewis Feuer, the author of a recent history of student revolts; S. M. Lipset, who had written several comparative studies on student radicalism—not to mention such knowledgeable conservatives as Russell Kirk and William F. Buckley, Jr.

by the sympathy of some faculty members and the vacillation of most administrators, offered varying amounts of support.

3. "Intellectual criticism is . . . the most neglected form of service that higher education is called upon to provide" (Edward Joseph Shoben, Jr.), and the demands of the radicals, however unfortunately expressed, often have some justice. The site of the university gymnasium, an issue that wracked the Columbia campus for months, was in Metzger's opinion one such half-legitimate grievance; but Mark Rudd, the head of the radicals (at the time of writing with the Weathermen faction of the Students for a Democratic Society and a fugitive from justice), publicly boasted that the controversy had been artificially contrived in order to generate dissension.

4. "The violence . . . is almost surely not a permanent phenomenon, . . . because no serious academic community can be sustained in the face of continuous obstruction by force and threats of force—whether from revolutionaries or reactionaries"[30] (McGeorge Bundy). In the face of spreading and increasing violence, that is to say, one must assume that it will soon abate—for the alternative is that the universities will be destroyed. Therefore no drastic countermeasures are necessary.

5. "The university has not only the right but also the obligation to put some limits on the freedom of the individual professor to develop his own research program" (Robert S. Morison, sympathetically reporting a supposed new consensus). "The university's research function should be circumscribed to exclude product development, market analysis, testing, or large-scale engineering. . . . The program agencies of government should be stripped of the power to offer incentives for faculty members, . . . [with such aid limited to] general support for higher education, to be administered centrally by each university" (Philip C. Ritterbush).

In the context of this essay, these proposed inhibitions to research are most pertinent. As long as the individual scholar (rather than the research team that later became typical) undertook a project based generally with no resources outside himself beyond a good library (rather than the elaborate and expensive equipment that is now usual if not required in virtually all disciplines), the freedom of academicians could be guaranteed with few ancillary problems. In the larger, more complex framework for research, this was often no longer the case. Some of the most

30 One might wonder who in this context would fall in the second category. Later in the essay Mr. Bundy personalizes the contrast—between Herbert Marcuse, a self-professed totalitarian (see in particular his contribution to *A Critique of Pure Tolerance,* Beacon, Boston, 1968), and Ronald Reagan, the Governor of California, whose constitutional, partial authority over the state university has been far less forceful or effective in restoring order than most of his constituents had hoped for.

prestigious professors received a double salary, one for the teaching they no longer performed and another (often larger) for contract research. Some universities adapted their rapid growth to the ready flow of research funds, so that any interruption was felt through every part of the institution. In the following discussion, as in the previous section on the invasion of privacy, such genuine difficulties are passed over in order to concentrate more fully on what are here taken to be more or less false issues.

Some of the first important attacks on university research were made in the context of Project Camelot, and it may be useful to review briefly that notorious fiasco.[31] Conceived in 1963 by some officers of the Army's Office of Research and Development, the Project was turned over to an organization that the Army had established specifically to conduct its research in the social sciences—the Special Operations Research Office, located on the campus of American University. Camelot's loosely defined objectives were to identify symptoms of societal breakdown and to specify acts that might forestall it. With an initial grant of $6 million, research on this politically delicate topic was to be undertaken in Latin America, the Middle East, the Far East, Western Europe, and Africa. Apparently by accident, the first steps in this worldwide survey of how to control insurgency were taken in Chile. Cooperation from sociologists there was sought by a Dr. Hugo Nuttini, who happened to be going to Chile on other business; he presented the Project to them as an academic effort and tried, eventually unsuccessfully, to hide the identity of the sponsoring agency. When this proved to be the U.S. Army, the Chilean Chamber of Deputies, some of whose members regarded Camelot as a *Yanqui* espionage plot to foster counterrevolution, formally investigated the whole matter. The United States ambassador, who first heard of this Army-subsidized research by reading of it in the Santiago press, reacted sharply. His protest resulted in a directive from President Johnson prohibiting any further government-

---

[31] The writings on Project Camelot are scattered, highly polemical, and difficult to evaluate. Among the most useful sources are: House of Representatives, Subcommittee on International Organizations and Movements, *Behavioral Sciences and the National Security*, Report No. 4; *Winning the Cold War: The U. S. Ideological Offensive*, Part IX, U.S. Government Printing Office, Washington, D. C., 1965; Irving Louis Horowitz, "The Life and Death of Project Camelot," *Trans-action*, 3 (November–December 1965), 3–7, 44–47; *The Rise and Fall of Project Camelot*, Irving Louis Horowitz, Ed., M.I.T. Press, Cambridge, Mass., 1967; Kalman H. Silvert, "American Academic Ethics and Social Research Aboard," American Universities Field Staff, *Report*, West Coast South America Series, 12, No. 3 (July 1965); Gideon Sjoberg, "Project Camelot: Selected Reactions and Personal Reflections," in *Ethics, Politics and Social Research*, Sjoberg, Ed., Schenkman, Cambridge, Mass., 1967, Chap. 6; Robert A. Nisbet, "Project Camelot and the Science of Man," in *Tradition and Revolt: Historical and Sociological Essays*, Random House, New York, 1968, Chap. 13.

funded research on other countries that in the opinion of the Secretary of State would damage the foreign relations of the United States.[32]

After Camelot's total collapse, its spokesmen were self-righteous in their explanations. They did not acknowledge that the failure was theirs, that they, acting professionally as social scientists, should have known (if indeed this background was requisite) that a study on the sources of civil disorders under the sponsorship of the U.S. Army was technically unfeasible in Latin America, of all places. Horowitz, similarly, regards the academicians as innocent, seduced into "assertions which clearly derive from American military policy objectives."[33] Even the *Report* of the House subcommittee is deferential to the guidance that these and other social scientists can give to national policy, critical only of the Army for wanting that guidance. In short, the principal conclusion from this experience was not that some social scientists are incompetent and these were more so than the rule, but that the political framework in which they operated was the entire cause of the Project's failure. And the conclusions that various policy makers drew in the subsequent period, only partly from the experience that Camelot afforded, set various kinds of restrictions to permissible research.

1. *No secret contracts.* From the beginning this was almost entirely a false issue. It has been all but forgotten that in fact the Army's sponsorship of Camelot was *not* secret, and that Nuttini lied to his Chilean associates when he asserted that the money would come from the National Science Foundation and "various scientific and governmental organizations in the United States."[34] The government guidelines already cited

---

[32] See "Government Guidelines for Foreign Areas Research," *Far Horizons*, 1, No. 1 (January 1968), U. S. Government Printing Office, Washington, D. C.

[33] On the other hand, Horowitz also averred that the Project's problems did not "derive from any reactionary character of the project designers. . . . The advisory board, the core planning group, the summer study group, and the various conference groupings . . . were more liberal in their orientation than any random sampling of the sociological profession." Moreover, the motivations and attitudes of Camelot's personnel were closely linked, according to Horowitz's analysis, with this left-liberal orientation. Not only were they joyful at having breached the gates to "the Establishment" but, as Nisbet put it, they looked forward to "the Platonic prospect of educating an elite . . . with peaceful and constructive aims, . . . of accelerating man's ascent to perfectibility through the humanization . . . of military power."

[34] It is not clear from the sources available to me whether he did this on his own initiative or following instructions from the Project director. In any case, his prevarication was divulged because Johan Galtung, a Norwegian sociologist who happened to be teaching temporarily in Santiago, had been approached earlier to join the Camelot staff, and he had in his possession a completely open and frank letter inviting him to a planning session. Once Galtung made this public, Nuttini protested that he had been

merely reaffirmed existent policy in stipulating that "the fact of government research support should always be acknowledged by sponsor, university, and researcher." Subsequently, in supposed reaction to Project Camelot and "other, primarily military-financed research with ends we consider interventionist, manipulative, or militaristic," a group of Latin Americanists pledged "to ourselves and to each other not to participate in such research," calling upon other academicians and universities and the United States government to take actions supporting their stand. Secrecy, according to their manifesto, is alien to academic research.

We shall not participate in any research or other activity ordered or paid for in whole or in part by any military or governmental agency or private corporation unless the involvement of such agency or corporation, and its objectives, is [sic] made clear and public.[35]

The same stand has been taken by a number of other academic groups. For example, according to the recommendations of the Committee on Research Policies at the University of Michigan:

The University will not enter into any contract which would restrain its freedom to disclose (1) the existence of the contract, (2) the identity of the sponsor and, if a subcontract is involved, the identity of the prime sponsor, . . . [and (3)] the purpose and scope of the proposed research.[36]

Since all parties generally agree that the existence of research contracts shall be publicized, in principle the barring of secret contracts does not inhibit the pursuit of knowledge.[37]

duped. The impression in Chile that "The Pentagon" was conducting American foreign policy was reinforced when "the Chilean Minister of the Interior good-heartedly but innocently absolved the American 'government' from blame, making the standard Latin American discrimination between the armed forces and the civil authorities" (Silvert, op. cit.).

[35] "Declaration of Latin America Specialists on Professional Responsibility," Transaction, 6, No. 9 (July–August 1969).

[36] "Classified Research at the University of Michigan," Report of the Senate Assembly Committee on Research Policies, January 16, 1968. A "Statement of Policy" adopted by the University of Minnesota, as another example, has almost exactly the same wording.

[37] In fact, however, this may not be the case in a university with a strong militant left. At Berkeley, for instance, the New Left conducts what it terms "Red Star Tours," in which newcomers are conducted from one office to another of those faculty defined as enemies, so that all radicals will know whom to harass or, on occasion, physically assault. With this kind of pressure to conform on university faculty and administrators, one could conceivably argue that only a man assured that his choice can be made privately truly enjoys academic freedom. I would hold, however, that secrecy is inherently destruc-

2. *Classified research.* If secret contracts are barred by the policies of both the government and most universities, is it possible nevertheless to conduct classified research on campuses? The committee at Ann Arbor, whose report we have already cited, recommended a compromise that would permit it under specified conditions. Since "in certain fields participation in classified research is vital to the professional development of the scholar, . . . selected classified research projects are acceptable for valid academic reasons." Each proposed project would have to be passed by a review committee, of which some members might not have security clearance. The impediments to classified research under such a system the committee accepted with equanimity, for it had no enthusiasm altogether for the university's participation in classified research. A similar set of guidelines was adopted at Princeton:

Contracts involving classified information shall be held to the minimum consistent with the interests and obligations of the members of the faculty and their departments for performing creative research in their respective fields. Contracts . . . undertaken at the request of the Government . . . shall be accepted only under the most pressing demands of national interest.[38]

Other universities have gone farther. At the University of Pennsylvania (as well as several others), no master's essay or doctoral dissertation may be based on classified research, and in general such projects are deemed admissible only in "unusual circumstances of urgent public importance":

The university . . . will not be a party to imposing any disadvantage upon any faculty members, student, academic, or policy-making officer because he seeks, or refuses to seek, or fails to obtain security clearance.[39]

At Stanford, the Senate of the Academic Council adopted a resolution barring classified research from the university altogether. After a 9-day sit-in at the Stanford Electronics Laboratory, all of its classified research (or an annual volume of more than $2 million, about two-thirds of the laboratory's total budget) was to be phased out.[40]

tive of the academic setting and that the remedy is rather to reestablish order on campus by expelling those bent on undermining it.

38 "Report and Faculty Resolutions with Regard to Security and Classification in Government-Sponsored Research," Princeton University, May 14, 1953; confirmed as university policy, January 16, 1967.

39 University of Pennsylvania, *Handbook for Faculty and Administration,* 1969, pp. 45–49.

40 Stanford University, *Campus Report* (April 30, 1969).

According to a recent survey, American universities are moving toward some general standards on this issue, which were summarized as follows:

1. Classified basic research is antithetical to the central purpose of institutions of higher learning: the development or extension of knowledge by free and open inquiry and the public dissemination of that knowledge.

2. . . . When applied research is classified, this seems further to restrict its value to the institution. Under such circumstances, the university must be especially sure that its own needs are met, not thwarted; its own functions fulfilled, not distorted.

3. In social science research, whether basic or applied, openness of purpose and activity are critically important, not only for the sake of the ultimate success of the particular effort and the sake of the institution's reputation, but for the sake of one of the oldest of academic traditions—respect for the dignity of man.

4. University-based research ideally involves students. . . . The further removed the research from learning and training opportunities for students, the less desirable is that research for the university.[41]

In response to this kind of pressure, there was a significant reduction in the amount of classified research at universities during the 1960s. Part of this was achieved by a change of ruling; a security classification had often been assigned not because of the character of the research but in order to give the principal investigator access to classified data, and in many such cases it was possible to separate the two. In other instances the Department of Defense has transferred classified research from universities to federal laboratories, federal contract research centers, or either commercial or nonprofit private laboratories. At the beginning of 1970, of the research contracts still in effect between universities and the Department of Defense, only about 5 percent were classified.[42]

3. *Sponsored research.* Apart from all of the polemics about classified projects, serious doubts have been raised about the amount, purposes, and consequences of any sponsored research at universities. Some have called for at least a partial return (as they see it) to laissez-faire in knowledge-gathering. This would permit universities to return to what such critics view as their main business, the maintenance and proliferation of a humanist point of view. For in arriving at any contract, the funding agency and the research team each bargains for its narrowly defined in-

41 Stephen Strickland and Theodore Vallance, "Classified Research: To Be or Not To Be Involved," in *Sponsored Research in American Universities and Colleges,* Stephen Strickland, Ed., American Council on Education, Washington, D. C., 1968, pp. 208–209.
42 Communication from S. Benedict Levin, Acting Assistant Director (Defense), Office of the Director of Defense Research and Engineering, Department of Defense, January 14, 1970.

terest, and the resultant compromise may not serve the university's needs. Criticism of Camelot, as vehement on campuses as anywhere else, resulted in the directive we have noted; but according to Professor Horowitz, "giving the State Department the right to screen and approve government-funded social science research projects on other countries, as the President has ordered, is a supreme act of censorship." Surely one might agree that it is the government's duty to see that public money is spent in the national interest, and it is the function specifically of the State Department to oversee such expenditures as they affect the relations between the United States and other nations. Any social scientist who objects to having the national interest, so defined, included in his professional orientation is entirely free not to apply for such funds. According to Blackstone's classic definition, a contract is "an agreement upon sufficient consideration to do or not to do a particular thing."

The more important question in this context is how the legitimate checks set by the President's directive worked in practice. As exercised by the State Department's Foreign Affairs Research Council, the control applies only to projects to be directly funded by the government, not to those paid for out of public money (in the sense that it is exempted from taxation) that private foundations administer. The only criterion in judging a proposal is "whether a given research project could adversely affect U. S. foreign relations with one or more countries. [The Council] has no authority to make any judgments on such substantive matters as the need, merit, or cost of a project." During the first 3 years the policy was in effect, about 1.6 percent of the projects reviewed were disapproved on this basis.[43]

Within only a couple of years, the opposition to "secret" or classified research, or to the supposed deleterious effects of any sponsored research at all on the university, was swallowed up in a vast effort to redirect the whole quest for knowledge. The issue is no longer who shall do what research under which conditions, but whether basic research is to be tolerated, and if so to what extent.

THE CALL FOR "RELEVANCE"

At one time it was routine to warn budding scientists that they should avoid bias in their research. One must conduct any quest for the empirical truth in such a way as to minimize the influence of preconceptions,

43 Communication from Donald Dumont, Deputy Director for Research Services, Office of External Research, Department of State, January 15, 1970. See also Foreign Affairs Research Council, "A Report on the First Three Years," August 1968 (mimeo); "Research Council Activities in FY '69—The Fourth Year," n.d. (mimeo).

whether on the observations, on the inclusion or exclusion of data, on the mode of analysis, or on the presentation of results. None of this implies that the scientist must lack the values involved in his study; "freedom from bias means having an open mind, not an empty one."[44] Max Weber, who wrote the classic essays defending this point of view, was almost as much a German nationalist as those who used their books and lectures to proselytize nationalism; the difference was that Weber rigorously separated professional analysis from political opinion.

The recent degeneration of objectivity in scientific research had been foreshadowed in postwar pronouncements by several of the physicists who had built the atomic bomb, and who after the fact felt personally culpable. Some of them founded the *Bulletin of the Atomic Scientists,* whose influence almost matched the high status of its main contributors. Today there exists a Society for Social Responsibility in Science "organized to foster throughout the world a tradition of personal moral responsibility for the consequences to humanity of professional activity, with emphasis on constructive alternatives to militarism." The association claims members in 20 countries, among them six Nobel laureates. Moral qualms are appropriate concerning modern weaponry. The point is not this specific issue but rather the fact that the writings of leading scientists challenging certain applications of their professional labors helped establish a general antiscientific mood.

One important index of this shift is the new style in the professional meetings of scientific societies. As recently as the early 1960s, these used to serve, more or less well according to the skill of the organizing committee, a double function: to provide a forum of colleagues who commented on early or partial research findings, and to afford a setting in which personal ties could be established and renewed among professionals from various universities. In the early 1970s it should be unnecessary to illustrate the new pattern at length, with anecdotes drawn from the meetings of humanists (such as the Modern Language Association), social scientists (whether sociologists, political scientists, anthropologists, or others), or natural and physical scientists. Perhaps the best example is the most general organization, the American Association for the Advancement of Science (AAAS).

In 1969, AAAS itself invited two graduate students to arrange a program as part of its annual meeting. Nine speakers declaimed on "The Sorry State of Science—A Student Critique." From the office that the Association furnished them, radical students organized "picketing, radical films, petition campaigns, and so on," including several violent disrup-

---

[44] Abraham Kaplan, *The Conduct of Inquiry: Methodology for Behavioral Science,* Chandler, San Francisco, 1964, p. 375.

tions of scheduled presentations. "A Columbia student screamed that the [professional] panelists were all 'war criminals' and that true disarmament could come only through revolution." Melvin Margulis, who identified himself as a former graduate student in engineering and presently a reporter for *Rat,* a New York "underground" newspaper, "took the microphone away from Charles Stark Draper of M.I.T.'s Instrumentation Laboratory and made a five-minute obscenity-punctuated speech denouncing the space program, among other things."[45]

At the 1970 meeting, the radical professors and students were organized into a loosely knit group called "Scientists and Engineers for Social and Political Action," with the slogan "Science for the people." With the routine violence and obscenity, they disrupted several sessions, prevented the president-elect of AAAS, Glenn T. Seaborg, former chairman of the Atomic Energy Commission, from speaking on a panel on "Science and the Federal Government." In his prepared but undelivered remarks, Mr. Seaborg would have denounced the "current anti-science, anti-technology, and anti-rational attitude." The keynote of the convention, one might say, was offered by folksinger Pete Seeger (whose presentation was not disrupted): "Here we are, knee-deep in garbage, shooting rockets at the moon."[46]

That AAAS permits a rabble to invade its meetings and denigrate its members is attributable, as also with other professional societies and universities generally, to the half-sympathy that some of its officers and members feel with the goals of the radical minority. In the often repeated phrase, the dissidents' purpose is good even if their tactics must be deplored. Many articles have been published recently in *Science,* the journal of AAAS, calling into question the value of scientific research. Public approval of science has slackened, according to one such paper, for the following reasons: (1) "The mere capacity to manipulate the world does not insure that it will be manipulated for the net benefit of mankind." (2) The increased production that science has made possible "comes at the cost of a rapid exhaustion of natural resources and increasing contamination." (3) Even the improvement of health has kept a larger number alive but in suffering. (4) The "ethical implications of advances in biological science . . . threaten the individual's command over his own life." (5) "Science is not as much fun as it used to be," for it no longer provides satisfying answers to fundamental questions about the natural world.[47]

45 James K. Glassman, "AAAS Boston Meeting: Dissenters Find a Forum," *Science,* 167 (January 2, 1970), 36–38; "Unprecedented AAAS Meeting," *AAAS Bulletin* (March 1970).
46 *Chronicle of Higher Education,* 5 (January 11, 1971), 1, 5.
47 Robert S. Morison, "Science and Social Attitudes," *Science,* 165 (July 11, 1969), 150–156. Dr. Morison is director of the division of biological sciences at Cornell University.

It is even more disturbing that, shortly after Dr. William D. McElroy was appointed as the new director of NSF, the government's main disbursing agency for the support of research in pure science, he voiced somewhat similar sentiments.[48] Shortly thereafter, NSF instituted a new program entitled "Interdisciplinary Research Relevant to Problems of Our Society." Dr. McElroy announced plans for a program in "student-initiated, student-planned, and student-directed research aimed at solving some of the pressing problems of our present-day society." Why at a time when the NSF budget was severely curtailed, when some legitimate projects could therefore not be funded, should a portion of the agency's smaller budget be diverted to students? Dr. McElroy explained the rationale behind the innovation: "University students are among those most concerned about society's problems. They have also been in the forefront of seeking solutions to those problems."[49] Later the emphasis on applied research at NSF was expressed in a wide range of new programs, all under the collective heading of Research Applied to National Needs (RANN).

It is even more indicative, perhaps, that Alvin M. Weinberg, the director of Oak Ridge National Laboratory, felt it necessary in the journal of AAAS to write a paper entitled "In Defense of Science."[50]

THE END OF UNIVERSITY RESEARCH?

The subhead is a manifest, and deliberate, hyperbole. Obviously, a certain proportion of the faculty will continue, as individuals, to extend the bounds of knowledge in their discipline. There may still be enclaves

---

In a similar vein, Murray Gell-Mann, winner of the 1969 Nobel prize in physics, called for a basic reorientation of science and technology. "It used to be true that most things that were technologically possible were done. . . . Certainly, in the future, this cannot and must not be so. . . . An essential element of engineering from now on must be the element of choice," quoted in *Science,* **166** (November 7, 1969), 723. Other important items in this journal's continuing campaign include Walter Orr Roberts, "After the Moon, the Earth!," **167** (January 2, 1970), 11–16; V. R. Potter et al., "Purpose and Function of the University," **167** (March 20, 1970); 1590–93; J. Alan Wagar, "Growth versus the Quality of Life," **168** (June 5, 1970), 1179–84.

[48] William D. McElroy, "Bewildering Questions for Science in the 1970s," National Academy of Sciences, *News Report* (November 1969). Dr. McElroy was later replaced as director of NSF by Dr. H. Guyford Stever, formerly president of Carnegie-Mellon Institute.

[49] National Science Foundation, "Interdisciplinary Research Relevant to Problems of Our Society," Important Notice No. 24, December 11, 1969.

[50] *Science,* **167** (January 9, 1970), 141–145.

in which large-scale research institutes remain viable. Whether the well-knit bond will last between graduate education and research, an association that on balance brought enormous benefits to both sides, has become questionable. In brief summary the factors that in combination pose this query are these:

1. Money is short for university research, both from government agencies and from the research and development budgets of private business. This depletion is partly attributable to what can be considered temporary causes—the war in Indochina, the government's efforts to control inflation, and so on. It is partly due, however, also to other, more lasting factors.

2. Money ostensibly allocated to research is being used—I would guess in increasing proportions—for other social purposes. Granted that in some instances the delincation cannot be sharp between research and teaching, or between social research and social reform; but fundamentally research—and not the others—is characterized by a conscious, disciplined effort to transgress the universal predilection to see not what is there, but what has been preconceived. The loudest spokesmen for American academia demand not intelligence in the solution of social problems, but "commitment," not knowledge but "passion." For by this view "ethical neutrality is a veneer for irresponsibility."[51]

Those that control the distribution of research funds, whether government agencies or the major private foundations, typically set "relevance" as a principal criterion of a proposal's worth, especially but not exclusively in the social sciences. A researcher who would like to study a matter of basic importance to his discipline thus is often constrained to disguise his absorption in fundamentals with a professed interest in the instant solution of the currently stylish social problem. Mere social concern is not enough if it is not modish. "Poverty" appeared in the United States when Harrington's book[52] created a general, exaggerated awareness; funds to study city problems, now almost inescapable, were difficult to get until the riots of the mid-1960s. "Relevance," in short, is defined largely by journalists, city mobs, or—within the social disciplines—New Left caucuses; they tell the professionals competent to do the research

51 Sydney Willhelm, "Scientific Unaccountability and Moral Accountability," in *The New Sociology*, Irving Louis Horowitz, Ed., Oxford Univ. Press, New York, 1964, pp. 181–187.
52 Michael Harrington, *The Other America: Poverty in the United States*, Penguin, Baltimore, 1962. Mr. Harrington, according to the blurb on his book, has an M.A. in English literature. He has worked as associate editor of *The Catholic Worker*, organizational secretary of the Workers Defense League, consultant to the Fund for the Republic, and a free-lance writer.

what problems they are to analyze. Perhaps the main argument, then, against permitting "relevance" to guide funding is that the research so designated often lacks pertinence. Unless we learn some of the underlying facts as yet unknown, and unless we can study more proximate data in an environment that is not supercharged with emotion, no expenditure of time and money is likely to increase knowledge significantly or bring about broad social reform.

The reallocation of research funds has also been effected indirectly. Late in 1969 Senators Mike Mansfield and J. William Fulbright offered an amendment that prohibited the Department of Defense from supporting research lacking a "direct and apparent relationship to a specific military function." The bill was enacted although not, in its sponsors' opinions, strictly enforced, and the Senate's leaders then demanded that top officials, starting with Deputy Defense Secretary David Packard, agree in writing to comply with the law. Previously, a considerable portion of Department of Defense funding had been for research marginal to the military enterprise narrowly defined (though often of high quality, in one case high enough to get a Nobel Prize for the researcher); and Pentagon research officials estimate that about one-tenth of the $260 million of Department of Defense funds going to university research will be permanently cut.

3. If and when funds become available in adequate amounts to support basic research, there will be little reason to channel them into what have become the nation's centers of violent dissent to scholarship. Not only has radical disruption often focused on research centers but many universities have accommodated to leftist blackmail, with consequent permanent changes in their institutional structure.

Several universities, notably Harvard since 1954, had evaded the ticklish issue of classified research on campus by formally banning it but in fact permitting those faculty members who wished to be involved to evade the ostensible controls. A typical device had been an off-campus site for such research, such as the Stanford Research Institute, with partial and ambiguous links to the main university. Once the New Left assault got into full swing, neither type of evasion proved to be an effective camouflage.

The issue—which affects to one degree or another most of the country's major universities—can be illustrated conveniently with the developments at M.I.T., perhaps the prime example of academic cooperation with the United States government in the furtherance of national goals. Associated with M.I.T. were two off-campus research institutions. Founded during World War II, the Instrumentation Laboratory (I-Lab)

—which its director, Dr. Charles S. Draper, had developed into one of the world's best research institutes in military and associated technology—had a budget of about $54.6 million in fiscal year 1969, about half each from the Department of Defense and the National Aeronautics and Space Administration (NASA). The Lincoln Laboratory was founded in 1950, also at the urging of government leaders, in order to develop radar, communications, and computer technology for air defense. The I-Lab was repeatedly picketed by mobs chanting, "Shut it down" and "Ho-Ho-Ho Chi Minh, the NLF is gonna win!" M.I.T. President Howard W. Johnson appointed a committee to reexamine the university's policy toward the I-Lab; its members included two students—Jonathan Kabat, a New Left extremist, and George Katsiaficas, a leader of the Rosa Luxemburg chapter of the SDS—as well as faculty (ideologically led by Professor Naom Chomsky) of a similar political orientation. After some months of deliberation (during which President Johnson's office was occupied and suffered some $6000 in damage), Dr. Draper was "fired" (in his words) as director of the I-Lab (which was renamed the Draper Laboratory), and the university agreed to sell it to a private corporation. For the time being, M.I.T. retained its connection with the Lincoln Laboratory, reportedly because its research was more basic and was "not directly related to specific weapons" (of its budget of $68.5 million in fiscal year 1969, all but $1 million derived from a single Department of Defense contract). In fact, one suspects, the reason is that the I-Lab, located in Cambridge, was convenient to M.I.T. radicals, while the disruption of its sister institution in Lincoln involves commuting. Meanwhile the university itself is in serious financial straits; as one official noted after the agreement was signed to divest itself of the Draper Laboratory, "We'll have to live by our wits."[53] In the middle of this battle, a project to furnish the Cambridge area with adequate computer resources, financed by the Department of Defense with $7.6 million over five years, began to founder in its second year. The project became "the subject of a university-wide debate at Harvard and M.I.T., involving the wider questions of the role of the Defense Department in funding any kind of social science or computer work (even basic and unclassified research), the role

53 "Defense Research on Campus: The Dimensions of a Dilemma," Technology Review (January 1970); "New Left vs. National Security," National Review, (January 13, 1970); "M.I.T. Officials Reject Demonstrators' Demands" (for an abolition of discipline procedure and a gift of $150,000 to the Black Panthers, among other items), New York Times (January 17, 1970); "M.I.T. Administration Makes Public Its Intentions," Science, 168 (May 29, 1970), 1074–75; "M.I.T. to Shift Defense Lab to Private Firm," Chronicle of Higher Education (June 1, 1970).

of technology in the development of the social sciences, and the effect of large-scale government funding on the university and its autonomy."[54]

4. The most fundamental reason that the quest for knowledge is likely to be divorced from universities is that these have become the foci of a growing distrust of knowledge. Man is seen by some of the faculty, typically influential beyond their numbers, as another sorcerer's apprentice, able to set the mops and brooms going but not to control the havoc they wreak.

Science is not a static "body of knowledge," but a knowledge-producing process, which time and again during the past several decades has breached the limits upon which the nineteenth-century compromise between empiricism and humanism was founded. The undeviating regularity of the Newtonian universe, once it was accepted as true, afforded man a psychological security, which is now shattered by Einstein's "relativity" and Heisenberg's "uncertainty." That recent explorations into the structure of matter also led to a weapon of terrifying force obviously did nothing to alleviate the unease. Early in the nineteenth century, Christian dualism had been challenged by Wöhler's synthesis of urea; with this demonstration that the animate and the inanimate are constructed out of the same elements, he founded organic chemistry. Today's new disciplines—biochemistry, biophysics, and their adjuncts—go much farther. With the purposeful manipulation of the gene that seemingly is in prospect,[55] the family, the school, the church, and any other institution designed to guard physical or cultural heredity become less significant. And, finally, among the marvels achieved by such applied sciences as medicine and engineering is the increase by many millions of the humans who live at the miserable edge of utter destitution. Thus, less than a decade after several prominent sociologists perceived "the end of ideology," we see instead the gradual conquest of empirical investigation and rational discourse by ideological intrusions into the main seats of learning.

Adam, who ate of "the tree of knowledge" and thereby lost his pristine innocence, sacrificed with it the paradise in which he was living. No

---

54 Judith Coburn, "Project Cambridge: Another Showdown for Social Sciences?" *Science,* **166** (December 5, 1969), 1250–53.

55 In January 1971, Dr. James D. Watson, testifying before the House of Representatives Science Subcommittee, described the recent work of two Cambridge University biologists and predicted that within a year it will be possible to implant in a woman's uterus an ovum fertilized in a test-tube. With the double authority of a Nobel laureate who wrote a best-seller, *The Double Helix,* Dr. Watson called on the United States to "take the lead now in forming an international commission to ask, 'Do we really want to do this?'" Perhaps, he suggested, steps should be taken to make the research illegal.

parable more clearly defines an age of faith, a time when man humbly set narrow limits to his potential. By this norm "he that increaseth knowledge increaseth sorrow" (Ecclesiastes 1:18). The modern era, one can justly say, began when knowing was redefined as good. When Kant wrote his famous essay, "What is the Enlightenment?," he defined it as man's emergence from this self-imposed subordination. The motto of the new age, he wrote, was *Sapere aude*—"Dare to know."[56]

Manifestly, it has not been the intent in this chapter to deny legitimacy to any and all limits to knowledge seeking. The point is rather that the limits actually imposed have often been ill chosen. There is good reason to fear the effect of mind-altering drugs on subjects' psyches, yet the supposed controls set by the psychological association hardly guard against serious abuses. The Census Bureau, which established probably the best record in Washington for unimpeachable probity, was subjected to a mindless attack that may have damaged the accuracy of the 1970 count. In the name of academic freedom, professional groups and universities have called for new restrictions on the right of academicians to do research.

The solution to problems, whatever they are, can only be by the application of informed intelligence. If, because of new political commitments we set new priorities, that is what politics has always meant. If, however, commitment replaces knowledge, confrontation replaces analysis, and ideology replaces science, then no problem can be solved.

---

[56] Immanuel Kant, "Beantwortung der Frage: Was ist Aufklärung?" *Werke*, Artur Buchenau and Ernst Cassirer, Eds., 4, 169–176, Bruno Cassirer, Berlin.

CHAPTER ELEVEN

Public and Private Opinions: Social Situations and Multiple Realities

Irwin Deutscher, Case Western Reserve University

There are two faces to the issue of confidentiality in social research. Attention among investigators has focused on the ethical dimension, including the rights of experimental subjects, ethnographic informants, and survey respondents. It is a proper concern of the social scientist that those who provide him with data be protected from possible self-incrimination, personal damage, or embarrassment as a consequence of their cooperation. The second face of confidentiality is, I believe, a neglected one. It is concerned not with ethical, but with methodological problems. The question raised from this perspective is, "In what ways does the definition of the research situation as 'confidential' alter or impinge upon the data obtained in that situation?" It is to this question that the present chapter addresses itself.

PUBLIC AND PRIVATE OPINIONS

This analysis originated in an effort to understand why utterances or acts made among intimates may vary from those made in public or among different publics.[1] The initial concern was with the methodology of survey research. We know from our everyday experiences that different opinions on the same subject can be elicited from the same people in different situations. Such opinions may at times be inconsistent with each other, but regardless of such apparent inconsistency all such opinions may be valid. All of them may be *real* opinions. An attitude that is likely to be expressed under conditions of actual social interaction is real and becomes a public opinion when it is expressed. As for our *private* opinions —basic, consistent, internalized orientations toward subjects—they rarely have an opportunity to find expression as public opinions or as actions.[2]

In a sense, then, such private opinions are rarely real. Exceptions occur in situations in which people can express themselves collectively with anonymity or in confidence among intimates. *This* public opinion then may be congruent with private opinion. Reston,[3] for example, once observed of Lyndon Johnson, "He is confusing what men say to the pollsters with what they say to their friends." Furthermore, the President "knows what his aides say to him personally, but he does not know what they say to their wives." More than most men, a president with long congressional experience should understand that men can hold to many honest opinions—opinions that are contingent upon the context within which they are called forth.[4] Thus in 1964 when United States congressmen were considering a sizeable increase in salary for themselves, a Republican

[1] This chapter is a revision of the paper "Public vs. Private Opinions: The 'Real' and the 'Unreal,'" read at the meetings of the Eastern Sociological Society, Philadelphia, 1966. A later mimeographed version was circulated under the title, "Evil Companions and Naughty Behavior: Some Thoughts and Evidence Bearing on a Folk-Hypothesis," (1968). Among the many critics who have influenced my revisions, I am especially grateful to Herbert Blumer, Lawrence Cagle, Lionel Dannick, Erving Goffman, Edward Sagarin, Alphonse Sallett, and Elbridge Sibley.

[2] For a divergent perspective, see Milton Rokeach, "Attitude Change and Behavior Change," *Public Opinion Quarterly*, 30 (Winter 1966–1967), 530–550.

[3] From his column appearing in the *San Francisco Examiner and Chronicle*, on May 1, 1966, under the title, "The Price Mr. Johnson Pays."

[4] President Kennedy appears to have been more aware of this than President Johnson. Robert F. Kennedy reports in *Thirteen Days*, "To keep the discussions from being inhibited and because he did not want to arouse attention, he [President Kennedy] decided not to attend all the meetings of our committee. This was wise. Personalities change when the President is present, and frequently even strong men make recommendations on the basis of what they believe the President wishes to hear." That this problem may be less serious with some presidents than with others, is suggested by the frequent "resignations" of high officials in the Nixon administration. Such situational constraints are not limited to presidents. Elsewhere in Washington D.C., streetcorner men have been observed to talk one way about women when in the company of their fellows, but to act quite differently when in the company of women. See Elliot Liebow, *Tally's Corner: A Study of Negro Streetcorner Men*, Little, Brown, Boston, 1967, p. 145.

attempt to eliminate the pay increase was thwarted by a vote of 125 to 37. Yet minutes later when the bill was voted on, a demand for a roll call succeeded, and the pay increase was overwhelmingly defeated.[5] Congressional voting behavior reflected one opinion as long as that behavior remained anonymous. However, these same men immediately reversed their votes when they knew they would be held individually accountable for them.

If exceptions to the reality of private opinions occur in such anonymous *collective* situations, they also can occur when people have the opportunity to express themselves *individually* with anonymity, as in such cases as nose-picking, voting, masturbating, the purchase of certain items of consumer goods, cheating oneself at solitary games[6]—or responding to a survey interview. As the case of the congressmen suggests, such private acts and opinions cannot be assumed to have any relationship to public acts or opinions. Paradoxically, then, one of the few instances in which an attitude is unlikely to be translated into an opinion or an act in any social context is when it is elicited in a rigorously controlled interview situation by highly trained interviewers employing a technically high quality instrument. Let us consider this paradox.

Rigorous Methods: The Quest for "Private" Opinion

So brash a statement demands explanation. Current research-interviewing technology assumes the desirability of sterile conditions in the interview situation; neither the interviewer nor the instrument should act in any way upon the situation. The question, ideally, should be so put and so worded as to be unaffected by contextual contaminations. The interviewer must be an inert agent who exerts no influence on response by tone, expression, stance, or statement. The question must be unloaded in that it does not hint in any way that one response is more desirable or more correct than any other response. It must be placed in the sequence of the instrument in such a way that the subject's response is not affected by previous queries or by his own previous responses. The respondent is provided with maximum assurances of anonymity and the implied guar-

---

[5] See Congressional Quarterly Service, *Congress and the Nation, 1965–1966,* Washington, D. C., 1966; and *Congressional Record,* 88th Congress, 2nd Session, 110, No. 45 (March 1964).

[6] Such cheating can occur not only in the obvious instances of solitaire or checkers but in self-deprivational games such as those involving smoking, drinking, dieting, or narcotics. Even in such relatively private acts there is, in a Meadian sense, a public quality in that interaction occurs between the "I," the "me," and the "generalized other."

antees of protection from sanctions. *In effect, the respondent is urged to reveal his most private opinions on an object without relating it to any other objects, or placing it in any context, with the assurance that the interviewer doesn't care what he says and no one else will ever know he said it.* We are confronted then with the paradoxical argument that we obtain an "unreal" opinion when a person is provided with the opportunity to state what he "really" thinks.[7]

The interview is structured in such a way as to maximize the opportunity to elicit a private opinion. The facts of social life are that real utterances of opinion always are *public* in the sense that they occur in the presence of others. They never occur in isolation, and one must always consider the consequences of having uttered them. In real life there is neither anonymity nor guarantee against possible sanctions. Public opinions are always uttered in a particular context, both in the sense of assessing the impact they are likely to have on others who are present and in the sense of resulting in part from, and being influenced by, what has immediately preceded their utterance in the flow of the action. Consequent overt behavior toward the object of the opinion also takes place in a social context and is as much constrained by others and by the actor's interpretation of the situation at the time as is the utterance of an opinion. Real expressions of attitude and overt behavior rarely occur under the conditions of sterility that are deliberately structured for the interview situation.

The survey methodologist views his instruments, his interviewers, and the interview situation as potentially contaminating elements. Nearly every volume of the *Public Opinion Quarterly* contains research notes and articles designed to help the pollster and survey researcher reduce the amount of variance in his results that is attributable to interviewer effect, instrument construction, and external features of the interview setting. Efforts are made to elicit opinions that are more purely "private" by using knowledge about situational effects for the purpose of removing or reducing those effects. In contrast to the approach of the social psychologist (see below), this is a strangely negative role of knowledge; the student of public opinion seeks to learn how people express their opinions and their behavior under real (public) conditions in order to alter these con-

---

[7] This is not to deny the "reality" of interaction in such an interview situation. I suggest only that the situation is so meticulously constructed and carefully managed by one party in pursuit of a clear goal (to obtain a complete interview) that it is difficult to imagine any routine social situation that resembles the formal interview. In short, responses to formal interviews inform us about behavior in a formal interviewing situation and little else. I attempt to apply such information in a constructive manner at a later point in this chapter.

ditions in such a way that they become unreal and thus facilitate his elicitation of private opinions.

At least one of the more sophisticated students of attitude and opinion research is clearly aware of this paradox. Hyman writes:

> . . . The general aim of modern opinion and attitude research has been to provide a situation in which the subject's "true" attitude can come out unhindered by any social barriers. Now there is perfectly good justification for being interested in the world of private, unhindered attitudes, but if our intent is to predict from test results to behavior, we should realize that the private attitudes revealed under test conditions may never be expressed in the more normal situations of everyday life.[8]

Although one's public opinions toward any given object may vary with the context in which they are called forth, and usually vary from one's private opinion (for any "sane" man), it has been suggested that in mass society the discrepancies grow even greater. Riesman and Glazer, for example, argue that in an increasingly other-directed society public opinion is something different from what it may have been in a tradition-directed or inner-directed society in which a man presumably was an atom with an opinion of his own.[9] Again we are confronted with a paradox; it is precisely in those societies in which rigorous efforts to assess public opinions are *most likely* to be perceived as necessary and to occur that the opinions they elicit are *least likely* to be real. It follows from the discussion so far that in more *gemeinschaftlich*—folk-type—societies there is less likelihood of divergence between public and private opinions.[10] These societies are hospitable to fewer publics, encompassing a limited variety of perspectives, and thus contain a narrower range of public opinions.

THE EVIDENCE

This chapter is an effort to document the argument proposed above by reviewing some of the relevant evidence. Such evidence can be derived

---

[8] Herbert Hyman, "Inconsistencies as a Problem in Attitude Measurement," *Journal of Social Issues,* 5 (Winter 1949), 38–42.

[9] David Riesman and Nathan Glazer. "The Meaning of Opinion," *Public Opinion Quarterly,* 12 (Winter 1948–1949), 631–48.

[10] This does not imply that the introduction of rigorous interviewing techniques into such societies is appropriate. To the contrary, the diffusion of American techniques into other societies may be most inappropriate for reasons I have discussed elsewhere. See Irwin Deutscher, "Asking Questions Cross-Culturally: Some Problems of Linguistic Comparability," in *Institutions and the Person: Essays Presented to Everett C. Hughes,* Howard Becker et al., Eds., Aldine, Chicago, 1968, 318–341.

from a variety of independent sources. If there is one common feature in all of the American community studies—from Middletown, to Yankee City, to Elmtown—it is the finding that people vary their opinions and their actions with the context in which they are observed. In his study of a small Kansas community, Warriner observes, on the one hand, a public affirmation of what he terms an "official morality," that is, that it is wrong to drink alcoholic beverages. On the other hand, "the majority did not feel that there was anything wrong with moderate drinking."[11] Warriner reminds us that "in most studies such an inconsistency is explained away by searching for some bias in the observational technique or by looking for some coercive, 'distorting' factor in the milieu."[12]

Warriner's insistence that the inconsistency is not a methodological artifact is a crucial point. The findings are not distorted by the instruments; people's views are distorted by their interpretation of the situation in which those views are called forth. A man can publicly support public morality by advocating prohibition and at the same time approve of drinking in the limited circle of his personal friends. Both of these attitudes are real in that social situations occur repeatedly in which these opinions are expressed and are followed by consistent action; the same man *votes* for prohibition and *consumes* alcohol at home. The only way we ever learn this man's private opinion is through his responses to a perfect interviewer, with a perfect questionnaire, in a perfect interviewing situation. But for what purpose would we want to elicit this private opinion? The respondent's real opinions are those manifested in the real situations in which he finds himself.

The irrelevance of private attitudes for conduct is documented in Wheeler's study at a reformatory for male felons.[13] His data suggest considerable private support among inmates for conventional values. However, this support is not acted upon. In like manner custodial officers reveal private opinions that are more like those of inmates than the inmates perceive them to be. Inmates are in constant contact with one another and feel the need to conform to what they believe the expectations of others to be:

Thus, the inmate is under pressure to conform to the expectations he per-

---

11 Charles K. Warriner, "The Nature and Functions of Official Mortality." *American Journal of Sociology,* 64 (September 1953), 165–68. A decade later wide variations in public and private morality in another small Kansas community were reported by Wayne Wheeler, "Backstage with Swedeholm's Youth," *Review of Religious Research,* 5 (Fall 1963), 1–5.

12 *Ibid.,* p. 168.

13 Stanton Wheeler, "Role Conflict in Correctional Institutions," in *The Prison,* Donald R. Cressey, Ed., Holt, New York, 1961, pp. 229–259.

ceives other inmates to hold. His perception of group opinion rather than his private feelings should serve as a model for overt conduct. So long as he perceives most inmates to be opposed to staff norms, his public behavior is likely to take the form of a conspicuous show of hostility toward the staff.[14]

The degree of influence persons in an interaction situation are able to exercise is subtly influenced by the actor's definitions of those other persons. Miller et al. report a study suggesting that perceived ability of others to reward has a greater effect on the actor's behavior than comparative perceptions of the ability of others to punish.[15] That the power of others in the situation is related to their influence is also evidenced by a study reporting the offense rates of military trainees to be related to the offense rates of their immediate superiors.[16] A further example is provided by Cole who documents the crucial influence of colleagues in the decisions of teachers to involve or not to involve themselves in a strike.[17] The volatility of attitudes—their vulnerability to external influences—is documented in a final illustration from an attitude experiment conducted by a pair of psychologists. Everything in their two trials is exactly the same, except the designation of the sponsor. In one case subjects are informed that the sponsor is "The Institute for the Study of Propaganda Effects"; in the other the sponsor is identified as "The Institute for the Study of Communication and Information Processing." Silverman and Shulman report "highly significant differences in attitude change scores" resulting from the change in sponsor designation.[18]

Compartmentalization

The ease with which people in a complex society can hold contradictory attitudes in insulated compartments, with no manifestations of dissonance or anomie, has been observed by field researchers among widely diverse publics. Kriesberg describes compartmentalization among steel distributors who participated in the gray market during the Korean War. "All the men in the gray market agreed with the government that national security was a prime consideration and the nation faced a danger-

14 *Ibid.*, p. 248.
15 Norman Miller, Donal C. Butler, and James A. McMartin, "The Ineffectiveness of Punishment Power in Group Interaction," *Sociometry*, 32 (March 1960), 24–41.
16 Jonah P. Hymes and Sheldon Blackman, "Situational Variables in Socially Deviant Behavior," *Journal of Social Psychology*, 65, No. 6, (Grn, 1965), 149–153.
17 Stephen Cole, "Teacher's Strike: A Study of the Conversion of Predisposition into Action," *American Journal of Sociology*, 74 (March 1969), 506–520.
18 Irwin Silverman and Arthur D. Shulman, "A Conceptual Model of Artifact in Attitude Change Studies," *Sociometry*, 33 (March 1970), 97–107.

ous threat to its security." According to Kriesberg, some of these men compartmentalized their evaluations from their conduct:

> Inconsistencies are not perceived, and if they are pointed out, the rejoinder is, "that's too deep for me." However, this shifting of perspectives from context to context cannot be regarded only as a way of escaping from the strain of conflicting obligations. The same inconsistencies, vagaries, and compartmentalizations are to be found among those who did not engage in activities they felt were condemned by the government.[19]

These observations suggest that compartmentalization occurs all the time. People compartmentalize consistent as well as inconsistent fragments of their social lives. It is a normal process to hold diverse opinions about an object—some of which may be contradictory. This must certainly be true of French Catholic Communist workers as revealed in Lipset's description of their voting behavior.[20] In my research with student nurses, I reported their ability to simultaneously assimilate the cold impersonal professional orientation and the warm, personal, helping orientation. Montague and I found compartmentalization to be "more common than the acceptance of one set of institutional values and the rejection of the other."[21]

In a study of attitudes toward Negro housing, Rose observes that "a given individual may hold a number of attitudes toward the same object, perhaps applicable to different segments, but logically incompatible if they should be confronted with each other in the same setting."[22] The most significant finding that emerged from this study, according to Rose, was that most of the expressed attitudes were contradicted by other expressed attitudes or by reports of behavior. Westie reports considerable inconsistency among Americans who voice agreement with the values of the American Creed but are inclined to devalue Negroes when situations

[19] Louis Kriesberg, "National Security and Conduct in the Steel Gray Market," *Social Forces*, **34** (March 1956), 274.

[20] S. M. Lipset, "Democracy and Working-Class Authoritarianism," *American Sociological Review*, **24** (August 1959), 482–501.

[21] Irwin Deutscher and Ann Montague, "Professional Education and Conflicting Value Systems: The Role of Religious Schools in the Educational Aspirations of Nursing Students," *Social Forces*, **35** (December 1956), 126–131.

[22] Arnold M. Rose, "Inconsistencies in Attitudes toward Negro Housing," *Social Problems*, **8** (Spring 1961), 286–282. Rose makes this observation in connection with an abortive attempt to measure the extent of opposition to fair housing legislation. He found so much inconsistency in response that he was forced to abandon the effort: "The chief finding that emerged from our questioning was that we could not, in fact, measure the extent of the opposition, as we got almost as many different results as we had approaches to the question."

are specified. Among the types of resolutions of this contradiction is *compartmentalization*.[23] This involves a conscious disconnection of the apparently inconsistent sentiments; similar to Kriesberg's gray marketeers, people are aware of them but see no relationship. Another type of resolution identified by Westie is "repression" which is distinguished from compartmentalization on the basis of awareness or consciousness. For my purposes, the distinction is not necessary; both types are compartmentalization.

One of the clearest field studies of compartmentalization and one that explains, in part, Rose's findings, was conducted by Lohman and Reitzes.[24] These investigators demonstrate empirically the manner in which the situation is defined differently for the same individuals in different settings—at home and at work. Their data reflect the manner in which white union members can be egalitarian and accepting of Negroes *at work* while simultaneously exhibiting prejudice and rejection of Negroes in their *neighborhood:* "The majority of the individuals studied were consistent in exhibiting what appeared to be an ambiguous and contradictory pattern in their identification with both the community and the union with regard to the race relations pattern."[25]

Such situational variation in behavior may appear to be inconsistent from the perspective of the "rational" detached observer, but from the perspective of the involved participant it may be that there is no inconsistency. This is a central theme in the ethnomethodological argument. Douglas, for example, builds on Garfinkel's position that

> . . . sociologists and other outsiders often see social actions as involving moral conflict because they assume the actors are (or *should* be) attending to certain abstract morals in a "rational" way, whereas there are generally understood, situated meanings or common-sense criteria of rationality specifying the appropriate processes of inference. However, it is also most important to note that most of us live highly compartmentalized moral lives: we have *situated moral and other meanings* for many different types of situations and feel relatively little need to relate the situations to each other via abstract meanings.[26]

Such inconsistencies are not to be easily dismissed as reflecting deception on the part of respondents or technical inefficiency on the part of the

23 Frank R. Westie, "The American Dilemma: An Empirical Test," *American Sociological Review*, 30 (August 1965), 527–38.
24 Joseph D. Lohman and Dietrich C. Reitzes, "Deliberately Organized Groups and Racial Behavior," *American Sociological Review*, 19 (June 1954), 342–48.
25 *Ibid.*, p. 342.
26 Jack D. Douglas, "The General Theoretical Implications of the Sociology of Deviance," in *Theoretical Sociology: Perspective and Developments*, John C. McKinney and Edward A. Teryakian, Eds., Appleton, New York, in press.

interviewing instruments. Anticipating the ethnomethodologists by several decades, Merton observed that internal tests of consistency assume rationality—that people never really hold inconsistent attitudes—and he concludes that "In making this assumption, the investigator is using *norms* of logic, not *facts* of sociology."[27]

And Sometimes Stress

The easy psychological device of compartmentalization is not the only way people deal with their lack of self-consistency. Awareness of subtle situational pressures to change one's opinion can create considerable stress. Gorden's study of members of a cooperative rooming house reveals the stress people undergo when they feel constrained to modify private opinions (i.e., previously elicited in an anonymous interview) in the presence of their fellow co-op members.[28] Gorden notes "an acute awareness of the presence of the other members of the group when they are asked to express their opinion. Confused efforts to appear nonchalant, efforts to escape the situation, and attempts to prevent others from hearing one's response are all telltale signs of the awareness of pressure."[29] Nevertheless, these individuals did tend to alter their private opinions to conform to their conception of the group norm when giving their public opinion.

These findings closely parallel those of Wheeler in his study of committed felons (see above). The major difference is that Gorden induced stress by entrapment of his subjects. Wheeler, however, demonstrates how stress is avoided by conformity to perceived expectations and suppression of private opinions. The evidence from the field studies suggests that one's private opinion is not likely to be the same as his public opinion, that one can hold a number of public opinions simultaneously, and, incidentally, that there is no necessary relationship between any kind of opinion about an object and subsequent behavior toward that object.[30] Referring to only one area of interaction, Kohn and Williams suggest, "There is now abundant research evidence of situational variability in

27 Robert K. Merton, "Fact and Factitiousness in Ethnic Opinionaires," *American Sociological Review,* 5 (February 1940), 13–28.
28 Raymond L. Gorden, "Interaction between Attitude and the Definition of the Situation in the Expression of Opinion," *American Sociological Review,* 17 (February 1952), 50–58.
29 *Ibid.,* p. 57.
30 I have dealt in more detail with the problem of the relationship between opinion and overt behavior elsewhere. See Irwin Deutscher, "Words and Deeds: Social Science and Social Policy," *Social Problems,* 13 (Winter 1966), 235–254.

inter-group behavior: an ever-accumulating body of research demonstrates that allegedly prejudiced persons act in a thoroughly egalitarian manner in situations where that is the socially prescribed mode of behavior, and that allegedly unprejudiced persons discriminate in situations where they feel it is socially appropriate to do so."[31]

Experimental Verification

Earlier in this chapter I referred to the strangely negative role played in survey research by knowledge of situational effects on behavior. For survey methodologists such knowledge is primarily viewed as useful for decontaminating their instruments and purifying the situation. Many social psychology laboratory experiments reflect interest in essentially the same problems, but psychologists assume a more affirmative stance toward their subject. Rather than attempting to *remove* contaminating effects in order to create private behavior, the psychologists attempt to *add* contaminations under controlled conditions in order to achieve a better understanding of public behavior.

Similar to sociological field studies and survey research, this body of literature is severely circumscribed as a source of evidence. However, its limitations are of a different order. Some psychologists are themselves aware of the artificiality of the situations and the contrived nature of the interaction typical of experiments in social psychology. Milgram insists that "eventually social psychology must come to grips with significant behavior contents that are of interest in their own right and are not simply trivial substitutes for psychologically meaningful forms of behavior."[32] Milgram deplores the use of such tasks as sorting IBM cards, making

31 Melvin Kohn and Robin M. Williams, Jr., "Situational Patternings in Intergroup Relations," *American Sociological Review*, 11, 21 (April 1956), 264–274.
32 Stanley Milgram. "Group Pressure and Action against a Person," *Journal of Abnormal and Social Psychology*, 69 (August 1964), 137–143. Although psychologists have long been aware of the possibility of contamination in their experimental findings, resulting from definitions of the experimental situation (Rosensweig, 1933), they have succeeded in ignoring the possibility until recent years. One group of scholars managed, in the early 1950's, to dispose of the problem of " 'realism' versus 'artificiality' " by redefining "real" to include "artificial." See Social Science Research Council, "Narrowing the Gap between Field Studies and Laboratory Experiments in Social Psychology: A Statement by the Summer Seminar," *Items*, 8 (December 1954), 38–39. I have no argument with the position that the experimental situation is a peculiar form of reality in which people occasionally find themselves. It does not follow, however, that since all situations are realities they are all the same. Although the choice of words may be unwise, the conceptual distinction intended between "real" and "artificial" is important. This last sentence also applies to my sometimes unhappy choice of words in such comparisons as "real" and "unreal" or "public" and "private."

paper dolls, or eating crackers—all of which have been employed in experiments conducted by his colleagues.[33] Hovland examined many such weaknesses of experimental research and reported efforts to overcome them in his own research program.[34]

Perhaps even more basic in the social psychological experiment is the underlying perception of the research "subject" as an "object." The fact of the matter is that people are not inert reactors to external pressures; they are *actors* who initiate action. Again, it is possible to find an occasional psychologist pleading with his fellows. Orne, for example, reports that in his efforts to set up an experimental situation he was unable to find a task boring enough to make subjects give it up in a reasonable length of time. In a thoughtful discussion he concludes that

The experimental situation is one which takes place within the context of an explicit agreement of the subject to participate in a special form of social interaction known as "taking part in an experiment." . . . Once a subject has agreed to participate in a psychological experiment, he implicitly agrees to perform a very wide range of actions on request without inquiring as to their purpose and frequently without inquiring as to their duration.[35]

Campbell, too, is concerned with the subject as an active agent. "Any measurement procedure," he states, "which makes the subject self-conscious or aware of the fact of the experiment can be suspected of being a reactive measurement."[36] In spite of such admonitions, it does not appear that most social psychologists are aware of the need to view the experiment itself as a form of interaction.[37]

Granting such serious shortcomings, the experiment is, nevertheless, often superior to survey research as a source of verification for field

[33] See J. R. P. French, H. W. Morrison, and G. Levinger. "Coercive Power and Forces Affecting Conformity," *Journal of Abnormal and Social Psychology,* 61 (July 1960), 93–101; and B. H. Raven and J. R. P. French, "Legitimate Power, Coercive Power and Observability in Social Influence," *Sociometry,* 21 (June 1958), 83–97.

[34] Carl J. Hovland, "Reconciling Conflicting Results Derived from Experimental and Survey Studies of Attitude Change," *American Psychologist,* 14, No. 1 (January 1959), 8–17.

[35] Martin T. Orne, "On the Social Psychology of the Psychological Experiment with Particular Reference to Demand Characteristics and Their Implications," *American Psychologist,* 17 (November 1962), 776–83.

[36] Donald Campbell, "Factors Relevant to the Validity of Experiments in Social Settings," *Psychological Bulletin,* 54 (July 1957), 297–312.

[37] Two important exceptions are Robert Rosenthal, *Experimental Effects in Behavioral Research,* Appleton, New York, 1966; and Neil Friedman, *The Social Nature of Psychological Research: The Psychological Experiment as a Social Interaction,* Basic Books, New York, 1967. Irwin Silverman and Arthur D. Shulman, *op. cit.* p. 106, cite a forthcoming volume which appears to the point: Robert Rosenthal and R. Rasnow, *Sources of Artifact in Social Research,* Academic, New York.

studies in at least three respects: (1) there is usually some theoretical framework to guide it and make it coherent; (2) the experiment generates "loaded" situations for study and thus to some degree simulates "real" interaction; and (3) conclusions drawn from experiments are interpreted in terms of a positive contribution to understanding human behavior. Even under the deliberately designed conditions of phantasy characteristic of many controlled experiments, there is no evidence that attitude, or opinion, or behavior remain stable through time or under changing conditions.[38] These experiments are so designed that their results can be interpreted as evidence that people react almost immediately to adapt themselves to perceived social constraints. The only conclusion I choose to draw from this body of research is that, similar to sociological field studies and methodological investigations in survey research, it suggests that *actors can harbor real attitudes which can be countervened in such a way that they become different—although still "real"—within a short period of time, as a consequence of redefinitions of the situation by the actor.*

As was true of the field studies, the experimental literature of social psychology provides hundreds of reports from which one can pick and choose in order to briefly review the manner in which this proposition can be documented. For example, since Sherif's pioneering experiments in the mid-1930s, there have been countless studies employing the autokinetic effect and practically all report the same results; when no point of reference is provided, people respond to suggestions from others regarding the direction of movement of a spot of light.[39] From the many variations on this theme, it is concluded that a subject's opinions are influenced by the interpersonal situation.

There are a few other basic design models, one of which was provided

---

[38] I have tried to select experimental evidence that does not suffer from the methodological handicaps mentioned above. Nevertheless, it remains possible that the evidence from these studies is an artifact of two widespread editorial practices in psychology journals. First, there is a selective reporting of experimental results as a consequence of the prevailing norm in that field that "negative" findings are not worth reporting because they reflect either theoretical naiveté or methodological errors. There are occasional and important exceptions to this norm, as, for example, Herbert Kelman, "Attitude Change as a Function of Response Restriction," *Human Relations*, 6, No. 3 (1953), 185–214. The second editorial practice is even more frightening in that it raises the spectre of a systematic selection of findings which are in error. These editorial policies, relating to significance levels required for publication are documented in David Bakan, *On Method: Toward a Reconstruction of Psychological Investigation*, Jossey-Bass, San Francisco, 1968 pp. 8–12. I have elaborated on their implications for knowledge. See Irwin Deutscher, "Buchenwald, Mai Lai, and Charles Van Doren: Social Psychology as Explanation," *Sociological Quarterly*, 11 (Fall 1970), pp. 533–540.

[39] Muzafer Sherif, "An Experimental Approach to the Study of Attitudes," *Sociometry*, 1 (July–October 1937), 90–98.

by Asch.[40] The Asch design was employed by Raven in an experiment with students which suggests that a member of a group who has deviant attitudes (1) tends to select and distort the content of what he communicates so as not to be rejected by the group, then (2) selects and distorts what he perceives so that it tends to be more and more in line with group norms, and (3) seeing more evidence to support the group norm, brings his attitudes into conformity with those of the group.[41] There are striking parallels between this laboratory experiment and Gorden's field study of members of a cooperative rooming house referred to earlier.

Much of this psychological research is concerned with the concept of "compliance" and is designed to investigate compliant behavior. Some of Kelman's earlier work and the later investigations by Goldstein and McGinnies provide examples.[42] That the effect of group pressure toward conformity in the experimental situation rapidly erodes—presumably as a consequence of exposure to other groups and other pressures—has also been documented.[43]

Some laboratory experiments have been designed to study the consequences of group pressures on behavior as well as opinion change. And among these a few have managed to create experimental situations involving relatively meaningful behavior. Such studies clearly demonstrate that private opinion has nothing to do with overt behavior in a "real" situation, that is, one that involves other people and which has meaning to the subject. Some of the best examples of this type of experiment are found in the work that takes Helson's notion of adaptation level as a point

[40] Unlike Sherif's, the Asch design does provide a point of reference and the subject is induced under group pressure to make objectively incorrect assessments. Recent sensitivity to experimental and experimenter effects has begun to raise doubts even concerning such widely replicated findings as those of Sherif and Asch. Alexander et al. report two experiments which show how the autokinetic effect is in part a function of "experimental expectations." See C. Norman Alexander, Jr., Lynn G. Zucker and Charles L. Brody, "Experimental Expectations and Autokinetic Experiences: Consistency Theories and Judgemental Convergence," Sociometry, 33 (March 1970), 108–122.

[41] B. H. Raven, "Social Influence on Opinions and the Communicator of Related Content," Journal of Abnormal and Social Psychology, 58 (January 1959), 119–28. Raven lists 34 references, dated from 1935–1958, to experiments on group pressures on opinions. These include a series by Asch and his associates and another series by Festinger and his associates. Raven briefly summarizes all of these studies.

[42] See Irwin Goldstein and Elliot McGinnies, "Compliance and Attitude Change under Conditions of Differential Social Reinforcement," Journal of Abnormal and Social Psychology, 68 (May 1964), 567–570; and Herbert Kelman, "Compliance, Identification, and Internalization: Three Processes of Attitude Change," Journal of Conflict Resolution, 2 (March 1958), 51–60.

[43] Op. cit. William A. Watts and William J. McGuire, "Persistence of Induced Opinion Change and Retention of the Message Contents," Journal of Abnormal and Social Psychology, 68 (March 1964), pp. 233–241.

of departure. Helson considers the various components of the situation, including the actor's personality, social constraints, and the meaning of the object toward which the attitude or behavior is directed. The experimental setup employed by Helson and others is such that the actual experiment is viewed by the subject as an extraneous incident occurring during the course of what he believes to be the actual experiment. The device is to have a student wander into the experimental setting during an interlude and solicit the subject's signature on a petition, in the presence of a confederate who has been instructed to either agree or refuse to sign the petition. The petition is presumably seen as real by the subject.

The conclusion reached by Helson, Blake, and Mouton is that the petition signing does not represent the inner convictions of the individual (what I have referred to as "private opinion") but rather the situational factors brought to bear upon the individual.[44] Himelstein and Moore report a variation of this design in which the petition is unloaded (designed not to elicit strong feelings), the race of the confederate is varied, and a different dimension of personality is tapped (prejudice rather than tendency toward submission).[45] "In general, the results indicate that both low- and high-prejudice Ss tend to be strongly influenced by the behavior of the confederate and to about the same extent. When the confederate, white or Negro, signs the petition, it is highly unlikely that S will refuse."[46] Their data "lend support to the statement of Helson, Blake, and Mouton that situational variables may be more important in the decision to sign or not to sign a petition than [either personality variables or] the nature of the petition itself."

Another experiment that provides clear evidence that the kind of private opinion sought by the survey researcher has little bearing on public behavior is reported by Milgram.[47] In effect, Milgram provides evidence in support of the notion that sometimes people do naughty (or good) things because of bad (or good) company. Unlike the Asch-type experiments, which show how groups influence attitude or opinion, and like the Helson-type experiments, Milgram has a diabolical design which shows how groups influence *action* (he makes the distinction between "sig-

[44] H. Helson, R. R. Blake, and J. S. Mouton, "Petition-Signing as an Adjustment to Situational and Personal Factors," *Journal of Social Psychology*, 48 (August 1958), 3–10.
[45] Philip Himmelstein and James C. Moore, "Racial Attitudes and the Action of Negro-and-White Background Figures as Factors in Petition-Signing," *The Journal of Social Psychology*, 16 (December 1963), 267–72.
[46] *Ibid.*, p. 270.
[47] Milgram's observation that different experiments impose the violation of different kinds of obligations on subjects, is important. See his comments on the subject-experimenter contract, Milgram, *op. cit.*, p. 142.

nal conformity" and "action conformity"). A naive subject works with two confederates planted by the experimenter in reaching joint decisions about how much voltage to use in shocking a "learner" when the latter makes a mistake. The drama is replete with howls of anguish and complaints of heart pains from the planted learner. Milgram found that subjects threw the switch on significantly more voltage under the influence of the confederates than they did otherwise.

Later in this chapter I will suggest the complementarity of field studies and laboratory experiments, but there is one serious weakness in experimental work that tends to impugn the credibility of the kinds of conclusions I am drawing from it. Unfortunately, this weakness is not adequately compensated in the field studies that reach the same conclusions. The observation that is most important in all these studies is that it is not personality, nor is it social structure, nor is it culture that appears to account for a large segment of the variance in human behavior. Rather, it is the actor's perception of the situation in which he finds himself—and especially his perception of others in that situation—that appears to provide much of the material from which he constructs his own line of action. To paraphrase Goffman, where else but in a social situation does action take place?[48] However, it is the central concept of Riesman's *The Lonely Crowd* that suggests the serious weakness I am addressing.[49]

Riesman delineated societies and eras which he described as other-directed, inner-directed, and tradition-directed. Societies may vary in the extent to which members' thoughts and actions are guided by their contemporaries (rather than by internalized constraints). There is also the suggestion that generations may vary in this respect, and the implication that in a mass society some segments may be more or less other-directed than other segments or strata. Riesman's thesis generally follows the tradition of the national character or personality and culture schools. Most of the literature we have reviewed as evidence of the extent to which the company one keeps is related to the behavioral choices one makes is based on experiments and observations of Americans, nearly all middle class, and frequently youthful college students. Do people in other parts of the world behave like Americans? Do lower or upper class Americans behave like middle class ones? Do middle-aged and older people behave like youngsters? There is considerable evidence that, at least in some respects, the answer to all of these questions is "no." Then, it is not safe to conclude that the tendency of people other than middle class American

---

48 Goffman actually asks, Where else but in a social situation does *speech* take place?
49 David Riesman, *The Lonely Crowd: A Study of Changing American Character,* Yale Univ. Press, New Haven, 1950.

college students is to alter their behavior so as to bring it more into line with what they perceive others around them to approve of.

Although scanty, some evidence does exist. Moving out of the laboratory into a situation involving people engaged in normal everyday activities and unaware that they were participating in an experiment, Dannick constructed a field experiment modeled after the Helson-type petition-signing experiments.[50] Furthermore, his subjects covered a wide age and socioeconomic range. Dannick demonstrated that pedestrians who ordinarily crossed against a stop light at an intersection tended to wait when a stranger (the experimenter) did so. In addition, those who ordinarily waited, tended to cross against the light when the bystander did. The decision to act or not to act appears in large part to be determined by the actor's assessment of the immediate situation and only in small part by any inner proclivity or private attitude. Although sex differences are observed, when age and social class are controlled, little variation occurs. Dannick provides some confirmation that what happens in the laboratory may also happen in everyday life and that this other-directedness of college students may also occur among other segments of the population.

Surely there exist some "strong" personalities who do "right" (or "wrong") regardless of their assessment of what others around them are thinking or doing. However, such firmly implanted inner convictions do not appear to explain very much of human behavior—at least in the United States. What of the rest of the world? Milgram has made an attempt to answer this question.[51] In a modification of the Asch group pressure experiments, Milgram reports a study of students in France and Norway. His subject entered the last of six booths under the impression that the other five were occupied by other subjects. What he heard through his earphones was five people consecutively reporting which of two tones sounded the longest. The confederates deliberately provided the wrong response on a certain number of trials. All five of the variations of this experiment resulted in large proportions of both Frenchmen and Norwegians conforming to the erroneous judgement—in most cases over

[50] Lionel Dannick, "The Relationship between Overt Behavior and Verbal Expressions as Influenced by Immediate Situational Determinants," Ph.D. Dissertation, Syracuse Univ., 1969. Some additional evidence can be found in the field experiments conducted by Helson and his colleagues. See Robert R. Blake, Milton Rosebaum, and Rich A. Duryes, "Gift Giving as a Function of Group Standards," *Human Relations*, 8 (February 1955), 61–73; Monroe Lefkowitz, Robert R. Blake, and Jane S. Mouton, "Status Factors in Pedestrian Violation of Traffic Signals," *Journal of Abnormal and Social Psychology*, 51 (November 1955), 704–706; and Anthony N. Doob and Alan E. Gross, "Status of Frustrator as an Inhibite of Horn-Honking Responses," 1966 (mimeo).
[51] Stanley Milgram, "Nationality and Conformity," *Scientific American*, 215 (December 1961), 45–51.

half. Also of interest, is the fact that the Norwegians were considerably more conforming than the Frenchmen, regardless of the experimental conditions. Unfortunately, Milgram provides no comparison with American students. "The experiment demonstrates," he concludes, "that social conformity is not exclusively a U. S. phenomenon, as some critics would have us believe." There is other (relatively weak) evidence to support this position.[52]

IMPLICATIONS: METHODOLOGICAL AND OTHERWISE

New Uses for Old Knowledge

This review of evidence suggesting the effect of the company one keeps on one's thoughts and acts, is not intended to be either exhaustive or representative. I have barely touched, for example, on the psychological literature dealing with "acquiescence response sets" (the inclination to go along with anything) and "social desirability" (the inclination to answer "right").[53] However, it is clear that the psychologist, like the sociological field worker whose evidence he confirms, is curious about how such phenomena enter into the behavior of his *subjects*, while the survey researcher abhors them and studies such phenomena for the purpose of eliminating them from his *respondents*. Nevertheless, survey methodological studies can provide a wealth of information if they are interpreted as providing opportunities for reclamation rather than the need for garbage disposal. Hyman, perhaps in a weaker moment, has implied as much:

Up to now, experiments providing data on the influence of the loaded question, the factor of anonymity, the group membership of the interviewer, the position of the question in a context of related questions, etc. have been regarded mainly as guides to the technician in the field of polling. In addition to the *practical* value of such experiments for technicians, there is the implicit

52 R. B. Zajonc and N. K. Waki, "Conformity and Need Achievement under Cross Cultural Norm Conflict," *Human Relations,* 14 (August 1961), 241–50.
53 For a discussion of these two concepts, the distinction between them, and evidence relating their operation to both personality tests and attitude scales, see James Bentley Taylor, "What Do Attitude Scales Measure: The Problem of Social Desirability," *Journal of Abnormal and Social Psychology,* 62 (March 1961), 386–90. More recently, Silverman and Shulman, *op. cit.,* pp. 98–99, have analyzed the interplay between "evaluation apprehension" and "subject motivation." They consider a series of decisions the subject must make as he participates in the experiment—decisions which are a function of factors "extraneous" to the experiment itself.

theoretical value for the student of inconsistencies between attitudes and behavior. The interview or test situation can be regarded as a miniature social situation in which certain forces may hinder the expression of the attitude. We can understand the problem of inconsistency if we re-examine such experiments and conceive of them as analogies to the way real life situational factors operate to influence the expression of attitude.[54]

I have been able to locate only two good examples of efforts in this direction. Although they have been reported 20 years apart, both are concerned with utilizing knowledge of interviewer effect and both deal with surveys of Negro communities. During World War II it was suspected that there might be some underlying discontent among Negroes with the Roosevelt administration and that this discontent could affect the 1944 elections in ways not revealed by the polls. On the basis of earlier NORC studies, Williams and Cantril knew that Negroes respond differently to Negro and to white interviewers.[55] They reasoned that Negroes were likely to hide race-sensitive opinions from white interviewers. Their study was designed to measure the extent of such opinions. Race-sensitive responses were to be identified by differences obtained when one-half of the Harlem sample was interviewed by whites and the other half by Negroes. They learned from this survey that the suspected underlying discontent did not exist and therefore would not distort predictions based on the polls.

The second study attempting to make use of knowledge of interviewer effect took place in an Illinois college town in the early 1960s. Bindman reports a wide range of discrepancies when Negro respondents previously interviewed by whites are reinterviewed by Negroes.[56] He is aware that such data are ordinarily interpreted as reflections of low reliability, but he recognizes this interpretation to be based on the assumption that there is only one "correct" answer. Bindman sees the discrepancies for what they are: different kinds of responses to different kinds of interviewers. A respondent may provide different truths (realities) to different guarantors of confidentiality. As a result of both his reinterviews and cross-interviewing similar to that of Williams and Cantril, Bindman was able to add new dimensions to his analysis. These are two examples of how "reliability" knowledge can be put to work for informative or theoretically relevant purposes.

[54] Herbert Hyman, *op. cit.*, pp. 40–41.
[55] Frederick Williams and Hadley Cantril, "The Use of Interviewer Rapport as a Method of Detecting Differences Between 'Public' and 'Private Opinion,'" *Journal of Social Psychology*, 22 (November 1945), 171–175.
[56] Aaron M. Bindman, "Interviewing in the Search for 'Truth,'" *Sociological Quarterly*, 6 (Summer 1965), 281–88.

Using knowledge of interviewer effect and controlling it in order to obtain new knowledge is only one of several means of obtaining "real" opinions. Mitchell, for example, suggests that "leading questions" can be used to help reduce the effect of the notorious courtesy bias in Southeast Asia polls.[57] I have argued elsewhere for the employment of popular stereotypes in the deliberate creation of "loaded" questions. In a survey of public images of the nurse, four independent tests of validity provided evidence that the opinions elicited by stereotyped—loaded—questions were *real*. At that time I observed that some of the better methodology texts grudgingly acknowledged—parenthetically, in footnotes, or as an afterthought—that "a 'loaded' question is not *necessarily undesirable. . . .*"[58] In this chapter, I am suggesting the obverse; under certain carefully specified conditions and with a specific deliberate purpose in mind, "unloaded" or objective questions are not *necessarily* undesirable. In describing the nurse survey, I wrote:

We asked "leading" questions and we asked "loaded" questions, because we were seeking neither superficial information nor testing the respondent's knowledge. We literally desired to "lead" the respondent into revealing his "loaded" feelings, rather than to obtain simpering cliches.[59]

Aurbach and his associates have reported the provocative manner in which deliberately loaded questionnaires (creating both positive and negative valences) can be used to establish opinion baselines in survey research.[60] Helson and his associates, in their petition-signing experiment, use the same model in the laboratory. They employed two petitions which were termed "positive" and "negative" on the basis of the degrees to which they attracted signatures in the absence of background factors. As a result, it became a relatively simple matter to determine the effect of those "background factors" when they were introduced. A rich bank of empirical data providing leads to understanding the manner in which situations influence behavior lies dormant in the methodological literature

[57] Robert Mitchell, "Survey Materials Collected in the Developing Countries: Sampling Measurement and Interviewing Obstacles to Intra- and International Comparisons," *International Social Science Journal,* **17,** No. 4 (1965), 665–85.
[58] This particular quotation is from Leon Festinger and Daniel Katz, *Research Methods in the Behavioral Sciences,* Dryden Press, New York, 1952, p. 347, italics added. See also Irwin Deutscher, "The Stereotype as a Research Tool," *Social Forces,* **37** (October 1958), 56–60.
[59] *Ibid.,* p. 57.
[60] Herbert A. Aurbach, John R. Coleman, and Bernard Mausner. "Restrictive and Protective Viewpoints of Fair Housing Legislation: A Comparative Study of Attitudes," *Social Problems,* **8** (Fall 1960), 118–125.

of survey research. Constructive reinterpretation of these data is needed if they are to enrich knowledge by complementing data provided from other sources.

On Individual and Collective Opinions

This chapter would be incomplete without reference to the fact that even if survey research and polling were to begin to elicit real *individual opinions,* the major problem of reality in *collective opinions* would remain (in terms of the likelihood of collective action following their expression). This issue was raised by Blumer in 1947 and remains unanswered. At that time, Blumer argued that "if public opinion is to be studied in any realistic sense its depiction must be faithful to its empirical character."[61]

Blumer's analysis rests essentially on the observation that, although every man may carry equal weight in the voting booth, every man does not carry equal weight in collective actions undertaken in a society. The opinions of the President of the United States and myself carry equal weight in the ballot box; there is, however, considerable disparity in the weight we carry in the formation of national policy. Blumer argues that "current sampling procedure forces a treatment of society as if society were only an aggregation of disparate individuals. . . . Certainly the mere fact that the interviewee either gives or does not give an opinion does not tell you whether he is participating in the formation of public opinion in the society."[62]

Eighteen years later, Angus Campbell writes, "It is curious that Blumer's hopes for the functional analysis of public opinion have been so little realized."[63] The comments of Blumer's discussants in 1947 make it clear that we were unable at that time to cope with his carefully developed argument, largely because we were so defensive about our scientific reputation—in and out of the academic community.[64] Perhaps now we can give it the serious attention it deserves.[65]

[61] Herbert Blumer, "Public Opinion and Public Opinion Polling," *American Sociological Review,* 13 (October 1948), 542–549.

[62] *Ibid.,* p. 546.

[63] Angus Campbell, Book Review, *American Sociological Review,* 30 (August 1965), 633.

[64] Theodore Newcomb and Julian Woodward, Discussion of Herbert Blumer's paper, *American Sociological Review,* 13 (October 1948), 549–554.

[65] For parallel interpretations of why important methodological critiques during the 1930s were ignored in both psychology and sociology, see Silverman and Shulman, *op. cit.,* p. 98; Irwin Deutscher, "Words and Deeds: Social Science and Social Policy," *Social Problems,* 13 (Winter 1966), 239–241; and Irwin Deutscher, "Looking Backward: Case Studies on the Progress of Methodology in Sociological Research," *American Sociologist,* 4 (February 1969), 35.

I am not attempting to argue that current public opinion polling and survey methods are never valid. In my discussion of loaded questions and, earlier, of essentially "private" acts, I have suggested that on occasion current methods are appropriate. Sometimes private opinions may have real consequences. Blumer points out that there are conditions under which every man's opinion does have equal weight:

. . . many actions of human beings in a society are of this nature—such as casting ballots, purchasing toothpaste, going to motion picture shows, and reading newspapers. Such actions, which I like to think of as mass actions of individuals, in contrast to organized actions of groups, lend themselves readily to the type of sampling that we have in current public opinion polling. In fact, it is the existence of such mass actions of individuals which explains, in my judgment, the successful use in consumer research of sampling such as is employed in public opinion polling.[66]

Blumer's observation provides a rationale for the use under certain conditions of the sterile, anonymous, unloaded, individual-oriented questionnaire. In an unpublished critique of public opinion research, Jordan makes the same observation: "This is why the concrete act of voting is closely related to behavior evoked in public opinion research—the psychological field of the polling booth is obviously very similar to the psychological field evoked by the public opinion poll." [67] In short, assurances of confidentiality in the interview simulate the assurances of confidentiality that characterize the polling booth. In my own efforts to understand the frequent lack of concordance between attitude and behavior, I have been struck by the fact that there is congruence in the very areas where Blumer suggests there should be: "Consumers sometimes do change their buying habits in ways that they say they will [and] people frequently do vote as they tell pollsters they will. . ."[68]

A Methodological Conclusion

There is a need for creative synthesis among the several discrete bodies of literature I have briefly reviewed. I have already noted, for example, that Raven, the psychologist, and Gorden, the sociologist, were both interested in the way in which members of a group who are aware of their own deviant attitudes alter those attitudes to preserve their group affilia-

[66] Herbert Blumer, *op. cit.*, p. 547.
[67] For a published set of Jordan's incisive critiques of contemporary social science, see Nehemiah Jordan, *Themes in Speculative Psychology*, Tavestock Publications, London, 1968.
[68] Irwin Deutscher, "Words and Deeds," *op. cit.*, pp. 235–254.

tion. Pursuing the problem independently and employing different methods, Raven and Gorden reach essentially the same conclusions. This, it seems to me, is evidence of convergent validity. Taken by itself, either study has enough weaknesses to leave its conclusions in doubt. However, *because the weaknesses of one are the strengths of the other,* they provide in combination very strong evidence in support of the hypothesis they share.[69] Many other such instances of convergence probably lie buried in the literature.

Hovland makes essentially the same point in his efforts to reconcile conflicting results derived from experimental and survey studies. Although he clearly identifies seven methodological artifacts that tend to bring about opposite results, he nevertheless concludes that "no contradiction has been established between the data provided by experimental and correlational [survey] studies." According to Hovland, it is "quite apparent . . . that a genuine understanding . . . requires both the survey and the experimental methodologies. At the same time there appear to be certain inherent limitations of each method. . . ."[70]

In 1954 the participants in a summer seminar discussing the possibility of narrowing the gap between field studies and laboratory experiments in social psychology arrived at some pessimistic conclusions. They suggest that a different orientation toward theory results in "noncorrespondence" between field and laboratory findings: "Conclusions reached through the two methods will not necessarily agree nor even be related. Field workers tend to speak a dialect different from that used in laboratories, and field and laboratory results are less often contradictory than incommensurable."[71] In view of some of the relationships and parallels suggested in this chapter and in view of increasing sensitivity to their own weaknesses on the part of some investigators in both disciplines, it may be that the situation is more hopeful a decade and a half later.

Social science to date has produced very few clearly demonstrable propositions concerning human behavior, and those that exist are of the grossest nature. Among them is the demonstrated tendency of an individual to interpret the situation as his context for committing himself either verbally or by other kinds of overt behavior. Regardless of the

[69] The logic of this notion of different sources of error in studies exploring the same problem, leading to an error cancelling process, is put another way by Eugene J. Webb, Donald T. Campbell, Richard D. Schwartz, and Lee Sechrest, *Unobtrusive Measures: Nonreactive Research in the Social Sciences,* Rand McNally, Chicago, 1966. See their discussion of "triangulation of measurement" which is introduced on p. 3 and appears repeatedly in Chap. 7.

[70] Carl J. Hovland, *op. cit.,* p. 14.

[71] Social Science Research Council, *op. cit.,* pp. 38–39.

basic assumptions, the methodology, or the disciplinary perspective, this simple fact consistently appears. What do people *really* think? This depends on where they are, who else is there, and what is going on. Do we want them to tell us what they think *in confidence?* This may depend on what it is we want to know.

Summary and Implications

Both the field studies and the experiments reviewed here provide evidence that a considerable proportion of the variance in human behavior can be explained by efforts (conscious or unconscious) on the part of people to bring their sentiments and acts into line with what they perceive the sentiments and acts of others in the immediate situation to be. If it is properly reinterpreted, further confirmation can be found in the methodological literature of survey research.

It is not my intention to argue that situational constraints explain all, or even most, of the variance found in human behavior. Such constraints do, however, appear to explain significant and frequently large amounts of that variance. The residue can probably be explained by such phenomena as cultural differences, social structural differences (differential location and participation in the society), personality differences (relatively enduring predispositions and values resulting from effective socialization), biological or genetic differences, and by idiosyncratic, whimsical, or "accidental" factors.

The social situation is a notion different in kind from the constructs, culture, social structure, and personality. These gross abstract forces not only provide little understanding of why people behave as they do in everyday life, but, unlike the social situation, they are fictions constructed by the social scientist; none of them in fact exists.[72] There is no culture out there which imposes upon us an imperative to act similarly to one another and differently from those located on other isolated patches of geography; there is no culture other than what the anthropologist has chosen to subsume under that rubric.[73] There is no personality which drives one

[72] This and the following paragraphs have grown out of a thesis I began to develop at an alumni lecture delivered in honor of the retirement of Professor C. T. Pihlblad at Columbia, Missouri, in May 1967. It was further developed in a public lecture delivered at Western Michigan University in November 1967. I am grateful to both institutions for the opportunity and to both sets of audiences for their stimulating reactions.

[73] The concept seems to me inherently ethnocentric. Culture is constructed by an outsider out of what appear to him to be all the odd and funny things that foreigners possess, say, and do. The contemporary urban anthropologist sometimes finds his data compelling him to recognize the limitations of the concept. For example, Liebow, *op. cit.*, p. 208, denies that lower-class Negro life can be understood "as mute compliance

to act along certain consistent lines which are different from those lines chosen by one's neighbor because he has a different personality; there is no personality other than what the psychologist has chosen to subsume under that rubric. There is no social structure in which one finds himself located and which coercively leads him to assume so-called roles and statuses which differentiate him socially from others in the society; there is no social structure other than what the sociologist has chosen to subsume under that rubric. These concepts are all inventions, myths, fantasies, which often blind the analyst to the very real constraints imposed by the immediate situation in which the actor finds himself. This is not to deny that such concepts have been and can continue to be sometimes useful. As some sociologists like to put it, they are heuristic devices.[74]

Let me supplement this concluding polemic with an analogy. It seems to me (as someone else once wrote) that all the world is a stage. The backdrop and the stage props provide the setting within which the action occurs. However, it is the script with its dialogue (both verbal and nonverbal) and its cues that provides the action. Culture, personality, and social structure, similar to the backdrop and the props, provide only the broadest suggestions of what range of action seems appropriate. An audience expects different action in a subway scene from what it expects in a bedroom scene, different action in an automobile from the action in a bordello, different action in a dining room from what would be expected in a store. Let us ignore or treat as "deviant" the fact that people occasionally do sleep in subways, make love in automobiles, and have breakfast at Tiffany's. The essential point of the analogue is that even within the restrictions of the backdrop and props there is an almost infinite number of dramas which can be constructed and played out. Likewise, within one's presumed cultural, personality, and social structural constraints, there are nearly infinite lines of action which can develop. To the extent that this is true, it follows that gross concepts throw little light on how or why we choose to act and interact as we do.[75] An appeal

with historical or cultural imperatives." In a footnote on pp. 208–209, he cites other examples among scholars of "a growing suspicion" of the concept of culture.

[74] All that I have suggested about these concepts applies equally to the verbs that presumably describe the processes by which they come about: to acculturate, to socialize, to condition, and the like.

[75] Acts, whether cognitive, verbal, or otherwise "overt," occur as a direct consequence of *interaction* (definitions of the situation being an integral part of any *interaction*.) Interaction, as the term is used here, is closely analogous to the statistical concept as, for example, in the analysis of variance. (The major weakness of the analogue is that the referent of interaction for me is actors; for the statistician the referent is variables.) The conduct displayed in any given act cannot be predicted by or anticipated by summing up the effects of any set of variables, regardless of how much variance they may

to authority on this matter is available simultaneously from three sources: Mills quotes a comment by Karl Mannheim on George Herbert Mead. The comment has reference to "Mead's program to approach conduct socially and from the outside. It keeps clearly in mind that both motives and actions very often originate not from within but from the situation in which indiviudals find themselves."[76]

The image of the tailor-made man—neatly fitted into his culture, hemmed in by his personality, and sewed down by the social structure— the "oversocialized conception of man," as Wrong calls it, is of limited utility.[77] Garfinkel refers more directly to the men created by sociologists and psychologists as psychological and culture dopes.[78] As long as social science posits an image of the tailor-made man, we are not only incorrect in our perception, but perhaps of greater consequence, our translation of knowledge into social policy will be couched in terms of creating better controls and constraints—to tailor the man so that he can be counted on to behave himself. When we free ourselves of this deterministic image of the culture-bound, personality-bound, or social struc-

appear to explain in isolation. This is somewhat different from our traditional causal model of thought and analysis. It is my impression that, in the statistical analysis of variance, significant interaction variances rarely occur unless one or more of the major variables involved also accounts for (explains) a significant amount of the variance. That is, it is mathematically possible to obtain significant amounts of interaction variance when none of the major variables explain a significant amount of variance, but in practice such an occurrence is highly improbable. In contrast to the statistical operation, the reverse is true of human conduct, that is, although it is possible to account for such conduct in terms of isolated variables, in fact it is highly improbable. Interaction, almost inevitable, explains the greatest amount of variance in conduct. As an aside, it is an interesting reflection on the priorities of statistical thinking that Fisher, in his earlier works on analysis of variance, lumped all interaction sources of variance in with "within cells" variance and called this "residual" variance—the denominator recommended for the F test of significance. The effect was to consider random (unexplained) variance and interaction variance as the same order of residual phenomena.

[76] C. Wright Mills, "Situated Actions and Vocabularies of Motive," *American Sociological Review*, 5 (December 1940), 904–913, reprinted in *Power, Politics, and People,* Irving L. Horowitz, Ed., Ballantine Books, New York, 1963, pp. 439–452. This quotation is from p. 444. The reference to Mannheim is *Man and Society*, p. 249. It may be that polemics, analogies, and appeals to authority provide arguments superior to the empirical research evidence presented earlier in this chapter. This possibility arises out of the reader's ability to more accurately assess and discount polemic, analogy, and authority than to assess and discount empirical research which is only fragmentally reported.

[77] Dennis H. Wrong, "The Oversocialized Concept of Man in Modern Society," *American Sociological Review*, 26 (April 1961), 183–93.

[78] Harold Garfinkel, *Studies in Ethnomethodology*, Prentice-Hall, Englewood Cliffs, N.J., 1967, pp. 66–68.

ture-bound man and replace it with the interacting, situation-assessing man, the translation into social policy then becomes couched in terms of designing roads to freedom—not to constraint. Hughes reminds us that this is the man Thomas would have called "creative" and Riesman "autonomous."[79] This man is no automaton, "not a reed blown about by the wind, but a man of many sensitivities who would attain and maintain, by his intelligent and courageous choice of the messages to which he would respond, by the choice of his 'others,' freedom of a high but tough and resilient quality."[80]

[79] Everett C. Hughes, "What Other," in *Human Behavior and Social Processes: An Interactionist Approach*, Arnold M. Rose, Ed., Houghton Mifflin, Boston, 1962.

[80] My great intellectual debt to Herbert Blumer requires acknowledgement. It is reflected in the following comment of his on the original draft of the paper which, several years later, was to evolve into this chapter. Blumer brought to my attention and spelled out for me the assumptions and implications of which I was not fully aware at the time: "I wonder if you realize some of the more far-reaching implications of your discussion. *Implicit* (italics added) in your treatment is a markedly different picture of the nature of human society from those which guide current sociological thinking and research. A recognition that human beings have significant ranges of variation in what they say and do inside of a supposedly organized and structured framework of group life throws definitely into question the view that the essence of human society is constituted by a structure of shared values and norms. The treatment points instead to a realization that life in a given society consists of a process of adjustment of talk and action by the participants to one another on the basis of how they handle the situations that confront them. It is evident to me that one may have a society of sizeable dimensions in which people differ widely in their so-called values, beliefs, and norms, yet they succeed remarkably well in fitting their on-going actions together in a workable and orderly fashion. To try to reduce such an area or activity by positing the existence of either a neatly and originally organized social structure or a neatly originally organized personal structure overlooks the simple and real point that people have to act in terms of coping with the immediate situations which call for their actions. Yet, unquestionably, current schemes of thought and analysis in our field, across the board, are anchored in the assumption that if one lays bare either or both the posited social structure and posited individual structure, one has the key to analyze the predicted human conduct." (Personal communication, April 5, 1966.)

CHAPTER TWELVE

The Case of Educational Research

Ronald G. Corwin and Saad Z. Nagi, The Ohio State University

In this chapter we focus on educational research in order to illustrate how some of the generic issues raised throughout the volume apply to a specific field. Several of the generic problems referred to in the preceding chapters are especially well illustrated in this field: difficulties inherent in interdisciplinary cooperation, conflict in priorities given to "applied" and to "basic" research, mounting demands on researchers to find immediate solutions to overwhelming problems now plaguing the schools, and rapidly accelerating change, all of which are contributing to ambiguities in the division of labor, uncertain standards of evaluation, and new career patterns. The analysis shows how two conditions, in particular, influence the types of research and research results—variations in the way research has been organized, and differences in the value systems of researchers' subcultures.

SCOPE OF THE PROBLEM

Educational research, although of recent development in this country, is no exception to the rapid growth rates documented elsewhere in this volume for other fields of research. Between the early 1950s and the mid-1960s, the annual research and development budget for the U.S. Office of Education (USOE) alone increased from $1 million to nearly $100 million, which accounted for nearly two-thirds of funded research and development (R & D) in this field. Over 85 percent of the funds spent by this agency during those 15 years has been appropriated in the latter 5 years.[1] USOE is only one of six federal agencies that support 95 percent of all federally funded educational research.[2] When the dollars spent by all of these agencies in the mid-1960s are considered, annual federal appropriations in the field exceed $170 million, and when non-federal sources are added, it reaches $250 million.[3] The level of funding has been expanding; however, it only represents less than one-half of 1 percent of the amounts spent annually on education. Throughout the 1950s and 1960s, trained manpower, although it experienced a high rate of growth, did not keep pace with expansion in funding.[4] Estimates are that between 1968 and 1976 the number of personnel in educational research funded by USOE and the National Science Foundation (NSF) will double; however, this will depend in large part on the picture of funding within these years. At any rate, positions in development and diffusion are expected to increase 2.5 times faster than positions in research.

Although researchers and auxiliary personnel from a wide variety of backgrounds are engaged in educational research, there are character-istic techniques in the field for problem solving and identifiable patterns of association and exchange among researchers, between researchers and practitioners, and in the conduct of the affairs of agencies of research support. These relationships are governed by shared, although at times conflicting, values and norms, and by distinct systems of reward and control. In other words, these research activities are organized into some type of sociocultural system which comprises a set of subsystems. It is this system that constitutes the subject of this chapter.

---

[1] The funds available from NSF for curriculum and development increased from $650,000 to $17 million over the same period. An additional $81 million is available for demonstrations and development from Title III of the ESEA. See Leila Sussman's interview with R. Louis Bright, *Sociology of Education*, 40 (Spring 1967), 162.

[2] OECD, *Educational Research and Development in the United States*, Government Printing Office, 1970, pp. 47–68; see also Hendrik D. Gideonse, "The OECD Policy Review of U. S. Educational R. & D.," *Educational Researcher*, 21 (April 1970), p. 3.

[3] *Ibid.*

[4] John E. Hopkins, "Scope of the Demand for Educational Research and Research-Related Persons," in a symposium presentation at AERA Annual Meeting, February 1967 (mimeo).

THE SOCIAL FUNCTIONS OF RESEARCH:
THE CONTEXT OF VALUES AND IDEOLOGY

Ideological conflict arises between the scientific community and the research support programs of "mission-oriented agencies" over the priority to be placed on basic and applied research. The agencies tend to expect more practical results than researchers have been able to deliver. The acute level that these controversies have reached is recognized in the following statement made a few years ago by officials of USOE.

We believe, however, that a strong and continuing tension exists between the conduct of research designed to increase our knowledge of basic learning processes, for example, and the pursuit of development projects designed to yield specific outcomes for instructional use. The demand for results has raised the appropriate and thoroughly justifiable concern of the academic and scholarly research community that such demands may tend to compromise the long-range efforts which are so badly needed. The continuing tensions between short-term and long-term requirements, between today's youngsters and tomorrow's, is real and constitutes one of the continuing nightmares of the research administrator.[5]

Commitments for development and demonstration are creating a squeeze on the existing basic and applied research programs. Growth of "individual project-support basic research programs" is slowing down in favor of expansion in programmatic support and large-scale development activities. Moreover, emphasis on the application of knowledge in education is increasing. Hence it can be expected that expansion in development activities, and to a lesser extent in diffusion, will account for much of the future growth in educational research activities. These trends will be reflected in the proportions of researchers engaged in basic and applied research and personnel involved in developmental activities.

Dimensions of Controversy

One element in this controversy concerns the utility of basic and applied research for solving the problems of education. Officials in charge of the research support operations in USOE take the position ". . . that

[5] R. Louis Bright and Hendrik Gideonse, *"Research, Development and Dissemination Strategies in Improving Education,"* 1967, pp. 29–30 (mimeo). We are not alluding here to the current controversy over whether social science can be or should be value-free. Critical scholarship must be distinguished from social action intended to implement that social criticism. The predicament is between scholarship and *action*, not between objective and critical forms of scholarship.

if research is to be valuable, it must be useable. Now this should be considered not only at the conclusion of a research project, but before the project is initiated."[6] Guba charges that "the kinds of questions which researchers have asked have had precious little effect on classroom practice."[7] Others contend that if research in the area of teacher personnel during the last 3 years were to vanish, education and educators would continue as usual, whereas if research in medicine, agriculture, physics, or chemistry were eliminated, our lives would be materially changed. However, agreeing with some of these conclusions, Griffiths disagrees with the implications and maintains that the reason for these limitations is that research in education has been *too* atheoretical and *too* practice oriented.[8]

Of course, champions of educational research refuse to accept that the impact of research has been negligible. They maintain that the early childhood educational movement, programmed learning, the new mathematics and physics curricula, bilingual education, renewed interest in schools serving low-income populations, and other social action programs were all strongly influenced by basic research on stratification, the learning process, the socialization process, the structure of knowledge, linguistic analysis, and other theoretical work from the social and behavioral sciences. They further argue that the impact of educational research has been limited partly by the reluctance of practitioners to adopt changes that certain research findings suggest should be made.

The controversy also involves a *time* dimension. It takes time to accumulate knowledge about educational problems. The central question therefore is whether or not technological development must await the results of basic studies. For example, it is asserted by Cronbach that "effective educational designs, with careful development and field trial, can emerge only from a deep understanding of learning and motivation."[9] Others have challenged this position, asking: "Are we to wait for the research before beginning to improve situations?"[10] Guba expounds this latter position, asserting that "innovation need not always be based on research . . . good research is, of course, to be encouraged . . . but it is not in every case essential to school improvement."[11]

[6] As quoted in *Educational Researcher* (February 1966), p. 3.

[7] Egon Guba, "A Matter of Survival," *Phi Delta Kappan* (October 1966), pp. 75–77.

[8] Daniel E. Griffiths, "Research and Theory in Educational Administration," in *Perspectives on Educational Administration and the Behavioral Sciences,* Center for the Advanced Study of Educational Administration, Univ. of Oregon, 1965, Eugene, p. 28.

[9] Lee J. Cronbach, "The Role of the University in Improving Education," *Phi Delta Kappan* (June 1966), 5–40.

[10] Guba, *op. cit.,* pp. 75–77.

[11] *Ibid.*

A third element in this controversy, and for many perhaps the most fundamental consideration, involves *competition* for funds, personnel, and other resources. The largest share of federal appropriations for research grants programs is intended to support developmental and social action research and demonstration activities. In fiscal year 1968, 42 percent of USOE funds were appropriated for development, 7 percent for dissemination, and 5 percent for training; most of the 42 percent for research went into applied research types.[12] This situation reflects the strong belief, on the part of some influentials, that the problems in the field are well delineated and that the solutions have been identified. Hence the need is for large-scale attacks on the problems to produce visible change. Some people who hold this position do not want research so much as social action. However, others view educational problems as too complex for quick and simple solutions. Again Cronbach, a past president of the American Educational Research Association (AERA), espouses this position, stating, "It is tragic that in the U.S. Office of Education the Bureau of Research has thrown its forces heavily on the side of 'practical products' and dissemination. While USOE is a passive patron of basic research, it has done nothing to formulate and sell to Congress a policy that will promote the healthy development of basic investigation."[13] It should be noted that the objections raised by advocates of basic research are not directed toward the support of well-conceived and well-executed applied research. Their opposition is aimed at premature efforts to be practical and the diversion of research funds into service programs under the rubric of development and demonstrations.

Accommodations

Partly under these pressures, in 1969 USOE inaugurated a program of basic research to support unsolicited proposals in psychology and the

---

12 OECD, *op. cit.*, pp. 128–129.

13 Cronbach, *op. cit.*, pp. 539–545. In reply to Cronbach's charges, Bright has said, "The schools cannot wait; there is an acute need for something to be done right now." See "The USOE and Research in Education: An Interview with Richard Louis Bright," *Phi Delta Kappan* (September 1966), pp. 2–5. However, J. Myron Atkin, Associate Dean of the College of Education at the University of Illinois, has charged that USOE research policies are short-term, highly mission-oriented, and developed without sufficient consultation with the academic community. Atkin believes that USOE is patterning itself more on a Defense Department model than on an NSF model. The result, he says, often seems to be a promulgation of educational facts through premature specification of development and dissemination programs; J. Myron Atkin, "The Federal Government, Big Business, and Colleges of Education," mimeo version of paper submitted to *Educational Forum* (Spring 1967).

social sciences, including history. For the first time the agency is making use of interdisciplinary panels of outside experts in the respective fields to review proposals. However, less than $4 million was appropriated for the program during fiscal year 1969–1970. In addition, the National Academy of Science, in cooperation with USOE, has sponsored a 3-year project to encourage and to fund research in all physical and social science disciplines involving basic research relating to education.

The two sides of the argument are also represented on the campuses of universities. Concerned about the effects of pressures for action and developmental work upon the traditional functions of universities, Cronbach suggested that independent institutions should be created to carry the main burden of demonstration, dissemination, and educational innovations.[14] The suggestion elicited a pithy response from Guba, who asked: "How can anyone espouse such an isolationist position in these times? . . . the demands will not go away; unless the university responds to them it will be bypassed and cut off from funds."[15] Few universities would take lightly that grim prospect.

The degree of accommodation that universities are making to the pressures for applied research depends upon such factors as the levels of support available for basic and applied work, alternative sources of support, the social distance between researchers in the basic discipline and the applied fields, the research priorities established by the funding sources, and the degree of articulation between their priorities and those of universities. In regard to the latter, it appears that when organizations become dependent upon one another in order to complete some task, it is in the interest of the organization that places the highest priority on that task to persuade its counterpart to raise its priorities; or failing that, to establish new relationships with other organizations that do have comparable priorities. Thus as long as research and development were minor responsibilities of the government, connected to related service activities, universities could handle the demand. However, since research is a part-time activity of universities and always in competition with teaching and service activities, universities have not been able to keep up with the growing, urgent demands for large-scale, applied research. The government-supported R & D centers and similar institute programs represent the accommodations worked out. Nevertheless, these accommodations do not appear to have been sufficient. USOE has begun to seek out and encourage full-time profit and nonprofit research corporations not affiliated with universities to submit research proposals. While universities

14 Cronbach, *op. cit.*, p. 544.
15 Guba, *op. cit.*, p. 76.

probably will continue to make more effective accommodations to the requirements of full-time applied work, in view of increased demands for teaching they are not likely to be willing to make the kind of major change that would permit them to maintain major responsibility for such research; and student militancy at times has made it difficult to conduct research on campus. Therefore it can be expected that a larger share of the funds will be allocated to nonuniversity research groups as the volume of funds for applied research grows.

These issues are pervasive, and they enter into decision making each time new commitments of funds, time, and energy are made. They affect the researchers, the educators, and the institutions in which they work, as well as the general public in the long run. However, the ideological conflicts that have resulted also have contributed to the emergence of new forms of research and various strategies for funding, which we now consider.

POLITICS, ECONOMICS, AND PEER GROUPS: THE CONTEXT OF CONTROL

The degree of success achieved in this field in closing the gap between science and technology has brought educational research into the center of the political and economic arenas in this and other countries. The result is an increased influence of political and economic factors in the picture of scientific reward and control.

Political Influences in Educational Research

Since government provides most of the research support, it sets at least some of the conditions. These conditions in turn are tied to political events. The commissioner's office of USOE has become one of the posts most vulnerable to political pressure. Controversies rage over the merits of bussing, desegregation guidelines, and the regionalization of programs of support—which includes regionalization of some research funds, especially funds used in some grants programs, and evaluation of federally funded local projects.* Research findings have begun to play an important role in these controversies. The renowned USOE Equal Educational Opportunities Study, as well as studies on the effects of bussing, computerized instruction, and alternative teacher training programs are all examples of studies in which competing industries, programs, and

---

* These projects are provided for in Titles I and III of the 1965 Education Act.

groups have a vested interest in the findings. Reportedly, the White House in recent years has been trying to obtain more control over the research arm of USOE; although the proposed National Institute of Education was first advocated by a past president of AERA, some observers fear that the effect of reorganization will be to place the Institute more directly under the influence of the White House than has been the case under a less centralized funding system.

Accommodations

In recognition of new political realities, AERA and certain other research-oriented associations, such as the National Research Academy have been increasing their lobbying efforts to influence the volume and direction of funding for educational research. Individual researchers are being asked to write to their congressmen about specific issues directly involving research funding patterns, and AERA is venturing to make public its stands on nonpartisan political issues. The problems faced by scholar-lobbyists, however, are severe. Manacker points to one of many obstacles. Federal aid of any kind is not primarily intended for the improvement of education per se.[16] Neither house of Congress has a standing committee devoted exclusively to education, and congressmen are adverse to long-term membership on the existing committees because of their low prestige. Educational interests therefore tend to become secondary to specific objectives to be accomplished through exploitation of the educational plant.

These developments go beyond and overshadow the more generic problems individual researchers must confront whenever a field becomes politically relevant. Educational researchers find that funds are more likely to be available to study the current causes—decentralization, minority group education, curriculum and materials development, urban schools, and so on. But more, they also sense that their colleagues are demanding "relevance" as well. Yet, at the same time, educational researchers, similar to other scientists, scorn "grantsmanship," "the operator," and "the empire builder," derogatory terms leveled at colleagues whose intentions either are not clear, or who are clearly motivated by political and economic rewards. Similar activities on the part of more established persons who have demonstrated their commitment to science may be the objects of praise and admiration.

Political intrusions have been further promoted by the vulnerable

16 Julius, Menacker, "The Organizational Behavior of Congress in the Formulation of Educational Support Policy," *Phi Delta Kappan* (October 1966), pp. 78–83.

financial condition of most academic institutions. As the volume of support has increased, "money" has become a more salient incentive, not so much in terms of personal financial gains but in the sense that research support has become a means of achieving recognition. Universities have come to rely upon the faculty's abilities to attract research funds; the research administrative and management units developed on campuses measure their effectiveness and success by the volume of research funds; universities are at times ranked on that basis also. Indeed, the economic aspects of research as symbols of achievement probably are taking precedence over the widely acclaimed "publish or perish" incentives for research. As research became better integrated into graduate training programs, academic institutions accepted and actually encouraged their own dependence upon government and industrial sources of support as sources of income, not only for students, but also for the faculty. About half of all funded educational research and development in 1968 was performed at universities and an additional 10 percent was conducted by university-based research and development centers.[17] In addition, USOE supported a $6 million research fellowship program to prepare new researchers for this field; but this latter program has been victimized from the beginning by political in-fighting over the distribution of funds—especially competition between colleges of education and the behavioral science departments, and Ph.D. programs versus M.A. and undergraduate programs—and was recently cut back to $2 million. In an effort to encourage universities to become more sensitive to the practical needs of educators for new curricula and related materials, USOE is encouraging training programs to place graduates in newly created regional laboratories and R & D centers which focus specifically on these more immediate needs.

In short, the increasing permeability of the boundaries between politics, economics, and science in this field, as in others, has introduced the competing elements of influence and finance into its reward and control structure, neither of which is entirely compatible with the peer groups' control over the allocation of rewards.

Government Reactions

Legislators have looked to research to provide guidelines for the solution of complex and threatening problems such as poverty, racial strife, and crime. By the same token, some are becoming disenchanted because they are convinced research in this field has not led to hoped for reform.

[17] OECD, *op. cit.*, p. 69.

The following quotations from statements made by congressmen introduced into the *Congressional Record* illustrate the point:

Judging from what is being studied, researched and fact-found all over the world, it is clear that as a civilization we no longer know how to do anything.[18]

Is it not about time to put our feet on the ground and concentrate fully on the learning experience and the classroom rather than to be awarding funds for projects, regional laboratories, research, and so forth, that seem to accomplish little more than create more educational jargon?[19]

Of course, not all congressmen are equally critical. Some have introduced into the *Congressional Record* remarks of prominent scholars and public officials who praised the debt of technology to basic science, who defended support for basic research, and who called for the protection of the strong tradition of intellectual freedom in American universities.[20] However, the basically pragmatic orientation of this society and its concern for solutions to practical problems are reflected in the congressional testimonies and actions regarding educational research. Officials in charge of the USOE research program have observed that "the testimony before the Congressional committees, or the legislative history, as it is called, made it very clear that the broadened authority (i.e., of the legislation authorizing funds for educational research) was to be used to bridge the gap between research and practice and to pay substantially more attention to the problems of implementing the knowledge derived from the research efforts to date and in the future."[21]

A report based upon a study commissioned by the Committee on Government Operations contended that social scientists in the federal agencies and in universities are more interested in the pursuit of knowledge for its own sake than in the use of research to evaluate or improve programs directed to the nation's social problems.[22] Charging that social research is trivial, small-scale, undirected, and without significant impact, its writers called upon social scientists to devote more effort to solving social problems in addition to merely studying their causes. In view of the potential influence Congress can exert over research through

18 *Congressional Record* (May 9 1967).
19 *Congressional Record* (March 20 1967), H2967.
20 *Congressional Record* (February 16 1967), Appendix; and *Congressional Record* (March 8, 1967), A1119 ff.
21 Bright and Gideonse, *op. cit.*, p. 3.
22 "House Research Subcommittee Release of Study on the Use of Social Research by the Federal Government," Congress of the United States, House of Representatives Committee on Government Operations, Friday, April 21, 1967.

its control of a large share of the support funds, it can be assumed that charges of this type contain substantial implications for the future development of this field.

Some Effects of the Linkage between Research and Politics

It is inevitable that political considerations leave their mark on the research community; the increasing influence of economic and political factors on the structure of research activities is bound to undermine the influence of scientific peers. In effect, other reference groups have evolved within the disciplines. These groups include some eminent people in various disciplines who have developed sympathies for the positions of the research support agencies and an appreciation for their concerns. These leaders constitute alternative significant others in the scientific community, whose response to the results of research becomes an important source of rewards. In fact, the research support agencies themselves and the administrative units of research in universities also have emerged as important reference groups for researchers.

It should be acknowledged that political pressures sometimes help to counteract pressures from conservative research groups which often seem reluctant to adapt to emerging social needs. Hence strong leadership from a funding agency, via the mechanisms described, can help to correct serious lags between new social needs and university research programs. However, there are also other, largely unintended consequences which can easily develop from the close ties between politics and applied educational research.

Perhaps the underlying problem is that applied research, especially when procured, threatens the researcher's autonomy. Leadership from Washington is intended to clarify the research objectives and, as Gordon suggests, as the goals of an organization grow more specific and immediate, the researcher's freedom decreases.[23]

Also, the competition for funds is distorting the usual boundaries between various research activities. As a result of certain compromises, under the rubric of "demonstrations" or "evaluation research," funds presumably intended for basic and applied research are diverted for purposes of social action and service projects to particular school districts in which research plays a minor role. Sieber and Lazarsfeld found that the tradition of service in education has been so dominant that the term

23 Gerald Gordon, and Sue Marquis, "Freedom and Control in Four Types of Scientific Settings," *American Behavioral Scientist*, 6 (December 1962), 39–42.

"educational research" continues to be applied to the nonscientific as well as to scientific activities.[24] When directors of educational research organizations were asked to select from a list of activities those they considered to be "educational research," more than half of them considered "school status studies" as research, while sizeable minorities regarded "designing" and "school surveys" as research. More than one-fifth of the research directors applied the term educational research to "dissemination" activities. There appeared to be a direct connection between their own involvement in service and their confusion between research and service activities. The research productivity of a unit was negatively related to the service organization of the unit.

Some research programs, then, are in effect fronts for what in reality are quasi-research activities. The extravagant claims sometimes made about the potential results from research and its utility in guiding social action further confuses the public about the nature of these activities. In addition, when support for research is grouped with action and developmental work, economic and political pressures tend to tip the appropriations in favor of the latter activities. Statements of administrators of the research support programs of USOE illustrate the point:[25]

While it is true that the justification for supporting research and related activities in education with public money can only be the eventual and significant betterment of the educational system as a whole, it is also true, happily, that the more we can demonstrate that research has affected school practices in a positive way, the more likely it will be that greater support for the entire research process will be forthcoming. Thus, we believe that such objectives are not only good public policy, but good politics as well.

Perhaps this situation is a prelude to the emergence of new forms of research. In the meantime, however, basic and applied research programs are becoming indistinguishable from these other, more favored quasi-research, social action programs. As the total budget of research and demonstration programs expands, a false impression is created about the actual volume of research relative to applied activities. Support for basic research relative to applied research actually constitutes a proportionately smaller share of the total research budget as these quasi-research activities increase.[26] Also, as the distinctions between research

[24] Sam D. Sieber and Paul Lazarsfeld, "The Organization of Educational Research," USOE Cooperative Research Project No. 1974, Washington, D.C., 1966.
[25] Bright and Gideonse, op. cit., p. 4.
[26] Cf. Bruce L. R. Smith, "The Concept of Scientific Choice: A Brief Review of the Literature," American Behavioral Scientist (May 1966), 27–35.

and action become obscured, research activities are subjected to the same criteria used in evaluating the effectiveness of action programs. It can be expected that research will share in the blame for the failures of social action programs as well as benefiting from their successes.

GROWTH AND DIFFERENTIATION:
THE ORGANIZATIONAL CONTEXT

Educational research has grown not only in terms of the number of people involved and the amounts of funds expended, but also in terms of the number of disciplines represented and the scope of studies undertaken. For example, the Equal Educational Opportunities Study funded by USOE at the level of $1.25 million involved more than 4,000 schools and 600,000 children. Understandably, highly complex relationships have evolved among the various participating groups and organizations.

Research Funding Agencies: Adaptations to Professional and Political Influence

As mentioned earlier, six federal agencies support 95 percent of federally funded research in this field: USOE, OEO, NSF, NIMH, NIDHD, and DOD. Programs supported by USOE include project grants and contracts, development, and demonstration, as well as continuing institutional grants for R & D centers and laboratories, research training, and information clearing houses. NSF concentrates on the production of teaching materials in mathematics and science, computer utilization in education and research, and fundamental research on learning, neurological processes, and related areas. OEO conducts evaluation studies of its instruction programs. The other three agencies support educational R & D only as by-products of other missions. In addition to these federal agencies, a few private foundations provide some support ($7 million in 1968). State education agencies provide a comparable amount.[27] In this discussion, however, we concentrate on government agencies since they seem to illustrate many of the issues so well.

These agencies are the flywheels of the system, tipping the balance of political power among competing factions of the academic and the lay audiences, that is, the producers and the consumers of research. They are understandably subject to the pressures of often incompatible orienta-

[27] OECD, *op. cit.*, pp. 61–65.

tions from the scientific and political communities. Program purposes are authorized by a Congress to which the agencies need to justify requests and performance, while research is actually conducted by professionals who in the main are employed by nongovernment institutions. Supporting agencies, then, find themselves in a mediating position. Some agencies have been able to buffer some of the political pressures more effectively than others but, in general, legislation and the financial dependence of funding agencies prevent their complete accommodation to either scientific or professional pressures.

The Office of Education

Bailey concludes that it is difficult to conceive of a federal agency more effectively surrounded by countervailing pressures, or temperamentally more eager to promote a working partnership with its variegated clientele, than USOE.[28] Indeed, he finds that in this era of rapid growth the agency's external policies have centered around a single word, "accommodation." USOE historically was a service agency dominated by practitioner-controlled organizations such as the National Education Association and the American Association of School Administrators. With the establishment of the Cooperative Research Program in 1958 and the increasing political importance of education in this country, the Bureau of Research became somewhat more sympathetic to academic orientations to research, although even in its early years it continued to place high priority on atheoretical studies and demonstrations as well. More recently the Bureau, under extensive reorganizations (and a new name) has reemphasized service through various forms of "social action research"; its new models include industry and nonprofit research groups which now receive over 10 percent of the funds allocated. Advocates expect that these last-mentioned developments will lead to a new synthesis between service and research, but at present all that can be said is that this agency is searching for models other than those traditionally provided by universities.

It seems likely that whatever the models finally adopted, they will influence the direction of university research. The nature of that influence will be shaped by both the structure of university and government organizations and the prevailing relationships between them. It may be instructive to consider some of these factors.

[28] Cf. Stephen K. Bailey, "The Office of Education: The Politics of Rapid Growth," paper delivered at the 1966 Annual Meeting of the American Political Science Association, New York, September 6–10, 1966 (copyright 1966, The American Political Science Association) (mimeo).

Types of Agencies

The vulnerability of a funding agency to political and professional sources of pressure depends in part upon its internal structure. An agency's top officials, professional subordinates, and the outside experts and clients it serves each has differing commitments to (a) professional norms, and to (b) the bureaucracy and (c) the political system. Assuming that political and professional forms of control are to some extent incompatible, we propose that an agency's vulnerability to *political* pressures increases with (1) centralization of decision-making authority within it, and (2) its autonomy from outside professional groups. The centralization of decisions in a specific office, such as a planning unit, provides outsiders with a critical point of entrée into the rest of the organization, while decentralization makes it more difficult for outsiders to reach the points of decision making within the organization. Centralization also can serve to insulate the top officials from the influences of their professional subordinates within the organization.

Various combinations of the decision-making structures and forms of participation by external groups can alter the balance between professional and political considerations, and the role of professionals is determined by the type of agency that employs them. Thus the priority given to technical standards, to the public's expectations, and to the form of participation of outside professionals in the organization all differ by type of organization. At least four primary types of agencies, or more precisely, situations that could occur within any agency, are identified in Table 1.

Table 1   Types of Funding Agencies Classified by Centralization of Decision Making and Participation of Outside Professionals

Relationship to Outside Professionals	Decision Making	
	Centralized	Decentralized
Autonomous	Political (type 1)	Bureaucratic (type 2)
Participative	Polarized (type 3)	Professional (type 4)

The Political Agency (Type 1)

In this type of situation, decisions are controlled from the top, and there is little participation in the organization on the part of outside professionals. Individual congressmen, powerful committees, and clients whose testimony before congressional committees could defeat the agency objectives, sometimes pressure funding agencies to support certain projects that have practical implications which could bring them favorable publicity, which have the backing of influential constituents, or which are likely to verify particular political viewpoints. Their primary leverage over a funding agency is through the budget. The vulnerability of an official to political pressure is likely to increase with his position in the government, and if he has been recruited from outside either the educational or the educational research community, he may not receive much protection from the professional community. The agency's clientele is also a factor. The fact that the big city school systems, which are often tied to city and state political machines, submit research proposals to USOE probably increases that agency's political sensitivity.

Strategies

A politically sensitive agency uses a few broad-gauged strategies and a large number of specific tactics to cope with the conflicting political and professional norms.

Strategic bargaining represents one strategy. For it must be recognized that government agencies are not powerless but have some leverage they can use with individual members of Congress. Congress may appropriate the budget, but the allocation of funds is primarily in the hands of the administrators of the various agencies. In order to carry out any bargains, agency officials must maintain a tight rein on professional subordinates who must be relied upon to carry out the commitments. Hence the more bargains made at the top, the more the subordinates are treated as technicians. Even highly technical judgments tend to be ignored when they fail to confirm decisions already made on other bases. It seems unlikely that such positions would attract the more technically qualified professionals. For these reasons the quality of research in such agencies can be expected to be relatively low. One alternative open to the professional in such an agency, however, is to attempt to use the same political channels to defend his own conception of the public interest or to block administrative actions that threaten to violate it.

Capitalization, or expanding the number of objectives for which a funding agency is responsible, represents another mechanism of adaptation to political and economic influences. Agencies are almost forced to pursue competing objectives. It is true that some agencies, such as NSF, have specialized in the support of basic research primarily oriented toward the development of knowledge in the researchers' disciplines, but such agencies have recently expanded their applied programs because of such pressures. However, USOE and the National Academy of Science have initiated basic research programs to counteract the emphasis on applied research, although such work is largely justified on the basis of potential long-range yield to the agencies' missions. These mission agencies also support some basic research as part of larger research or demonstration projects of a more applied nature. USOE has also gained broad legislative authority through which it has undertaken responsibility not only for basic and applied research, but for development, demonstration, dissemination, and research training as well. By increasing the scope and diversity of its responsibilities in this way, it seeks to enhance the probability of having some effective and visible programs and to gain greater flexibility and reduce the impact of cutbacks in the budgets of certain programs as priorities shift. Furthermore, broadening the scope of the operation enhances its bargaining position.

A third mechanism through which the strain from political factors can be reduced is through the *cooptation* of members of the research community. As one measure, a granting agency may employ persons trained in each of the disciplines supported. The intent of course is to have represented persons who know the trends, substantive problems, and normative orientations of each discipline and the prestige system and communication networks. Also, selected representatives of the various disciplines have been regularly included in allocating funds and planning research support programs and in assessing one another's activities and yield. Scientists from the different disciplines, too, are usually used by these agencies as experts in advisory capacities on program matters.

This participation takes a variety of forms. In some agencies review panels, constituted of representatives of related disciplines and professions, are appointed for the purpose of evaluating new research proposals and assessing the progress of on-going work. These panels may have primary authority over determining the priority projects should receive. Other agencies, including USOE, seek the opinions of "field readers" who independently evaluate the proposals. Although agencies using this approach are required to "solicit the advice of non-federal experts," the authority to exercise final judgement is retained in the hands of their staffs. Still other agencies use combinations of review panels, consultants, and field readers. The system provides a defense to the agency against political pressures to fund technically unsound proposals. However, by the same token, even though an agency may select its own consultants, the panel system limits its maneuverability.

This participation seems to have made some researchers more sympathetic with the problems and objectives of agencies and resulted in greater appreciation for research problems of an applied nature. For some, their work in social action and technological programs has made them less conscious of, and less concerned about, distinctions between basic and applied research, while it has made others more acutely aware of some of the issues involved.

Tactics

Within the scope of these general strategies, certain, more specific tactics used by USOE and other agencies can be identified. For example, the general *guidelines* for submitting unsolicited proposals usually outline very broadly the criteria of evaluation and the agency's domain of research interests as specified by its "mission," which serves as a means of keeping research in line with political realities. However, these guidelines in themselves state only the official, stable aspects of the agency's policy. Since they are designed for unsolicited proposals, they must provide flexibility. For this reason the guidelines cannot give an accurate picture of the many specific internal needs and the immediate fluctuating pressures on the agency for particular types of research. Moreover, it is extremely difficult for an agency to develop a comprehensive research program and to justify it to Congress by relying exclusively on the unsolicited proposals of researchers constrained only by such guidelines.

As the pressure increases to demonstrate that a program is having an impact, agencies tend to exert more control over researchers by soliciting *procured research.* The procurement of research is similar to procuring any other service; government staff members identify the problems, plan a coordinated attack, write the specifications, and solicit bids for contracts. The general notion is that coordinated attacks on important problems are more effective than the laissez-faire efforts of individual researchers. To maximize visibility and effect, government-conceived projects are likely to be large in scale with substantial social action components. USOE has been following a policy of funding fewer but larger procured projects, primarily for development and demonstration purposes. During some recent years the bulk of USOE's uncommitted research funds was used for procured R & D projects relating to model teacher training programs, model schools, computerized teaching, and related projects.

Planning is the key to a successful procurement system. Several new planning institutions have been developed by USOE as it has leaned more heavily on procurement. In addition to strengthening its program planning and evaluation offices, it has funded several external "centers" which gather policy-planning information for the agency.

Planning means establishing an enforceable *priority system,* which is the agency's way of recognizing popular problems and current research "needs" and "fashions." Since Congress holds the funding agency responsible for its research program, it is to the agency's advantage to establish the priorities internally without too much reliance upon researchers, except as the agency may wish to solicit their advice. However, researchers understandably attempt to influence them. Bailey concludes in this connection that, although there are some dangers of federal control over education, the real danger is that Congress will define categorical priorities.[29] In testimony before the Research and Technical Programs Subcommittee in Government Operations, Richard Dershimer, Executive Officer of AERA, expressed grave concern that the Bureau of Research was given too much responsibility for determining priorities without the necessary increases in staff size and competency.[30] Julian Stanley, a past president of AERA, told the same committee that he favors free competition in the open market of ideas rather than "earmarking" of funds for favorite topics. Dershimer added, "Some researchers in the field are beginning to doubt that the U.S. Office of Education is the agency through which the educational research program should be administered . . . Federal officials must remain sensitive to political demands and pressures." He advocated keeping the engineering and development functions in USOE and transferring basic research to NSF or a similar agency.[31]

Priorities also serve to announce the agency's intention to stake a claim over popular problem areas that Congress is likely to support. When one agency successfully pioneers an area, as the Office of Economic Opportunity (OEO) pioneered early childhood education, other agencies are tempted to move in on it. Shifts in the priorities therefore can alter the fortunes of government agencies (as well as of research specialists) as they compete for, and withdraw from, one another's functions. The (former) USOE Bureau of Research, for example, initiated its Indian Education Research Program at a time when the Bureau of Indian Affairs' educational program was being critically appraised, and it has taken over research on early childhood education pioneered by OEO.

An alternative means of encouraging coordinated attacks on problems of concern to the research support agencies, without relying totally upon either the interests and initiative of researchers or internally initiated procured research, is through long-range R & D centers and labora-

29 *Ibid.*
30 See *Educational Researcher,* p. 2 (February 1967).
31 *Ibid.*

tories. The purpose of the USOE program of R & D centers was explained as follows.[32]

> . . . it became apparent that the individual research projects as a whole, while of acceptable levels of quality individually, did not fit together well enough to be considered coordinated approaches to substantive problems in education. The Research and Development Centers were in part created in response to this need . . .

The USOE regional laboratories are also supposed to provide coordination of efforts. They differ from R & D centers in that their primary responsibilities are to develop new products and disseminate them within their respective regions.

The R & D centers and laboratories offer to scientists and other professionals the advantage of greater continuity in support and longer-range planning, while providing a medium through which sponsoring agencies can influence research. However, because these functions are not entirely compatible, these programs have experienced certain problems. It is difficult to attract researchers with the prospect of continued work in narrowly specified areas. Several centers have either settled for less renowned researchers or have become umbrellas for a series of unrelated projects. Others have been forced to make continual alterations in their initial objectives. Dean Theodore Sizer of Harvard University's School of Education disagreed with the insistence by USOE that the goals of the Harvard R & D center be precisely defined. Sizer's idea of a research center was to assemble respected scholars and educators and let them probe toward discovery; these activities, he maintained, cannot be programmed in advance. It is not surprising that this R & D center was phased out.[33]

Other problems were encountered by regional laboratories in which the emphasis upon innovation sometimes aroused the suspicion and resistance of local educational authorities. Although considered by some as most promising developments, the laboratories have been the subject of criticism by the educational community and Congress. Koerner expresses one point of view when he calls regional laboratories marriages of convenience: "No one can expect these regional labs as now constituted to lead the way toward significant change or, to use one of their own factorite nouns, 'innovation' in American education. An assortment of professional educators and administrators—who share a common background as well as a certain interest in the *status quo* and who make no

[32] Bright and Gideonse, *op. cit.* See also, "The USOE and Research in Education, p. 2.
[33] Cf. *Boston Sunday Globe* (January 27, 1967), A-7.

use of the scientific-intellectual-artistic community, not to say the community at large—cannot come up with anything but routine answers to educational problems."[34]

At the same time, because of the method by which these centers and laboratories are funded, and the long-term commitments involved, USOE has not been able to influence their activities as much as might have been expected. It is probably no accident that, as such problems have become more apparent and, in the absence of an "intramural" research program of its own, USOE has begun to rely more heavily on its own planning staff and procurement procedures.

Finally, as one tactic of defense, some agencies employ *special* personnel to examine research projects for potentially adverse political repercussions. The USOE Bureau of Research, for example, employs a staff to examine questionaires and other data-gathering instruments for possible invasions of the public's privacy and for politically sensitive questions.[35] Both the Ruess Committee Report and the President's Office of Science and Technology have publicly opposed the clearance of questionnaires by government agencies, but the procedures are rationalized by USOE under the Federal Reports Act of 1942. That Act stipulates that only projects specifically solicited by USOE should undergo such clearance. USOE's real authority comes from a bargain with a congressional committee which has agreed to leave the policing functions to USOE as long as it maintains effective control over researchers. USOE officials believe that they are in this way heading off even more restrictive legislation. The fact that the agency can unilaterally determine the information that can be legitimately obtained by researchers using public funds (there is no explicit appeal procedure) raises awesome questions. Since the agency cannot anticipate with certainty Congress' reaction to particular projects, it is possible that it will be even more conservative in its judgements than intended by Congress.

The Professional Agency (Type 4)

In direct contrast to the political agency, this type of agency is the most vulnerable to pressures from the professional community. Professional subordinates here are likely to have considerable influence, while

[34] James, Koerner "EDC: General Motors of Curriculum Reform," *Saturday Review* (August 19, 1967), p. 70.
[35] Cf. Herbert S. Conrad, "Clearance of Questionnaires with Respect to 'Invasion of Privacy,' Public Sensitivities, Ethical Standards, etc.; Principles and Viewpoint in the Bureau of Research, U.S. Office of Education," *Sociology of Education,* **40** (Spring 1967), 170–175.

professionals outside the agency also participate extensively in its affairs. Professional standards are probably more effectively represented in the outside panel review and consultant system, even though the agency selects the membership of these panels, than when it is left to professional employees within the agency to represent the profession. The particular professionals employed by the agency do not necessarily represent the most influential segment of the profession. For, although they are likely to be more prestigeful than those attracted to the first type of organization, government employment seems to be rated lower, at least by the social science research community, than university settings in which there is purportedly more academic freedom. As they move up in the system and find it to their personal advantage to identify with their supervisors, they are likely to find even less incentive to identify with their profession. Rotating appointments, which are used by some agencies, probably counteract some of this.

It should be noted that the concern of professional researchers with the integrity of standards, technical and theoretical considerations, professional jealousies, and self-interest introduce elements of rigidity in such agencies. Indeed, without political pressure, there probably would be even more disparity than presently exists between the research the public wants and the activities of educational researchers.

The Bureaucratic Agency (Type 2)

In this type of organization, the professional employee can develop a great deal of autonomy. On the one hand, in the absence of outside experts, he can claim to be "the technically competent" employee. On the other hand, decentralized authority gives him a sphere of control and insulates him from the close scrutiny of his supervisors and from political repercussions of his decisions.

While professionals in these positions have an opportunity to defend professional norms, they are strongly tempted to reduce role conflicts by disaffiliating themselves from their professions. They are not in a good position to solicit support from professional colleagues in the field, which could give them leverage over the organization. At the same time, they are rewarded for closely monitoring research projects and for being conservative about requests for contract amendments and for enforcing contract deadlines and procedures. They are constrained by the necessity of working through a hierarchy, by deadlines, and by competition within various parts of the agency for available funds.

Moreover, their hands are tied by the internal system of reciprocities. Their obligations to people in the field are not reinforced by the service departments (e.g., the contracts officers) upon which they must rely in order to fulfill commitments to the field; service departments are more concerned with other echelons and departments of government. Thus professionals in a bureaucratic agency are left with obligations to clients not shared by other supporting units within the organization. For example, to fulfill commitments to clients, these employees must have the backing of the fiscal and contracting offices which are likely to be more obligated to other administrative units in higher levels of administration than to the outside clientele. As a result, such organizations tend to be even more "bureaucratic" than the more centralized organizations.

The Polarized Agency (Type 3)

This type of agency is probably typical. Its structure facilitates compromises between contending political and professional norms. Both professional subordinates and agency officials have authority, and both function as mediators between the interests of researchers and the political contingencies. As an integral part of the decision-making structure, the professional subordinate is able to bring his professional standards to bear on decisions, but in this political context he is also very much aware of the political price of decisions made on purely technical grounds. He is forced to calculate the net gains to the agency and to his profession that accrue from trade-offs between the political and professional norms. No single project under political fire is considered to be worth jeopardizing the entire program. Politically controversial projects are likely to be sacrificed in order to spare other projects and the agency's budget. Similarly, however, a decision to fund a poor project for political reasons must be weighed against possible repercussions from the professional community.

While technical considerations carry weight in this type of agency, there is always the danger in this setting that the merely adequate projects with political support will crowd out the technically soundest ones which are without backing. Ironically, the professional subordinate is forced to lower technical standards sufficiently to qualify some substandard proposals, or face the probability that available funds will be used up on even poorer quality proposals having political backing. One factor that affects the priority given to technical criteria is the ratio of supply of funds to the demand. As long as sufficient funds are available, technical criteria can be used as the exclusive basis for selection. As funds become limited, however, some other selection principle is necessary to select from among worthy proposals; that is, "priorities" must be established. It is the process of setting priorities that opens the door to the influence of government agencies, industry, the profession, and the various educational organizations.

In this type of agency, too, there is some tension between top administrators and professional subordinates. Top officials are still responsible for handling political pressures, but their power is limited by the autonomy and outside backing of their professional employees. These employees, in a position to influence the way the funds are distributed by employing technical criteria and calling upon colleagues for backing, can sometimes block attempts to fund projects on nontechnical grounds. The fact that top officials need the aid of professional subordinates, and the parallel dependence of professionals upon the officials, means that each group has some leverage but must be willing to bargain with the other level.

Research Operations and Administration

In turning from the national to the local level, it is clear that in recent years the scope of research activities has changed considerably. Some of the identifiable patterns of research activities and the influences that have shaped them deserve examination.

Patterns of Research Organization

Universities still receive over half of all appropriated funds in this field, but research is also conducted in independent research organizations, several regional laboratories, and a few commercial organizations. There are differences in pace and predictability of outcome in these various settings.[36] For example, the development of instructional programs is more amenable to procurement and routinization than is the discovery of how learning takes place in a classroom. Also, there are differences within and among universities. Colleges of education traditionally have placed a higher priority on the transmission of knowledge than on its production. This is also true of many of the liberal arts colleges, and it is becoming more true of state universities. That conflicts in requirements for the two activities are usually resolved in favor of teaching is evident in patterns of appointments, for example. Most teach-

---

[36] For a discussion of some of the problems of doing research in bureaucratized settings, see Alfred McClung Lee, "Individual and Organizational Research in Sociology," *American Sociological Review*, 16 (1951), 701–707; also, Arthur Vidach and Joseph Bansman, "The Springdale Case: Academic Bureaucrats and Sensitive Townspeople," *Reflections on Community Studies*, Wiley, New York, 1964.

ing appointments are provided for by "hard money," while a much larger proportion of the research appointments are made on "soft" grant funds; and perhaps as important, there are comparable differences in tenure, faculty membership, and so on. There are other strains in government, in regional laboratories, and in industry. In general, it seems that only in a limited number of settings have organizational patterns compatible with the requirements of research and the expectations of the researchers involved.

Several organizational patterns have evolved for administering research operations in this field as in others. The entrepreneurial pattern is found in government and industry but is more prevalent in institutions of higher learning where research development is generally left to the initiative and interests of the faculty. Since the major objective of educational institutions is the transmission of knowledge, research activities in these institutions are organized around this objective. This pattern is also consistent with the normative orientation of science.

The bureaucratic patterns can be found in both "profit" and "nonprofit" research corporations, in nine USOE R & D centers, several regional laboratories, institutes and, increasingly, in large-scale university projects. Some are specialized in the type or areas of research such as curriculum development, computerized learning and other forms of programmed instruction, or cognitive development. As university research becomes more bureaucratic, it can be expected that an increasing amount of tension will develop between entrepreneurial and bureaucratic types of researchers on campuses.

Continuity in Research

Full-time research scientists whose careers depend entirely on research especially need stability in funding policy. The pattern of supporting research on a "project" basis, then, creates arbitrary disruptions in the continuity of long-range research, imposes time limitations, and forces project directors to defend prematurely their achievements in academic institutions; and the fact that research activities are considered the researchers' rather than the institutions' responsibilities aggravate this situation. It is often facetiously remarked that for studies with 3 years' duration, which seems to be the modal period, the first year is used in the recruitment and training of staff and most of the last year is spent by the staff in looking for other jobs.[37]

37 Cf. Warren G. Bennis, "The Effect of Academic Goods on Their Market," *Comparative Studies in Administration,* Univ. of Pittsburgh Press, Pittsburgh, 1959.

Another influence favoring continuity of on-going research emanates from the granting agencies themselves, which have learned that dependence upon proposals based exclusively upon the interests and initiative of scientists in the field not only results in serious gaps in knowledge but also contributes to their own budgetary instability. With the encouragement of certain investigators and universities, granting agencies began to experiment with long-range programs supported on a "programmatic" basis (such as the R & D centers and regional laboratories). Although funds are appropriated annually, commitments are made for a longer duration. In addition to giving universities more continuity in their own programs, programmatic support for research usually involves larger amounts of funds. However, programmatic support tends to circumvent the usual review procedure by delegating many of the funding decisions to program directors who acquire discretionary powers to evaluate and fund individual projects within their programs.

A distinction should be made between the continuity of the research *process* and the continuity of particular research *organizations* and university *programs*. Most funding programs are based on the implicit assumption that organizations and not individuals are primarily responsible for fulfilling the research contract or grant. While there is some truth in this, and it is sometimes possible to replace a principal investigator, in practice most research programs, even programmatic ones, are entrepreneurial in origin, the offspring of a certain investigator whose own zeal and imagination is instrumental to the project or program. Academic mobility is of much concern to agency officials who initially chose to fund a particular university because of the research talent concentrated there. In the case of mobility of a principal investigator, the agency must decide whether to continue a commitment it can no longer justify, or to transfer the funds with the principal investigator, thus admitting the fictional basis of a presumably institutional program.

On the Dissemination of Findings

Given the explosion in educational research during the past two decades, results are fragmentary and in need of periodic synthesis. Communications often develop in closed circuits of communication in which researchers communicate their findings to colleagues in their own specialties and practitioners to other practitioners. That researchers from the basic disciplines are only infrequently concerned about the implications of their research for practical problems in the applied fields makes it difficult for mission-oriented granting agencies, which support research largely in the hope that it will contribute to the improvement of practices in the fields of interest, to justify their support of certain disciplines. This problem receives further attention as we now consider the operational context of research.

COLLABORATION AND ACCESS: THE OPERATIONAL CONTEXT

Applied fields such as educational research must draw upon principles from the various basic disciplines, such as the physical, the biological, and the behavioral sciences. The task of educators is to apply these principles to certain problems and populations. This division of labor requires collaboration between scientists and practitioners. Other types of collaboration are required between people in different disciplines because of the fact that no one discipline can cope with all aspects of a complex problem area. However, collaboration is hampered by differences in conceptual frameworks and methodological approaches. This lack of integration within the fabric of knowledge has resulted in a more "multidisciplinary" rather than "interdisciplinary" approach to the applied fields.

Interdisciplinary Rivalry and Monopoly

Tyler estimates that over the past 40 years the number of disciplines involved in educational research increased from three to twelve, and that inquiries have considerably expanded in scope and increased in complexity.[38] These various disciplines are split by both ideological disputes and struggles for control. Some disciplines, such as psychology, have had a longer tradition in this field, but no one discipline any longer has a monopoly. The majority of research proposals submitted to USOE come from researchers outside colleges of education. Sieber and Lazarsfeld reported that over the years 1956–1963 the number of proposals submitted to USOE from noneducators increased fourfold while the number submitted by applicants located in schools of education remained fairly stable, and that over the eight-year period the proportion of proposals submitted by educators decreased from 66 to 40 percent.[39] Moreover, a

---

[38] Ralph W. Tyler, "The Field of Educational Research," in *The Training and Nurture of Educational Researchers*, Egon Guba and Stanley Elam, Eds., Phi Delta Kappa, Bloomington, Ind., 1965.

[39] Sieber and Lazarsfeld, *op. cit.*, p. 49. However, Bargar's sample of 3500 educational researchers reveals that only 7 percent of them are social scientists, most of whom are

reorganization of USOE in 1966 greatly weakened the influence of educators and educational psychologists within that agency. The long-run prospects for increased support for the various social sciences are favorable. In addition to research on curriculum and students, more attention is being paid to the home environment, community, and school organization.

The field is growing and changing so rapidly that it is difficult to determine just who the "educational researcher" is. Most research has focused on students, but a sociological study of educational social mobility, or an anthropological investigation of acculturation and socialization, also constitutes educational research. Whatever the boundaries, it is safe to say that the different producers of educational research do not systematically interact, even though they have a common audience of practitioners and to some extent share common concerns and problems. Hence, while the body of knowledge is interdependent, separate monopolies and rivalries have impeded effective interdisciplinary cooperation. Psychologists have been closely identified with the study of school children, while anthropologists have dominated the study of ethnic groups, particularly the American Indians. Black communities seem to have become the almost exclusive domain of sociologists.

This tendency of disciplines to monopolize certain problems and populations is responsible for at least two practical problems. First, shifts in political priorities—such as from the mentally retarded to the talented, and more recently to the educationally disadvantaged—bring unintended changes in the fortunes of the various disciplines. Educational problems connected with the civil rights movement have now thrust sociologists into new positions of responsibility for educational research.[40] A second practical consequence of rivalry between and within disciplines is that they have become so divided among themselves that they cannot wield significant political influence.

The Roots of Rivalry

Several factors promote interdisciplinary rivalry. A few of the more salient ones in this field are discussed here. These include differences in

sociologists. Eighty-eight percent of those responding majored in education or psychology. Three-fourths of them are located within educational units, mostly in universities. Only 20 percent of the researchers in Bargar's sample are likely to have been trained in a research-oriented department. Typically, regardless of department, they devote less than one-third of their time to research. Robert Bargar, "Who Is the Educational Researcher?" in Guba and Elam, *op. cit.*

40 James Coleman, et al., *Equality of Educational Opportunity*, U.S. Office of Education, Government Printing Office, Washington, D.C., 1966.

the isolation from and closeness to practitioners, the value placed on research, differences in typical research strategies, and traditions of individualism and control.

RELATIONSHIP TO PRACTITIONERS.   For one thing, disciplines differ in their relationships with practitioners and can be classified according to their degree of isolation from educators and their identification with the academic community. Some disciplines are more closely identified with practitioners and give greater priority to basic research than others. Compared to researcher-educators, social scientists are not as likely to be familiar with the daily problems of schools and, in any event, tend to interpret education from the perspectives of their own disciplines. This difference in relationships with practitioners also influences the accessibility of the subjects to the researcher. Studies of learning theory (the largest single topic of research in this field) are attractive partly because students and classrooms are accessible and students can be easily manipulated.

VALUE OF RESEARCH.   Also, disciplines differ in the priority given to research. Sieber and Lazarsfeld report that college of education faculties place less emphasis on research than college and university administrators, and it is probably also safe to conjecture that they value research less than do social science faculties because colleges of education traditionally have been more oriented to teaching and service. Deans of education report that their faculties are more favorable toward service than research and that personnel are drawn away from research by field service work. Directors of service-oriented units also report less difficulty in recruiting than do directors of research units.[41] Fattu reported in 1960 that of 94 colleges and universities that grant the doctorate in education only 10 could be said to be making a serious effort to encourage educational research, probably because of the dominance of practitioners in most of these institutions, who attained their influence by means other than scholarship and scientific skills.[42] Only 36 percent of the education professors in Fattu's study said that the typical doctoral candidate is adequately prepared to do research independently. He summarizes discussions with 29 persons from other disciplines by characterizing educational research as poverty-stricken—that is, poverty of ideas, experience, personnel, influence, support, and qualifications. Educational research, according to these outsiders at least, has suffered from poor standards of

[41] Sieber and Lazarsfeld, *op. cit.*
[42] N. A. Fattu, *A Survey of Educational Research and an Appraisal by Scientists From Other Fields*, USOE Cooperative Research Report No. 525, 1967.

scholarship and the tendency of educators to ignore criticism. They felt that too much emphasis was being placed upon immediate "practical" solutions and isolated problems at the expense of sustained efforts to develop systematic knowledge.

Clark is as harsh in his appraisal of educational research for the past 30 years. He concludes that research in colleges of education typically involves piecemeal studies on a wide variety of areas rather than systematically focusing on one line of development. Furthermore, few faculty members doing research have had little significant training in research and, he contends, these same "unqualified persons" do a poor job of teaching classes of future researchers. He concludes that colossal USOE funds entice a great many poorly qualified persons to engage in vaguely conceived, sloppily conducted, and ad hoc research projects.

Interestingly, the bulk of the USOE research training programs are located in colleges of education rather than in behavioral science departments. It is not known whether such programs in education departments have improved the quality of research in these settings.

DIFFERENCES IN RESEARCH STRATEGIES. The disciplines also differ in their truth strategies and their use of various research technologies. Distinctions were made earlier between two general aspects of research activities—the creative and the technical aspects. The root of the technical differences is a difference in strategy for seeking truth or, more specifically, rules about verification of knowledge. Thompson and his associates have identified four truth strategies which seem to underlie many differences among the various disciplines.[43] His typology is based upon the scholar's reliance on sensory experience (either high or low) and the kind of reasoning used to analyze and arrange the experience (either codified and systematic or otherwise). Table 2 gives a simplified version of his typology.

Table 2   Typology of Truth Strategies

Strategy	Reliance on Experience	Type of Reasoning
Scientific	High	Codified
Direct	High	Uncodified
Analytic	Low	Codified
Inspirational	Low	Uncodified

43 James D. Thompson, Robert W. Hawkes, and Robert W. Avery, "Truth Strategies and University Organization," paper read at the American Sociological Association, New York, 1960.

This typology applies to differences that exist *within* disciplines as well as differences among them. Experimental psychology and conventional sociology probably fall predominantly under the "scientific" category, where strong reliance is placed on precoded tests, questionnaires, short structured interviews and surveys; the vast majority of most psychologists submitting proposals to USOE intend to use some kind of test. It should be noted that the prestructure, which instruments impose on observations, seems to suppress the experiential component and places even more stress on the sensory experience than Table 2 indicates. There is also a strong analytic orientation among many sociologists who rely on statistical procedures and frequently use secondary sources of data, such as census information and records.

The tradition of cultural anthropology seems to be much closer to the direct approach, with strong reliance placed on direct observation, participation, and informal unstructured interviewing. By contrast to the psychologists, anthropologists exert less "control" over their subjects but in return are able to obtain more extensive information. A personal equation between the anthropologist and his subjects sometimes makes it difficult for him to remain sufficiently uninvolved and to avoid taking sides in disputes. By contrast, the social distances involved in the scientific approach have encouraged some scientists to do research on a "hit-and-run basis," ignoring any responsibility for the aftermath of their work.

Cutting across both sociology and anthropology is an inspirational strain being advocated by a select group of creative malcontents in each discipline. This approach, which has been labeled by some sociologists as the "new sociology," is actually a return to a blend of humanism and science formerly characteristic of these disciplines. This orientation is characterized by strong overtones of social criticism, advocacy of social reform, and a preference for literary and speculative approaches to analysis. These less structured approaches to research are not always compatible with the needs of mission-oriented funding agencies which want reliable *information* that will be of use to practitioners at least as much as they want new "insights."

In each discipline, then, there are competing truth strategies along side the dominant one, and the dominant strategy of one discipline may be adopted by some researchers within another; some anthropologists are adopting mathematical approaches, in keeping with the new universal popularity of technologies that can be adapted to computers, while some sociologists periodically rediscover the utility of observational techniques. Finally, a growing number of social scientists have become cosmopolitan enough to tolerate and even use a combination of truth strategies in their own work.

A SPECIALTY IN RESEARCH METHODOLOGY.   Forty-seven percent of AERA members belong to a division devoted to measurement and research methodology, which is one of the three largest of the seven divisions in the Association. Although research strategies and techniques are taught in specialized ways within the framework of each discipline, common features of these techniques have become highly developed as a separate speciality in itself. Many books are available, and various courses are taught about designs for sampling, statistical and other analytical techniques, the presentation of tables, the construction of questionnaires and interview schedules, interviewing, and so on. For example, techniques of survey studies have evolved almost as a specialty in their own right. The result is a core of research technicians, many of whom are willing to work on a variety of problems or to limit their work to the execution of already planned studies. The emergence of this type of specialty in research operations has facilitated the already noted trend toward procurement of research by funding agencies. It has also had the effect of creating a group of transient researchers who do a few studies in educational research and move on to other fields without developing a long-term commitment to the improvement of the field as such.

OTHER RESEARCH TRADITIONS.   Finally, there are different traditions of individualism and control in the various disciplines. According to the Sieber and Lazarsfeld study, a majority of directors of research units within colleges of education prefer the bureaucratic to the entrepreneurial type of research. A study of a USOE-supported interdisciplinary R & D center found that researchers connected with the college of education were "organization men," serving the structure of the organization itself, whereas social scientists gave more priority to individualism. The social scientists were more concerned with the research function, looking upon the center merely as a place to get their work done. They seldom communicated with colleagues from education, while educators functioned to hold the organization together. Their desire for structure seemed to represent a threat to social scientists who were jealous of their freedom of inquiry.[44]

[44] Alfred G. Smith, *Communication and Status: The Dynamics of a Research Center,* Center for the Advanced Study of Educational Administration, Univ. of Oregon, Eugene, 1966.

Interdisciplinary Structure

There are few *formal* mechanisms to support collaboration and overcome the barriers. In this field, however, three structures have been used to sustain relationships between researchers from education and the other disciplines—namely, joint appointments with colleges of education, R & D centers, and professional associations.

JOINT APPOINTMENTS.   Nearly half the colleges of education in Sieber and Lazarsfeld's study reported either joint teaching or research appointments of scholars from outside education; indeed, their data reveal that one-fourth of all new staff members of colleges of education in recent years have come from the behavioral sciences. Evidence reported in that study suggests that joint relationships are related positively to the quality of research. Nevertheless, educators were seldom jointly involved in the research with educators. This fact suggests the inadequacies of relying on joint appointments to encourage collaborative efforts.

Not the least of the problems is that isolated social scientists can be expected to encounter some role strain in settings in which the traditions of service overshadow research and in which there are strong pressures to engage in applied research on predefined problems. Moreover, the erratic tradition of research in colleges of education and the pressures in these settings to research problems identified by educators can easily cancel any potential contributions a social scientist might make by following leads from his own discipline's unique perspectives. His discipline often leads him to focus on variables not easily *controlled* by educators who then regard the research as unuseful to their immediate needs.

Also, the institutional, mission-oriented approach to research, which in fact underlies the whole notion of a separate field of "educational research," discourages social scientists from taking a comparative institutional approach to education, even though in the long run such an approach could yield very fruitful results. Neither the mission agencies nor colleges of education encourage or support systematic comparative research of schools, hospitals, churches, and so on, within the same research design.

The way researchers on joint appointments resolve these conflicting expectations would provide a study in itself. In this connection, research is needed on career patterns in basic and applied research settings, on the characteristics of people who choose to work in each setting and on the quality of the work produced in each. In the absence of this research, it can be anticipated that it is difficult for a person to maintain the discrepant roles for long without shifting his standards of reference. One might conjecture that his present position outweighs the effects of his prior training. However, it is also possible that hybrids evolve in such settings, blending characteristics of both the discipline and the practical setting.

R & D CENTERS. The problems of interdisciplinary research converge even more forcefully in R & D centers designed as multidisciplinary attacks on a given problem area. Centers are typically based on the premise that no one discipline can solve educational problems. However, in practice, a given discipline tends to dominate a center. "Involvement" of members of the other disciplines then often amounts to attempts by the dominant discipline to coopt them sufficiently so that they are willing to apply their technical skills to preformulated problems. Nevertheless, the social scientists' need for access to data that can be provided through collaboration with colleges of education can be a powerful incentive for collaboration.

The representation of educators on funding agency staffs and their advisory committees, and the strings that agencies attach to funds, can be used as a leverage to encourage collaboration between colleges of education and the disciplines. Since the latter are typically the reluctant partners, colleges of education have been given some leverage. In some cases proposals from social science departments for an educational research training program, or for an R & D center on an educational problem, have not been approved by USOE until promises are made that the local college of education will play a central role in the program.

PROFESSIONAL ASSOCIATIONS. Some of the tensions that develop between interdisciplinary teams working together on a sustained basis, in a given setting on a narrow set of problems, can be minimized in other settings. Membership in a common professional association is one alternative. AERA (under the leadership of its past presidents and its executive secretary, Richard Dershimer) has attempted to organize rather reluctant, unwieldy groups of researchers from the behavioral sciences into a newly formed division within the Association. Its members are broadly concerned with the social context of education. Although at present dominated by sociologists, an interdisciplinary membership is sought, and the Association has planned a new social science journal. However, there are already signs of cleavages within the division between members of different disciplines and between those researchers whose interests are primarily theoretical and those of a more applied, social action bent. It is not clear at this time whether such an organization will be able to overcome obstacles to communication and cooperation among disciplines in the field.

Strains between Researchers and Practitioners

Data gathering is a cultural contact situation in which the researcher attempts to extend his subculture into an operational setting. As pointed out elsewhere in this volume, the producers of research and the consumers of it participate in different reward systems and must satisfy different audiences and reference groups. Basic researchers, and many applied researchers, are less interested in rendering a local service to educators than in making a contribution to their respective disciplines (or in just publishing), while practitioners usually want to derive some tangible benefit from their cooperation in research projects. Since educators do control the access to school systems and are represented in funding agencies, they have some leverage.

Perhaps the most fundamental issues arise over the question of who will define the problems. Social scientists and educators are not likely to agree on the important problems. Educators are more oriented to the solution of practical problems they meet in their daily practices. Researchers are usually oriented to patterns of similarities and differences among events, often on a more abstract level than is directly applicable to immediate problems. Practitioners often lament that while researchers from the basic disciplines may be well acquainted with the principles of their disciplines they are much less acquainted with the facts in the applied fields. By the same token, practitioners are often more preoccupied with the myriad of facts and less familiar with the underlying explanatory principles. Besides aggravating problems of communication between the two, this situation is also responsible for the inadequacy of many research proposals. Proposals that exhibit elegance in conceptual framework and methodological design often demonstrate ignorance about the workings of the systems to be studied. Or, at the other extreme, many of the proposals addressed to important practical problems lack theoretical and methodological sophistication.

This suggests another area of difference between researchers and practitioners concerning the way they view knowledge. As others have suggested, researchers view their work as conditional, tentative, and subject to testing, verification, and extension. Practitioners, however, must act and so accept existing knowledge with greater finality. Indeed, they must make a degree of commitment to the knowledge upon which practices are based. The more fundamental the assumptions challenged by the researchers and the more pervasive their implications, the more difficult cooperation is to attain and the more likely that the results of research will be ignored by practitioners, or criticized on methodological grounds for lack of conclusiveness. There are always ample bases for criticism.

This last point suggests another important source of conflict between researchers and practitioners, which stems from the need for controls in conducting research, especially in experimental work. As mentioned, a large share of the work in this field is in the area of demonstration and social action projects. Legislation has provided a substantial amount of funds for local schools seeking to try out innovative programs. Myriads of evaluation studies of these projects have been completed. Most of them are inconclusive. One reason is that the procedures necessary for establishing and maintaining such controls at times interfere with the freedom and routine activities of practitioners. It may be deemed necessary to withhold from practitioners much of the information related to the study in order to guard against the introduction of bias. Compromises in research design, for example, in the needed controls, can make it impossible to determine the validity of findings.

A prime source of tensions surrounding applied projects within operational settings arises from the combinations of innovation and conformity implicit in such efforts. Such projects sometimes begin with the purposes of testing hypotheses, demonstrating the effectiveness of a change, and assisting the local system all at the same time. Furthermore, while the objectives may be fixed in advance, often the procedures for achieving them must be developed during the course of the project. Some of these conditions require innovation, freedom, and flexibility; but testing and demonstration in particular require close control over both the subordinate researchers and the practitioners. Centralized control is needed to implement a tight research design, or to facilitate the adoption of procedures once developed, but a more diffuse style of organization is better suited to the development and service components.

Pressures on infant programs for sheer survival constantly threaten to crowd out the research component and to divert research funds to the support of unplanned program costs. By the nature of the operational setting, such projects often violate certain scientific norms. These programs are not necessarily conceived from a theoretical basis and often do not have observable behavioral objectives. Moreover, the inability of researchers to control the operational situations makes it nearly impossible for them to implement fully the ideal research design. Research projects in operational settings are apt to lose personnel and encounter lack of cooperation from program people upon whom they depend.[45] Further-

---

[45] Cf. Gwen Andrew, "Some Observations on Management Problems in Applied Social Research," *American Sociologist* 2 (May, 1967), 84–89; Harlin L. Voss, "Pitfalls in

more, difficulties are to be expected in securing good researchers for 2- or 3-year projects on other than a part-time basis. It is equally difficult to coordinate the separate tasks of many part-time researchers normally separated by their own specialities and harried by the pressures of other activities.

A typology of change strategies proposed by two veteran educational researchers places these problems in perspective.[46] They distinguish two implementation strategies (the use of existing and temporary organizational structures), and two control structures (control at the director's and at the operating levels). (See Table 3.)

Table 3   Typology of Change Strategies

Control	Implementation	
	Existing Structures	Temporary Structures
Director's level	Type I	Type II
Operating level	Type III	Type IV

Type-I strategy is probably the most typical. It entails across-the-board impact in which control of the project is centralized. There appear to be strong pressures in favor of this approach because it avoids the accusation of preferential treatment that sometimes appears to be shown to experimental groups and because it demonstrates that projects can succeed outside special "hothouse" conditions. However, this approach disturbs the system and so encounters the greatest resistance from the practitioners, who may not have been involved in its initiation. The type-II strategy avoids this latter problem, but is usually not convincing, since the innovation has been sheltered from the "typical" operating conditions. Moreover, there may be no way to incorporate the procedures of projects initiated in sheltered temporary structures into the permanent organization. In type III the subordinate researchers and the practitioners are given responsibility for carrying out a project whose objectives have been set by higher levels of the administration remote from the operating scene. Conflicts between freedom and control resulting from relatively fixed objectives and the need to develop procedures are particularly acute in this situation. Type IV shifts the responsibility for both the objectives of the project and its procedures to the individual researchers and the practitioners. This is likely to

Social Research: A Key Study," *American Sociologist,* 1 (May, 1966), 136–140; Julius Roth, "Hired Hand Research," *American Sociologist,* 1 (August, 1966), 190–196.
[46] Warland Bessent and Hollis A. Moore, "Affects of Outside Funds on School Districts," in *Prospectives on Educational Change,* Richard I. Miller, Ed., Appleton-Century-Crofts, New York, 1967, pp. 101–117.

stimulate new ideas, but because the people involved are not constrained by project orientation it loses direction and is as poorly suited for a comprehensive approach as for implementing ideas once developed.

Facing the obstacles mentioned, it is no wonder that a well-intentioned, innovative project often becomes transferred into what Gouldner and Miller call a problem-solving ceremonial—in effect, a ritual undertaken so that basic change will not have to occur.[47] Indeed, any attempt to maintain technical standards under these adverse conditions is likely to be inimical to the objective of immediate change—which often could be accomplished more effectively through administrative and political influence than by research and development. Any improvements accomplished by such projects are probably as much a tribute to the native ingenuity, good intentions, and influence of particular people as to the guidance provided by research.

Another source of contention between researchers and practitioners arises from the fact that they have different investments in the ongoing system. The researcher is almost always an alien in the educational subculture and in the school or community he studies. Moreover, the ultimate purpose of most applied research, and implicitly of much basic research, is to evaluate present practice in order to improve it, which may mean advocating changes in the behavior of precisely the people to be studied. The practitioner may have much to lose from criticism and suggested reforms which can result from research and has virtually no way to defend himself from conclusions drawn about him by researchers. Moreover, the subjects of theoretical research are likely to feel that they are being exploited unless some immediate, practical problem is to be attacked in a way that they can understand. Social scientists tend to do "hit-and-run" research with very little accountability or regard for the possible consequences of their research on the people they have studied, who must live with the questions and conclusions long after the researchers have left. At the same time, a researcher is likely to have been engaged by vested interests (e.g., a government agency, a school board, or an administrator) who may very well want to use his research to justify their own positions. In addition, since researchers often have vested interests of their own, they may be more intent upon changing the behavior of *other* people than scrutinizing and improving their own professions.

Understandably, then, sometimes the actual source of practitioners' resentment goes deep and has more to do with the potential threat of

47 Alvin Gouldner and S. M. Miller, *Applied Sociology*, Free Press, New York, 1965, p. 16.

the researcher's conclusions than his reluctance to apply his work to their problems. The practitioner wants some control over the research process itself so that he will not be at the mercy of the viewpoint of the researcher; but since giving the practitioner such control threatens to transform the researcher into a mere technician, he resists.

The theoretical explanations offered by researchers can conflict with the practitioner's commonsense definition of the situation. Compared to educational psychologists, social scientists are at a special disadvantage in this regard. People are in the first place more accustomed to the individualistic, personalized explanations of psychology (e.g., drives and motives) than to impersonal societal forces, such as the control structure or the value systems. Probably more important, psychological characteristics of individuals simply appear to be more easily manipulated than the systemic variables that are of interest in social science, such as social class, organization, culture, values, and community power structure. The uncomfortable fact that the practitioner cannot control these factors means that *he* might have to adjust to *them*. For example, new information on differences between lower-class and middle-class styles of learning provides the basis for criticizing current practice, which makes such research threatening to middle-class teachers. The fact that it is more difficult to check the validity of case studies made by an individual social scientist than to check the psychological experiments, questionnaires, and interviews probably increases the practitioner's suspicions about this form of social research.

This suspicion of social scientists is easily reinforced by the liberal, critical views known to be held by many of these scholars.[48] A recent survey of 386 members of AERA demonstrates that a substantial proportion of educational researchers hold relatively liberal views toward critical social problems. Two-thirds of the sample listed their highest degree in education, and less than one-fourth were from the behavioral and social sciences (most of these from psychology). Education faculties are typically among the more conservative members of universities. Nevertheless, one-fourth of this sample believed that the United States should withdraw immediately from the Vietnam war; 72 percent agreed that where de facto segregation exists black people should be assured of control over their own schools; 48 percent agreed that white racism is the main cause of Negro riots in the cities; and over 60 percent of the sample classified themselves as "liberals." Furthermore, over half of the

48 Richard Wisniewski and Matthew B. Miles, "Educational Researchers and Social Values: A Preliminary Report," paper read at AERA meetings, Minneapolis, Minn., March 1970. That social scientists tend to be liberal is documented in Paul Lazarsfeld and Wagner Thielans, *The Academic Mind,* Free Press, New York, 1958.

sample (56 percent) believed that a scholar's teaching and research inevitably reflect his political values.

A diffuse sense of personal alienation among many researchers in this field leads them to reject or exaggerate much of what they see and, often, to advocate extreme alternatives. This is especially true of social scientists. This implicit threat of applied research was illustrated in a recently completed nationwide USOE-sponsored study of equal educational opportunities in public schools.[49] Because of the emotional moods surrounding questions about the school performance of minority groups and the distribution of educational resources in major cities, studies of these issues are likely to raise controversies and may promote negative feelings about participation on the part of practitioners.*

---

[49] Coleman, et al., *op. cit.*

* Some anthropologists, fired with a sense of social indignation, have become personally involved in the disputes of the people they are studying in their *own* society (even while refusing to take sides when studying other cultures). This kind of issue was involved in an anthropological field study of the education of a minority group. The researchers happened to pick a community in which the traditional power structure was being challenged by some of the "young Turks" within the community. Under any circumstances an outsider who sought to study the community would have been viewed with suspicion, and in this case the principal investigator's personal disapproval of the power structure apparently prompted him to ignore it, or at least so the leaders interpreted his action. He was accused of taking sides against the official leaders who, without adequate information about the project, readily identified this basic research effort with a social action program that had been upsetting the status quo in the community.

Caught in this crossfire, the granting agency involved sought outside advice. A team of respected social scientists together with government professional employees went to the site in a visit which satisfied the community leaders that they were being listened to. The presence of nonfederal employees helped to protect the agency from political pressures and gave professional sanction to the decision that was made; the social scientists were understandably concerned that they would not be used as a front to sanction an essentially political decision and confined their evaluation to the professional merits of the project. The strategy finally used was to examine the feasibility of obtaining valid and reliable information in the community under such formidable opposition to the study; this seemed to be one criterion that overlapped with both professional and political considerations, and which the principal investigator might be willing to accept.

The case illustrates the interplay of professional and political considerations in ongoing research. As important, however, it demonstrates the close tie between social action research and politics, for if the project had not become identified with a particular coalition within the community and with the social action program there, the political problems probably would not have developed. The case points up some of the difficulties likely to arise when social scientists become heavily involved in programs dealing with the solution of social problems. The loss of the appearance of neutrality and detachment on the part of researchers can become a major source of obstacles in their research. However, a high degree of detachment can be interpreted by practitioners as

THE RELATIONSHIPS OF RESEARCHERS TO SUBJECTS:
THE MORAL CONTEXT OF RESEARCH

In considering the researcher's relation to the practitioner, we have already entered the moral context of research. For these relationships are the heart of the ethical and moral concerns. They involve the researcher's proper relationship to data, including norms of honesty, objectivity, and the public's right to know research findings. Since these norms and the ways to implement them have been the subject of much of the methodological literature, our attention here is focused upon the relationships to subjects. Two areas of concern are briefly considered here: experimentation involving human subjects, and confidentiality.

The Issue of Experimentation

Experimentation involving human subjects has been an issue in medical research for some time, but recently it has been raised with respect to educational research and, more generally, to the social and behavioral sciences. There are two major inherent dilemmas in this area. The *first* is caused from strains created by two contradictory expectations of science. On the one hand, experimentation is a principal means of certifying knowledge before it is applied on a wide scale to human subjects who could be harmed by it; for example, a new reading curriculum based on faulty principles could injure a whole generation of school children if introduced prematurely. On the other hand, the fact that experimentation involving human subjects is being more closely scrutinized restricts the opportunity for and quality of experimentations needed to certify knowledge. Moreover, the experiment is criticized both because it necessarily entails risk to the subjects, and yet, to the extent the experimental approach being tested is believed to be superior to conventional ones, those who are not included in the experimental groups complain of being denied the superior services or educational methods.

Methods typically used to cope with these issues include informing the subjects about the research objectives and the risks involved, and obtaining their consent regarding participation. Stumpf raises the important question, Is the consent of the subject actually the decisive issue

disinterest with their values and practical problems. The delicate balance between involvement and detachment is not easy to maintain. However, this balance is precisely what the social scientist needs to gain access to credible data and information without at the same time arousing antagonisms that can undermine his objectives.

in research? Referring to the area of medicine, he asks, "Does the patient have the right to permit a physician to do what, for other reasons, the physician ought not to do?"[50]

Informing the subject about the study in which his participation is sought raises the *second* dilemma related to the issue of research involving humans. Knowledge about the objectives of a study may defeat the purposes for which it is designed. This need not necessarily be the result of a conscious attempt on the part of subjects.[51]

The same issues involved in experimentation are also implicit in surveys, research, demonstrations, and action programs. Such work usually entails either implications for practice or the direct introduction of innovations designed to change people's behavior and lives. Questions can be raised about the right of a researcher to suggest policy changes that can have favorable consequences on some group at the expense of others, or to attempt to alter behavior of which he disapproves, in the name of science. This has become an acute question as social scientists have rushed into areas of "urban education" to study the schools and communities of ethnic and minority groups.

Wisniewski and Miles sample of AERA members identified the issue of race and education as the one most deserving of their attention.[52] AERA members were concerned not only with studying the issues as passive observers but in "doing something" about them. Over three-fourths of the sample disagreed with the statement that it is up to others to implement the findings of research. One in five believed that distinctions between applied and basic research are "to a great degree actually rationalizations used by some researchers to avoid controversial issues that must be researched," and an additional 42 percent said that it is true "to some degree." More important, 38 percent of the sample said that they had been very much involved in efforts to bring about educational reform, and another 45 percent said they had been at least "somewhat" involved. When asked about their participation in different activities (such as speaking at meetings on controversial issues, supporting strikes, teach-ins, and so on), only 12 percent said that they had been involved in none of these activities; half of the sample reported involvement in over three activities.

At the same time, it is important to recognize that less than two percent of the above sample is nonwhite. It can be assumed that these

---

[50] Samuel Stumpf, "Some Moral Dimensions of Medicine," *Annals of Internal Medicine,* **64** (1966), 460–470.
[51] "Privacy and Behavioral Research," A preliminary report of the Panel on Privacy and Behavioral Research, *Science,* **155** (1967), 534–538.
[52] Wisniewski and Miles, *op. cit.*

researchers bring with them not only the perspectives of their disciplines, but of their predominately middle-class backgrounds. They are typically funded by agencies and groups against whom the more militant minority group members have grievances. Hence minority groups are becoming alarmed that their points of view are not being fairly represented in the research designs. For example, a high dropout rate from school may be interpreted in terms of the dropouts' personal shortcomings, for example, poor grades, lack of incentive; or it can be interpreted in terms of the failures of schools to adapt curriculum and procedures to the needs of the minority group. Each interpretation would lead to very different policy implications.

One example of such a controversy is found in Moynihan's report to the United States government which cited the weak family structure among blacks as the primary reason for the problems encountered by this group.[53] Critics of the report point out that segregated schools and job discrimination are equally plausible explanations. A more recent example is the bitter attacks leveled against educational psychologist Jensen's conclusions from his research in which he attributes failure in compensatory educational programs among black children to genetic differences between blacks and whites.[54]

Because of the dilemmas involved in these controversies, it has been difficult to prescribe clear-cut policies and equally difficult to establish methods of enforcement. The USPHS issued certain guidelines and rules regarding research involving human subjects, which in effect delegated the responsibility of guarding the rights of subjects to the institutions employing researchers. The mechanisms devised for this purpose have in most situations boiled down to either an additional set of rituals, or to a routine expression of confidence in a researcher by his peers.

Some educational researchers believe that professional associations have a clear obligation to make public statements about the validity of controversial research that is likely to be used in setting educational policy. However, others believe that such a practice would constitute a form of intimidation which could lead to serious infringements on academic freedom. One middle course advocated by some is that professional groups should publish in popular journals critiques of these controversial studies in order to alert laymen to all sides of the controversies. Others maintain that members of the ethnic group or other

53 Daniel P. Moynihan, *The Negro Family: The Case For National Action*, U.S. Department of Labor, Office of Policy Planning and Research, U.S. Government Printing Office, Washington, D.C., March 1965.
54 Arthur Jensen, "How Much Can We Boost I.Q. and Scholastic Achievement?," *Harvard Educational Review*, (June 1969).

groups being studied should be included in research, not only as consultants, but more centrally as members of steering committees responsible for identifying the broad policy questions dealing with research projects. Presumably, they would help to formulate research questions and to write recomendations that flow from the findings. They also would be employed on research projects whenever possible.

The Issue of Confidentiality

The issue of confidentiality in the handling of research material is multifaceted, but probably the most widely discussed aspect is related to questions about "invasion of privacy." People have the right to be secure in their attitudes, opinions, and actions within limitations set by law. Private attitudes, opinions, and personal histories of deviance are an integral part of the study of educational problems, and yet they obviously concern the very facts that respondents may not wish to have known.

Even though, in one sense, assuring anonymity of respondents and institutions studied has been a strict norm of research, for purposes of checking reliability, historical studies and accounts have to include references to places and the names of those who shape events. Another important aspect of this issue relates to the eventual use of data. If the data were to be used as a basis for reform and action programs involving the respondents, a question of propriety may be raised. The use of data voluntarily furnished for research purposes in determining the relationships of respondents to given programs may entail a violation of the subjects' rights unless they have been fully informed of the consequences. For example, a teacher might volunteer information to a researcher that exposes widespread violations of state education standards in a particular school. If such information, given freely in response to research questions, were submitted to the school board or the state agency for use for its own program purposes, it would pose profound questions, especially if the subjects had not been informed about such an eventuality.

The confidentiality issue is not only related to the knowledge of others about the characteristics of individuals in question, but also the knowledge of these individuals about their own characteristics. One problem associated with this issue relates to the self-fulfilling prophecy. The influence of the group's definition of the situation upon an individual's expectations of himself is among the more established generalizations about human behavior. Knowledge about the personal characteristics of an individual often becomes the basis for grouping or stereotyping him into categories which in turn can influence his behavior in a direction that conforms to the stereotypes. In fact, the situations themselves often are structured by others in a way that would produce the stereotyped characteristics. Examples can be found in the use of I.Q. tests, questions about a child's feelings toward his parents, and employment experiences of ex-mental patients and others who had a history of criminal and deviant behavior. This is particularly important in the case of acute social stigma, such as in mental illness and lower levels of intellectual functioning.

SOME CONCLUSIONS

Students and observers of science and research must come to the conclusion that the normative structures are in transition. Although it may be said that the normative structure of *science* has matured and stabilized, that of *research* is still in a condition of flux. This relative instability of expectations is a primary characteristic of research, especially of interdisciplinary fields as in education. This is an important source of many of the conflicts that arise among researchers in basic disciplines and those in such fields.

The poor articulation among basic, applied, and social action research persists in face of the apparently widespread belief that the effectiveness of each can be improved if they are closely linked. The problem is aggravated by a tradition of isolation among different subcultures of research. However, there is no guarantee that better integration will actually result in substantial improvements. The history of the social and behavioral sciences abounds with instances of basic research from which there have been no clearly discernible practical outcomes, and of practical innovations which apparently were developed independently of results of such research.[55]

Universities and research support agencies are perhaps the institutions most affected by the changing patterns of the organization of research in education, and by the conflicting demands and expectations. Expansion in public and private support for educational research and

[55] Hendrick W. Bode, "Reflections on the Relation between Science and Technology," in *Basic Research and National Goals*, National Academy of Sciences, March 1965. See also in the same volume, George B. Kistiakowsky, "On Federal Support of Basic Research." Conversely, a recent study of the utilization of science and technology by the Department of Defense in developing weapon systems, called "Project Hindsight," concluded that the contributions from research since 1945 were greatest when the effort was oriented, and that basic research had relatively little discernible impact on the development of modern weapon systems; C. W. Sherwin and R. S. Isenson, *First Interim Report on Project Hindsight (Summary)*, Office of the Director of Defense Research and Engineering, Washington, D.C., October 1966.

increased awareness of the role of knowledge in the solution of applied problems has brought about pressures upon universities to shift from their traditional long-range interest in systematic knowledge in order to accommodate a variety of competing research activities. The way universities and support agencies are organized affects their vulnerability to incompatible pressures from political and scientific pressure groups. Funding agencies have developed a variety of mechanisms to deal with such pressures.

As mentioned in several places in this volume, the intrusion of economic and political factors into research activities, as in the case of educational research, has meant not only that new elements have been introduced in the system of sanctions and rewards, but that new reference groups and organizations have evolved. The probability that a researcher will encounter role conflicts increases with the number and saliency of his audiences, and with the degree of incompatibility between his primary audience and his sources of support. It would be useful to examine the ways in which researchers reconcile these conflicts. The academic and lay norms are likely to receive different priorities in universities and government agencies; but the academic norms are likely to have more priority in either of these institutional settings than in more operational settings.

It might be argued that these changes have made researchers more responsive to audiences outside their disciplines, with the result of sacrificing systematic inquiry in favor of immediate and expedient results. It also can be argued that the sensitization of researchers from the various disciplines to others in the applied fields has been a source of stimulation and an influence toward bridging the gaps between theory and facts. Regardless of positions on this issue, the existing relationships between researchers and practitioners clearly pose important obstacles in the planning and conduct of research and in the utilization of research results. Articulation between the competing norms of researchers and practitioners must occur in settings in which both are present, although that is not sufficient. Funding agencies probably could do more than is presently done to promote such cooperation.

In conclusion, it should be evident that, in a field such as educational research, in addition to the individual researcher's personal decisions, a variety of social forces within and outside the research community converge to influence the research activities. It should also be clear that while educational research shares many common problems and characteristics with other types of research, it represents certain uniqueness. Perhaps, it would be only appropriate to conclude an analysis of the social structure and processes of research by emphasizing the great need for comparative research on research.

Author Index

Numbers in brackets indicate the pages on which authors appear in the footnotes.

General Index

Numbers in brackets indicate the pages on which authors appear in the footnotes.

403